JAN HERMANN

CITY SECRETS®

NEW YORK CITY

ROBERT KAHN

EDITOR & SERIES EDITOR

THE LITTLE BOOKROOM

NEW YORK

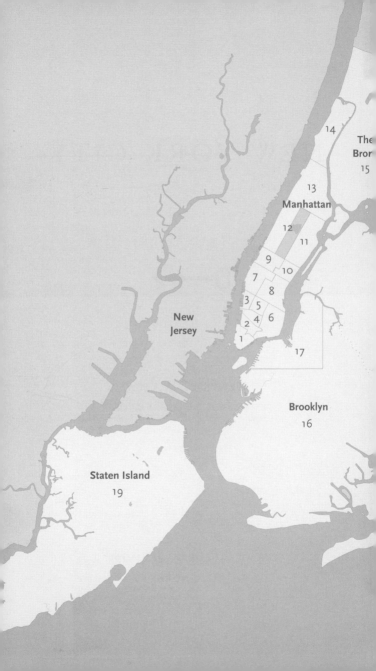

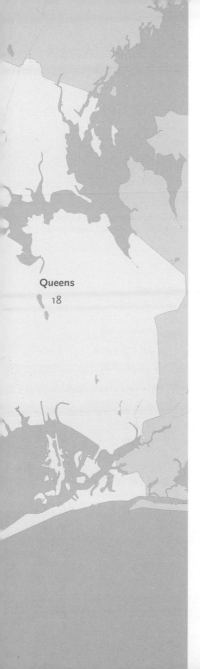

Queens

18

©2002 Robert Kahn
Series Editor: Robert Kahn
Editorial Staff: Nadia Aguiar, Lana Bortolot, Jane Fisher, Nalini Jones,
Dave King, Anne Young
Editorial Interns: Lizzie Tannen, Caitlin Petre
Book Design: Homans Design, New York, NY,
Katy Homans with Christine M. Moog
Original series and imprint design: Red Canoe, Deer Lodge, TN,
Caroline Kavanagh and Deb Koch
Map Production: Jenny King
Production: Elissa Stein, Ingrid Bromberg, Stefanie Silverman
Key: Based on a design courtesy of E. R. Butler & Co., New York
Chapter divider pages: *New York in the Nineteenth Century: 317 Engravings
from* Harper's Weekly *and Other Contemporary Sources*, by John Grafton. New
York: Dover Publications, Inc., 1980.

Special thanks to Fiona Duff Kahn

Eighth Printing
Printed in China by South China Printing Company Ltd.

Library of Congress Cataloging-in-Publication Data

New York City / Robert Kahn, series editor.

    p. cm. -- (City secrets ; 4)

    Includes bibliographical references and indexes.

    13-DIGIT ISBN: 978-1-892145-08-6   10-DIGIT ISBN: 1-892145-08-1

    1. Art, American--New York (State)--New York--Guidebooks.

    2. Amusements--New York (State)--New York--Guidebooks. 3. New York
(N.Y.)--Guidebooks. I. Kahn, Robert, 1950- II. Series.

N6535.N5N37 2002
917.47'10444--dc21

                                                        2001050392

City Secrets is registered in the U.S. Patent and Trademark Office.

Published by The Little Bookroom
1755 Broadway, Fifth floor
New York NY 10019
212 293-1643; fax 212 333-5374
editorial@citysecrets.com
www.citysecrets.com

HOW TO USE THIS BOOK

This is a highly subjective guidebook which reflects the personal tastes and insights of its contributors. We asked architects, writers, curators, and other cultural figures to recommend an overlooked or underappreciated site or artwork, or, alternatively, one that is well-known but about which they could offer fresh insights, personal observations, or specialized information. Respondents were also invited to describe strolls, neighborhoods, events, shops, and all manner of idiosyncratic and traditional ways of spending time in New York City. These recommendations have been organized into 19 areas. Each area has an accompanying map, keyed to the text by numbers. The numbers appear in boxes **3.9** and include an item number and a map number (which is also the chapter number). For example, a box with the number 3.9 denotes item number 9 from Chapter 3, which appears on Map 3.

In addition, three icons appear throughout the book to reference restaurants ¶¶, shops ⊛, and transportation Ⓜ.

The editors are delighted with the high number of unusual and delightful recommendations included here. At the same time, we acknowledge that New York City provides an endless number of rich experiences, and that this book, though full, is not exhaustive. It is our hope that you will be inspired by the enthusiasm of our contributors to explore even further and discover secrets of your own, and when you do, please let us know. We would love to hear about your city secrets—in any city, anywhere.

Finally, every care has been taken to ensure the accuracy of the information in this book. The publisher and the series editor are not able to accept responsibility for any consequences arising from use of the guide or the information it contains. If you do encounter a factual error, we hope that you will let us know.

Please contact us at www.citysecrets.com if you are interested in receiving a City Secrets newsletter.

TABLE OF CONTENTS

PREFACE

E.B. White wrote that New Yorkers have "... the sense of belonging to something unique, cosmopolitan, mighty and unparalleled." Although much has changed since he wrote these words over fifty years ago, the heart of the message remains as true now as it was then.

Whether entering this great city for the first time or the hundredth time, it is difficult not to be awed by the possibility of New York. From afar, there is the exhilaration and grandeur of a great metropolis, yet within, there is the comfort and familiarity of one's own neighborhood. The city is made up of thousands of small villages connected by streets and avenues, parks and playgrounds, bridges and tunnels. For many, no neighborhood is more important or more interesting than their own. New Yorkers take great pride in knowing their particular corner of the city and, as this book demonstrates, in telling others about it. This willingness to share personal "secrets" does not surprise me, for I have found New Yorkers to be generous and gracious people. I know of no other city that so quickly accepts anyone choosing to be a part of it—perhaps because it is a city that rarely forgets that it was built by and for immigrants. New York can be inconvenient, preoccupied with commerce and success, at times overwhelming ... yet we New Yorkers cannot imagine living anywhere else. This sense of belonging was never more evident than in the days and months following the tragedy of September 11, 2001. On that day, New York became everyone's city. This book is a reminder that the city exists as a continuum of the people that live here and the places they inhabit. What follows are the personal insights of our extraordinary contributors—a love letter to New York.

Robert Kahn
New York City

LOWER MANHATTAN

I

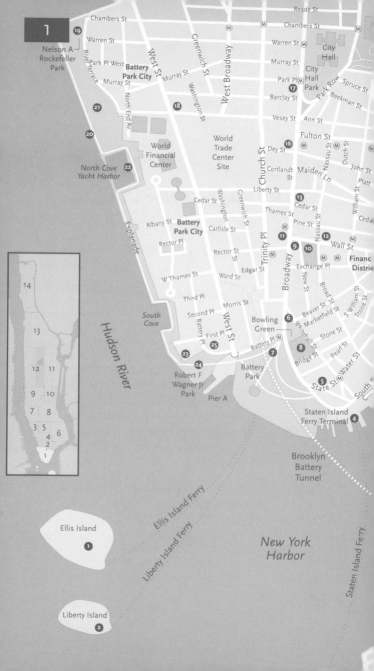

Ellis Island, Statue of Liberty, Financial District, Fulton, World Trade Center Area & Battery Park City

ELLIS ISLAND & STATUE OF LIBERTY

1.1 **Ellis Island National Monument and Ellis Island Immigration Museum**
1900, Boring & Tilton; 1991, restoration by Beyer Blinder Belle and Notter Finegold & Alexander
Ellis Island information, ☎ 212 363-3200
Open daily 9am-5pm; ferries depart at least once an hour from Battery Park; last ferry 3:30pm
Ferry, ☎ 212 269-5755
Ⓜ Bowling Green (4/5); Whitehall Street (N/R)

Not exactly a "city secret" this, but a visit to Ellis Island is so rewarding that it should not be missed by anyone curious about the history of New York or, indeed, the United States. About 100 million Americans, roughly 40 percent of the population, are related to someone who entered the country through Ellis Island. The museum presents the history of this extraordinary story, good and bad, in an intelligent, moving, and entertaining way.

You enter through the Baggage Hall. Suitcases and bundles stacked onto original baggage carts set the scene. You climb the stairs that, had you been an immigrant, would (unbeknownst to you) have been your first medical test. Any sign of distress and your coat would have been marked with a chalk code to alert the doctors to investigate further. America wanted immigrants, but she wanted them healthy.

At the top of the stairs is the impressive Registration Room with its vaulted tiled ceiling. The museum designers have been clever here: the room is restored, but left more or less empty, save some of the original inspectors' desks and some benches the immigrants would have waited on. Looking down on this space from the balcony, one imagines today's tourists almost in the role of extras; as they shuffle around, it's easy to imagine them as immigrants waiting their turn to be registered.

The historical information is presented upstairs in a series of small former inspection rooms. Here you can hear audio recordings of Ellis Island immigrants.

Not only is a visit to Ellis Island informative, it is also a great day out. The view back to the island of Manhattan is alone worth the trip.

CHARLES MARSDEN-SMEDLEY
Museum and exhibition designer

1.2 Statue of Liberty National Monument

1871-1886, Frédéric Auguste Bartholdi, sculptor; Alexandre Gustave Eiffel, engineer; Richard Morris Hunt, architect of the base
Liberty Island information, ☎ 212 363-3200
Open daily 9am-5pm; ferries depart at least once an hour from Battery Park; last ferry 3:30pm
Ferry, ☎ 212 269-5755
Ⓜ Bowling Green (4/5); Whitehall Street (N/R)

Although it is often thought of as a tourist trap, the Statue of Liberty is also a magnificent monument to dichotomy in architecture. It is at once both metal and masonry, frame and load bearing, literal and abstract. As a representation of old and new, the lady has better folds and warped surfaces than anything in current architectural fashion, and is in contrast to the finely composed base by Richard Morris Hunt. The star fortress below is just an added attraction. With contributions by Hunt, Eiffel, and Bartholdi, "base-middle-top" has never been played better and there is no finer example of "firmness, commodity and delight."—Vitruvius

ROBERT LIVESEY
Architect

Yes, you'll be on a boat with a thousand tourists, surrounded by seagulls that won't leave you alone. Yes, it's kind of corny. Still, I'm always surprisingly moved by the entire experience and it reminds me that I'm proud to be an American.
ERIC STOLTZ
Actor

FINANCIAL DISTRICT & FULTON

1.4   Staten Island Ferry

South Street at foot of Whitehall Street, ☎ 718 815-2628
Ferries run 24 hours
Ⓜ Bowling Green (4/5); Whitehall Street (N/R)

We were very tired, we were very merry
We had gone back and forth all night on the ferry.
—Edna St. Vincent Millay

The best free ride in the world, a round trip on the Staten Island Ferry offers unparalleled views of the Statue of Liberty, Governors Island, Ellis Island, New York Harbor, and the downtown skyline. The ferry connects lower Manhattan with St. George in Staten Island for 70,000 commuters and tourists 24 hours a day: during rush hour at 15-minute intervals, at 30-minute intervals most of the day, and hourly late at night. It was the sole lifeline to Staten Island until 1964, when the Verrazano-Narrows Bridge opened. For decades the fare was just a nickel; now it's free. Peter Minuit Park, named to honor the man and the 24 dollar deal that enabled the Dutch to buy (steal) Manhattan from the Indians, fronts the Staten Island Ferry Terminal. The terminal was designed by Walker & Morris in 1907, but a series of subsequent additions and renovations has all but obliterated the original structure. Imagine that it once looked exactly like its magnificent neighbor, the landmarked Battery Maritime

Building. Board the ferry after work with your sweetheart and uncork a bottle of champagne. On the way over, watch the sun set behind the Statue of Liberty. On the way back, you'll see the downtown skyline and a thousand twinkling lights.

FREDERIC SCHWARTZ
Architect

1.5 New York Unearthed

17 State Street between Pearl & Whitehall Streets
☎ 212 748-8628
Monday-Friday noon-5pm; closed Saturday, Sunday
Ⓜ Bowling Green (4/5); Whitehall Street (N/R)

New York Unearthed is a little-known museum and conservation laboratory with a display of artifacts from New York City archaeological sites. Its location—across from Battery Park, with access to Ellis and Liberty Islands—is fantastic for a New York visit, and the museum is charming. School tours can be arranged. Visitors can also see conservation of artifacts "in action," so to speak. Run by, but not at, the South Street Seaport Museum.

JOAN H. GEISMAR
Urban archaeologist

Melville's Manhattan

Herman Melville may have written *Moby Dick* while looking at a mountain out his window in the Berkshires, but he was born and lived most of his life in New York City. Melville liked islands (England, Tahiti) and never got too far from "the insular city of Manhattoes." His best friend Ishmael wonders why people, island people in particular, are so attracted to water, and why it is that on a Sunday you will find countless citizens congregating at the Battery simply staring at the water. This water-gazing is as true now as it was in 1851, when Melville wrote *Moby Dick*, ►

▶

or back in 1819 when he was born only yards away
from the Battery, on Pearl Street, so named because of the
glistening oyster shells strewn upon it. People are water-
gazers, and the Battery is still the place to stroll along the
breezy promenade, lean against the rail, and watch people
looking beyond the Statue of Liberty (in full view) for
the opening to New York's bay (just out of view), and the
rolling Atlantic beyond.

Of course, the rail you lean against rests on landfill. As
a toddler Melville never witnessed the grass and trees that
now intervene between the house of his nativity and the
promenade; it was all water then. But the view is much the
same: ships, pleasure craft, birds, and people bumping into
each other because they are gazing at the water. The home
at 6 Pearl Street where Herman learned to walk has vanished
and is now the site for an insurance company's skyscraper
and a modest museum for city archaeology (see New York
Unearthed, p. 15).

Melville died farther uptown, at 104 East 26th Street,
in the Gramercy Park area. That home is also gone. He
had returned to Manhattan after his Berkshire years (13 in
all), and spent close to three decades ignored and virtually
unknown, writing poetry and *Billy Budd*. Before his death
in 1891, he would take the trolley with his granddaughter
to Central Park to watch her run on the meadows and
jump from rocks, and to listen to the flapping of her skirts.
They sounded much like sails.

JOHN BRYANT
Writer and editor

1.7   Battery Park

Southernmost tip of Manhattan

Ⓜ Bowling Green (4/5); Whitehall Street (N/R)

This is the place in lower Manhattan that makes one forget
all about that other, bigger, more central park to the north,
especially if you are drawn to the water and especially if

you happen to be a runner. Battery Park combines sweeping green lawns, lush flowerbeds, and a whiff of the city's energy from nearby Wall Street with a continuous view of the mighty Hudson. If you squeeze your eyes and look out between Governors Island and Staten Island and the Statue of Liberty, you can almost convince yourself that you are alone in New York City, staring at your own private section of the Hudson River.

KATHLEEN DEMARCO
Writer and film producer

The Wilds of New York Nature Tour

Manhattan:

1.8 **National Museum of the American Indian**
Alexander Hamilton U.S. Custom House
1 Bowling Green between Whitehall & State Streets
☎ 212 514-3700
Monday-Wednesday, Friday-Sunday 10am-5pm;
Thursday 10am-8pm
Ⓜ Bowling Green (4/5); Whitehall Street (N/R);
Broad Street (J/M/Z)

5.43 **Merchant's House Museum**
29 East 4th Street between Lafayette Street & Bowery
☎ 212 777-1089
Thursday-Monday 1pm-5pm; closed Tuesday, Wednesday
Ⓜ Bleecker Street (6); Broadway-Lafayette Street (F/S/V)

12.17 **Belvedere Castle**
Central Park, mid-park at 79th Street
Wednesday-Monday 11am-4pm; closed Tuesday
Ⓜ West 81st Street (B/C); East 77th Street (6)

14.18 **Inwood Hill Park**
Northwest corner of Manhattan above Dyckman Street
Ⓜ Inwood-207th Street (A); 207th Street (1)   ▶

▶

The Bronx:

15.15 **Orchard Beach**
Pelham Bay Park, ☏ 718 885-2275
Summer 7am-8pm; rest of year 7am-dusk
Ⓜ Pelham Bay Park (6) or NY Express Bus/Pelham Bay
to Pelham Bay Park, to BX12 bus (summer only) to beach

Brooklyn:

16.8 **Prospect Park**
1873, Frederick Law Olmsted & Calvert Vaux
☏ 718 965-8999
Open daily from dawn to dusk
Ⓜ Grand Army Plaza (1/2); Eastern Parkway-Brooklyn
Museum (1/2); Prospect Park (Q/S); Parkside Avenue (Q)

16.4 **Old Stone House**
Originally built, 1699; rebuilt, 1935
336 3rd Street between Fourth & Fifth Avenues,
in James J. Byrne Memorial Playground, ☏ 718 768-3195
Call for hours
Ⓜ 4th Avenue-9th Street (M/N/R/F)

16.20 **Salt Marsh Nature Center**
3302 Avenue U between Burnett Street & East 33rd Street
☏ 718 421-2021
Summer 10:30am-5:30pm; winter 9:30am-4:30pm;
closed Wednesday
Ⓜ Avenue U (Q), to B3 bus west

While many come to New York City to see its granite
grandeur and the splashy commercialism for which it is
so widely known, one shouldn't overlook the city's natural
side. New York lies at the intersection of several migratory
pathways and the juncture of several ecotypes. The city
holds treasures and relics reflecting nearly a thousand years
of human occupation; secreted within its emerald necklace
of parks are various jewels containing fragments of its

distinguished natural history.

Be brave and, in a car, trace the city's cultural and natural heritage. Start at the National Museum of the American Indian. Located at Bowling Green Park in lower Manhattan, the museum holds an incredible collection of artifacts from the various people who originally occupied this area. Then head north. If it's autumn, stop at Belvedere Castle in Central Park to see the hawk migration. Thousands of raptors pass over the park on cold fronts in September and October, and there is a ranger available to help you identify in-flight raptors, as well as eagles, falcons, harriers, and accipiters. Then, on to Inwood Hill Park (also see p. 403) in upper Manhattan, where you will find the island's last great forest, surrounding a series of caves used for eons by Native Americans. Cross the Bronx and stop at Orchard Beach. If you walk all the way eastward on the boardwalk, you will come to a newly refurbished nature center that opens out onto a splendid beach, a back-bay salt marsh, and a beautiful upland forest that still contains vestige populations of American chestnuts. The beach sand was barged in from southern Long Island by Robert Moses, just so northern New Yorkers could have a beach as nice as any in Brooklyn or Queens. Have a seafood lunch on City Island—you'll think you're in Mystic. Head south across the Whitestone Bridge, take the BQE to Prospect Park (also see p. 432), enjoying the park's sylvan scenery. It's worth your while to pause at the Old Stone House (also see p. 430) nearby for a taste of New York during the Revolutionary War. See where General Alexander badgered George W. into a hasty retreat and listen to how 400 Marylanders saved the Colonial Army so it could fight again another day. Off again now, farther south to the shore. Stop in at the Salt Marsh Nature Center in Marine Park. Here is one of the great hidden treasures of the city: a brand-new nature center facing a vast marsh that turns bronze each fall and is always teeming with wildlife. It also hosts unique exhibits and creative ▶

▶

programs prepared by park rangers and the National
Geographic Society. Once you're back in Manhattan, wrap
up this epic journey by stopping off at East 4th Street to
visit the Merchant's House Museum (also see p. 125). This
cozy brownstone contains whale oil lamps, secret passages
for the Underground Railroad, and great furnishings from
the late 19th century.

ALEXANDER R. BRASH
Chief Park Ranger

`1.9` Bank of New York (originally Irving Trust Company)

1932, Voorhees, Gmelin & Walker
1 Wall Street at Broadway
Ⓜ Wall Street (1/2/4/5); Rector Street (N/R);
Broad Street (J/M/Z)

The building is well known, but the "red room" banking
hall, a superb blend of red terrazzo, dark purple marble,
and sparkling red-to-orange-to-gold mosaic tiles, is one of
the best surprises in New York. This masterpiece deserves
a special trip, especially if you're looking for New York
Art Deco.

DAVID M. CHILDS
Architect

`1.10` Wall Street Wall

Steeped in city, national, and international history for
nearly four centuries, the world's best-known address was
actually once a wall. In 1653, the city's slaves were ordered
to build a protective barricade with logs "twelve feet long,
eighteen inches in circumference, sharpened at the upper
end" from river (Hudson) to river (East) across Manhattan
Island. Demolished in 1699, its first official market was an
East River depot constructed in 1711 for the sale of slaves.
In 1791, brokers and investors began meeting under a

buttonwood (sycamore) tree at Broad and Wall Streets, and a year later founded a market for the buying and selling of stocks and securities.

CHRISTOPHER PAUL MOORE
Author and historian

1.11 **Trinity Church**
1846, Richard Upjohn
Broadway at Wall Street, ✆ 212 602-0800
Ⓜ Wall Street (1/2/4/5); Rector Street (N/R);
Broad Street (J/M/Z)

Trinity Church, the principal church of New York's first Episcopal parish, is worth a visit as much for its Wall Street context as for its extraordinary architecture. The most impressive 19th-century Gothic monument in New York, Trinity was completed in 1846 to the design of Richard Upjohn. The brownstone church and its graveyard seem to hold their own in the canyon of vintage skyscrapers at Broadway and Wall Street. The inside of the church, with its marble altar and reredos memorializing William B. Astor, completes this Gothic vision from the age of Melville.

PETER PENNOYER
Architect

A Perfect Evening

2.25 **The Peking Duck House**
28 Mott Street between Pell Street & Chatham Square
✆ 212 227-1810
Open daily for lunch and dinner
Ⓜ Canal Street (J/M/N/Q/R/W/Z/6)

2.11 **City Hall**
1812, Joseph François Mangin and John McComb Jr.
City Hall Park between Broadway & Park Row
Ⓜ Park Place (1/2); Brooklyn Bridge-City Hall (4/5/6);
City Hall (N/R); Chambers Street (J/M/Z)   ▶

►

1.11 **Trinity Church**
1846, Richard Upjohn
Broadway at Wall Street, ☎ 212 602-0800
Ⓜ Wall Street (1/2/4/5); Rector Street (N/R);
Broad Street (J/M/Z)

1.12 **George Washington Statue**
1883, James Quincy Adams Ward, pedestal by Richard Morris Hunt
26 Wall Street, near Broad Street
Ⓜ Wall Street (1/2/4/5); Rector Street (N/R);
Broad Street (J/M/Z)

1.6 **Wall Street Bull**
1989, Arturo di Modica
Broadway at Bowling Green
Ⓜ Bowling Green (4/5); Whitehall Street (N/R)

1.4 **Staten Island Ferry**
South Street at foot of Whitehall Street, ☎ 718 815-2628
Ferries run 24 hours
Ⓜ Bowling Green (4/5); Whitehall Street (N/R)

Whenever friends come to town and go to see the Statue
of Liberty, I feel deeply ashamed. I know New York the
way I know my oldest friends, all the secret back corners
and all the bad stuff, too, but the places I know least are
the ones that visitors usually see. The closest I've been to
the General Assembly of the United Nations is the press-
room, and the last time I took the Circle Line boat around
Manhattan was 20 years ago, and then only because
of a reporting assignment.

The New York I know and love is less eventful and more
unremarked, less monument and boulevard and more row
house and alleyway. And here is how I used to spend a
perfect evening with my husband before we had children.

We would go to dinner at a place on Mott Street in
🍴 Chinatown called the Peking Duck House, where you can
eat Peking duck without ordering it in advance. We would

browse in the little shops that sell cheap Chinese dishes, sandals, and fans.

We would walk south past the courts and the municipal buildings and into the pocket park that stands in front of the prettiest city hall in America, a graceful, oddly diminutive building with a beautiful floating staircase inside.

We'd continue toward the end of the island, passing through the area that was called Five Points when Manhattan was young, a neighborhood that 250 years ago was a den of thieves, prostitutes, and street gangs, all of whom have now moved largely uptown. We would pass the spire of Trinity Church (also see p. 21), the neo-Gothic house of worship that was once the tallest point in the city, and cross over Wall Street, which is named after a wall the earliest immigrant New Yorkers, the Dutch, built to keep out the earliest New Yorkers, the Indians.

We would arrive at the giant statue of George Washington that commemorates his inauguration in New York and the giant statue of a bull that commemorates Wall Street's most recent incarnation. And suddenly we would run out of land at the point of Manhattan, where the ferry terminal stands. So of course we would take the ferry to Staten Island.

We never stayed on Staten Island, just used its best-known, most romantic form of mass transit to see the city strung around us like a hive of hyperactive fireflies. (Staten Island actually has its own little aboveground subway system called the SIRT, which is as different from the rest of the subway as Staten Island is from the rest of the city. But that's another story.) Then we would take the ferry back again.

This constitutes a practically perfect experience, even better than taking the subway to Coney Island (see p. 444), looking at the beluga whales in the New York Aquarium, and having a hot dog and fries at Nathan's.

ANNA QUINDLEN
Writer

1.14 Bridge Cafe

279 Water Street at Dover Street, ☎ 212 227-3344
Monday-Friday for lunch and dinner; Saturday for dinner only;
Sunday for brunch and dinner
Ⓜ Brooklyn Bridge-City Hall (4/5/6); Chambers Street (J/M/Z)

🍴 There's nothing that will make you feel more like a real
New Yorker than being one of the lucky few who knows to
head down to the Bridge Cafe the moment the first snow-
flakes of winter start to cover Manhattan's streets. Cozy up
with an Irish coffee in the tin-ceilinged room and watch out
the big windows as the snow dusts the 200-plus-year-old
cobblestone streets, and the lights on the Brooklyn Bridge,
practically within touching distance, twinkle through the
flakes. And think about what it was like when Water Street
really fronted the East River and Prohibition-era guests
slipped Irish whiskey into their coffees, right where you sit.
MARYELLEN GORDON
Writer and editor

RECOMMENDED READING
Joseph Mitchell, *Up in the Old Hotel and Other Stories*, Random
House, 1993.
Caleb Carr, *The Alienist*, Bantam Doubleday Dell, 1995.

1.15 Brooklyn Bridge

1867-1883, John A. Roebling & Washington Roebling
Park Row (Manhattan) to Adams Street (Brooklyn)
Ⓜ Manhattan: Brooklyn Bridge-City Hall (4/5/6);
Chambers Street (J/M/Z). Brooklyn: High Street (A/C)

The Brooklyn Bridge celebrates the simple act of passage,
elevating the commonplace to a ritual. Always a threshold
to the city that is an island, the bridge normally is tra-
versed by car, and during rush hour it is as rushed and full
and bustling as any other downtown street. On the pedestrian walk, however, traffic is slowed to an almost stillness.
The wooden platform stretches between two remarkable
Gothic piers, pacing and dividing the excursion into three

parts. The true privilege is in being able to use it this way, not as a special event but as an everyday occurrence.

FREDERICK BIEHLE
Architect and professor of architecture

There is a component of Roebling's engineering design that I find so emphatically lyrical and marvelously beautiful that I almost prefer to keep it to myself. I have in mind a major structural feature that presents itself most dramatically from the Manhattan approach—namely, the great low-slung follow-through whereby the main cable, descending from the towers, sweeps down below the roadway only to sweep back up again without missing a beat, securing itself in the stone abutment. It strikes me as utterly modern—not pre-modern, but absolutely modern. I have long been convinced that this mathematical chord-like structural form inspired the governing motive of Albert Gleizes's curiously hearty 1915 Cubist painting, *Brooklyn Bridge*, now in the Guggenheim Museum.

JOSEPH MASHECK
Art historian and critic

WORLD TRADE CENTER AREA

1.16 **Former American Telephone & Telegraph Company**
1923, William Welles Bosworth
195 Broadway between Dey & Fulton Streets
Ⓜ Fulton Street-Broadway Nassau (A/C/J/M/Z/1/2/4/5)

The lobby is a forest of Doric columns, in true hypostyle fashion, on an approximate 15-foot grid—an exquisite room, the way one should enter a grand and proud corporation. Beautiful craftsmanship and detailing, even though four panels created for this space by Paul Manship are no longer there. (Evelyn Beatrice Longman's *Genius of the Telegraph*, popularly known as "Golden Boy," once perched on the building's pinnacle, later was moved to

their lobby in Philip Johnson's "Chippendale" tower at 550 Madison Avenue, and is now regretfully sentenced to their suburban New Jersey complex.)
DAVID M. CHILDS
Architect

1.17 **Woolworth Building**
1913, Cass Gilbert
233 Broadway between Park Place & Barclay Street
Ⓜ Park Place (1/2); City Hall (N/R); Brooklyn Bridge-City Hall (4/5/6); Chambers Street (J/M/Z)

At 792 feet, the Woolworth was the tallest building in the world until 1930, when the Chrysler Building surpassed it. The massing became a model for skyscrapers—a soaring, slender campanile of glazed terra cotta. Gilbert remarked, "a skyscraper, by its height, makes its upper parts appear lost in the clouds, whose masses must become more and more inspired as it rises." The lobby of this Gothic "cathedral to commerce" vibrates with mosaics, murals, and marble. Brendan Gill waxed that it was "one of the most sumptuous in the country...a bedazzlement of marble walls and gilt bronze doors with a vaulted ceiling of blue and gold mosaics." One whimsical carving includes caricatures of Gilbert with a model of the building and five-and-dime founder F.W. Woolworth counting his nickels.
FREDERIC SCHWARTZ AND TRACEY HUMMER
Architect and Writer

American Modernism

2.11 **City Hall**
1812, Joseph François Mangin and John McComb Jr.
City Hall Park between Broadway & Park Row
Ⓜ Park Place (1/2); Brooklyn Bridge-City Hall (4/5/6); City Hall (N/R); Chambers Street (J/M/Z)

1.17 **Woolworth Building** (see above)

It's 1913. Put together John Marin, the Woolworth Building, and City Hall, and you're right at the divide between safe Gothic skyscraper style and an insurgent American modernism. Then jump 20 years to see Alfred Stieglitz, modernism's major progenitor, promoting these insurgent impulses in Depression-era America.

First, go down to City Hall with a book of John Marin's city drawings. Stand on the steps of City Hall and look across Broadway to the ornamented Woolworth Building, then to Marin's drawings of the building, made in 1913, just after the then-tallest building in the world opened.

The building itself has a regal look, quite proud of its height, design, and dripping ornament. But the drawings, a kind of abstraction, show the building bending, swerving, dancing. Marin said he made the building move because people move and people give it life, in itself a distinctly humanist expression of the modernist impulse. Alfred Stieglitz hailed these drawings and immediately hung them at 291, his gallery. One day Cass Gilbert, the building's architect, came to see them. He walked in, looked around, and was so horrified that he stomped out—a perfect example of the clash between architecture's formalist entry into the 20th century and painting's break-loose modernist spirit.

Add 21 years to the same scene and you see Stieglitz, usually pigeonholed as elitist and formalist, striving to deepen modernism's place in the American consciousness. It's May 8, 1934, sunny and spring like. A crowd of 2,000 looks up at the steps of City Hall, where Stieglitz, the main speaker, is standing with Lewis Mumford and John Dewey. The three, spokespersons for Artists for Democratic Action, a communist front, demanded of Mayor La Guardia a municipal center of art where artists and the people of New York might exhibit, teach, learn, socialize—and feed America's creative soul. The center never happened. But the next day Mumford and Stieglitz ▶

►

congratulated each other for the crowd's vision—and for their own performances.

JUDITH MARA GUTMAN
Writer

RECOMMENDED READING
Judith Mara Gutman, *Raging Bull of American Culture, A Life of Alfred Stieglitz* (forthcoming).
John Marin: New York Sketches, exhibition catalogue published by Kennedy Galleries, 1990.

1.18   New York Telephone Company (Barclay-Vesey Building)
1927, McKenzie, Voorhees & Gmelin
140 West Street between Barclay & Vesey Streets
Ⓜ Chambers Street (A/C/1/2)

A favorite of Le Corbusier's and the frontispiece for his *Vers Une Architecture*, this trendsetting building, designed by a leading early modernist, Ralph Walker, concretely illustrates the bold massing of the 1916 zoning laws as best rendered by Hugh Ferriss in 1922. Massive, uplifting, uninterrupted skyward brick piers alternate with recessed vertical stripes of windows and spandrels capped by stone Art Deco motifs. Walker's preliminary massing studies pre-date the design of Rockefeller Center. As the architect who introduced the "urban twist," he acknowledged the city's powerful grid by anchoring the parallelogram base to the local streets while twisting its tower for a citywide reading. Don't miss the Guastavino vaults under one of the city's only public sidewalk arcades.

FREDERIC SCHWARTZ
Architect

RECOMMENDED READING
Le Corbusier, *Towards a New Architecture*, Dover Publications, 1986.

BATTERY PARK CITY

Battery Park City Esplanade
Battery Park City along the Hudson River from
Chambers Street to Battery Place, ☎ 212 267-9700
Ⓜ Chambers Street (A/C/1/2)

1.19 **"The Real World"**
1992, Tom Otterness

1.21 **"Inscribed Writings"**
1994, Mark Strand and Seamus Heaney

1.22 **North Cove Yacht Harbor Railing**
(see p. 30)

1.23 **Museum of Jewish Heritage**
18 First Place, Battery Park City, ☎ 212 509-6130
Sunday-Wednesday 10am-5:45pm; Thursday 10am-8pm;
Friday and eve of Jewish holidays 10am-3pm; closed Saturday
and Jewish holidays
Ⓜ Whitehall Street (N/R); Bowling Green (4/5);
Broad Street (J/M/Z); Wall Street (1/2)

Run down Hudson River Park to the Battery Park City
Esplanade along the river. Besides all the joggers and
bicyclists, there's much to see. In the northeast corner of
Governor Nelson A. Rockefeller Park (at Chambers Street),
there is the wonderful world of sculptures called *The Real
World* by Tom Otterness. Groupings of funny Lilliputian
animal-humans reflect our own world of work with humor
and parody. Just above North Cove is the Lily Pool, with
inscriptions by Mark Strand from *The Continuous Life*,
and Seamus Heaney from *Death of a Naturalist*. Farther
south at North Cove Yacht Harbor is a metal rail fence
with the words of Frank O'Hara and Walt Whitman,   ►

▶

and right past the Japanese gardens, where Robert F. Wagner Jr. Park begins, is the new Museum of Jewish Heritage.
GAIL KRIEGEL
Playwright and librettist

1.22 North Cove Yacht Harbor Railing
1986, Walt Whitman and Frank O'Hara
West of World Financial Center on the Hudson River
Ⓜ Chambers Street (A/C/1/2)

At the beginning of a group of marble benches at the marina, you will see a rail resplendent with gold letters. Follow these words as you view the docked yachts and sailboats with Ellis Island as a backdrop. In these evocative phrases you may discover two of the most apt descriptions of New York City.

City of the world (for all races are here,
All the lands of the earth make contributions here;)
City of the sea!
City of wharves and stores—city of tall façades
    of marble and iron!
Proud and passionate city—mettlesome, mad,
    extravagant, city! —Walt Whitman

For a different take on the city's charms, follow the words on the other side of the marble stairs.

One need never leave the confines of New York
to get all the greenery one wishes—I can't even
enjoy a blade of grass unless I know there's
a subway handy, or a record store or some other
sign that people do not totally regret life.
—Frank O'Hara

THERESA CRAIG
Writer and editor

RECOMMENDED READING
Walt Whitman, "City of Ships," from *Leaves of Grass.*

1.24 Robert F. Wagner Jr. Park

1989, Olin Partnership; Machado & Silvetti; Lynden Miller
Foot of Battery Park City

Ⓜ Bowling Green (4/5); Whitehall Street (N/R);
Broad Street (J/M/Z); Wall Street (1/2)

Robert F. Wagner Jr. Park is just steps from one of the
city's oldest tourist locations, Castle Clinton in Battery
Park, and one of its newest museums, the Museum of
Jewish Heritage, which includes the Living Memorial to
the Holocaust. Featuring a beautifully landscaped setting of
well-tended flower gardens, lawns, and walkways, the
waterfront Robert F. Wagner Park offers spectacular views
of the harbor. At its center is Gigino (20 Battery Place,
☏ 212 528-2228), the perfect place for an al fresco lunch
or dinner, where the loudest noise is not the backfire of
a truck but the low rumble of passing tugboats. Joggers,
skaters, and a few sunbathers complete the tranquil
outdoor scene.

BOB COOK
Lawyer

"Ape & Cat (At the Dance)"

1993, Jim Dine

In the middle of Robert F. Wagner Jr. Park is a circular
English garden, a patch of beauty and serenity with a
majestic brick pavilion and wide walkways that look out
onto the river. In the winter, the frozen peaks of the waves
are sublime. On the lawn, in front of the pavilion, is my
favorite piece: two human-size, graceful bronze figures
called *Ape & Cat (At the Dance)* by Jim Dine. I never tire
of looking at the details of their clasped hands, their regal
clothes, their kind faces. One can't help feeling tenderly
toward this elegant "mixed" couple standing in the grass
at the edge of the city.

GAIL KRIEGEL
Playwright and librettist

Sunset Jam on the Hudson
July (starting the Friday after July 4th)-August (at least
through mid-month) Friday 6:30pm-8:30pm
☎ 212 267-9700; www.bpcparks.org

On summer nights, you can hear drums beating in lower
Manhattan. These aren't ghosts from the island's Native
American past, though old and new worlds collide happily
in Wagner Park. This lovely spot marks the southernmost
point of the esplanade at Battery Park City, which didn't
exist until the latter part of the 20th century. Here, the
harbor where New York began stretches before you, with
spectacular views of the Statue of Liberty and Ellis Island.
The towers of Wall Street loom to the north and east. Oh
yes, the drumbeats. On Fridays in July and August, park
employees bring a cartful of drums to the lawn, around
6 p.m. You can use one of these, or bring your own. A
leader sets the rhythm. As the sun slowly sets behind the
Statue of Liberty, a motley crowd combines into an
impromptu percussion band. For New Yorkers, this is perfect relaxation: mellowness induced by rapid movement.
JULIE SALAMON
Author and critic

RECOMMENDED READING
Walt Whitman, "City of Ships," from *Leaves of Grass*.

Floating the Apple
Various locations, ☎ 212 564-5412
www.floatingtheapple.org

This organization rows in beautiful old-time rowboats, not
little chunky modern things, but 25 feet long, the kind of
boats that raced out to bring passengers in from the latest
sailboat over from Europe in 1820.
PETE SEEGER
Musician

1.25 The Skyscraper Museum

39 Battery Place, ☎ 212 968-1961
Opening late 2002

Ⓜ Whitehall Street (N/R); Bowling Green (4/5);
Broad Street (J/M/Z); Wall Street (1/2)

Founded in 1996, this can-do museum has put on exhibitions whose subject matter ranges from downtown
New York to an international survey of the world's largest
buildings. Thankfully, it will have a new high-concept
permanent home, designed by Skidmore, Owings &
Merrill, in the Ritz-Carlton Downtown located in lower
Manhattan—the birthplace of the skyscraper.
WALTER CHATHAM
Architect

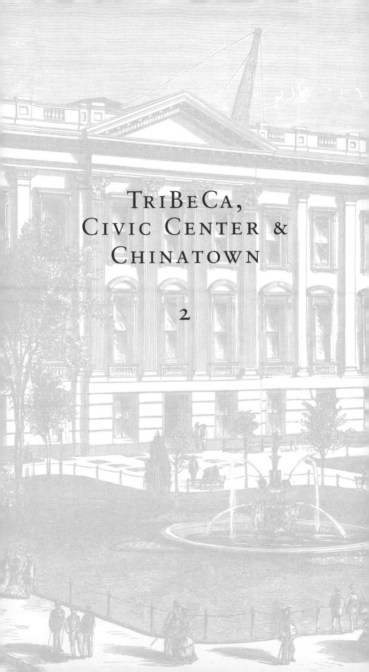

TRIBECA, CIVIC CENTER & CHINATOWN

2

TRIBECA

1 Hudson River Park
2 Downtown Boathouse
3 Miniature Golf
3 Games House
3 Fishing
4 American Express Stables
🍴 5 Walker's
🍴 6 Danube
🍴 7 Taste of TriBeCa
8 Washington Market Park
🍴 9 Morgan's Market
🍴 10 Odeon

CIVIC CENTER

11 City Hall
12 Old NY County Courthouse
13 Emigrant Savings Bank
14 Surrogate's Court
15 Municipal Building
16 African Burial Ground
17 U.S. Courthouse
18 NY County Courthouse
19 Criminal Courts Building

CHINATOWN

🚇 20 Canal Street
🍴 21 Pacifica Restaurant
22 Tunnel
🍴 23 Nom Wah
🍴 24 Canton Restaurant
🍴 25 Peking Duck House
🚇 26 Kam Kuo Food Corp.
🍴 27 Ten Ren's Tea Time
🍴 28 Saint's Alp Teahouse
🍴 29 Ice Cream Factory
🚇 30 Mott St. General Store
🍴 31 Hong Kong Cake Co.
32 Columbus Park

Tribeca, Civic Center & Chinatown

TRIBECA

2.1 **Hudson River Park**
Along the Hudson River from 59th Street to Battery Park City

At one time, downtowners wishing to run, skate, bike,
or power-walk had to go uptown to Central Park. Now
the Hudson River Park, a long strip of interconnected
parks and gardens from West 59th Street to Battery Park
(and growing), provides traffic-free space and relatively
fresh air filtered off the Hudson. Watch the ferries shut-
tling people between New Jersey and the Financial District
while the Statue of Liberty looks on. Plantings along the
path are in full bloom during the spring and summer, and
in the winter Canada geese graze. Along the way are the
famous Stuyvesant High School, an open field to rival
Central Park's Great Lawn, a children's park, a pier where
boats of the rich and famous dock, a wooden boardwalk
where fishermen cast their lines year round, and, right
before Battery Park, the Museum of Jewish Heritage. A
nearby set of steps provides a great view of the river and
Ellis Island. Walk the steps slowly or run up like Rocky
Balboa, on top of the world.
ADAM BERLIN
Writer

Kayaking on the Hudson
Daily status line, ☎ 646 613-0740
www.downtownboathouse.org
Seasonal and weather permitting: Saturday, Sunday, holidays,
and some weekday evenings

2.2 **The New York City Downtown Boathouse: Pier 26**
On the Hudson River at North Moore Street
Ⓜ Franklin Street (1/2); Canal Street (A/C/E)

7.2 **The New York City Downtown Boathouse: Pier 64**
On the Hudson River at West 24th Street
Ⓜ 23rd Street (C/E)

Well off the beaten path psychologically, but easily accessible, is the Downtown Boathouse, which offers free kayaking in two locations in a city more known for crowded subways, noisy buses, rushing taxis, and busy sidewalks. Just show up on a summer weekend and you'll find a free kayak to use, basic instruction, and access to a relatively protected portion of the Hudson River. For more advanced kayakers, show up before 8 a.m. on the weekend (Pier 26 only) for a three-hour paddle to the Statue of Liberty or the *U.S.S. Intrepid*. Although there are often more people than boats for these longer trips, it's a great chance to get back to nature in a dramatically man-made city.
THORIN TRITTER
Historian

2.4 **Former American Express Stables**
1867
Collister Street between Laight & Hubert Streets
Ⓜ Franklin Street (1/2)

The American Express Company was originally an express company; that is, it hauled things. Its headquarters were located in the then newly commercial part of New York west of Broadway and south of Canal, which today is once again becoming residential. The company built a handsome marble-faced building at the southwest corner of Hudson and Jay Streets, now gone, though the present building on that site was also built by American Express in the 1880's. But American Express has left a small remnant where the keen-eyed observer can see it, at the northeast corner of

Hubert and Collister Streets, and likewise at the southeast corner of Collister and Laight Streets. The handsome building that runs along Collister Street was the stable for its superb horses, and at either end of the building, high up in the steep gable, are circular reliefs with what are supposed to be dogs (the emblem of the company before that vapid centurion) surrounded by the words AMERICAN EXPRESS CO. The dog on Hubert Street looks more like a bear or a large cat with odd jaws; the dog on Laight is far more dog-like, but oddly like a Chihuahua. They were supposed to be bulldogs, sources say, but neither one achieves proper bulldogginess. What's even odder is that they don't match. The building itself is a lovely brick composition, massive and confident, with splendid Palladian windows on the second floor.

ROBIN CLEMENTS
Teacher

RECOMMENDED READING
Oliver E. Allen, *Tales of Old TriBeCa: An Illustrated History of New York's Triangle Below Canal*, The TriBeCa Tribune, Inc., 1999.

Summer in New York

2.1 **Hudson River Park**
Along the Hudson River from 59th Street to Battery Park City

2.2 **Kayak Rental**
The New York City Downtown Boathouse: Pier 26
On the Hudson River at North Moore Street
Daily status line, ☎ 646 613-0740
www.downtownboathouse.org
Ⓜ Franklin Street (1/2); Canal Street (A/C/E)

2.3 **Miniature Golf: Pier 25**
On the Hudson River at North Moore Street
Manhattan Youth, ☎ 212 732-7467
Ⓜ Franklin Street (1/2); Canal Street (A/C/E)

2.3 **Games House: Pier 25**
On the Hudson River at North Moore Street
Hudson River Park Trust, ☎ 212 533-PARK
www.hudsonriverpark.org
Manhattan Youth, ☎ 212 732-7467
Ⓜ Franklin Street (1/2); Canal Street (A/C/E)

3.19 **Games House: Pier 40**
On the Hudson River at West Houston Street
Pier Park & Playground, ☎ 212 989-3764
www.pier40.org
Ⓜ Houston Street (1/2)

2.3 **Fishing: Pier 25**
On the Hudson River at North Moore Street
Hudson River Park Trust, ☎ 212 533-PARK
www.hudsonriverpark.org
Ⓜ Franklin Street (1/2); Canal Street (A/C/E)

3.19 **Fishing: Pier 40**
On the Hudson River at West Houston Street
Hudson River Park Trust, ☎ 212 533-PARK
www.hudsonriverpark.org
Ⓜ Houston Street (1/2)

1.20 **Ferry Dock**
World Financial Center at Vesey Street
Ⓜ Chambers Street (A/C/1/2)

1.22 **North Cove Yacht Harbor**
West of World Financial Center on the
Hudson River
Ⓜ Chambers Street (A/C/1/2)

1.23 **Museum of Jewish Heritage**
18 First Place, Battery Park City, ☎ 212 509-6130
Ⓜ Bowling Green (4/5); Whitehall Street (N/R); Broad Street
(J/M/Z); Wall Street (1/2)

►

1.24   **Robert F. Wagner Jr. Park**
Foot of Battery Park City
Ⓜ Bowling Green (4/5); Whitehall Street (N/R);
Broad Street (J/M/Z); Wall Street (1/2)

Take a bike and ride to the lower west side of Manhattan
along the path that hugs the Hudson River and runs to the
tip of Battery Park City. While this esplanade is still evolving and is by no means any competition for Frederick Law
Olmsted, it attempts to open a new area of the city for
exploration, allowing New Yorkers and visitors access to
the lower Hudson River and revealing the ongoing development of a part of Manhattan built entirely on landfill.

Starting at 23rd Street, this ride runs along the old piers
of the lower Hudson River. It passes a variety of attractions along the way, including a boathouse for kayak
rental, a tiny homemade mini-golf course, games houses
where you can rent all manner of outdoor games, the ferry
dock for rides to New Jersey, cafes and restaurants surrounding the yacht harbor at the World Financial Center,
and the newly completed Museum of Jewish Heritage,
before arriving at the jewel-like Robert F. Wagner Jr. Park
at the foot of Battery Park City. Here one is thrilled by a
magnificent view of New York Harbor and one of the
great sculptural achievements of the 19th century—the
captivating Statue of Liberty. This tiny park, designed by
the firm of Machado & Silvetti, works beautifully. A
🍽 little cafe (Gigino, 20 Battery Place, ☎ 212 528-2228)
open in the summer months, with tables and umbrellas, is
tucked gently into the base of the brick observation deck.
Below stretches a plane of perfect green grass.
CAROLYN CARTWRIGHT
Feature film set decorator and interior designer

2.5 Walker's

16 North Moore Street at Varick Street, ☎ 212 941-0142
Open daily for lunch and dinner; bar open until 4am
Ⓜ Franklin Street (1/2); Canal Street (A/C/E)

🍽 This is the requisite no-frills bar/restaurant in TriBeCa.
Walker's has three rooms, big windows, great fries, and a
decently expanded menu that makes this the place to go
when sophisticated restaurants with sophisticated pricing
seem just too much of a hassle and what you really want
is to be in a comfortable place with relaxed people and
good food.
KATHLEEN DEMARCO
Writer and film producer

2.6 Danube

30 Hudson Street at Duane Street, ☎ 212 791-3771
Monday-Saturday for lunch and dinner; closed Sunday
Ⓜ Chambers Street (A/C/1/2)

🍽 The bar at Danube is an over-the-top Viennese dream-like
fantasy. David Bouley's masterpiece is sheer elegance, beauty,
and romanticism in a setting of high ceilings, warm candle-
light, rich fabrics, mauves against gold, and mosaics—just
imagine walking into a Gustav Klimt painting. Bring a date
for the most romantic (and most expensive) drinks downtown. Maybe you'll get lucky—I did.
FREDERIC SCHWARTZ
Architect

2.7 Taste of TriBeCa

Duane Street between Greenwich & Hudson Streets
www.tasteoftribeca.com for information, date, and time
Ⓜ Chambers Street (A/C/1/2)

🍽 In this annual event, world-class local restaurants and
catering firms provide a mouth-watering outdoor buffet
luncheon. Dozens of TriBeCa's finest chefs prepare their

signature dishes so that, on a late May Sunday from end of morning until mid-afternoon, they may be sampled by diners who stroll down Duane Street. Participating restaurants have included Chanterelle, Danube, Capsouto Frères, and TriBeCa Grill, to name just a few. In terms of cuisine, no ordinary street fest. First held in 1996 in an effort to raise money for art in the neighborhood's public schools, Taste of TriBeCa was conceived by its founders as a moment and place where, on a beautiful day in spring, their passion for great food and art and their children's education would converge.

JANE FISHER
Independent consultant

2.10 Odeon

145 West Broadway between Duane & Thomas Streets
☎ 212 233-0507
Open daily for lunch, dinner, and late-night meals
Ⓜ Chambers Street (A/C/1/2)

🍴 Once the trendiest restaurant in the city (think long ago, like the 80's), this place has remained popular because they just do everything right: big dining area, great food, an atmosphere that remains comfortably chic but not off-putting.

KATHLEEN DEMARCO
Writer and film producer

CIVIC CENTER

Civic Center Stroll

Ⓜ Brooklyn Bridge-City Hall (4/5/6); City Hall (N/R);
Chambers Street (A/C/J/M/Z); Park Place (1/2)

2.11 **City Hall**
1812, Joseph François Mangin and John McComb Jr.
City Hall Park between Broadway & Park Row

2.12 **Old New York County Courthouse ("Tweed" Courthouse)**
1872, John Kellum and Thomas Little
52 Chambers Street between Broadway & Centre Street

2.13 **Former Emigrant Industrial Savings Bank Building**
1912, Raymond F. Almirall
51 Chambers Street between Broadway & Elk Street

2.14 **Surrogate's Court/Hall of Records**
1911, John Rochester Thomas and Horgan & Slattery
31 Chambers Street between Centre & Elk Streets

2.15 **Municipal Building**
1914, McKim, Mead & White
Centre Street opposite Chambers Street

2.17 **U.S. Courthouse**
1936, Cass Gilbert and Cass Gilbert Jr.
40 Centre Street at Pearl Street

2.18 **New York County Courthouse (New York State Supreme Court)**
1927, Guy Lowell
60 Centre Street between Pearl & Worth Streets,
in Foley Square

2.19 **Criminal Courts Building and Men's House of Detention**
1939, Harvey Wiley Corbett and Charles B. Meyers
100 Centre Street between Leonard & White Streets   ▶

►

1.15 **Brooklyn Bridge**
1867-83, John A. Roebling & Washington Roebling
Park Row (Manhattan) to Adams Street (Brooklyn)

1.17 **Woolworth Building**
1913, Cass Gilbert
233 Broadway between Park Place & Barclay Street

I recommend an incredible group of buildings that I have
often taken friends and students to visit. The tour can be
done in an hour unless one is detained by the many
interesting aspects of this visit. It has to be done during
business hours, as the interiors are of as much interest
as the exteriors and are not open on the weekend.

I like to start at the front of City Hall, in the newly
renovated City Hall Park. City Hall has an elegant 1812
French Renaissance facade by Joseph F. Mangin and John
McComb Jr. and a dramatic interior hall with a twin
circular stair and dome.

One used to be able to go out the back door to the
"Tweed" Courthouse, on axis behind City Hall. In 1876,
C.L.W. Eidlitz added a Romanesque cast iron hall with
glass walkways and a steel truss skylight that once held
stained glass. You can leave Tweed Hall by the basement
door in the front.

Across the street, on axis, is the former Emigrant
Industrial Savings Bank Building, designed by Raymond F.
Almirall in 1912. One can enter this interesting double
tower building to see an impressive banking hall.

Just east on Chambers Street is the Surrogate's Court
building. This Beaux Arts building has entries from both
Chambers and Elk Streets. From Chambers, one passes
through a double colonnaded entry to the center skylighted
hall. There is an elegant and complex stair at the end of
the hall that appears to be independent of its container.
It begins with a symmetrical center entry and becomes

asymmetrical as it rises above the skylit center court.

From here, one is confronted with the Arch of Constantine screen in front of the U-shaped Municipal Building. The Municipal Building is split by Chambers Street, with a vaulted space in the form of the entry to the Palazzo Farnese in Rome. This urban solution forced two lobbies and two elevator banks rising to the colonnaded top where stands the statue *Civic Fame*.

Now walk north on Centre Street; at Foley Square is the U.S. Courthouse, with its pyramided tower by Cass Gilbert and Cass Gilbert Jr. North of that is the New York County Courthouse, designed in 1912, but built 15 years later. The hexagonal plan has a great interior hall surrounded by a colonnade.

Continue north to the Art Deco Criminal Courts Building and Men's House of Detention—the Tombs (also see p. 48). Peek into the formidable center hall, then turn back to City Hall Park. This time, passing the screen of the Municipal Building under the south arm of Guastavino tile work, one can look down the axis of the Brooklyn Bridge (also see p. 24).

Saving a walk over the bridge for another time, cross the park with eyes on the Woolworth Building (also see p. 26). The delicate exterior is complemented by the glass mosaic lobby, which seems like a cross between a Byzantine street system and the proclaimed "cathedral of commerce."

JON MICHAEL SCHWARTING
Architect

2.14 **Surrogate's Court/Hall of Records**
1911, John Rochester Thomas and Horgan & Slattery
31 Chambers Street between Centre & Elk Streets
Monday-Friday 9am-5pm
Ⓜ Brooklyn Bridge-City Hall (4/5/6); Chambers Street (A/C/J/M/Z); City Hall (N/R); Park Place (1/2)

The next best thing to seeing the Paris Opera House is a visit to the lobby of the Surrogate's Court. Open to the public during regular court hours, this spectacular granite building was begun in 1899 and completed in 1911. The courtrooms on the fifth floor, made of mahogany and English oak, are well worth the elevator ride. The building also houses the archives of the City of New York.
JAMES J. BRUCIA
Justice (retired), New York State Supreme Court

`2.16` African Burial Ground Memorial
c. 1690
Corner of Duane & Elk Streets
Ⓜ Brooklyn Bridge-City Hall (4/5/6);
Chambers Street (A/C/J/M/Z)

Unearthed during construction of the federal office building at 290 Broadway in 1991, the Colonial-era cemetery once spanned more than five acres or about five city blocks. Archaeologists estimate more than 20,000 men, women, and children were once buried at the site, which included the preserved portion at the corner of Duane and Elk Streets.
CHRISTOPHER PAUL MOORE
Author and historian

`2.19` Criminal Courts Building and Men's House of Detention (the Tombs)
1939, Harvey Wiley Corbett and Charles B. Meyers
100 Centre Street between Leonard & White Streets
Ⓜ Canal Street (6/J/M/Z)

Go to night court and listen to the pleas of a parade of pimps, prostitutes, petty thieves, and, every once in a while, a murderer. It's gritty and it's real. The Art Moderne design by Harvey Wiley Corbett is a poor man's Rockefeller Center. Named the Tombs after its Egyptian Revival predecessor across the street, it lived up to its name for decades as symbol of the deplorable condition of correctional institutions.

FREDERIC SCHWARTZ
Architect

CHINATOWN

2.20 Canal Street

This bustling, traffic-riddled crosstown thoroughfare originally functioned as a canal and is now virtually a linear flea market starting east at the Manhattan Bridge, running through the Lower East Side, Chinatown, Little Italy, SoHo, and TriBeCa and ending west at the Hudson River. You can buy anything under the sun (and more), it seems, as vendors spill out on the sidewalks hawking their wares from sunrise to sundown. Brush up on your bartering skills before buying the knockoff handbags and watches that abound, and also watch your pockets. A great place to score the requisite NYC T-shirts and ball caps at way below Midtown prices. Treat yourself to the best café con leche in New York at the Westside (corner of Church and Lispenard).

FREDERIC SCHWARTZ AND TRACEY HUMMER
Architect and Writer

2.21 Pacifica Restaurant

138 Lafayette Street between Howard & Canal Streets
☎ 212 334-9003
Open for breakfast, lunch, and dinner
Ⓜ Canal Street (J/M/N/Q/R/W/Z/6)

One of the best-kept secrets about Chinatown is this second-floor restaurant in the Holiday Inn. The windows overlook the teeming neighborhood, yet inside it is quiet and the service is great. When our Asian friends

come to visit we always take them here because the
food is authentic and always fresh and exciting.
GAIL KRIEGEL
Playwright and librettist

Chinatown Walk

Ⓜ East Broadway (F); Canal Street (J/M/N/Q/R/W/Z/6)

2.22 **Tunnel**
5 Doyers Street between Pell Street & Bowery

2.23 **Nom Wah**
13 Doyers Street between Pell Street & Bowery
☎ 212 962-6047
Open daily 9:30-8pm

2.24 **Canton Restaurant**
45 Division Street between Bowery & Market Street
☎ 212 226-4441
Wednesday-Sunday for lunch and dinner; closed
Monday, Tuesday

Try this short historical walk, followed by a top-flight meal.
    Pre-dinner, head for Pell Street, where at Number 16
you'll find a bronze placard reading "Hip Sing
Association." Pell Street has been home to the Hip Sing
Tong, or association, since the 1880's. The Hip Sing were
fierce rivals of the On Leong Tong (who were headquar-
tered in the Pagoda on the southwest corner of Mott and
Canal). From the late-19th century through the 1930's,
these tongs would regularly erupt in battle over gambling
turf and other interests of the day. These conflicts, referred
to legendarily as the Tong Wars, were full of shootings and
stabbings that spilled over from Pell Street onto adjoining
Doyers Street. Number 5 Doyers, site of the Old Chinese
Opera House, was the scene of an especially gruesome
power play in 1906, when Hip Singers fired into an audience of On Leongers. The attackers made their getaway

through Chinatown's network of ancient tunnels, and you can enter one of them at 5 Doyers Street today.

Take the staircase below ground and follow the tunnel until you exit at Chatham Square, farther to the south. What you'll encounter en route currently, however, is a dingy arcade of small businesses that include not only Tin Sun Metaphysics and Chinese Medical Science, but also employment and insurance agencies and an English-language-learning site. Still, it doesn't take too much fantasizing to conjure up images of blood, battle, and flight in this corridor a century ago. If you double-back and exit on Doyers Street, make mental note, for a future outing, of Nom Wah—New York's oldest (1920) dim sum parlor—at Number 13.

Now you're ready for some heavenly Chinese fare, which you will consistently encounter at Canton. The food is sublime (though more expensive than customary in Chinatown), the service indulgent, and the circumstances simple, clean, and serene. Canton specializes in Cantonese banquet-style dishes, so ideally you'll be a party of six or more. Permit your hostess to select your menu, then settle back for course after delicious course.

JANE FISHER
Independent consultant

2.26 Kam Kuo Food Corp.

7 Mott Street between Chatham Square & Mosco Street
☎ 212 349-3097
Open daily 8:30am-8:30pm
Ⓜ Canal Street (J/M/N/Q/R/W/Z/6)

New York's Chinatown has grown tremendously in recent times, taking over the old Little Italy and reaching into the Lower East Side. In some ways, it is a city within a city and exploring it can be daunting. One good place to get started is the Kam Kuo Food Corp. From the street this looks like an ordinary small store, but once inside you'll realize that it's as large as a suburban supermarket and it has a second floor as well.

It's definitely not a tourist spot. Most people there are just doing their regular grocery shopping, and unless you ask for help, you will be left alone. Begin at the collection of bins in front. Mixed in with the usual bulk goods is more unusual fare, such as shredded squid, pickled tangerines, and preserved dry olives. One row offers six different kinds of ginseng, ranging from 16 to 63 dollars a pound. There are some familiar brands on the shelves—Carnation, Nestlé—but these are products made for the Asian market, not the ones you see in America. Then there are the brands manufactured and sold in Asia, with Western names chosen to sound exotic in their target markets: Kewpie mayonnaise, Mickey Mouse haw candy, Bull-Dog Worcestershire sauce, Beefeater pukka tea.

Kam Kuo is a good source for hard-to-find foods from many Asian countries. They have a wonderful selection of ready-made foods; especially worth trying are the frozen steam buns. Try to leave with at least one product that you've never heard of before. It shouldn't be too difficult. On a recent visit some items to be considered were white fungus with pineapple, grass jelly drink, toddy palm seeds, shrink-wrapped preserved quail eggs, canned rambutan, sapota, jackfruit, "odour frying fish with chili," peanut gluten, salted croaker (a kind of fish), medlar chrysanthemum drink crystal, honey fritillary and loquat beverage, pickled mayom, as well as some foods whose names are translated only into Latin because there isn't an English equivalent.

Upstairs they sell mostly cookware and a few household appliances. You can find cheap, high-quality pots and utensils and beautiful dishes here. If you're having a banquet for 50 people, their banquet room has all sorts of little tables and chairs. And if you need an industrial-sized soybean drink press or a melonseed cracker, you will find one here.

JANET B. PASCAL
Writer and editor

Mott Street Stroll

Ⓜ Canal Street (J/M/N/Q/R/W/Z/6)

2.27 **Ten Ren's Tea Time**
79 Mott Street between Canal & Bayard Streets
☎ 212 732-7178
Sunday-Thursday 11am-11pm; Friday, Saturday 11am-midnight

2.28 **Saint's Alp Teahouse**
51 Mott Street between between Bayard & Pell Streets
☎ 212 766-9889
Open daily 11am-11:30pm

2.29 **Chinatown Ice Cream Factory**
65 Bayard Street between Mott & Elizabeth Streets
☎ 212 608-4170
Open daily until 10pm; late-nights Friday, Saturday, Sunday
and all summer

2.30 **Mott Street General Store**
32 Mott Street between Pell & Mosco Streets
☎ 212 962-6280
Monday-Friday 8am-7pm; Saturday 8am-8pm;
Sunday 8am-6pm

2.31 **Hong Kong Cake Company**
On Mosco Street between Mott & Mulberry Streets
No regular hours

2.32 **Columbus Park**
South of Bayard Street between Mulberry & Baxter Streets

🍽 Most people think of Chinatown as a noisy, sprawling
🏯 market of trinkets, gadgets, street vendors, and odd-
looking food. But if you know where to go, you can enjoy
the neighborhood at a slow pace, taking in its quiet
moments in unexpected ways.

Enter the gateway to old Chinatown at the southern
intersection of Mott and Canal Streets. Head south on   ►

►

Mott, where you'll soon see a cluster of new teahouses boasting the latest drink innovation: flavored tapioca teas or "bubble tea." These candy-colored teahouses are the new social clubs for young Asians, who are a few generations removed from the old benevolent societies their grandparents patronized. You may choose from a number of fruits and flavors (mango, chocolate, peanut), but all the drinks have giant black pearls of tapioca (hence the nickname, "bubble tea") bobbing on the bottom. Sucked up through a giant straw, the gummy beads pop into your mouth and require considerable chewing before you can swallow them (kids love this part). The tea bars are similar, but the social scenes are most lively at Ten Ren and Saint's Alp, which were among the first to introduce the new drink to New York.

Continuing south, just to the left on Bayard Street, is a tried-and-true institution, the Chinatown Ice Cream Factory. Forget about 31 flavors, the nearby Häagen Dazs, or those two guys from Vermont; the ice cream here is made fresh daily, and many flavors, such as almond cookie, chrysanthemum tea, and lychee, are from ancestral Chinese recipes. Try these flavors you won't find in the supermarket freezer: ginger, taro, red bean, and green tea. Get a cone or a dish and return to Mott Street.

Tempting shops line the street, but forge ahead to the Mott Street General Store, a tiny storefront owned by the original family that set up business here in 1891. It's the oldest retail presence in Chinatown, and it still looks much as it did more than 100 years ago. Formal portraits of Chinese women hang on the walls, the original clock still ticks on, and the apothecary shelves display traditional Chinese goods such as rice bowls, tea sets, and jade dragons. The carved woodwork at the back twists around a handsome counter, from which herbal remedies were once sold. Many stores and restaurants in Chinatown had similar carvings to ward off evil spirits, which, flying straight, would be captured in the tangle of peacocks and lucky fish.

Save room in both your backpack and your stomach for the Hong Kong Cake Company, on Mosco Street, just off Mott. A tiny wooden stall with no formal hours, it's easy to miss, but when you see long lines of people on the sidewalk, you'll know you've found it. They're all waiting for Mrs. Tam's little cookies, which she makes on the spot, on a griddle. While you're waiting in line, you can marvel at the simple efficiency of this one-person operation: there's room enough only for her, the griddle, and a mixing bowl. Like a crepe in texture and a fortune cookie in taste, the small, soft, warm cookies come about 12 for 1 dollar.

Follow Mosco to Columbus Park, an outdoor living room and salon for the community. The sounds of the city disappear here, not for the peace, but for the loud chirps of birds, the buzz of hundreds of people talking, and the clapping of mahjong tiles on the tables. Throngs of Chinese sitting on cardboard boxes and milk crates socialize here all year round, testing their skills and fortunes. They're young and old, male and female, but the activities seem to be segregated: the women play cards, the men play dominoes. Along the wire fence, fortune-tellers hang their red banners and point to mysterious battered books and long, thin reeds, devices used to divine the future. As few of the "wise women" speak English, having your destiny revealed may not come easy.

LANA BORTOLOT
Writer

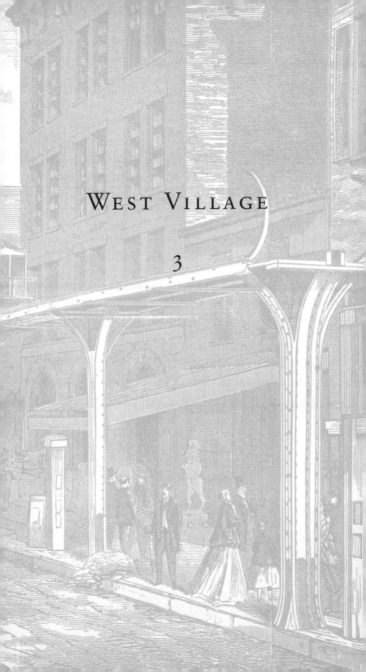

WEST VILLAGE

3

WEST VILLAGE

West Village

3.1 **The High Line**
Gansevoort Street to 34th Street between Tenth
& Eleventh Avenues
Ⓜ 14th Street (A/C/E/1/2/3); Eighth Avenue (L)

From Gansevoort Street and Tenth Avenue, amid the
remnants of the meatpacking district, you can see the current southern terminus of the High Line elevated railway
about 30 feet up in the air to the west. The structure runs
overhead all the way up to 32nd Street, 1.3 miles of steel,
as it pushes through old manufacturing buildings and
bisects the streets between Tenth and Eleventh Avenues—
follow it, and it will take you meandering through Chelsea
and up into Hell's Kitchen. Occasionally a spur of this
abandoned railway snakes east or west and ends inexplicably, stranded in a time when Chelsea's art galleries housed
New York's heavy industry and luxury liners embarked
from Chelsea Piers.

   The meatpacking district provides hints of the High
Line's past: built in the 1930's under an agreement among
the New York Central Railroad, New York State, and New
York City, the High Line's goal was to elevate dangerous
and congesting railroad traffic above city streets. The final
freight train that ran on its rails carried three carloads of
frozen turkeys in 1980.

   Imagine a new time, when the High Line could be used
again, this time as a landscaped public promenade, a place
to stroll and see the city skyline from a new perspective.
Friends of the High Line's mission is to save the High Line
from destruction and convert it to a unique public space
like the Promenade Plantée in Paris's 12th arrondissement.
PHILIP E. AARONS
Principal and founding partner, Millennium Partners

Why it's not a "real" city park is beyond me—enjoy it
before some genius tears it down.
ERIC STOLTZ
Actor

What's the Password

3.2 **APT**

419 West 13th Street between Ninth Avenue & Washington
Street, ☎ 212 414-4245
Open daily 6pm-3am
Ⓜ 14th Street (A/C/E); Eighth Avenue (L)

4.26 **SubMercer**

99 Prince Street at Mercer Street, ☎ 212 966-6060
Wednesday-Saturday 10pm-4am; closed Sunday-Tuesday
Ⓜ Prince Street (N/R); Broadway-Lafayette Street (F/V/S);
Spring Street (6)

Milk and Honey

Location, secret

🍴 Nightclub challenges: difficult to find or tough to gain
entry to, once located. But each is distinctive and worth
a bit of effort.

APT is in the meatpacking district. Even if you can
find the metal warehouse entry door, there is no guarantee
you will be admitted through the second door, which
leads to APT (referred to as "A-P-T"). It is designed as
an actual retro apartment with an old black-and-white
television set playing 70's sitcoms. The only clues that
you aren't in someone's pad are the small bar and the
dance floor downstairs.

You may know the trendy Mercer Hotel in SoHo and
its equally trendy and very delicious restaurant, the Mercer
Kitchen. But it may surprise you to find hidden there, one
floor below the basement restaurant, a mini nightclub
called SubMercer with a capacity for 35 clubgoers. Very ►

►

exclusive, it's supposedly open only to hotel guests. But if you're well dressed enough and can drop a few names, you can get in. You'll find a DJ, a disco ball, a VIP lounge, and a stripper pole for kinky visitors.

Many wonder if Milk and Honey even exists. Its location is secret and its telephone number changes weekly. It is six tables, four barstools and an expert mixologist with a plethora of drink specials. No menu. Only freshly squeezed juices, crushed ginger, sprinkled spices, and other all-natural ingredients are allowed. Vodka? How gauche! Find someone to take you there after dinner at Rao's. It will be a memorable evening, that's a promise.

ALEXANDER DUFF
Restaurateur

RECOMMENDED READING
Charles Schumann, *American Bar: The Artistry of Mixing Drinks*, Abbeville Press Inc., 1995.

3.4 **Corner Bistro**

331 West 4th Street at Jane Street, ☎ 212 242-9502
Open daily for lunch, dinner, and late-night meals
Ⓜ 14th Street (A/C/E/1/2/3); Eighth Avenue (L)

🍴 Located on the corner of one of the most maddeningly tangled sections of the West Village: the intersection of Eighth Avenue and West 4th and Jane Streets. It is, how-ever, quite easy to find "the Bistro." Inevitably, there will be people pouring out of it, walking into it, and, depend-ing on the weather, lounging outside of it. Forget everything you've heard about fancy service and sleek decor (there is a reason everything is so cheap) and order one of the Bistro's legendary hamburgers, fries, and a beer. A particular American species, Frat Boy, mistakenly believes it owns this place, but just push right by him and head for the back tables. You may look up one night (it doesn't close until the wee hours of the morning) and see Bruce Springsteen having dinner, right next to a bunch of businessmen, next to an in-love couple, next to a man who won't stop smiling. If it weren't always so crowded, it would be perfect.

KATHLEEN DEMARCO
Writer and film producer

3.5 The Village Vanguard

178 Seventh Avenue South between West 11th & Perry Streets
☎ 212 255-4037
Sets daily at 9:30pm and 11:30pm; Saturday additional set at 1am
Ⓜ 14th Street (1/2/3)

The legendary club that Miles Davis used to play in is dark, a little uncomfortable, and absolutely delightful.

ERIC STOLTZ
Actor

3.6 Smalls

183 West 10th Street between West 4th Street & Seventh Avenue South, ☎ 212 929-7565
Friday-Saturday 7:30pm-8am; Sunday-Thursday 10pm-8am
Ⓜ Christopher Street-Sheridan Square (1/2); West 4th Street (A/C/E/F/S/V)

If Charles Mingus were ever to call me on the telephone and ask me to go to Minton's Playhouse up in Harlem, I would say, "But Charlie, Minton's is closed," and I would take him to Smalls. Smalls is a jazz club pinched between Seventh Avenue and West 4th Street, at the bottom of a stairwell that twists into the basement. The music at Smalls almost never stops. It starts every night at about 7:30 or 8 p.m., and flows like a glowing current of electricity until musicians can no longer honk, bleat, or swing, and sunlight cracks your eyes as you climb the stairwell and stumble back out into the street.

Sometimes on cold winter evenings, people will stand for hours holding plastic bags filled with imported beer or wine bottles, in a line so long that it wraps around the corner onto West 4th Street. They'll wait and wait until it's their turn to pay the 10 dollar cover charge to Mr. Borden, the man at the door, who is probably reading poetry or playing his violin. The inside of Smalls is smoky and very dark, and there's room for about 50 people. There's no stage, and musicians perform in the front of the club, in an area about the size of a phone booth. The club's brick walls are covered by black-and-white photos of jazz legends. Patrons sit at small, round, candlelit tables, on padded benches, or at the bar, which serves only fruit juice and iced tea. Musicians are paid entirely from the sale of CDs, but applause is also a valid form of currency. Mounted on the wall, behind where the drums are usually set up, is an old photograph of Louis Armstrong, sitting cross-legged on the ground, smiling gloriously because his ears are delighted.

ALEX FRENCH
Writer

West Village à la Carte

Ⓜ West 4th Street (A/C/E/F/S/V); Christopher Street-Sheridan Square (1/2)

3.3 **Pastis**
9 Ninth Avenue at Little West 12th Street, ☎ 212 929-4844
Open daily for breakfast, lunch, dinner, and late-night meals
Ⓜ 14th Street (A/C/E); Eighth Avenue (L)

3.7 **Mary's Fish Camp**
64 Charles Street at West 4th Street, ☎ 646 486 2185
Monday-Saturday for lunch and dinner; closed Sunday

3.11 **Taylor's Bake Shop**
523 Hudson Street between West 10th & Charles Streets
☎ 212 378-2890
Monday-Friday 6am-9pm; Saturday, Sunday 7am-9pm

3.15 **Garden of the Church of St. Luke-in-the-Fields**
487 Hudson Street between Barrow & Christopher Streets, entrance on Barrow Street
Tuesday-Friday 8am-7pm; Saturday, Sunday 1pm-4pm; closed Monday

3.16 **Grange Hall**
50 Commerce Street at Barrow Street, ☎ 212 924-5246
Open daily for lunch and dinner

3.17 **Cherry Lane Theater**
38 Commerce Street at Barrow Street, ☎ 212 989-2020

5.12 **Pearl Oyster Bar**
18 Cornelia Street between Bleecker & West 4th Streets
☎ 212 691-8211
Monday-Friday for lunch and dinner; Saturday for dinner only

5.13 **Blue Hill**
75 Washington Place between Sixth Avenue & Washington Square West, ☎ 212 539-1776
Open daily for dinner

5.14 **Washington Square Park**
Foot of Fifth Avenue

5.22 **Murray's Cheese Shop**
257 Bleecker Street at Cornelia Street, ☎ 212 243-3289
Monday-Saturday 8am-8pm; Sunday 9am-6pm

🍴 Greenwich Village: the best place in Manhattan! Grab a lobster roll at Mary's or Pearl or a panini at my place, Murray's, and eat it outside on the bench. Try a maple danish and coffee from Taylor's and savor it in St. Luke's Garden (also see p. 69). Have a late dinner on a summer evening at Blue Hill restaurant, then sit on a bench and watch the people go by in Washington Square Park (also see p. 109). Have brunch at Grange Hall, catch a Sunday matinee at the Cherry Lane Theater next door, and   ►

▶

marvel at the most beautiful residential architecture in
Manhattan. Stay up really late and have a bite to eat at
Pastis in the meat market, then hit the local nightclubs.
ROBERT KAUFELT
Proprietor of Murray's Cheese Shop

3.8 Magnolia Bakery

401 Bleecker Street at West 11th Street, ☎ 212 462-2572
Sunday, Monday 10am-11:30pm; Tuesday-Thursday
9am-11:30pm; Friday 9am-12:30am; Saturday 10am-12:30am
Ⓜ Christopher Street-Sheridan Square (1/2); 14th Street
(A/C/E/L/3)

🍴 If your only goal is to taste the cupcakes those *Sex and the
City* girls carried on about, then you can visit Magnolia
Bakery any time you please. Magnolia's cupcakes are so
popular that fresh batches are on constant rotation from
the kitchen, and the bakery's other highlights—old-
fashioned icebox cake in op-art striations of whipped
cream and chocolate wafer; and a kind of lush, pastry
chef's piña colada with the sweet name of hummingbird
cake—only improve as they repose under their bell jars.

But for the full Magnolia experience, you must go after
dinner, say around 10:30 p.m. Then this little corner is the
brightest thing on Bleecker Street, and a steady stream of
sweet-toothed epicures is drifting towards the light. Inside,
Jimi Hendrix or Dick Dale or Muddy Waters is blasting
and there's a sense of mingled hilarity and chaos. The line
runs out the door—well, it's a smallish shop—and bakery
boxes are stacked by the window. The cashier stares into
space and one of the bakers, oblivious to the swarming
clientele, has commandeered an entire table for the icing
of more goodies. In the middle of everything, busy as the
Tasmanian Devil in those old Warner Brothers cartoons,
a single staff member is seeing to customers. But the
counter guy's good, and it turns out the chaos is merely an
illusion; the instant you've made your choice he's ready for

you: packing brownies, pouring cups of milk, dishing out a slab of that heavenly hummingbird.

So you can't eat inside because the icer's busy at your table. There are chairs and benches outside the store, but on summer nights no one's anxious to wander off too quickly. You could carry your sweets to a moody little parklet just catercorner from the bakery, where a cluster of benches stand tucked beneath overhanging trees. A coterie of Village types hangs out here, and maybe they drink a little, but they'll give you no guff.

DAVE KING
Writer

Not much of a secret anymore (alas!), but still the place to go in the West Village for authentic cupcakes like your mom used to make... or you can try the delicious banana pudding with Nilla wafers... or the sumptuous red velvet cake... or the super-light coconut frosted angel food cake... the list goes on and on... as does the line in this crowded little corner bakery, but when you see people leaving in a sugar haze, licking icing from their lips, they'll seem so happy you will rush to join them.

KATHLEEN DEMARCO
Writer and film producer

3.10 Betwixt
245 West 10th Street between Bleecker & Hudson Streets
☎ 212 243-8590
Monday-Friday 11:30am-6:30pm; Saturday 11am-6pm;
Sunday noon-5pm
Ⓜ Christopher Street-Sheridan Square (1/2); West 4th Street (A/C/E/F/S/V)

🎁 Buying clothes for girl kids between the ages of 7 and 12 is a little like studying Karl Marx in your spare time. The world of girl kid clothes seems hopelessly divided along grim and rigid class lines. The downtrodden proletariat wear Gap, Old Navy, or one of all those other variations

on khaki and sweatshirts that look like Red Guard uniforms gone suburban (read: cheap). The ruling-class elitist
oligarchs get their togs at Jacadi, Prince and Princess, or
Bonpoint and look like family members from a Darien
Christmas card photo. Is there some escape from this
totally humorless duality?

Sure, turn those little monsters loose in Betwixt, located
in liberated Greenwich Village next to the police headquarters of the Sixth Precinct. It's a hip clothing alternative for
little girls who can't wait to be big girls. Let 'em dress in
black stovepipe jeans, suede sport coats, Diesel-brand
denim, Miss Sixty, Mavi, Juicy, Monkeywear, and all that
other cool stuff you remember fitting into but, what with
commuting and everything...

The staff at Betwixt is young, knowledgeable and, most
importantly, able to stifle laughter at fathers who mean
well but don't have a clue what they are talking about.
ANDREW S. PAUL
Attorney

3.12 Taka

61 Grove Street between Bleecker Street & Seventh Avenue
South, ☎ 212 242-3699
Tuesday-Sunday for dinner only; closed Monday
Ⓜ Christopher Street-Sheridan Square (1/2);
West 4th Street (A/C/E/F/S/V)

🍴 Living in Greenwich Village, I am surrounded by restaurants of all sorts, but my favorite is a tiny Japanese
restaurant called Taka. Taka herself is an artist as well as
a sushi chef, and her sushi is in every way exquisite. You
will find me there, with my notebook and pen, enjoying
the early bird special, almost every day except Monday.
OLIVER SACKS
Neurologist and author

3.13 Chumley's

86 Bedford Street between Grove & Barrow Streets
📞 212 675-4449
Monday-Friday for dinner only; Saturday, Sunday for brunch
and dinner

Ⓜ Christopher Street-Sheridan Square (1/2); West 4th Street
(A/C/E/F/S/V)

🍴 Chumley's looks today much as it did in the 20's. In
deference to its speakeasy past, there is still no identifying
sign on the facade—only a small barred window in the
otherwise anonymous entrance door. Inside, the wooden
tables still display initials carved in the 20's by illegal
drinkers, and the walls are still adorned with jackets of
books authored by its once well-known patrons. On the
tables, lamps have replaced candles, and—Edna St. Vincent
Millay notwithstanding—burn only at one end.
ALIX KATES SHULMAN
Novelist

3.15 Garden of the Church of St. Luke-in-the-Fields

487 Hudson Street between Barrow & Christopher Streets,
entrance on Barrow Street
Tuesday-Friday 8am-7pm; Saturday, Sunday 1pm-4pm,
closed Monday

Ⓜ Christopher Street-Sheridan Square (1/2)

Walk through the street gate and follow the path to the
walled garden. A walled garden—the kind so many of
us imagined as children! In the center, a flowering tree,
paths through lilac and tulips and roses (tended by bands
of invisible volunteers), a few benches, squirrels, singing
birds. It feels safe and sacred—a broken-off piece of
paradise. If you're hungry, walk up Hudson Street to
🍴 Taylor's (see p. 64), a little take-out place where you can
get coffee and muffins or a small salad and bring it back
to eat in the garden.

The garden is lovely in all seasons—in winter with snow falling, in spring, when the first crocus comes up. People seem to talk softly and to smile and nod to one another as people do in churches, but it's also a good place for a kiss. I've seen commuters striding to the PATH train in the early morning stop and stare from the sidewalk, as if looking back into paradise from the fallen world.

MARIE HOWE
Poet

3.18 Former Home of Edna St. Vincent Millay

1873
75 1/2 Bedford Street between Morton & Commerce Streets
Not open to the public

Ⓜ Christopher Street-Sheridan Square (1/2); West 4th Street (A/C/E/F/S/V)

This house on Bedford Street is the smallest row house in Greenwich Village, once known as the "Edna St. Vincent Millay Doll's House" because the famous poet lived there with her husband Eugen Boissevain during the 1920's. It is said that the original house consisted of one narrow room on each of its floors, but it had the advantage of a closed-in backyard that gave easy access to a neighboring house occupied by Edna's one-time lover and lifelong friend, the poet Arthur Davison Ficke, then married to another dear friend, Gladys Brown.

EDMUND KEELEY
Novelist, translator, and critic

Celebrated Women

6.24 Former Home of Emma Goldman

210 East 13th Street between Second & Third Avenues
Not open to the public

Ⓜ 14th Street-Union Square (L/N/Q/R/W/4/5/6); Third Avenue (L)

3.18 **Former Home of Edna St. Vincent Millay**

75 1/2 Bedford Street between Morton & Commerce Streets
Not open to the public

Ⓜ Christopher Street-Sheridan Square (1/2); West 4th Street
(A/C/E/F/S/V)

3.13 **Chumley's**

86 Bedford Street between Grove & Barrow Streets

☎ 212 675-4449

Ⓜ Christopher Street-Sheridan Square (1/2); West 4th Street
(A/C/E/F/S/V)

Two houses—one a tenement in the East Village, one a
tiny townhouse in the West Village—still stand in lower
Manhattan, much as they were in the early decades of
the 20th century, despite occasional renovations. Each
memorializes the vibrant labors of a celebrated woman,
each of whose creative accomplishments contributed to
the exuberant spirit of an era.

At 210 East 13th Street, Emma Goldman (1869-1940),
the anarchist organizer, feminist agitator, birth-control and
free-love advocate who was tagged by FBI chief J. Edgar
Hoover "the most dangerous woman in the world," lived
for a decade. She moved to her "oasis in the desert," as she
called it, in 1903, soon after she emerged from hiding,
following President William McKinley's assassination in
1901 by a deranged anarchist whom Goldman was falsely
accused of abetting. In the living room/bedroom, which
also became her office, she launched her anarchist journal
of art and politics, *Mother Earth*, in 1906; it appeared
monthly for 12 years, interrupted only by occasional police
interference. In that dashing era of the New Woman,
Goldman's cold-water flat quickly became one of the city's
liveliest centers of feminist agitation and radical thought.
"There was always someone sleeping in the front, someone
who had stayed too late and lived too far away or who
was too shaky on their feet or needed cold compresses ▶

►

or who had no home to go to," wrote Goldman in her autobiography, *Living My Life*. The apartment was described by one friend as "a home for lost dogs," and lauded by another (Wobbly labor leader Big Bill Haywood) for its coffee "black as night, strong as the revolutionary ideal, sweet as love."

Across town and some blocks south stands the house of Edna St. Vincent Millay (1892-1950), another New Woman. Her 1922 poem,

my candle burns at both ends;
it will not last the night;
but ah, my foes, and oh, my friends—
it gives a lovely light!

was taken up as the anthem of a generation. This celebrated poet, playwright, and advocate of women's sexual freedom was one of three famously beautiful sisters who took bohemian Greenwich Village by storm. They acted at the Provincetown Playhouse on MacDougal Street, sometimes in Millay's own plays. A decade after gaining national attention for a long poem she published at age 20, Millay won a Pulitzer Prize in poetry in 1922, the first awarded to a woman. Her one-time lover, the influential critic Edmund Wilson, described her as "almost supernaturally beautiful" and her readings as "thrilling," noting ruefully that she was more interested in poetry than in men. After half a dozen years spent in various Village apartments with her sisters and sometimes their mother, Millay married in 1923 and moved for a while to the one-room-wide, three-story house—reputedly the city's narrowest—at 75½ Bedford Street. In her eighties, Millay's sister Norma told me that back during Prohibition the sisters would sometimes tend bar as a favor to their friend Lee Chumley, owner of Chumley's (also see pp. 69, 85), the popular speakeasy at 86 Bedford, diagonally across the street from Millay's house.

If Lee Chumley was away, Norma confided, they invited
their friends in for an evening of free drinks.
ALIX KATES SHULMAN
Writer

RECOMMENDED READING
Edna St. Vincent Millay, "First Fig," *A Few Figs From Thistles*, 1922.

Stargazing

After several decades, the brick facades of many row
houses built in New York during the Federal period began
to fatigue and buckle, and it became necessary to "tie" the
brick back to the joists with metal rods, which were then
capped by iron plates on the outside walls. Early versions
of these plates, which functioned like large washers, were
made in straightforward utilitarian shapes—a couple of
crossed iron strips, or perhaps a simple rondel. By the end
of the Civil War, however, ironworkers began making them
from melted-down cannonballs and casting them in the
shape of stars to honor the enduring Republic. You'll find
these utilitarian but beautiful symbols on brick walls
throughout lower Manhattan and the Village—affecting
examples of turning swords into plowshares.
ANGELA HEDERMAN
Editor and publisher

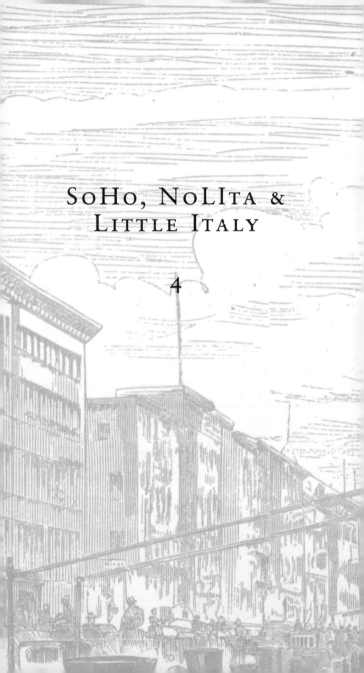

SoHo, NoLIta & Little Italy

4

SOHO

1. Film Forum
2. Pétanque competition
3. Joe's Dairy
4. St. Anthony of Padua
5. Richie's Candy Store
6. Pepe Rosso to Go
7. Pino's Prime Meats
8. The New York Earth Room
9. Raoul's
10. Vesuvio Bakery Shop
11. Anonymous Hair Salon
12. Joovay
13. Sullivan Street Bakery
14. Ear Inn
15. The Broken Kilometer
16. Palačinka
17. Broome Street Bar
18. Vintage New York
19. Ted Muehling
20. E. Vogel Inc.
21. Putnam Rolling Ladder Co.
22. Patina
23. K. Trimming & Zippers
24. Singer Building
25. Fanelli Cafe
26. Mercer Hotel
27. Balthazar
28. Savoy
29. E.R. Butler & Co.

NOLITA & LITTLE ITALY

30. St. Patrick's Old Cathedral
31. Storefront for Art & Architecture
32. Bowery Savings Bank

SoHo, NoLita & Little Italy

SOHO

4.1 **The Film Forum**
209 West Houston between Sixth Avenue & Varick Street
☎ 212 727-8110
Ⓜ Houston Street (1/2); Spring Street (C/E)

Don't worry about what's on the bill at this intimate
three-theater complex. Just trust the programmer's taste
and go. Whether it's a quirky low-budget job, a pristine
new print of an American classic, or a contemporary
foreign film, these folks find and screen the best. The
atmosphere is unpretentious, the crowd is smart and
appreciative, and they have the best popcorn in New York.
GREGORY MOSHER
Director and producer

4.2 *Pétanque* **competition**
MacDougal Street between Prince & West Houston Streets
Competition held on July 14th, Bastille Day
Ⓜ Houston Street (1/2); Spring Street (C/E); Prince Street (N/R)

The visitor who finds him- or herself in Manhattan on July
14th shouldn't miss the Bastille Day *pétanque* competition
on MacDougal Street. Just for the day, the entire block is
covered with sand and partitioned into a dozen or so courts
in which teams from the city's French restaurants go up
against each other. (Where they practice the rest of the year
is a total mystery.) The fun isn't the feeling that you're in
France. The fun is that you could only be in New York.
ROSLYN SCHLOSS
Editor

Note: The competition was organized by Provence
(38 MacDougal Street, ☎ 212 475-7500) in celebration

*of the restaurant's fifth anniversary more than a decade
ago. Now an annual charity event, it benefits the
Children's Museum of the Arts (182 Lafayette Street,
☎ 212 941-9198).*

4.3 Joe's Dairy

156 Sullivan Street between Prince
& West Houston Streets, ☎ 212 677-8780
Tuesday-Saturday 9am-6pm; closed Sunday, Monday
Ⓜ Houston Street (1/2); Spring Street (C/E); Prince Street (N/R)

If you're a mozzarella snob or just like a good Italian
sandwich, you will do well to make a stop at Joe's Dairy.
It's a tiny, old-fashioned storefront, a vestige from the days
when this neighborhood was the western half of Little Italy
(split by what is now SoHo). Inside you'll find an ample
cheese selection along with other dairy staples such as
milk, mascarpone, and ricotta. Filling the shelves are a
sampling of olive oils and dried pastas. But the real reason
to make the pilgrimage is the mozzarella—unsalted, salted,
and smoked. You may never taste better outside Italy. If
you're lucky, you'll catch the cheese makers in action in the
back, stirring and stretching the gooey white stuff in enormous soup pots. If you happen to walk by and see smoke
billowing out of the place and the entire staff hanging
around outside, don't bother calling the fire department...
it's only the smoked mozzarella being made. Grab a half
of a smoked for a tasty snack, or take an unsalted home
for the perfect, rich, velvety accompaniment to a fresh
tomato and sprig of basil. Joe's sells a nice mozzarella
sandwich and also will grate your just-cut piece of
Parmigiano Reggiano.

SARAH CAPLAN
Designer and graphic artist

Sullivan Street Stroll

Ⓜ Houston Street (1/2); Spring Street (C/E);
Prince Street (N/R)

4.4 **St. Anthony of Padua Roman Catholic Church**
c. 1888
155 Sullivan Street at West Houston Street

4.5 **Richie's Candy Store**
156 Sullivan Street at West Houston Street
☎ 212 982-7572
Monday-Friday 7am-9pm; Saturday 8am-midnight;
Sunday 8am-8pm

4.6 **Pepe Rosso to Go**
149 Sullivan Street between West Houston & Prince Streets
☎ 212 677-4555
Open daily for lunch and dinner

4.7 **Pino's Prime Meats**
149 Sullivan Street between West Houston & Prince Streets
☎ 212 475-8134
Monday-Saturday 8:30am-6pm; closed Sunday

4.11 **Anonymous Hair Salon**
105 Sullivan Street between Prince & Spring Streets
☎ 212 966-6806
Open daily 11am-7pm

4.13 **Sullivan Street Bakery**
73 Sullivan Street between Spring & Broome Streets
☎ 212 334-9435
Open daily 7am-7pm

🍴 There's a street, Sullivan Street, that was the spine of an
🎁 Italian-American neighborhood now devoured by the
advance of SoHo. But if you start at Houston and walk the
three blocks south to Broome, a few places that remain can
give you the flavor of what was.

Start at the church of St. Anthony of Padua. On a good Saturday you can catch an old-fashioned Italian-American wedding, with the chance of a horse and buggy or at least the longest white stretch limo you've ever seen. Across from the church is Richie's Candy Store. Egg creams, the racing sheet, newspapers, magazines, a television going, some guys just hanging out, and Richie... if Richie's busy, one of the guys will take your money and help you out. Walk past Depression Modern, which used to be Canapa's Bakery. Across the street is Pepe Rosso to Go, which used to be Rocky's Vegetable Store. The butcher shop's another leftover, with sawdust on the floor and a butcher block from years ago. Pino took over for Mario, but the flavor's the same. There used to be another butcher on this street, as well as two bakeries, two grocery stores, a club, some storefronts, and some stores that were just for rent to keep baby carriages and bicycles.

Cross Prince Street and keep walking and you'll come to a sign that reads Anonymous Hair Salon. Go in on a Saturday morning and you'll be back in the old neighborhood. All the seniors come to get their hair washed and set and teased into bouffants that will hold all week. You'll get all the gossip: who died, who's sick, who's been naughty and who's been nice, plus you'll get a good haircut. Ask for Pat. She'll order you coffee and a sandwich at lunchtime. But be nice... you gotta be nice in the neighborhood.

Afterwards, go down one more block to Sullivan Street Bakery and have a coffee and a piece of the old-fashioned pizza like they used to make—no cheese. Then shop all you want in the SoHo everybody knows.

LOUISA ERMELINO
Writer

RECOMMENDED READING
Louisa Ermelino, *The Black Madonna,* Simon & Schuster, 2001.

4.8 Dia Center for the Arts: *The New York Earth Room*

1977, Walter De Maria

141 Wooster Street between West Houston & Prince Streets

☎ 212 473-8072

Wednesday-Saturday noon-3pm and 3:30pm-6pm; closed
Sunday-Tuesday; closed summer

Ⓜ Broadway-Lafayette Street (F/S/V); Prince Street (N/R)

If the urban shuffle is making you pine for pastoral environs
or if you just want a place to reflect, the Earth Room—
a sanctuary in a SoHo loft—is the answer. Created in 1977
by American artist Walter De Maria, it is filled with 250
cubic yards of rich, dark topsoil weighing 280,000 pounds
and standing 22 inches high. Originally one of three Earth
Rooms—the other two created by De Maria in Germany—
this is the only one still remaining, sponsored and maintained
by the Dia Center for the Arts (see p. 165). Prepare to be
transported by an incredibly unique experience.

CHRISTINE MOOG
Graphic designer

4.9 Raoul's

180 Prince Street between Sullivan & Thompson Streets

☎ 212 966-3518

Open daily for dinner and late-night meals

Ⓜ Spring Street (C/E); Prince Street (N/R)

🍴 For someone who finds comfort in the gloriously faded
past while being entirely immersed in the present, Raoul's
is a godsend. I remember pulling up to the bar when I was
a young writer and feeling as though I'd arrived home.
Countless evenings have been spent enjoying long, winding
discussions with friends, surrounded by straight talkers and
abstract expressionists, gumshoes, and rock stars. Fifteen
years after my first steak au poivre at Raoul's, I still look
forward to every visit—every greeting from Eddie, maitre
d' and dear friend; every walk through the hectic kitchen
to the back room; every journey up the precarious circular

staircase leading to the restrooms. I've enjoyed dinners for 15 in the front room settled comfortably into the seemingly ancient long banquette, as well as simple dinners for two, hidden away at a table under the skylight. Raoul's seems to get better every year, even though it hasn't changed a bit.

ANDY SPADE
Creative director and fashion designer

4.10 Vesuvio Bakery Shop

160 Prince Street between Thompson Street & West Broadway
☎ 212 925-8248
Monday-Saturday 7am-7pm; closed Sunday
Ⓜ Prince Street (N/R); Spring Street (C/E)

🎁 Vesuvio Bakery Shop was established in 1920, and Anthony Dapolito carries on the tradition of his parents in presenting a treasure of delicious homemade Italian bread and tarellas (pepper biscuits). This small bakery shop has a nostalgic, Depression-era ambience. Anthony is a fixture in SoHo and Little Italy. The shop has been used as a background in corporate ads in *Fortune* and *Forbes* magazines, as well as in films, including *The Prince of Tides*.

NICHOLAS ARCOMANO
Attorney

4.12 Joovay

436 West Broadway between Prince & Spring Streets
☎ 212 431-6386
Open daily noon-7pm
Ⓜ Spring Street (C/E/6); Prince Street (N/R)

🎁 Sometimes, in a strange city, it's the small stuff that seems mysterious and just out of reach: where to buy nice underwear? If you're downtown in SoHo there's a very small, dear store called Joovay. It has fine lingerie at pretty good prices, and the women who work there are gracious, helpful, and unpretentious.

MARIE HOWE
Poet

Vintage Bars

4.14 The Ear Inn

326 Spring Street between Greenwich & Washington Streets

☎ 212 431-9750

Open daily for lunch, dinner, and late-night meals

Ⓜ Spring Street (C/E); Houston Street (1/2)

🍴 Originally located on the banks of the Hudson River and originally known as the James Brown House, the Ear is one of the few remaining two-story, wood-framed, Federal-style buildings in Manhattan. One of the oldest taverns in the city (circa 1817), the Ear served as a halfway house for runaway slaves during the Civil War. Not only a beautiful and historic landmark, it's also the best meal for your money below Houston Street. The daily fresh fish special cannot be beat. A friendly, loud, and eclectic downtown neighborhood crowd that includes workers, bikers, artists, and musicians, spills out on the sidewalk on summer evenings.

4.25 Fanelli Cafe (also see p. 154)

94 Prince Street at Mercer Street, ☎ 212 226-9412

Open daily for lunch, dinner, and late-night meals

Ⓜ Prince Street (N/R); Broadway-Lafayette Street (F/S/V); Spring Street (6)

🍴 Though there is much debate about which is the oldest bar in the city (Fraunces Tavern, 1762; Bridge Cafe, 1794; Ear Inn, 1817; Pete's Tavern, 1864; McSorley's Ale House, 1854), Fanelli's is surely one of the oldest and best. Serving food and drink continuously since 1847, it operated as a speakeasy during Prohibition from 1920 to 1933. Perhaps the most beautiful back bar in the city, it faces a wall of original boxing photos and portraits dating from the turn of the century. Fanelli's was once my friendly local neighborhood watering hole, but as SoHo has changed, unfortunately so has the crowd (and boy, is it crowded).

So, go very late at night after the tourists, shoppers, and the bridge-and-tunnel gang have gone to bed and try hard to engage Bob the bartender in conversation. A retired former prizefighter, he once fought Bob Chavalo for the Canadian heavyweight championship and was smart enough to turn down a fight with mean Sonny Liston. If you get Bob going, then you're in for an education loaded with vicious one-liners and lots of laughs.

3.9　**The White Horse Tavern**
567 Hudson Street at West 11th Street, ☎ 212 989-3956
Open daily for lunch, dinner, and late-night meals

Ⓜ Christopher Street-Sheridan Square (1/2); 14th Street (A/C/E/3)

🍴 Once a speakeasy, this historic tavern has been a favorite of locals, workers, artists, and writers since 1880 (including such neighborhood notables as Jack Kerouac, Norman Mailer, and Bob Dylan). Fact: in 1953, Dylan Thomas, on a two-day binge, drank himself to death here. ("I've had 18 straight whiskeys and I believe that's the record.") Sit outside at the corner table on a lazy Saturday afternoon and watch Jane Jacob's neighborhood stroll by. Stick to the beer, a good bacon burger, or my favorite, the tuna melt.

3.13　**Chumley's** (also see p. 69)
86 Bedford Street between Grove & Barrow Streets
☎ 212 675-4449
Monday-Friday for dinner only; Saturday, Sunday for brunch and dinner

Ⓜ Christopher Street-Sheridan Square (1/2); West 4th Street (A/C/E/F/S/V)

🍴 Bet you can't find this 1920's sawdusted former speakeasy. If you like frat boys, go early; if not, go late on a snowy winter night, sit in front of a roaring wood-burning fire, and carve your sweetheart's name in a table. Writers once met here, and dusty jackets of their novels grace the　▶

▶

walls. A diverse and expansive selection of beers is on tap, including my local favorite, the Brooklyn Brewing Co. lager.
FREDERIC SCHWARTZ
Architect

4.15 **Dia Center for the Arts: *The Broken Kilometer***
1979, Walter De Maria
393 West Broadway between Spring & Broome Streets
📞 212 925-9397
Wednesday-Saturday noon-3pm and 3:30-6pm; closed
Sunday-Tuesday; closed summer
Ⓜ Spring Street (C/E/6); Prince Street (N/R)

Walter De Maria's 500-piece work is both the bright golden reflection you see and the silence you hear in the white room it inhabits: a weightless, drifting space. Looking left to right, the building's row of cast-iron columns gives comparison to scale, and divides the work into two rows of bars on one side, and three on the other. From foreground to background, all weight, dimension, and shape disappear into light. The rear bars float off the floor and the wall drops behind the horizon. The work's calm, mystical euphoria owes everything to its simple perspective in pictorial space. It feels huge and timeless and exists in a pure state of relativity. Seeing and understanding its specific physicality becomes a way of thinking while you are there, which is then claimed quickly by memory once you exit through the short maze and return to the outside.
JAMES L. BODNAR
Architect

4.16 **Palačinka**
28 Grand Street between Sixth Avenue & Thompson Street
📞 212 625-0362
Open daily 10:30am-11:30pm
Ⓜ Canal Street (A/C/E/1/2)

¶⍭ Czech for "little pancake," Palačinka is a Prague-meets-Paris creperie in south SoHo offering the city's best sweet and savory. The look of this small cafe is as simple as its fare, and the mood is set with grainy jazz recordings or the latest from Stereolab. Wait for the coveted cozy corner table and linger over a late breakfast. You cannot go wrong with the basic butter, sugar, and fresh lime.

TRACEY HUMMER
Writer

4.17 **Broome Street Bar**
363 West Broadway at Broome Street, ☎ 212 925-2086
Monday-Friday for lunch and dinner; Saturday, Sunday for brunch and dinner
Ⓜ Spring Street (C/E/6); Prince Street (N/R)

¶⍭ A wonderful no-frills restaurant located smack in the center of SoHo. After too much shopping at Prada and too much looking at disparate art galleries and too much walking and people-gazing and all the rest of the things people do in SoHo, go to the Broome Street Bar, sit back, order a beer, look out the window, and be so happy that there are places like this in the city where comfort reigns and pretension is permanently barred.

KATHLEEN DEMARCO
Writer and film producer

4.18 **Vintage New York**
482 Broome Street at Wooster Street, ☎ 212 226-9463
Monday-Saturday 11am-9pm; Sunday noon-9pm
Ⓜ Spring Street (C/E/6); Prince Street (N/R)

🎁 The Sunday night blues: 7 p.m. and no wine in the house. Vintage New York to the rescue. How? The savvy owners also run Rivendell Winery, which operates under a vineyard license. Thus they're permitted to open on Sunday. True to its name, the shop sells only New York wines—

about 200—including reds, whites, sparkling wines, dessert wines, and fruit wines, as well as cider and mead. There's even a bar at the back where for a buck per (tiny) gulp you can taste any wine they carry. Vintage New York also carries native delicacies such as toothsome cheeses from Sprout Creek Farm in Poughkeepsie and Germantown's Highland Farms venison prosciutto.

DANY LEVY (AND EDITORIAL STAFF OF DAILYCANDY.COM)
Founder of DailyCandy.com

Howard Street

4.19 **Ted Muehling**
27 Howard Street between Broadway & Lafayette Street
☎ 212 431-3825
Tuesday-Saturday noon-6pm; closed Sunday, Monday
Ⓜ Canal Street (J/M/N/Q/R/W/Z/6)

4.20 **E. Vogel Inc.**
19 Howard Street between Broadway & Lafayette Street
☎ 212 925-2460
Monday-Friday 8am-4pm; Saturday 8am-1pm; closed Sunday
Ⓜ Canal Street (J/M/N/Q/R/W/Z/6)

4.21 **Putnam Rolling Ladder Co. Inc.**
32 Howard Street between Broadway & Crosby Street
☎ 212 226-5147
Monday-Friday 8am-4pm; closed Saturday, Sunday
Ⓜ Canal Street (J/M/N/Q/R/W/Z/6)

🎁 Although almost every fashionable woman I know owns at least one pair of beautiful earrings from Ted Muehling's elegant workshop on Howard Street, the origin of these treasures remains somehow mysterious. Maybe it's because ownership of a pair is like membership in an exclusive club. Or maybe because, like me, husbands refuse to tell their wives the location of this never-fail "get-out-of-jail-free" card. Whatever the reason, Ted Muehling has resisted the temptation to go "wide," and the quality and design remain unsurpassed. Though mostly abstract, these earrings, necklaces, bracelets, and pins find their inspiration in organic forms such as berries, rice, shells, nuts, and eggs. The shop also carries beautiful ceramic pieces designed by Mr. Muehling and manufactured by the great Nymphenburg porcelain factory in Germany. Highly recommended as a source of simple beauty.

While on Howard Street, look in on two other establishments devoted to Old World craftsmanship. At Number 19, visit the three-story brick townhouse, home to E. Vogel, and order a pair of made-to-measure jodhpurs or a pair of custom dress shoes. You will be in good company; this fourth-generation establishment (32 years in its present location, to which it moved from its 1879 Warren Street home) has made riding boots and shoes for General Pershing, Charles Lindbergh, Paul Newman, and Jacqueline Onassis, as well as for Olympic equestrian teams, and kings and queens.

At Number 32, you will find the Putnam Rolling Ladder Company. Their model Number 1—think library ladder sliding along a brass rail—has been in continuous production since 1905. The ownership is in its third generation, having taken possession of the company in 1946 when Mr. Putnam sold it to his long-time employee. The shop has been on Howard Street at its current whereabouts since the 1930's and, with the exception of one i-Mac computer, nothing appears to have changed much. Even the sign above the shop is from Mr. Putnam's horse-drawn carriage. Current clients range from Barnes & Noble to President and Mrs. Bush.

ROBERT KAHN
Architect

4.22 Patina

451 Broome Street between Broadway & Mercer Street
☎ 212 625-3375
Monday-Saturday noon-7pm; Sunday 1pm-6pm
Ⓜ Spring Street (6); Prince Street (N/R)

🏛 This unique SoHo shop features items that reflect the
passions of its energetic owner, Lenore Newman. Hand-
selected vintage clothing and accessories, unusual jewelry,
ceramics, tableware, and glassware (both old and new)
are available. Displays, in the form of amusing vignettes,
are constantly changing, and new merchandise enters the
store regularly. Perfect for that hard-to-find gift.
SUSAN TUNICK
Artist and writer

4.23 K. Trimming & Zippers

519 Broadway between Spring & Broome Streets
☎ 212 431-8929
Sunday-Thursday 9:15am-6:30pm; Friday 9:15am-1pm;
closed Saturday
Ⓜ Spring Street (6); Prince Street (N/R)

🏛 Take your daughters to K. Trimming & Zippers, an old-
time notion store that has managed somehow to hold on
in the thick of SoHo's endless reinvention. In addition to
fabrics and buttons galore, you'll find all sorts of elastic
for ballet slippers and beyond, every imaginable kind of
trim (what scavenging grounds for Greek princesses and
other school-play characters!), colorful boas for dress-up,
and above all, a treasure trove of ribbons. Choose any
width you desire, from satin to grosgrain, solids of every
hue to little white hearts on a cheery pink background.
Jazz up pigtails or upgrade a present. And while you shop,
you'll experience a bit of what the neighborhood used to
be. There is nothing faux about the distressed floors or the

dusty, untended window display. But you'll come away
with something just right, I'm sure, and spend next to
nothing in the process.

JANE FISHER
Independent consultant

4.24 Singer Building
1904, Ernest Flagg
561 Broadway between Prince & Spring Streets
Ⓜ Prince Street (N/R); Broadway-Lafayette Street (F/S/V)

The two facades of Ernest Flagg's 1902-04 Singer Building
(the second facade pops out on Prince Street) rank among
the most innovative structural and material expressions of
New York architecture. Combining glazed and buff terra-
cotta tiles, florid wrought iron and structural steel, and
large panes of glass in different planes, the building is one
of the most sophisticated responses to a strain of French
architecture usually overshadowed by the Beaux Arts. It
provided a richly suggestive direction for New York's high-
rise architecture, yet had a disappointingly small progeny.
Ten years later, Flagg offered a more refined variant on the
theme in his building for Scribner's Bookstore (now a
Benetton) on Fifth Avenue at 48th Street.

BARRY BERGDOLL
Architectural historian and professor, Columbia University

RECOMMENDED READING
Mardges Bacon, *Ernest Flagg: Beaux-Arts Architect and Urban
Reformer*, MIT Press, 1986.

WNYC
820 AM or 93.9 FM

The best way to wake up and get your news—never too
harsh or hyped, a gentle nudge into your day.

ERIC STOLTZ
Actor

Savoir Fare

4.27 **Balthazar**

80 Spring Street between Broadway & Crosby Street

☎ 212 965-1414

Open daily for breakfast, lunch, and dinner

Ⓜ Spring Street (6); Prince Street (N/R)

4.28 **Savoy**

70 Prince Street at Crosby Street, ☎ 212 219-8570

Monday-Saturday for lunch and dinner; Sunday for dinner

Ⓜ Prince Street (N/R); Spring Street (6)

🍽 There are two restaurants that I rely on for sustenance when I am in New York. The busy, often crowded Balthazar is a terrific place for breakfast. When you walk in you can pick up a *New York Times*, bring it to your table and read it over a cappuccino or a bowl of café au lait. You can also, if you wish, have delicious rolls—plain or sweet—or eggs Benedict or whatever pleases you. It is easily the most relaxed breakfast that I know. I sometimes go to Balthazar for dinner, and I like to be seated near the entrance. If I am early, I can catch the stylish and often outrageously attired guests making their entrance.

Perhaps my favorite place in which to eat, at least in downtown Manhattan, is the very intimate and not overly expensive Savoy. One has a choice of eating downstairs in a comfortable atmosphere, selecting a meal from a varied menu, or upstairs, in a smallish room with logs burning in the fireplace, where one eats from a prix-fixe menu. Whether one chooses downstairs or upstairs, the food will be delicious. The wine list is small but brilliantly selected. In all the years I have been eating there, I have not been disappointed with any meal. The people who work at Savoy are without question the friendliest yet least obtrusive of restaurant personnel. It is a great place to finish off the day.
MARK STRAND
Poet

4.29 E. R. Butler & Co.

75 Spring Street between Crosby & Lafayette Streets
℡ 212 925-3565
By appointment only
Ⓜ Spring Street (6); Prince Street (N/R)

🎁 Shopping at this hardware showroom is like a visit to Berry Brothers & Rudd Ltd., wine merchants to the Queen—you sit at a lovely mahogany table (in Butler's case, designed by the fine furniture maker Chris Lehrecke) and the hardware is brought to you. It feels more like a museum of architectural hardware than a place to buy a latch set and a pair of hinges. Whether you are looking for a traditional, authentic early-American door handle or one designed by the philosopher Ludwig Wittgenstein, the Bauhaus master Walter Gropius, or the contemporary architect Richard Meier, you will find it here. If it exists, they have it; if it doesn't, they will make it for you, in any of 75 hand-finished metal patination formulas, including sterling silver. (And should you need to jot down a thought, the notepads are engraved.)

Behind this quiet and elegant showroom is a high-tech and sophisticated enterprise, including state-of-the-art CNC machines, prototype development, as well as antique conservation and restoration. There is even a library with 5,000 rare trade catalogs, 6,000 original drawings, and thousands of original hardware patterns.

The only catch (so to speak) is that the showroom is open to design professionals and their clients by appointment, and to the rest of you by pleading.

ROBERT KAHN
Architect

NOLITA & LITTLE ITALY

`4.30` St. Patrick's Old Cathedral

1815, Joseph Mangin
260-264 Mulberry Street between Prince & East Houston Streets
Ⓜ Broadway-Lafayette Street (F/S/V); Spring Street (6);
Prince Street (N/R)

Old St. Patrick's is a very charming brick church with
a lot of greenery around it, an unexpected piece of the
19th century. Formally opened in 1815 to a crowd of more
than 4,000 worshippers and dignitaries, it was New York's
first cathedral, the second Roman Catholic church in
America, and the first house of worship in the United
States to be dedicated to Ireland's patron saint, Patrick.
The building was engulfed by a fire in 1866, which
destroyed all but the outer walls, but was reconstructed in
two years' time. It is surrounded on Mott, Prince, and
Mulberry Streets by a beautiful brick wall, built to protect
the cathedral from the frequent brawls and street riots
between Protestants and Catholics. When the Cardinal's
seat was moved uptown to the new St. Patrick's Cathedral
on Fifth Avenue, dedicated in 1879, the historic St.
Patrick's downtown became a parish church.
JOAN SILBER
Writer

`4.31` Storefront for Art and Architecture

1993, Steven Holl and Vito Acconci
97 Kenmare Street at Cleveland Place, ☎ 212 431-5795
Tuesday-Saturday 11am-6pm during exhibitions;
closed Sunday, Monday
Ⓜ Spring Street (6); Bowery (J/M); Broadway-Lafayette
Street (F/S/V); Prince Street (N/R)

On a small plot of land at the crossroads of SoHo, Little
Italy, and Chinatown, a storefront facade uniquely defines
its turf. In renovating a space to be dedicated to showing

architectural schemes and urban plans, utopian or dystopian, Holl and Acconci conceived a wall that transforms itself from a blank surface into a geometric plane, hinged within to allow for bold opening sections that pivot out into the street. Windows and a door appear, then disappear, reverting to the planar surface from which they emerged. But the intellectual excitement of all this is in the realization of a kind of paper architecture in the very materials of the facade itself.

MARJORIE WELISH
Writer

The design of this gallery provides New York with a genuine stage for urban theater. The unfolding wall establishes a threshold that takes art into the street and brings people close to the exhibits.

IAIN LOW
Architect

GREENWICH VILLAGE

5

GREENWICH VILLAGE

5.1 Strand Book Store

828 Broadway at East 12th Street, ☎ 212 473-1452
Monday-Saturday 9:30am-10:30pm; Sunday 11am-10:30pm;
rare book room closes at 6:20pm daily

Ⓜ 14th Street-Union Square (L/N/Q/R/W/4/5/6)

For more than 20 years I've lived within a three-minute
walk to the Strand Book Store, which means I've had to
contend with more than two decades of sheer temptation.
The Strand's celebrated claim of "over eight miles of used
books" certainly can no longer be true; I've purchased at
least a mile's worth myself.

Now almost the last remnant in what used to be a
thriving district of used book and print shops, the Strand
boasts a splendid selection of used books in all fields,
along with extensive discounted offerings of review books.
In addition, I will confess to enjoying a vicarious kick by
purchasing discarded volumes from distinguished owners;
my shelves contain books once owned by Elizabeth
Hardwick, Aileen Ward, John Simon, and Joseph Alsop,
among others.

Big, dusty, sometimes a bit confusing, often crowded, and
resolutely un-air-conditioned, the Strand remains a stalwart
institution dedicated to the hopelessly addicted bibliophile.
RICHARD LAVENSTEIN
Architect

5.2 Forbes Magazine Building and Galleries

1925, Carrère & Hastings and Shreve & Lamb
62 Fifth Avenue at 12th Street, ☎ 212 206-5548
Galleries open Tuesday, Wednesday, Friday, Saturday
10am-4pm; Thursday 10am-4pm, preregistered tours only;
closed Sunday, Monday

Ⓜ 14th Street (F/V/1/2/3); 14th Street-Union Square
(L/N/Q/R/W/4/5/6)

The Forbes Building was built as the American headquarters for British publisher, Macmillan. Architect Thomas Hastings of Carrère & Hastings (The New York Public Library) died before completion; the successor architects were Shreve & Lamb (Empire State Building). Elements of both firms' styles are visible here. The member of the Macmillan family who selected architects and oversaw construction was Harold Macmillan, who left publishing to go into politics when he returned to the U.K. and ended up Prime Minister. The building and adjacent 1840's brownstone were acquired by Forbes Inc. in 1964; the ground floor now houses the Forbes Magazine Galleries. Shortly after the entire ground floor of the building opened as the Forbes Magazine Galleries in 1986, a friend of my father turned to him and laughingly observed, "Malcolm, that's the happiest sequence of non sequiturs I've ever experienced." Featuring the world's largest collection of Fabergé's fabled jeweled Easter eggs created for the last czars, a staggering archive of American historical documents, the earliest surviving renderings of the game Monopoly, an armada of toy boats, platoons of toy soldiers, inscribed trophies, and rotating exhibitions of paintings and photographs, the galleries are an evolving manifestation of the diverse collecting enthusiasms of three generations of Forbeses.

CHRISTOPHER FORBES
Vice chairman, Forbes Magazine

My vote for the best little jewel of a museum (and free to boot) is the Forbes Galleries in the lobby of the Forbes Magazine Building on Fifth Avenue. Apparently Malcolm Forbes's interests in collecting crossed many borders. If you are a fan of Fabergé, you will find a trove of royal Easter eggs, jewelry, and other accoutrements that the great jeweler created for the Romanovs. There is also a fabulous collection of historical memorabilia, including the bill for Paul Revere's ride (who knew he was a consultant?) and

Lincoln's opera glasses. The collection of toy tin soldiers and boats and the prototypes for the original Monopoly game are also wonderful.

MARIA MANHATTAN
Artist

5.4 Second Cemetery of the Spanish and Portuguese Synagogue

1805-1829

72-76 West 11th Street between Fifth & Sixth Avenues

Ⓜ 14th Street (F/V/1/2/3); 14th Street-Union Square (L/N/Q/R/W/4/5/6)

In the middle of frenetic Manhattan, along one of the loveliest tree-lined streets in Greenwich Village, it is possible to miss one of the city's most unusual little gems if you walk too quickly. There, nestled along the south side of 11th Street, just a few feet from the streaming traffic along Sixth Avenue, is a tiny triangle that comprises one of the city's few Spanish Portuguese Jewish cemeteries. Scattered haphazardly on the small plot are a handful of simple weathered tombstones—somehow, in the midst of Manhattan's mad rush for development, this sacred corner of the dead survived intact. Today, occupying a tiny slice of real estate, this is a completely different stop for any city visitor. When finished, go to French Roast on the corner of West 11th Street and Sixth Avenue, and toast the dead with a good glass of house wine.

GERALD POSNER
Writer

It is typical of New York that unlike any other major city in the world, it does not have a recognizable and accessible cemetery. No Highbury, no Père-Lachaise, no San Michele. Maybe this lack of graveyard gravitas comes from the famous Gotham mercenary attitude; the lust for power and wealth have little to do with bones moldering six feet under.

There is, however, a tiny Jewish cemetery on West 11th.

The men and women buried there came to New York in the early 19th century as refugees from South America in the wake of upheavals surrounding independence. There are a couple dozen headstones with Hebrew writing, two tombs, and an ivy-strewn brick walkway that meanders through the plots. But the walkway has nowhere to go. The cemetery is a triangle, no more than 30 feet in any direction, appallingly hemmed in on all sides by the city— by an apartment building, a brick wall, and a sidewalk. The hemming-in was so violent that more than one grave-stone is a part of the brick wall that lies on its western and southern edge. The forces of real estate were so powerful that someone simply built walls through the gravestones.

The cemetery has a sad appearance, especially in a downpour, this forgotten place, no one to come to tend to the graves, and no one alive who knows any of the people resting there.

JAMES ZUG
Writer

Greenwich Village Stroll

5.6 Milligan Place
1852
Sixth Avenue between West 10th & West 11th Streets
Ⓜ West 4th Street (A/C/E/S); 14th Street (F/V/1/2/3); Sixth Avenue (L)

5.7 Patchin Place
1849
Off West 10th Street between Greenwich & Sixth Avenues
Ⓜ West 4th Street (A/C/E/S); 14th Street (F/V/1/2/3)

3.14 Grove Court
1854
Grove Street between Bedford & Hudson Streets
Ⓜ Christopher Street-Sheridan Square (1/2); West 4th Street (A/C/E/F/S/V) ▶

►

3.18   **Former Home of Edna St. Vincent Millay**
1873
75 1/2 Bedford Street between Morton & Commerce Streets
Not open to the public
Ⓜ Christopher Street-Sheridan Square (1/2); West 4th Street
(A/C/E/F/S/V)

5.11   **Former Home of W.H. Auden**
7 Cornelia Street between Bleecker & West 4th Streets
Not open to the public
Ⓜ West 4th Street (A/C/E/F/S/V); Christopher Street-
Sheridan Square (1/2)

6.29   **Former Home of W.H. Auden**
77 St. Mark's Place between First & Second Avenues
Not open to the public
Ⓜ Astor Place (6); First Avenue (L)

Let me take you away from the hurly-burly of Broadway,
the elegant shops of Madison Avenue, and the dazzling
corridors of art offered by the Metropolitan Museum.
And where shall I lead you? Downtown on a 10-minute
walk to some of the smallest and most poetic streets in
Manhattan's Greenwich Village. Each is a gated cul-de-sac,
tucked away from the furors of urban life and festooned
in a quiet otherworldliness. The first and smallest is
Milligan Place; you will need to look really sharp to espy
it on the west side of the avenue, opposite Jefferson
Market. There, inside the marked gate, a wee cluster of
homes appears to belong to a private world. Built in the
1850's, they were conceived as boarding houses for Basque
waiters and workers employed nearby. Farther west, off
10th Street, is Patchin Place—with two rows of diminutive
dwellings dating from 1848; they, too, were built as
boarding houses for toiling New Yorkers. At Number 4,
near the gate, lived the poet E.E. Cummings, and at various times Patchin Place was the home of Djuna Barnes,
Theodore Dreiser, and Padraic Colum. Continue west on

10th Street, turn south on Seventh Avenue, and west on Grove Street, mindful to keep looking sharp. Between Bedford and Hudson Streets you will come to Grove Court with its row of Victorian houses built in the mid-1850's, again for the working class. Compared with the heft of skyscrapers profiling the city, you will surely find the houses in each of these charmed groves doll-like in their proportions. You are also likely to comment on the irregularity of the early property lines that define them—no right angles here. Leon Trotsky, who arrived as an exile in New York in 1917 looking for working-class quarters and found them in the Bronx, characterized the dominant geometric pattern of New York's layout as "a triumph of Cubism." In an earlier century, Thomas Paine, the ex-corset maker from England turned eloquent revolutionary, found refuge during the final years of his life at various addresses amidst the wavering property lines of the West Village area. A brilliant proponent of American independence and author of *Common Sense* (1776), Paine died sad and lonely in the year 1809 in the back room of a frame dwelling on the site of what is now 59 Grove Street. But sadness will not be yours in the beckoning, small-street intimacy that defines the Village. There are colorful crowds, lively art galleries, and shops throughout, as well as cafes aplenty for a lingering cappuccino and conversation. Artists and writers who made—and still make—the Village their home are too numerous to mention, but you should take a look while you are in this area at the narrowest house in the Village located at 75½ Bedford Street (also see pp. 70, 71). In the early 1920's, it was the home of the poet Edna St. Vincent Millay, who was moved to write that,

The trees along this street . . .
make a sound as thin and sweet
As trees in country lanes.

▶

►

W.H. Auden chose the Village as the locus of his several dwellings here and abroad, living at 7 Cornelia Street and then at 77 St. Mark's Place. In 1969 he declared,

My Eden landscapes and their climes
Are constructs from Edwardian times.

GLORIA DEAK
Writer

5.8 **Jefferson Market Library and Garden**
1877, Frederick Clark Withers and Calvert Vaux
425 Sixth Avenue at West 10th Street, ☎ 212 243-4334
Ⓜ West 4th Street (A/C/E/F/S/V); Christopher Street-Sheridan Square (1/2)

Smack in the middle of bustling, downtown Sixth Avenue, you will find a magnificent and elaborate concoction of a building, the Jefferson Market Library. Originally a courthouse (1876-1945) with an adjacent prison and market (both torn down in 1929 and replaced by a Women's House of Detention), this neighborhood library is a wonder of arches and turrets and stained-glass windows. It looks, as my daughter says, like a castle in a fairy tale. There is even a clock tower. In rare, quiet moments, you can hear the bell, which once summoned volunteer firemen, chime out the time.

The country's attention was focused on the original courthouse in 1906, when Harry K. Thaw was tried here for the murder of architect Stanford White. White's affair with chorus girl/model Evelyn Nesbit before her marriage to Thaw was the motive in this crime of passion, an episode captured by E.L. Doctorow in *Ragtime*.

Behind the library, largely hidden from view on Sixth Avenue, is the Jefferson Market Garden—a beautiful oasis in the middle of city gridlock. In the early 1970's, the Women's House of Detention on this site was closed, then demolished, creating the opportunity for this garden, now a beloved feature of the Greenwich Village Historic District. You will find wooden benches hidden among flowers, a small pond with fish and a fountain, and an arch with climbing vines marking the garden's perimeter path. Flower beds, dripping with color and scent, continue to change throughout the seasons. A luscious green lawn fills the middle—not to walk on, just to gaze upon.

The entrance to the garden is on Greenwich Avenue, and when the gates are open, there is a table with a volunteer or two, and a donation box, out front. Walk slowly along the garden path, and note the labels identifying the wide variety of flowers. If you are lucky, you may snag a bench for a little while. The city and its traffic never completely disappear, but they are held at bay in this garden, behind its lovely wrought-iron fence, a recent bequest of the Astor Foundation.

ELISSA STEIN
Graphic designer and writer

5.9 Three Lives & Co.

154 West 10th Street at Waverly Place
℡ 212 741-2069
Monday, Tuesday noon-8pm; Wednesday-Saturday
11am-8:30pm; Sunday noon-7pm
Ⓜ Christopher Street-Sheridan Square (1/2); West 4th Street
(A/C/E/F/S/V)

🎁 Three Lives & Co. is one of the great small bookstores in the world. It is staffed by avid, eccentric readers, any one of whom, if asked, will recommend books on any subject. They are often books of which you have never heard; they are always revelations. Three Lives stocks a catholic selection of new books and a smattering of old ones, but trying to describe it in terms of its stock and even its remarkable staff is a little like trying to describe a face by offering the precise locations of the mouth, nose, and eyes. Three Lives is magical, utterly mysterious; it is enormously hospitable; it shines. I go there not only to buy books but sometimes simply to be reminded of why one writes books. I once asked the former owners if I could someday be buried there, under the floorboards in the southwest corner, but they told me they weren't zoned for that.

MICHAEL CUNNINGHAM
Writer

5.10 Patisserie Claude

187 West 4th Street between Sixth & Seventh Avenues
☎ 212 255-5911
Open daily 8am-8pm
Ⓜ West 4th Street (A/C/E/F/S/V); Christopher Street-Sheridan Square (1/2)

Patisserie Claude is coincidentally owned and operated by a permanently taciturn man named Claude. Patisserie is the key word here: walk in and innocently ask for bread and Claude or one of his minions, if they are feeling kindly that day, will inform you that they know how to spell *boulangerie* and do you see *boulangerie* in the name of the store, you *Américain stupide*? No bread, only pastry and maybe you should go away for a while.

First impressions can be telling. When I first met Claude some 15 or so years ago, I was intimidated by his gruff manner and thought him to be cold, aloof, and disdainful. I now know that he *is* cold, aloof, and disdainful. Which doesn't mean a thing because Claude does make the best croissant, brioche, and pain au chocolat in the city. His fruit tarts are near equals to the tarts my wife's great aunt, Marie-Rose, used to cook up in Cannes, and to get them you don't have to sleep on that lumpy mattress and listen endlessly to Charles Trenet.

Claude has a simple rule. Less is more may fly in certain architectural circles, but not for Claude. Claude, like Albert Einstein, sought a central unifying theme to the universe. Unlike Albert, Claude found it, and it is called butter. More is better. Each croissant has at least a stick of butter in it and is the better for it. My visiting French relatives and friends generally drop their bags at the house and make a beeline for Claude's because they claim it is very difficult to get croissants, etc. that good in Paris anymore.

Claude's has a couple of perfunctory tables up front where you can sip your coffee, look pensive in your beret, and eat the best patisserie in the city. But whatever you do, don't ask for bread.

ANDREW S. PAUL
Attorney

5.14 Washington Square Park
Foot of Fifth Avenue
Ⓜ West 4th Street (A/C/E/F/S/V); 8th Street-NYU (N/R)

"The Secret Worlds of Washington Square" would be an essay describing the multiple societies that coexist yet seldom interact in this treasured and abused public space. Here are drug sellers and their customers, dog owners (large and small, separated by different exercise yards), chess players, musicians, amateur gardeners, students, lonely squirrel and pigeon feeders (each jealously guarding her bit of pavement), photographers, runners, bocce players...all dutifully recorded by busloads of tourists. As an N.Y.U. professor who has lived in the West Village for 40 years, I pass through the park almost daily and love it as one who has seen—and participated in—its struggle against oblivion. Practically every book about the city repeats the facts and myths that have accumulated since the area was, first, a graveyard for slaves, then a drill ground for Revolutionary troops. N.Y.U.'s usurpation of the park for its graduations, watched with resentment by

all those who assume they "own" the park, provides a
lively bit of annual street theater before and after the event.

GEORGE C. STONEY
Filmmaker and professor

Fountain

When the city sizzles, and it's impossible to find a spot
of concrete at any public pool, the Washington Square
Park fountain offers a downtown oasis. With its wide
seating area and five mighty water jets, it's one of the few
fountains where jumping in and getting soaked is customary.
The spot is never overcrowded (nearly empty before noon)
and a midday splash is akin to a Midwestern run through
the front yard sprinkler (though at 100 times the power).

SKOT HESS
Actor

Theater al Fresco

5.14 **Washington Square Park**
Foot of Fifth Avenue
Ⓜ West 4th Street (A/C/E/F/S/V); 8th Street-NYU (N/R)

5.15 **Provincetown Playhouse**
133 MacDougal Street at West 3rd Street, ☎ 212 998-5776
Ⓜ West 4th Street (A/C/E/F/S/V)

Washington Square Park is always alive, especially on the
weekends, with music, acrobats, clowns, stand-up comics,
people hanging out, every breed of dog being walked, kids
on swings. In the summer nights you might stumble across
a group of young actors doing a Shakespeare play by
flashlight. And there's the statue of Garibaldi, reminding
us that the leader of the Risorgimento, the revolutionary
movement that united Italy, lived right here in New York
and worked in Staten Island at a candle factory. Cut down
MacDougal Street and look in at the Provincetown Playhouse, where modern American theater was born, thanks

to Eugene O'Neill. (Until a couple of years ago the original set for *The Emperor Jones* was still part of the permanent structure of the stage.) Now you're in the Village, and it's still the best part of town.

JOHN GUARE
Playwright

5.16 Second Childhood

283 Bleecker Street between Seventh Avenue South
& Jones Street, ☎ 212 989-6140
Monday-Saturday 11am-5:30pm; Sunday noon-5pm
Ⓜ Christopher Street-Sheridan Square (1/2); West 4th Street
(A/C/E/F/S/V)

🎁 One of the last great repositories of vintage stuff, lovingly displayed and beautifully maintained, this is a toy store like no other. The proprietor, Grover Van Dexter, has kept this shrine to nostalgia open for decades, but nothing about the establishment feels old or musty. In addition to the dolls, tin soldiers, metal trucks, toy trains, and puppets, he also sells vintage signs and point-of-purchase displays.

Facing a bustling Bleecker Street, his window is an oasis of joy in a row of commercial merchants. Which is not to say things are not for sale. Everything is a bargain away, and once one piece is gone, another gem takes its place.

STEVEN HELLER
Co-chair of MFA/Design, The School of Visual Arts

Village Breadbasket

Ⓜ West 4th Street (A/C/E/F/S/V); Christoper Street-Sheridan
Square (1/2)

5.17 Ottomanelli & Sons

285 Bleecker Street between Seventh Avenue South
& Jones Street, ☎ 212 675-4217
Monday-Friday 8am-6:30pm; Saturday 7:30am-5:30pm;
closed Sunday

5.18 John's Pizzeria

278 Bleecker Street between Jones & Morton Streets
☎ 212 243-1680
Open daily for lunch and dinner

5.19 Cones

272 Bleecker Street between Jones & Morton Streets
☎ 212 414-1795
Sunday-Thursday 1pm-11pm; Friday-Saturday 1pm-1am

5.20 Bleecker Street Cafe

271 Bleecker Street at Morton Street, ☎ 212 255-3855
Monday-Thursday 10am-11pm; Friday 10am-1am;
Saturday, Sunday 10am-11pm

5.21 Zito & Sons Bakery

259 Bleecker Street between Cornelia & Jones Streets
☎ 212 929-6139
Monday-Saturday 6am-7pm; Sunday 6am-3pm

5.22 Murray's Cheese Shop

257 Bleecker Street at Cornelia Street
☎ 212 243-3289
Monday-Saturday 8am-8pm; Sunday 9am-6pm

5.23 Faicco's Pork Shop

260 Bleecker Street between Morton & Cornelia Streets
☎ 212 243-1974
Tuesday-Thursday 8:30am-6pm, Saturday 8am-6pm;
Friday 8:30am-7pm; Sunday 9am-2pm; closed Monday

5.24   **Pasticceria Bruno**
245 Bleecker Street between Leroy & Carmine Streets
☎ 212 242-4959
Sunday-Thursday 7am-11pm; Friday, Saturday 7am-2am

5.25   **Rocco's Pastry Shop**
243 Bleecker Street between Leroy & Carmine Streets
☎ 212 242-6031
Monday-Thursday, Sunday 7:30am-midnight; Friday
7:30am-1am; Saturday 7:30am-1:30am

5.26   **Winston Churchill Square**
West side of Sixth Avenue where Downing Street
meets Bleecker Street

5.27   **Minetta Triangle**
East side of Sixth Avenue, just north of Bleecker Street

5.28   **Father Demo Square**
Intersection of Carmine & Bleecker Streets
& Sixth Avenue

In the area popularly considered Little Italy, the Italian
inhabitants are now only a memory. Except for a couple
of tenacious survivors and a row of tourist restaurants,
the area is now, for all practical purposes, part of
Chinatown. If you want a sense of Little Italy as it used
to be, go to Bleecker Street between Sixth Avenue and
Seventh Avenue. From the turn of the century to the
1940's, this block, which has been called the "breadbasket
of the Village," was choked with pushcarts selling provi-
sions to the primarily southern Italian population.
Following the passage of stricter sanitary laws, much of
this commerce moved indoors; several stores established
at that time still survive.

Beginning at Sixth Avenue, on the north side of Bleecker,
is Ottomanelli & Sons, the butcher shop. The Ottomanelli
family immigrated to New York from Bari in 1900 and   ▶

▶

established itself in the wholesale meat business. Their store opened on Bleecker Street in the 1940's. Since that time, it is substantially unchanged—it remains a real, old-fashioned butcher shop, with a long counter, huge hams and sides of beef hanging in the window, and personal service.

Across the street is John's Pizzeria. Founded in 1929 by John Sasso, John's famously does not sell single slices. But that's okay—the pizza is so good you'll want a whole one. The restaurant is now run by the nephew of the original John, and it's a good celebrity-spotting site, frequented by Woody Allen, Johnny Depp, Danny DeVito, Jack Nicholson, Mary Tyler Moore, and Matt Dillon, among others.

Next door is Cones, which is only three years old but too good to miss. Self-described "ice-cream artisans" Oscar and Raul D'Aloisio make what is arguably not only the most authentically Italian gelato but the best ice cream of any kind in the city. The brothers come from Buenos Aires, where there is a large Italian community. Oscar says that when he tasted Häagen Dazs ice cream, he thought, "This is the best America has to offer?" and decided to come over and show us what ice cream should be. The flavors, especially the fruit flavors, are startlingly intense and authentic. I also recommend the zabaglione.

Back across the street is the Bleecker Street Cafe. Although a relative newcomer on the block, this is worth a visit both because of their excellent pastries and because the television over the counter is always tuned to the Italian-language station—usually a soccer game.

A few doors farther east, you come to Zito's bread bakery, the longest continuously occupied store on Bleecker Street. Founded by Anthony Zito in 1924, the bakery is now run by his son and grandson. With no preservatives, their bread won't keep longer than a day, but it is very cheap and tastes like bread is supposed to. Zito's concentrates on a few basic kinds of bread—white and whole wheat, in round or long loaves, and focaccia. Despite its unappealing name, their savory lard bread, a bagel-shaped loaf studded with bits of prosciutto and sausage, is exceptionally good and makes a simple, substantial lunch.

Next door is Murray's Cheese Shop. Founded in 1940 as a wholesale vendor of butter and eggs, Murray's used to be around the corner on Cornelia Street. The new, larger shop may not be as quaint as the old one, but it no longer has a perpetual line of waiting customers spilling out the door. They stock more than 250 different kinds of cheese from countries all over the world; if you've heard of a cheese, they have it. They also sell delicatessen fare such as olives, salami, prosciutto, and prepared foods.

Back on the south side of the street is another deli, Faicco's Pork Shop. As the blue pig on the storefront sign proudly announces, this store was founded in 1900, making it the oldest on the block (although it only moved from Thompson Street to its present location in the 1940's). Originally they sold only pork, and although they now sell a range of other Italian foods, too, their glory is still their pork sausage, which you can watch them make right in the shop.

For about 80 years, the Sixth Avenue end of the block was distinguished by its two side-by-side pastry shops—Bleecker Street Pastry and Rocco's. Bleecker Street Pastry was recently replaced by Pasticceria Bruno, and is now very elegant and upscale, although it retains the old decor. But Rocco's continues the same as ever. If you've ever been to Italy, the smell of anise as you walk in the door will take you right back. As an Internet guide from Milan comments, *"si riconoscono da lontano per i profumi tipici dei nostri fornai."* ("You can recognize them from far away by our bakeries' typical aromas.") Everything in Rocco's is extraordinarily cheap and un-self-consciously Italian, from the nuclear-blue and hot-pink decorations on some of the cakes to the hand-filled cannoli to the pink-and-green neon decor. Particularly noteworthy is their freshly baked, authentic tasting panettone—a hard-to-find treasure ▶

▶

outside of Italy except during the Christmas season. In the summer they offer refreshing Italian ices, of which the hazelnut is especially good.

If you live near Bleecker Street, you can still do your shopping the old-fashioned way, with daily trips to the butcher, the baker, the dairy, and the greengrocer. If you're from farther away, try coming down on a nice day and assembling a picnic lunch as you walk down the block. Where Bleecker intersects Sixth Avenue, several tiny parks have recently been redesigned and offer restful places to eat. In the triangle formed by Downing and Bleecker Streets, Winston Churchill Square offers winding paths and benches around a sundial in the form of an armillary sphere. On the other side of the avenue, the even smaller Minetta Triangle has a few shady, secluded seats. Or if you prefer a grittier, more urban atmosphere, the older Father Demo Square between the two is an open brick plaza with trees, benches, and lots of street life and pigeons.

JANET B. PASCAL
Writer and editor

Father Demo Square
Ⓜ West 4th Street (A/C/E/F/S/V)

5.28　**Father Demo Square**
Intersection of Carmine & Bleecker Streets & Sixth Avenue

5.26　**Winston Churchill Square**
West side of Sixth Avenue where Downing Street meets Bleecker Street

5.29　**Minetta Street**
South of West 3rd Street, between Sixth Avenue & MacDougal Street

5.30 Joe's Pizza

233 Bleecker Street at Carmine Street, ☎ 212 366-1182

Open daily 10am-5am

5.31 Bagels on the Square

7 Carmine Street between Bleecker Street
& Sixth Avenue, ☎ 212 691-3041

Open 24 hours

5.32 Trattoria Spaghetto

232 Bleecker Street at Carmine Street, ☎ 212 255-6752

Open daily for lunch and dinner

5.21 Zito & Sons Bakery

259 Bleecker Street between Cornelia & Jones Streets

☎ 212 929-6139

Monday-Saturday, 6am-7pm; Sunday 6am-3pm

5.33 Da Silvano

260 Sixth Avenue between Bleecker & West Houston Streets

☎ 212 982-2343

Open daily for lunch and dinner

5.34 Bar Pitti

268 Sixth Avenue between Bleecker & West Houston Streets

☎ 212 982-3300

Open daily for lunch and dinner

🍴 Arrive hungry: you are at the threshold of great treats.

🏛 But before you indulge, pause a few moments in this
charming piazza. More triangle than not, this étoile stands
at the crossroads of Sixth Avenue, Bleecker, Carmine,
Downing, and Minetta Streets. Father Demo, the Italian-
born pastor of nearby Our Lady of Pompeii Church, was
lauded for his Herculean efforts during the famed Triangle
Shirtwaist Company Fire of 1911 (see p. 127). In thanks,
the Borough of Manhattan commemorated his life's work
with this brick-paved homage.

Bordered to the southwest by the majestic single-   ►

►

domed church, the square spills onto Downing Street, at whose feet sits tiny, impeccable Churchill Square—a reference to the London abode of the only Prime Minister with a New Yorker mother. Folded into an adjacent corner of the park is a typical neighborhood playground, complete with whimsical frog and seal sculptures for climbing. (Discover, in a few paces' stroll along Downing Street, some of lower Manhattan's most interesting single-family residences.) Your bench on the east side of the piazza will provide an inimitable view north of both Jefferson Market Library and the Empire State Building. Also of note: Minetta Street, where Al Pacino's Serpico lived; and on the southeast corner of Bleecker Street and Sixth Avenue, the Little Red School House, an enduring neighborhood private school made famous by both Auntie Mame and the Rosenbergs.

And now you may eat, for Father Demo Square is home not only to Joe's Pizza and Bagels on the Square—both Village classics—but also Trattoria Spaghetto, where the finest bowl of minestrone soup on the island can be consumed with a loaf of Zito's (also see p. 112) finest bread. And if there's time for a proper meal, then by all means cross Sixth Avenue to the south and invest a couple of hours sitting outside at either Da Silvano or Bar Pitti. Known fondly to regulars as "first-class and coach," the relationship is as magnetically charged as that of Paris's Café de Flore and Les Deux Magots. Silvano costs more and takes major credit cards; Pitti is cheap and takes only cash. Both are delicious. Whichever you choose, you will not be sorry.

RACHAEL HOROVITZ
Film producer

5.35 **Monday Night Magic**
Formerly at the Sullivan Street Playhouse
☎ 212 615-6432
Call ahead to verify location
Performances, Monday at 8pm
Ⓜ West 4th Street (A/C/E/F/S/V)

Fun! Thrills! Comedy! Magic! Imagine a different full-length magic show presented each week in an intimate setting and you've got Monday Night Magic, where the best magicians from all over the world come to perform for an appreciative and enthusiastic audience. In addition to performances on the stage, with no seat more than four or five rows away, intermission features close-up magic where the miracles happen right in front of your disbelieving eyes. In addition to magicians, you'll often find sideshow performers, escape artists, comedy-magicians, jugglers, and Wild West whip-crackers on the bill. This is New York's longest-running magic show.

MATTHEW FIELD
Reviewer for Genii *and editor of magic books*

The art of magic at a very high level.
DON CAMP
Photographer

RECOMMENDED READING
Ricky Jay, *Learned Pigs and Fireproof Women*, Farrar, Straus & Giroux, 1998.

Best Tuna

5.36 'ino
21 Bedford Street between Sixth Avenue & Downing Street
☎ 212 989-5769
Monday-Friday 9am-2am; Saturday, Sunday 11am-2am
Ⓜ Houston Street (1/2)

2.9 Morgan's Market
13 Hudson Street at Reade Street, ☎ 212 941-7578
Open 24 hours
Ⓜ Chambers Street (1/2)

2.8 Washington Market Park
Greenwich Street between Chambers & Duane Streets
Ⓜ Chambers Street (1/?)

▶

5.37   **The Grey Dog's Coffee**
33 Carmine Street between Bleecker & Bedford Streets
℡ 212 462-0041
Open daily 7am-midnight
Ⓜ West 4th Street (A/C/E/F/S/V); Houston Street (1/2)

🍴 As one who loves the city deeply, I offer you here this favorite
thing (of many) about New York: the tuna sandwich.

I want to omit any mention of tuna "steak," the slabs
of rare tuna on toast (the Odeon! my favorite; see p. 44).
What I prefer to recommend are tuna salad sandwiches,
those that originate in a can and are easy to eat with one
hand while turning pages of a book or properly folded
newspaper. Here are three personal favorites:

1. The tuna tramezzini at 'ino. Tuna in a bit of oil with
caperberries and black olive pesto on Pullman bread with
the crust removed. Two subway cars side by side could just
fit into this little room with a scuffed floor on an aging
side street. Have wine and coffee with your sandwich and,
after lunch, stumble left to the Village or right into SoHo.

2. Tuna with lettuce on a pita at Morgan's Market
in TriBeCa. Kind of creamy, kind of plain, kind of perfect
tuna salad. There's no place to sit down here (it's a
market). You can carry your lunch bag a block down
Reade Street to Washington Market Park, a nice patch
of tree-lined grass with a playground and benches. Hudson
River Park (see p. 38), only two long blocks west, is right
on the water.

3. The Number 8 at Grey Dog. Dense, happy tuna with
lettuce and tomato and one secret ingredient—relish—on
sponge sized slabs of big fresh bread. This little piece of
college town is wedged between Our Lady of Pompeii and
a selection of record stores (Vinylmania! no CDs!). Order
your sandwich at the counter and find a little table. FM
music and doggie biscuits; it's loud and dimly lit, in a good
way, with moms and writers and the occasional EMS girl or
well-known actress, a little-known painter, a suit, a teacher,

a couple of kids. Ain't life grand; it's that kind of place.

STACY COCHRAN
Writer, director, and producer

5.38 Village Comics

214 Sullivan Street between Bleecker & West 3rd Streets
☏ 212 777-2770
Monday, Tuesday 10am-7:30pm; Wednesday-Saturday
10am-8pm; Sunday 11am-7pm
Ⓜ West 4th Street (A/C/E/F/S/V)

There are comics stores in New York such as Forbidden
Planet that cater to the superhero, alternative, and weirdo-
comics aficionado, and then there's Village Comics, which
appeals to the rest of us. Though not a big comic-book fan
myself, I have a voyeuristic interest in the countercultures
that comprise this fan base.

Village Comics is something of an epicenter for the
underground, overground, and middle earth of comics. It
sells the usual fare of DC and Marvel, the unusual oddities
by the likes of Chris Ware, and for this voyeur, comic
models—plastic, resin, and dolls galore. But don't let the
habitués hear you say the word "dolls": they prefer the
state-of-the-art term "action figures."

The store is fully stocked with action figures that you'll
never see at Toys "R" Us, representing troops from the
Civil War, World War II (German and American), Vietnam,
members of SWAT teams, special forces, and more. The
avid recreationist who builds large dioramas and vignettes
in which these figures play will find a wall covered with
doll clothes and miniature weaponry. Also in stock for the
art enthusiast are resin models, samples of which are precisely constructed and displayed in glass reliquaries.
Models on hand run the gamut from classic Revel snap-
togethers of cars, ships, and planes to variations of odd
comics characters in revealing, if not kinky, garb. There is
also the requisite Adults Only section, which I have never

dared enter, given the fact that whenever I'm in the store, I feel just like a kid.
STEVEN HELLER
Co-chair of MFA/Design, The School of Visual Arts

5.39 University Village
1966, I.M. Pei & Partners
From Bleecker Street to West Houston Street,
between LaGuardia Place & Mercer Street
Ⓜ Bleecker Street (6); Broadway-Lafayette Street (F/S/V)

Escape the hodgepodge of Greenwich Village into I.M. Pei's urban utopia. The three simple concrete towers stretch above the neighboring horizon, injecting light, air, and space into the otherwise crowded cityscape. Follow the rough-cut stone drive from Bleecker Street to a central square. Here you will be greeted by an enormous, 36-foot-high cast-stone-and-concrete *Portrait of Sylvette* by Pablo Picasso. (This enlargement of Picasso's much smaller sculpture is the 1970 work of Carl Nesjar.) The combination of massive forms, idealism, and simplicity is truly impressive. A visit to this austere oasis never fails to leave me at peace.
GEORGIA O'NEAL
Designer

5.40 Bayard Building (originally Condict Building)
1899, Louis Sullivan
65 Bleecker Street between Broadway & Lafayette Street
Ⓜ Bleecker Street (6); Broadway-Lafayette Street (F/S/V)

This is the only Louis Sullivan building in New York and is pretty and calming to look at. I have always thought of it as the wedding-cake building. When it was built, architectural critic Carl Condit (not to be confused with the building's first owner, Silas Condict), supposedly said, "Who would expect an aesthetic experience on Bleecker Street?"
JOAN SILBER
Writer

The only building in New York designed by Louis H. Sullivan is best viewed from the corner of Houston and Crosby on a sunny day when the filigreed terra-cotta-clad facade beams white. On the skyscraper of his time, Sullivan wrote: "It must be tall, every inch of it tall. The force and power of altitude must be in it." Commanding all of 13 stories, the supporting columns indeed shoot skyward, giving way to arches, porthole windows, and heavy-handed ornamentation. Bring your binoculars to catch the dragon-fly women—with arms and wings outstretched. They're the high altitude caryatids that carry the cornice and were reportedly added to the design against Sullivan's wishes.

FREDERIC SCHWARTZ AND TRACEY HUMMER
Architect and Writer

5.41 **Il Buco**

47 Bond Street between Lafayette Street & Bowery
☎ 212 533-1932
Tuesday-Saturday for lunch and dinner;
Sunday, Monday for dinner only
Ⓜ Bleecker Street (6); Broadway-Lafayette Street (F/S/V)

🍴 One of the most gracious dining experiences in Manhattan is, without doubt, Il Buco. In the capable hands of its proprietors, Donna Lennard and Albert Avalle, I have eaten many of my most memorable New York dinners. This unassuming gem serves an Italian-Mediterranean cuisine with strong Spanish influence in a cozy, yet lively setting. The owners are avid antiques collectors, and the decor of Il Buco is constantly changing as they share with their customers the bounty of their many trips to Italy, Spain, and Pennsylvania. Ask for tips on the wine menu, as their steward is most knowledgeable and insightful. Octopus carpaccio is nicely paired with a glass of prosecco to start, moving on to roasted baby beets and goat cheese followed by any number of fish or pasta dishes accompanied by a beautiful, hot, crusty fresh bread soaked in deep green, first-press olive oil. Ask to eat in the wine cellar, which served as the inspiration for Edgar Allen Poe's "The Cask of Amontillado." Call early for reservations, as this treasure has been discovered.

CAROLYN CARTWRIGHT
Feature film set decorator and interior designer

5.42 The Cooper Union for the Advancement of Science and Art Foundation Building

1859, Frederick A. Peterson

7 East 7th Street at Cooper Square, ☎ 212 353-4195

Ⓜ Astor Place (6); 8th Street-NYU (N/R)

Cooper Union is steeped in history. On February 27, 1860, Abraham Lincoln spoke in the Great Hall, effectively beginning his first presidential campaign. Abolitionist and women's rights activist Frederick Douglass spoke several times in the same hall. As a child, my maternal grandmother walked in yellow lamplight through a snowstorm with her parents, from her house on West 10th Street to Cooper Institute, to catch a glimpse of Lincoln. That walk still takes a visitor past some of New York's oldest and most charming houses.

PETER BURCHARD
Writer

Although he had little formal education himself, the industrialist and philanthropist Peter Cooper envisioned a college of the first rank for the working-class and immigrant children of New York City. Strategically and symbolically placed between the Bowery and the more prosperous neighborhoods uptown, the tuition-free college was intended by its founder to break through the class boundary. As pointed out in a characteristic passage by Horatio Alger Jr., the building has entrances uptown and downtown, but the clock and its light face the Bowery.

A national and city historic landmark, the Italianate Foundation Building was designed by Frederick Peterson and, in 1859, was the tallest building in New York City. As the first thoroughly fireproof structure in the city, it set a standard for public safety in construction. It also included the round shaft requested by Peter Cooper in anticipation of the invention of the elevator. When the interior of the building was completely rebuilt in the 1970's, modern technology permitted the old rectangular elevator to be replaced by a cylindrical one.

Abolitionist William Lloyd Garrison and feminists Susan B. Anthony and Victoria Woodhull rallied against the injustices of their time and spearheaded great change in their speeches in the Great Hall of the Foundation Building, and it was there that Albert Einstein presented his transcendent ideas in physics.

GEORGE CAMPBELL JR.
President, The Cooper Union for the Advancement of Science and Art

5.43 Merchant's House Museum

1832
29 East 4th Street between Lafayette Street & Bowery
☎ 212 777-1089
Thursday-Monday 1pm-5pm; closed Tuesday, Wednesday
Ⓜ Bleecker Street (6); Broadway-Lafayette Street (F/S/V)

In 1835, for 18,000 dollars, the merchant Seabury Tredwell bought an elegant three-year-old Greek Revival/Late Federal-style house on the outskirts of New York, at East 4th Street, and moved in with his large family, including five daughters and two sons. Five years later, his last daughter, Gertrude, was born. Seabury, whose ancestors had come over on the *Mayflower*, was a stern and devout man, and when Gertrude wanted to marry an Irish Catholic doctor, he forbade her. She never married and continued to live in the house her whole life, first with her parents, then with three spinster sisters, and finally, when her money was gone, with paying guests. She died in the house in 1933 at 93 years of age. By then the area had changed from a wealthy and respectable suburb to one of the Lower East Side's crowded tenement neighborhoods, known for its bars and brothels. Outside the house, the world was altered completely, but inside, time stood still. Except for a very few modernizations, the house remained as it had been when Gertrude was young. According to one legend, Gertrude's haunting story was the inspiration for Henry James's *Washington Square*.

After her death, the house was given to the city, and it has been a museum ever since—one of the few places where you can see, not a re-creation of Victorian life, but the real thing. The lower floor houses the pantry, the family dining room, and the kitchen, where dishes and cookware still sit. The room is dominated by the black woodstove (which replaced the original fireplace). The sink is worked by a pump connected to a cistern filled with rainwater. Next to it stands the little round tub the family used for bathing. The legs on the pie safe are corroded where they were stood in glasses of water to keep vermin from the baked goods.

Visitors came to the elegant ground floor, containing the dining room and formal parlor decorated with columns, elaborate plasterwork, and magnificent marble fireplaces. To satisfy the Greek Revival desire for symmetry, the parlor was built with two heavy wooden doors—one to use, and a dummy that opens onto a blank brick wall, revealing the structure of the walls. Mrs. Tredwell redecorated in the 1860's to show the family's prosperity—she was trying to marry off six daughters. (Only two ever married.) The piano the girls used to entertain their guests, with an extra pedal meant to imitate an organ, stands by the window.

Upstairs are a small guest room and two separate bedrooms for Mr. and Mrs. Tredwell, connected by a private passageway. Mrs. Tredwell's mirror is lit by gas jets shaped to look like morning glories twining around the edge. The effect is very pretty, but it's a little frightening to imagine her doing up her hair just inches from two open jets of

flame. Although the rooms are large and expensively decorated with gilded pressed-tin ornamentation, there are
no closets. Houses were taxed according to the number of
rooms, and closets counted as rooms. After Gertrude's
death, the magnificent red damask bed curtains were found
to be too decayed to salvage, but there was no need to
try a modern re-creation; bolts of the original fabric were
still stored in the attic.

There is a charming little garden in back, which now
looks out on brick walls and barbed wire, but once backed
onto the Vauxhall Pleasure Garden. You can see the domed
top of the cistern, fed by a drainpipe from the roof, but the
outhouse has been removed.

If you want to pretend you're a Victorian, the Old
Merchant's House is the place to do it. And if you want to
be reminded why you're glad you're not a Victorian, consideration of the throne-like mahogany commode in the
bedroom, the small hand-filled and hand-emptied bathtub,
or Gertrude's terrifyingly narrow corset should do it.

JANET B. PASCAL
Writer and editor

5.45 Former Asch Building, now the Brown Building

29 Washington Place at Greene Street

Ⓜ 8th Street-NYU (N/R); Astor Place (6)

On March 25, 1911, a fire in the Asch building, one block
east of Washington Square, took the lives of 146 garment
workers, most of them young women, some little more
than children. The Triangle Shirtwaist Company occupied
the top three floors of the 10-story building. The company's vast workrooms were packed with seamstresses and
flammable materials. It was nearly quitting time when fire
broke out on the eighth floor and spread swiftly to the
upper floors. Flames blocked the only unlocked exits. A
New York Times reporter wrote: "The girls rushed to the
windows and looked down at Greene Street, 100 feet

below them. One poor little creature jumped. Then they all began to drop. A girl, who waved her handkerchief at the crowd, leaped from a window. Her dress caught on a wire and the crowd watched her hang there until the dress burned free and she came toppling down."

Social worker and reformer Frances Perkins, who was in the neighborhood when the fire alarms were sounded, rushed to Greene Street, where she saw heaps of broken bodies lying on the slate sidewalk. Outraged by the carelessness and greed that had made escape impossible, Perkins joined a campaign to eliminate the irresponsible and cruel labor practices that had led to the disaster. Workers like Rosie Yussum, who survived the fire, made it impossible to forget the people who had perished. Rosie said, "They didn't want to jump. They was afraid. They was saying their prayers first, and putting rags over their eyes so they should not see."

PETER BURCHARD
Writer

Lower East Side
& East Village

6

Lower East Side & East Village

LOWER EAST SIDE

6.1 **Angel Orensanz Foundation**
1850, Alexander Saeltzer
172 Norfolk Street between Stanton & East Houston Streets
☎ 212 780-0175
Open daily 9am-8pm
Ⓜ Lower East Side-Second Avenue (F/V); Delancey Street-Essex Street (J/M/Z)

Designed under the spell of Hegel, Schinkel, Schiller, Heinrich Heine, and the German Romantic movement, this building was erected at the time of the great buildings of central Berlin of the 1840's—the Altes Museum, the Neue Museum, the Berlin Opera, the Berlin Concert Hall, Humboldt University, the Friedrichswerdesche Kirche, and others. The German Jewish community that arrived in Manhattan in the 1840's asked Berlin architect Alexander Saeltzer to build a synagogue on Norfolk Street that would replicate the glory of the Cologne cathedral and the humanistic splendors of central Berlin. From here, the Jewish Reform movement would transform the cultural horizon of New York and the country.

Angel Orensanz Foundation, formerly the Congregation of Ansche Chesed, has a neo-Gothic main space of about 7,000 square feet with 50-foot-high cathedral blue ceilings and soaring balconies. There is also an Assembly Room of about 4,000 square feet. In 1986, the Angel Orensanz Foundation, established by sculptor Angel Orensanz, rescued the building from demolition. Some of New York's most creative recent projects have been staged here, including *City, Garbage and Death* by Rainer Werner Fassbinder; Alexander McQueen's first American fashion show; Mandy Patinkin's *Mamaloshen*; and George Frederick Handel's

Esther, in its first full staging since the 18th century. This unique, breathtaking space has been used by a diverse group of people in the arts: Philip Glass, John Zorn, Lou Reed, the Kronos Quartet, Whitney Houston, Mariah Carey, Spike Lee, Cecil Taylor, Elie Wiesel, Maya Angelou, Erica Jong, and Jacques Derrida, among others. As a space for culture, spirit, and high learning, the Orensanz Foundation sustains the vision and dream of those 19th-century reformers and humanists.

AL ORENSANZ
Director, Angel Orensanz Foundation

Loisaida

Ⓜ Lower East Side-Second Avenue (F/V); Delancey Street-Essex Street (J/M/Z)

6.2 Russ & Daughters

179 East Houston Street between Orchard & Allen Streets
☎ 212 475-4880
Monday-Saturday 9am-7pm; Sunday 8am-6pm

6.3 Katz's Delicatessen

205 East Houston Street at Ludlow Street
☎ 212 254-2246
Open daily for breakfast, lunch, and dinner

6.6 El Castillo de Jagua

113 Rivington Street between Essex & Ludlow Streets
☎ 212 982-6412
Open daily 8am-midnight

6.7 First Roumanian American Congregation Synagogue

89 Rivington Street between Ludlow & Orchard Streets
☎ 212 673-2835

6.8 Rosario's Pizza

173 Orchard Street at Stanton Street, ☎ 212 777-9813
Sunday-Wednesday 10:30am-3am; Thursday 10:30am-4am;
Friday, Saturday 10:30am-5am

▶

►

6.9   **Sara D. Roosevelt Park**
East Houston Street to Canal Street between Chrystie
& Forsyth Streets

6.10   **Yonah Schimmel's Knishes Bakery**
137 East Houston Street at Forsyth Street
☎ 212 477-2858
Open daily 8:30am-7:30pm

For every American of Jewish descent there is a one-in
three chance that they had an ancestor who, upon arrival
in this country, lived in the Lower East Side. One in three
Puerto Ricans who have settled in the continental U.S. has
a relative who has lived in that crowded corner of Lower
Manhattan. The same one-in-three odds also apply to
parents all over the U.S. who may have had a child run
off to New York to be an artist. Unlike many sections of
Manhattan where ethnic or cultural groups come and go,
usually leaving nothing more than a few plaques or
cleverly named coffee shops to commemorate their
presence, the Lower East Side (LES), or Loisaida if you're
Latino or "down," still pulsates with the energy of each
of these groups.

Begin at Houston Street (pronounced HOW-stun) and
Orchard, which used to be the center of the Lower East
Side when its boundaries extended north to 14th Street.
(The blocks between Houston and 14th Street east of the
Bowery are now called "the East Village," a designation
begun in the 1950's to compete with the hip West Village.)
Now Houston and Orchard is the northernmost part of
the LES. Though there is no official signpost, two neon
fish glowing over 179 East Houston Street can serve as
your markers. They're perpetually swimming over Russ
& Daughters, the last and best of the smoked fish and
delicacy stores that used to dot the neighborhood. Though
the space has remained small and unassuming, Russ &
Daughters' selection and quality make stores like Zabar's

and Dean & DeLuca look like, as my grandmother would say, "they don't know from fish." The place is a true microcosm of the LES, with Latin countermen who can banter with customers in Spanish-laced Yiddish (Spiddish) and the owner of the store, Mark Russ Federman, who manages it all with his Colombian wife, Maria. More Jews swear by their whitefish salad than they do by the Torah. Order a bagel to go, or get a few pounds of Gaspé salmon packed in ice and a tub of their incomparable whipped cream cheese. With one foot in 1900 and another in the present, you can grab an old-fashioned licorice whip and a cappuccino as you walk out the door.

A block east, on the corner of Ludlow, is Katz's Deli. Since 1888, Katz's has been churning out the best pastrami and corned beef in the city. You'll be given a ticket as you enter—your bill, which you will be expected to produce when you leave. Start at the counter on the far right with a hot dog, so you have something to nosh while countermen with flashing knives prepare your sandwiches. When a chunk of pastrami flies your way, it's not a mistake, you're being offered a taste (be sure to tip). You can even eat your sandwich in the same spot where Meg Ryan faked an orgasm in *When Harry Met Sally* (or the same chair in which my Uncle Irving did not fake it in 1944 over a particularly good brisket on rye).

Take a right upon leaving Katz's and stroll south down Ludlow. Remarkably, the 30 or so new bars that have sprung up over the past few years have not seriously impacted the authentic tenement feel of the street. Many original shop signs remain, though the stores they advertised are long gone. Have a drink at any of these hipster bars. There's a 50-50 chance that the grungy-looking kid sitting next to you is either an artist you just read about in *The Times* or an N.Y.U. student cutting class.

A couple of blocks south at 113 Rivington Street on the corner of Essex is one of the best inexpensive Latin restaurants in the city, El Castillo de Jagua. As a paroled friend ▶

►

of mine once said, "Any place where you can frequently find six or seven Latin cops eating has to be good." If matzo ball soup can cure a cold, their chicken (sopa de pollo) could raise the dead. It's just how your Jewish grandmother would have made it if she were Dominican, and yucca and cilantro had been available anywhere near Kiev. Castillo is especially known for seafood, so try their paella Valencia (yellow rice with seafood). And be sure to spend at least a dollar on the jukebox to get a crash course on the hottest salsa music. Unlike many other bars and restaurants in the city, you will have no problem hearing your selections playing, even a couple of blocks away. Any Jewish patrons feeling guilty from too much roast pork or arroz con longosta can walk a few blocks west to 89 Rivington to the First Roumanian American Congregation Synagogue. Though not packed the way it would have been 90 years ago, there's rarely trouble getting a minyan for the 5 p.m. daily services.

About a block north on the corner of Stanton and Orchard is Rosario's Pizza, a neighborhood institution for more than 38 years. The place is run by Salvatore Bartolomeo, who will also be heating up your slice, the best in the city. You'll recognize Sal because the walls of Rosario's are covered with photos of him, taken by numerous appreciative neighborhood photographers whom Sal feeds late into the night, even after he's posted the Closed sign.

Now take a slice three blocks west and one north to Sara D. Roosevelt Park, which runs from Houston to Canal between Chrystie and Forsyth. On the way, stop into any of the neighborhood bodegas and brown-bag a 40-ounce beer. Make it a malt liquor. Plant yourself on a park bench within this island of towering trees and basketball courts. You can watch a game of pick-up or read Henry Roth's *Call It Sleep* and let the Yinglish of the kids in the book who played in the neighborhood 80 years ago mingle in your mind with the Spanglish of today's inhabitants.

For dessert, walk about 20 steps east to 137 Houston, since 1910 home of Yonah Schimmel's Knishes. As you ascend the step into the doorway of the shop, you'll see an interior barely changed since its opening. You could be in Poland or Russia of a hundred years ago, except for the fact that punk rockers were probably having sex in that very doorway only hours before. Substitute Cossacks for punks and cross the threshold. Order a cheese knish. It's as though you've stepped into an Isaac Bashevis Singer novel, but better. In the schtetl you wouldn't hear motor-cycles revving outside of the Hell's Angels' headquarters a few blocks north or the Puerto Rican man on the corner, scraping a huge block of ice to make mango-flavored snow cones.

DAVID BAR KATZ
Writer and director

6.2   **Russ & Daughters**

179 East Houston Street between Orchard & Allen Streets
℡ 212 475-4880
Monday-Saturday 9am-7pm; Sunday 8am-6pm
Ⓜ Second Avenue (F/V)

🎁 You want deli, you got deli. Smoked sable, olives of plenty, dried mushrooms depending from the grottoed walls. Grandpa Russ started the business as a pushcart in 1914, it's now in the third generation of the family and still they argue. So you won't see Jackie Mason there. Better, you'll see his lox.

BRUCE DUCKER
Novelist

6.4   Orchard Corset Center

157 Orchard Street between Rivington & Stanton Streets
📞 212 674-0786
Sunday-Thursday 10am-6pm; Friday 10am-3pm;
closed Saturday
Ⓜ Delancey Street-Essex Street (F/J/M/Z)

🎁 If you get your thrills wearing daring little pearl thongs,
this is not the place for you. If, on the other hand, you prefer
more serious support, then pay a visit to Ralph Berk at the
Orchard Corset Center. Berk has an uncanny talent for
serious bra counsel: from the outline of your shirt he'll
guess your size with remarkable accuracy. And the prices!
Wacoals—those French gifts to D-cups—are always on sale.
DANY LEVY (AND EDITORIAL STAFF OF DAILYCANDY.COM)
Founder of DailyCandy.com

6.5   Economy Candy

108 Rivington Street between Ludlow & Essex Streets
📞 212 254-1531
Sunday-Friday 9am-6pm; Saturday 10am-5pm
Ⓜ Delancey Street-Essex Street (F/J/M/Z)

🎁 Started in the midst of the post-Depression era when
candy still came in barrels, Economy Candy is a rickety
little Lower East Side spot owned by Jerry Cohen, a grizzly
New York City native with an auctioneer's voice and an
attitude to match. This vintage candy warehouse brims
floor to ceiling (literally—a stepladder is required) with
jawbreakers, licorice whips, chocolate-covered raisins, root
beer barrels, Chiclets, Pixy Stix, kosher gourmet jellybeans,
and other Willy Wonka-like delicacies. A favorite of Jerry
Lewis, Red Buttons, and Tony Curtis, Economy Candy
was described by *Gourmet* magazine as "the penny-candy
store elevated to an art form."

Other favorites include rock-candy swizzle sticks (red,
blue, amber, yellow, pink, and green), Jordan Almonds,
Atomic Fireballs, candy necklaces, 18 kinds of halvah,

chocolate-covered pretzels (milk, dark, and white), and Pez in every imaginable size and form. In fact, the only candy you won't find here is Chunky. "It's my favorite," says Cohen. "I don't sell it because I'd eat it all day long." At least the man shows some restraint.

DANY LEVY (AND EDITORIAL STAFF OF DAILYCANDY.COM)
Founder of DailyCandy.com

6.11 **Lower East Side Tenement Museum**
90 Orchard Street at Broome Street, ☎ 212 431-0233
Guided tours only; call for hours
Ⓜ Delancey Street-Essex Street (F/J/M/Z); Grand Street (S)

This is a breathtaking discovery, perfectly preserved on a busy Lower East Side street. You can touch and smell the world of the original immigrants and see what was overcome to succeed in New York City.

Here is the Lower East Side as gateway to America: the heart of this museum, the tenement at 97 Orchard Street, was home to an estimated 7,000 people from more than 20 nations between 1863 and 1935. It is now a National Historic Landmark. Visit and tour carefully-restored tenement apartments of actual past residents: German Jews (1870's), Eastern European Jews (1900's), and Italian Catholics (1930's). There is also a living-history program focusing on Sephardic Jews from Turkey (1916). There will soon be apartments that interpret an 1893 sweatshop and an Irish family in residence during the Civil War.

JOHN PENOTTI
President, GreeneStreet Films

This museum is not your conventional installation of precious objects. Instead its apartments are more like a collection of time capsules ranging from the Civil War era to the early part of the 20th century, each bearing witness to succeeding generations of immigration into the Lower East Side. Furnished with authentic period furniture and artifacts, these humble shelters for the genteel working poor give the visitor an almost eerie sense of association with the families who called these apartments home.

Be sure to take the complete tour with one of the very knowledgeable and enthusiastic guides. Any wait time can be put to good use wandering the narrow old streets nearby and maybe heading for one of the few remaining ethnic delis for some New York specialties. You'll feel like you're on the set of the *The Godfather*.

EVELYN AND PETER KRAUS
Proprietors, Ursus Books and Prints

6.11 Guss' Pickles

At press time, temporarily located in the Tenement Museum
97 Orchard Street between Broome & Delancey Streets
Sunday-Thursday 9am-6pm; Friday 9am-4pm; closed Saturday
Ⓜ Delancey Street-Essex Street (F/J/M/Z)

🎁 At the risk of letting out the cat, try Guss's pickle emporium for the best pickles in the galaxy.
BRUCE DUCKER
Novelist

6.12 Tonic

107 Norfolk Street between Delancey & Rivington Streets
☏ 212 358-7501
Tuesday-Sunday sets at 8pm, 10pm; Thursday-Saturday sets at 8pm, 10pm, midnight; open Sundays at 1:30pm for brunch; open some Mondays
Ⓜ Delancey Street-Essex Street (F/J/M/Z)

Tonic, on the Lower East Side of Manhattan, is one of the premier venues of the downtown avant-garde jazz scene. Formerly a kosher wine cellar (hence the name), Tonic's main performance space is on the ground floor, while the basement is now a bar complete with huge wine barrels that have been converted into huts with

tables and chairs for a very private atmosphere. Check out the Klezmer Brunch on Sundays.
JON MADOF
Musician

6.13 Williamsburg Bridge
1903, Leffert L. Buck
Delancey & Clinton Streets (Manhattan) to Washington Plaza (Brooklyn)
Ⓜ Manhattan: Delancey Street-Essex Street (F/J/M/Z)
Brooklyn: Marcy Avenue (J/M/Z)

South Passage
Manhattan entrance at Delancey & Ridge Streets
Brooklyn entrance at Broadway & Roebling Street

In a rapidly gentrifying city, this temporary metal mesh cage provides a glimpse of the gritty, graffiti-covered dystopia of the 1970's. Built to protect bikers and pedestrians during the bridge's interminable reconstruction, this poor man's Pompidou offers the river and skyline to the south and the wheels and sparks of the adjacent J train to the north.
SEBASTIAN HARDY
Urban planner

6.14 Doughnut Plant
379 Grand Street between Essex & Norfolk Streets
☏ 212 505-3700
Tuesday-Sunday 6:30am until the doughnuts sell out
Ⓜ Delancey Street-Essex Street (F/J/M/Z)

🎁 Sandwiched between a thrift shop and a row of brick apartments, Doughnut Plant's storefront is easy to miss. But what lies within puts the franchise doughnut stores to shame.

One day, while sifting through boxes, Mark Isreal happened on some of his grandfather's recipes, so he whipped up a batch of doughnuts and tried selling them to his local coffee shop. The orders poured in literally overnight, and today Mark's doughnuts grace the counters at, among others, Dean & Deluca, Zabar's, and Balducci's. But for the real experience, head down to Grand Street and meet the man behind the doughnut.

This is not your average cop food. Flavors range from classic vanilla bean to ginger, lime, pistachio, and rose water, all hand-cut, hand-rolled, and fried in canola oil. Best of all, each doughnut measures roughly the size of a human head. In the words of *The New York Times*'s Florence Fabricant, "a plusher chocolate doughnut than his Valrhona would be hard to find."

DANY LEVY (AND EDITORIAL STAFF OF DAILYCANDY.COM)
Founder of DailyCandy.com

6.15 Eldridge Street Synagogue

1887, Peter Herter & Francis Herter
12 Eldridge Street between Canal & Division Streets
Eldridge Street Project, ☎ 212 978-8800
Tours: Sunday on the hour 11am-3pm; Tuesday, Thursday
11:30am and 2:30pm; or by appointment
Ⓜ East Broadway (F); Grand Street (S); Canal Street
(J/M/N/Q/R/W/Z/6)

Completed in 1887, Eldridge Street was the first synagogue in America built by Eastern European Jews. Which is to say, this synagogue, in disrepair but coming back to life through an ongoing restoration project, is a link to an older New York that everybody knows about, some have family ties to, and hardly anyone has any contact with. The building itself, with 70-foot ceilings, Moorish design, and a vast skylight, is beautiful. The fact that it still stands, and, amazingly, is still used for worship, is incredibly moving. The Eldridge Street Project hosts readings, concerts, and educational events at the synagogue; on Sundays, Tuesdays, and Thursdays, volunteer docents lead

tours, complete with details that summon the old neighborhood and the synagogue's central place in its life. Imagine:
mounted policemen were required for crowd control on the
high holidays; people paid rent to reserve their seats in the
pews. After exploring the synagogue, which also has a display of signs advertising rabbinical services and a collection
of plaques depicting the Ten Commandments under the
guard of carved lions—made by the same craftsmen who
made the elaborate carousel horses then popular—take
a look around the neighborhood. Part of Chinatown now
(albeit far off the tourist track), it continues to serve new
arrivals and provide an anchor for the next generation
of New Yorkers.

MARTHA SCHULMAN
Writer and teacher

6.16 East River Park Tennis Courts

FDR Drive north of Delancey Street
Open daily 7am-dusk
Ⓜ Delancey Street-Essex Street (F/J/M/Z)

For me, the quintessential New York experience must
involve playing tennis. Where Delancey Street meets the
river, there are 12 outdoor hard-surface courts at the Brian
Watkins Tennis Center, in East River Park under the
Williamsburg Bridge.

The most amazing thing about the experience of playing
there, aside from seeing the same cronies every time
(the guy who never has a racket or tennis shoes, but beats
anyone and everyone, the "coach" who gives lessons but
looks like he's too large to move around the court, the
rooster who feeds on platters of rice and beans) is the
incredible urban context in which the courts are situated.
To one side is the East River with its stream of maritime
traffic; above, the never-ending road-and-rail din of the
Williamsburg Bridge; to the south, gatherings of family
and friends, with music of the Caribbean islands, Puerto

Rico, and the Dominican Republic often blaring from loudspeakers; and to the west, the East River Drive, a frequent route for fire engines and police cars.

With all this around you, it's imperative you work out some type of sign-language system with your partner for communicating (you can forget about even trying to hear the ball bounce!). Yet, despite the dissonance, one whiff of "sea" breeze can relax even the most stressed-out New Yorker.

All it requires is a 50 dollar permit (good for one season, April 15-October 15, at any city park court) available at Paragon Sporting Goods (867 Broadway between 17th and 18th Streets, ☎ 212 255-8036) and the courts in Central Park. Get there at least 45 minutes before the hour to secure a court. If the winter is mild, the nets don't come down and you can play all year long. Diehards have been known to show up with their own.

STEFANIE SILVERMAN
Architect and graphic designer

EAST VILLAGE

6.17 **East River Park**
East 12th Street to Montgomery Street between the East River & FDR Drive
Ⓜ First Avenue (L); East Broadway (F)

Grand Street Park, as it was known back then, was enlarged in 1946 when Marshall Plan Aid was taking food to bombed-out Europe. They needed ballast on the way back for the empty boats. When they got back to New York, they had to get rid of the ballast. The cheapest way was to dump it in the East River, off Grand Street Park, and enlarge the park. This kind of thing has been done for 300 years, you know. Manhattan had about 10 percent less acreage back

in those days, maybe even less. Now when kids hopscotch in the park, they're doing it on Hitler's bunker.
PETE SEEGER
Musician

Community Gardens
Ⓜ First Avenue (L); Lower East Side-Second Avenue (F/V)

6.18 La Plaza Cultural
632 East 9th Street at Avenue C

6.19 Tower
East 6th Street at Avenue B

Weave your way along the numbered streets between First Avenue and Avenue C. You'll see any number of community gardens growing where empty and rubbage-filled lots once stood. Some gardens are just a single lot-width wide, others are graced by stands of weeping willows. One, La Plaza Cultural, has a stone-built amphitheater, another a 30-foot tower built of community and personal throwaways. This vernacular tower is a totem for the garden's many individually cultivated plots. You'll probably see somebody turning the garden's mulch, someone else readying its arbor. Most gardens post hours for outsiders' visits.
JUDITH MARA GUTMAN
Writer

6.20 **Lakeside Lounge**
162 Avenue B at East 10th Street, ☎ 212 529-8463
Open daily 4pm-4am
Ⓜ First Avenue (L)

🍴 When the Lakeside Lounge opened a few years ago, word spread pretty quickly that the owners weren't looking to run another East Village dive for kids to invade on

weekends, like the rest of the "hotspots" that had moved into the neighborhood over the past few years. In fact, they opened the smoky, low-ceilinged hangout as an antidote to those spots. Lakeside was generally meant to be a locals' kind of place and specifically meant as a haven for those locals old enough to understand the humor in a 2 dollar can of Old Milwaukee (served icy cold). A so-bad-it's-cool collection of garishly colored Adirondack lake scene paintings was hung on the walls. Most importantly, a jukebox was installed, filled with bands like MC5, the Dictators, early Ramones, Howlin' Wolf, The Flaming Groovies, and assorted other five-miles-of-bad-road rock 'n' roll bands and Depression-era country and blues guys that no one's ever heard of. It got the point across about who was welcome at Lakeside Lounge: if you don't like our jukebox, you probably shouldn't be here. And it pretty much worked. Now, on any given night, you can catch honky-tonk-tough local bands' sets on one side of the U-shaped bar and admire the jukebox's still-scorching attitude. Remember the night with a stash of black-and-white snapshots from one of the last working photo booths in town.
MARYELLEN GORDON
Writer and editor

6.21 Tompkins Square Park

1834
East 7th Street to East 10th Street between Avenues A & B
Ⓜ First Avenue (L)

Slocum Memorial Fountain
Mid-park near 9th Street

When you walk through Tompkins Square Park, you pass clusters of old Ukrainians, old Italians, and old Slovaks; young Latino families, picnickers, skaters, people walking their dogs (or vice versa), "artsy" kids paying 1,800 dollars a month or more for studios in Old Law tenement buildings in the neighborhood, and a multitude of homeless folk.

If you walk east through the park on the path closest
to 10th Street, until you are almost all the way to Avenue
B, you will come to a small Parks Department building.
If you look north through the walkway of this building,
you will see a rose-colored eight-foot marble stela with
a small lion-head fountain and a shallow relief image
of children looking out to sea on its south face. The
inscription on this face reads: "They were earth's purest
children, young and fair."

The stela was "dedicated by the Sympathy Society of
German Ladies" in "the year of Our Lord MCMVI...in
memory of those who lost their lives in the disaster to the
Steamer *General Slocum*" on June 15, 1904.

In 1904, Tompkins Square was in the very center of a
neighborhood called Kleindeutschland or Little Germany.
The neighborhood was home to more than 150,000
Germans and German-Americans; a German free library,
hospital, town hall, and schools; numerous German
Socialist organizations; and the thriving congregation of
St. Mark's Evangelical Lutheran Church on East 6th Street.

On June 15, 1904, St. Mark's Evangelical Lutheran
Church leased the *General Slocum* to take the women and
children of the congregation to their annual Sunday school
picnic in Locust Grove, Long Island. Somewhere around
125th Street, the boat caught on fire. It is still not known
what caused the fire, although various sources cite a galley
fire, illegally stowed hay placed too near kerosene, a cigar
smoked near oil cans, and a fallen match or cigarette.
What is known is that the captain did not heed the warn-
ings that the boat was on fire until it was too late to pull
into safe harbor on one of the many working piers along
the way, the crew had not been trained in emergency
procedures, the boat's original hoses had never been
replaced and were no longer functioning, its six lifeboats
had been painted and wired to the ship and could no
longer be pried free, its life vests crumbled and sank when
used, and—although scores of people saw the burning

boat and battled the East River currents and the intense heat from the flames to try to reach it—by the time the *Slocum* pulled into North Brother Island, at least 1,021 women and children had been drowned, killed by the churning wheel of the steamship as they tried to escape the boat, or burnt to death.

Almost every family in Kleindeutschland lost a family member to the disaster and within a very short time Kleindeutschland was no more. The Germans moved uptown to the previously smaller German community of Yorkville, where they could be both closer to the cigar factories where many of them worked and far away from the devastating memories of June 15, 1904—making numerous apartments between the East River and the Bowery, and between Division, Grand, and 14th Streets, available for the next wave of immigrants, many of whose now-aged children can be found sitting and chatting in the park today.

There are a few mementos left of the old German neighborhood: the sign for the free German library ("Freie Bibliothek u. Lesehalle") above the doorway of the Ottendorfer Branch of the New York Public Library on Second Avenue between St. Mark's Place and 9th Street, and the sign for the German hospital ("Deutsches Dispensary") above the doorway of Cabrini Medical Center's Stuyvesant Polyclinic next door. But the Germans themselves are long gone, and today fewer and fewer people know about either the *Slocum* disaster or the monument to its victims in Tompkins Square Park.

KATE HARTNICK
Marketing consultant

RECOMMENDED READING
Eric Blau, *The Hero of the Slocum Disaster*, Mosaic Press, 1997.

6.22 ## Tompkins Square Park Dog Run
9th Street entrance, near Avenue B

One of the best dog runs in the city, complete with a giant
wooden statue of a bone.
ERIC STOLTZ
Actor

6.23 ## Russian Turkish Baths
268 East 10th Street between First Avenue & Avenue A
📞 212 473-8806
Monday, Tuesday, Thursday, Friday 11am-10pm; Wednesday
9am-10pm; Saturday, Sunday 7:30am-10pm; men only Sunday
before 2pm; women only Wednesday before 2pm
Ⓜ Astor Place (6); First Avenue (L)

You've been tramping around the city and it's finally
beginning to get to you: the noise, the traffic, the constant
press of human beings. You want to do something that will
put you in a completely different frame of mind. Go to the
Russian baths. You are surrounded mostly by people in
their sixties, seventies, and eighties, many of them speaking
Russian. You sit in a hot steam room and every once in
a while you leave and jump into a cold pool.

There are small surrounding rooms where you can get
different types of massages. The most unusual is the one
using branches of oak leaves. You lie on a slab in the main
steam room and an attendant rubs and massages your
body and beats you with wet oak leaves; as you heat up
from the steam, the attendant pours cool water on you and
continues to beat and rub. I sent a friend of mine who
described it as a religious experience.
MARGOT ADLER
Correspondent, National Public Radio

Go up the red steps. At the register, deposit your money
and jewelry into a safe deposit box. Go behind a curtain,
take a cotton robe and a pair of plastic slippers, and put

your clothes, along with your modesty, into a locker. Don your robe and slippers and go down a flight of steps to the Russian Turkish baths, where you may enter a traditional sauna, a sauna with a pull-chain shower, a steam room, an ice-cold pool, or—best of all—the radiant heat room. The first time I went into the radiant heat room, I was handed a bucket of icy water. Puzzled, I entered a stone room lined with two tiers of wooden benches. I have never experienced such intense heat. Within seven minutes I had overturned the bucket on my head; it was wonderful. For a modest fee you can spend hours at leisure. Founded in 1892, the baths are a rare New York treat, but the days and hours vary for single-sex and co-ed bathing; call to be sure.

MARGARET A. BRUCIA
Latin teacher and scholar

6.25 St. Mark's-in-the-Bowery Church

1799
131 East 10th Street at Second Avenue
Poetry Project information: www.poetryproject.com
Ⓜ Astor Place (6); Third Avenue (L)

When it was completed in 1799, St. Mark's-in-the-Bowery was already more than 100 years old, having started in 1660 as a Dutch chapel on Peter Stuyvesant's farm. It stands today as the second-oldest site of worship in New York City after St. Paul's Chapel. The Bowery, to the left of St. Mark's, was the road leading to the New Amsterdam governor's farm.

If slightly weary from all the changes around it, St. Mark's is still the most vocal member of the community. The old bronze bell tolled for John F. Kennedy and Martin Luther King, and rang to celebrate the end of the Vietnam War. Cracked in the fire of 1978, it now sits in the courtyard. After years of fund-raising, the church was restored and rededicated in 1983.

There is a sublime simplicity to St. Mark's. The inside of the church looks more Quaker than Episcopalian. The sun streams into the large white room over wooden floors—a place where one is as likely to hear the voices of poets as prayers. There is little sign of the arboreal splendor that marked the Stuyvesant farmland, but beautiful trees still grace the courtyard with a skyline of green. With your back to Stuyvesant Street, you can imagine the small colonial town of 1650. Just as easily, you will feel the history of community involvement and countercultural movements. Always a forum for common and radical beliefs alike, St. Mark's is a symbol of peaceful acceptance as well as protest.

St. Mark's has been home to the Poetry Project, scene of the only joint reading by Robert Lowell and Allen Ginsberg, since its founding in 1966. Readers have included Amiri Baraka, John Ashbery, Yoko Ono, Kenneth Koch, Adrienne Rich, and many adventurous unknowns. A small dogwood in the courtyard honors Allen Ginsberg, who wrote. "The Poetry Project burns like red hot coal in New York's snow." Nearby, flowering trees memorialize W.H. Auden, Paul Blackburn, and Frank O'Hara. A brass plate on the Parish wall quotes Auden: "Thousands live without love, not one without water."

I love St. Mark's for the two women eating lunch on the porch and the man practicing tai chi in the courtyard, the gravel barely moving under his light but deliberate steps. Growing up, we used the vault markers as bases. I walked quickly past Peter Stuyvesant's bust as if he were the authoritative parent of a friend. I kissed my first kiss amidst the charred stones. St. Mark's church—eternal home to seven generations of Stuyvesants—reminds us that among the hustle and bustle of Second Avenue, poetry thrives and New York, with its gritty past, is still beautiful.

LAURIE DUCHOVNY
Teacher and author

6.26 Cinema Classics

332 East 11th Street between First & Second Avenues
☎ 212 677-5368; www.cinemaclassics.com
Ⓜ First Avenue (L); Astor Place (6)

Bacall taps her cigarette on her silver case and gazes wistfully at Bogart. Bogey leans in with his lighter...

Ever wish the atmosphere in the multiplex were a little more like the action onscreen? At Cinema Classics, it is. Here you can curl up in a comfy chair and watch vintage film while enjoying what may be the world's largest cup of coffee (we're talking kiddie pool!). Movies are available to rent, buy, or watch. The current thing is the 10 o'clock Mock on Thursday nights, which involves a really bad B-flick and a comedy troupe making fun of the movie as it plays. Happy hour is from 4 p.m. to 7:30 p.m. daily, with beer prices that date from the era when they actually paid stars to smoke in public.

DANY LEVY (AND EDITORIAL STAFF OF DAILYCANDY.COM)
Founder of DailyCandy.com

6.27 Second Avenue Deli

156 Second Avenue at East 10th Street, ☎ 212 677-0606
Open daily for breakfast, lunch, and dinner
Ⓜ Astor Place (6); Third Avenue (L)

🍴 Go for a hot pastrami sandwich at the Second Avenue Deli, where you can also find the best matzo ball soup in town.
MAIRA KALMAN
Author and illustrator

Lower East Side Memories
Ⓜ Astor Place (6); Third Avenue (L)

6.27 Second Avenue Deli
156 Second Avenue at East 10th Street, ☎ 212 677-0606
Open daily for breakfast, lunch, and dinner

6.28 Veselka
144 Second Avenue at East 9th Street, ☎ 212 228-9682
Open 24 hours

🍽 The Lower East Side has its ghosts. The Second Avenue
of the Yiddish theater, Ratner's, Rappaport's, and the cafes
where intellectuals, impoverished writers, and Yiddish
impresarios drank tea and thought about art and the hard-
earned dollar, has been replaced by multiplex movie houses
and gentrified restaurants. But the Second Avenue Deli still
boasts footprints of yesterday's celebrities and Veselka still
offers pierogi, blintzes, and the excitement of new theater
projects being hatched alongside the stuffed cabbage and
the beet borscht (hot or cold). Orchard Street still has great
clothing bargains and still offers a pickle barrel as briny as
that of the 1920's (see Guss' Pickles, p. 140). Old syna-
gogues are living, beseeching ghosts, and streets like Willett
have all but vanished but still speak to my heart.
ARTHUR SAINER
Writer

RECOMMENDED READING
Henry Roth, *Call It Sleep*, Farrar, Straus & Giroux, 1991.
Michael Gold, *Jews Without Money*, Carroll & Graf Publishers,
Inc., 1996.

6.30 Gem Spa Newsstand
131 Second Avenue at St. Marks Place, ☎ 212 995-1866
Open 24 hours
Ⓜ Astor Place (6)

🎁 Stupid name, great egg creams. In my opinion this Manhattan
newsstand serves the best version of that world-famous

concoction of milk, seltzer, and syrup that is often described as the quintessential New York beverage. Once you've got the proportions and ingredients right, the trick to a great egg cream is using very, very cold milk, and Gem Spa keeps theirs in an ice cream freezer. The mixologists at Gem Spa have one fault, however. They will ask you what flavor you want. Scoff at them. Any real New Yorker knows that egg creams only come in chocolate.

MICHAEL MISCIONE
Writer

Best Old Barrooms

6.31 **McSorley's Old Ale House**
15 East 7th Street between Second & Third Avenues
☎ 212 473-9148
Monday-Saturday 11am-1am; Sunday 1pm-1am
Ⓜ Astor Place (6)

4.25 **Fanelli Cafe**
94 Prince Street at Mercer Street, ☎ 212 226-9412
Monday-Thursday 10am-2am; Friday, Saturday 10am-3am;
Sunday 11am-2am
Ⓜ Prince Street (N/R): Broadway-Lafayette Street (F/S/V);
Spring Street (6)

8.12 **Old Town Bar and Restaurant**
45 East 18th Street between Broadway & Park Avenue South
☎ 212 529-6732
Open daily for lunch and dinner
Ⓜ 14th Street-Union Square (L/N/Q/R/W/4/5/6)

🍴 McSorley's Old Ale House, the "wonderful saloon" chronicled by Joseph Mitchell and painted by John Sloan, may be the last remnant of a New York we all dreamed about long ago. "To a devoted McSorley customer, most other New York City saloons are tense and disquieting,"

Mitchell wrote. "It is possible to relax in McSorley's. For one thing, it is dark and gloomy, and repose comes easy in a gloomy place... Also, there is a thick, musty smell that acts as a balm to jerky nerves; it is really a rich compound of the smells of pine sawdust, tap drippings, pipe tobacco, coal smoke, and onions." Despite a few modifications, including the first female face behind the bar, McSorley's is much as it was when Mitchell brilliantly captured it for *The New Yorker* almost 60 years ago; much as it was when the doors first opened in 1854. Dim and crowded (avoid it at all costs on Saint Paddy's Day), it has the same bar taps, the same pot-bellied stove and it serves just two kinds of beer—McSorley's own light and dark.

If McSorley's is the place to be pleasantly melancholy, then Fanelli's is the place to be happy. It's practically the last genuine establishment left in SoHo, once a gritty factory neighborhood and now full of relentlessly trendy shops. The beautifully intact speakeasy interior hasn't changed much since the repeal of Prohibition. And even though the gallery-goers and local loft-dwellers who dart in and out may whip out Palm Pilots at the drop of a hat, Fanelli's remains without pretensions, offering generous drinks and plates of honest grub at fair prices. A friend once compared it to the bar in *Cheers*, but to my mind it's more like the bar in *Northern Exposure*: completely non-judgmental. Prada and Yohji Yamamoto rub elbows with well-worn workshirts and the seersucker jacket and madras tie on the gentleman to your left.

If you've seen the opener of *Late Night with David Letterman*, with that grand sweep of mahogany bar (it seats 40), then you've seen the Old Town. It's pretty great. And when it comes to being conducive to talking (or eavesdropping), there is nothing like it. Go early, when the serious drinkers are there, and slide into one of the intimate booths opposite the bar. There's a good selection of brew on tap, but there's something about the tone of the place that makes the choice of Bud in a bottle almost ▶

▶

automatic. And the food—burgers, real bar sandwiches, terrific fries—is popular with neighborhood loyalists.

JANE DANIELS LEAR
Senior editor, Gourmet

RECOMMENDED READING:
Joseph Mitchell, *McSorley's Wonderful Saloon*, Pantheon Books, 2001.
Geoffrey R. Bartholomew, *The McSorley Poems: Voices from New York City's Oldest Pub*, Charlton Street Press, 2001.

6.32 Sonali Indian Restaurant

326 East 6th Street between First & Second Avenues
☎ 212 505-7517
Open daily for lunch and dinner
Ⓜ Lower East Side-Second Avenue (F/V); Astor Place (6)

🍴 In Manhattan's East Village on 6th Street between First and Second Avenues there is an entire block lined with Indian restaurants. There are a few more off-block, along Second and First Avenues, but of all the eateries of any ethnicity located in this diverse neighborhood, my favorite is a mere slip of a place on East 6th Street called Sonali. It is no wider than a coffin, yet the food provides sustenance for a joyous life. The reddened chicken fresh from the tandoor is extraordinary; never dry, ever moist. It is a pleasure to savor its ground spices and yogurt flavors with a 20-ounce Taj Mahal beer. I love the luminous decor of this place, its subtle glow. A walk up the front stairs of this old rowhouse is a walk into another land.

DENNIS BARONE
Writer and professor of English

Where DJs Go

6.33 Dance Tracks

91 East 3rd Street between First & Second Avenues

☎ 212 260-8729

Monday-Thursday noon-8pm; Friday noon-10pm;

Saturday noon-8:30pm; Sunday noon-7pm

Ⓜ Lower East Side-Second Avenue (F/V); Bleecker Street (6)

5.44 Other Music

15 East 4th Street between Broadway & Lafayette Street

☎ 212 477-8150

Monday-Friday noon-9pm; Saturday noon-8pm;

Sunday noon-7pm

Ⓜ Bleecker Street (6); 8th Street-NYU (N/R); Broadway-

Lafayette Street (F/S/V)

🎁 Hey DJs, you want vinyl? Then Dance Tracks is where
you want to be. Always busy and always abuzz. You better
know what you're looking for or you'll get the look. For
those interested in CDs, go to Other Music—they carry the
cool stuff.

ALEXANDER DUFF

Restaurateur

RECOMMENDED READING

Flaunt, DJ Times

CHELSEA &
THE GARMENT
DISTRICT

7

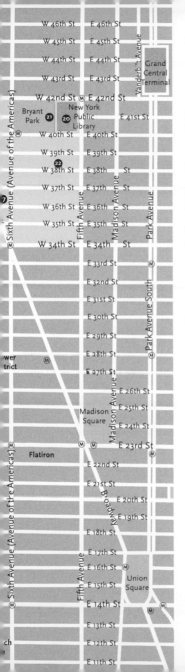

CHELSEA

1. Starrett-Lehigh Building
2. Downtown Boathouse
3. Art Gallery District
4. Comme des Garçons
5. Printed Matter
6. Bottino
7. Grand Sichuan
8. Dia Center for the Arts
9. General Theological Seminary
10. Chelsea Market
11. Port Authority
12. La Taza de Oro
13. El Quijote
14. Capitol Fishing Tackle Co.
15. Biricchino

GARMENT DISTRICT

16. The Circle Line
17. Greenwich Savings Bank
18. Drama Book Shop
19. Empire Theater
20. New York Public Library
21. Bryant Park
22. Tinsel Trading

Chelsea & Garment District

CHELSEA

7.1 **Starrett-Lehigh Building**
1931, Russell G. Cory & Walter M. Cory, and Yasuo Matsui
601 West 26th Street between Eleventh & Twelfth Avenues
Ⓜ 23rd Street (C/E)

The streamlined Art Moderne Starrett-Lehigh Building anchors a full city block like a hulking dry-docked tanker. Russell and Walter Cory and Yasuo Matsui designed the 2.5 million-square-foot shipwreck for the Starrett Brothers (contractors for the Empire State Building) and the Lehigh Valley Railroad. An early modernist landmark work of the Machine Age, its gently curved corners are wrapped with nine miles of strip windows and brick. Freight train cars ferried across the Hudson River, rode the elevated High Line rail inside and were hoisted to the upper floors fully loaded by super-powered Otis elevators. For a brief moment, the former factory and warehouse housed hundreds of dot.coms. Remaining tenants include the do-it-yourself diva Martha Stewart, who delights in driving door-to-door (via the freight elevator) to her empire designed by architect Dan Rowan, and advertising legend Jay Chiat's Screaming Media, designed by the Huts Sachs Studio.
FREDERIC SCHWARTZ AND TRACEY HUMMER
Architect and Writer

7.3 Chelsea Art Gallery District

West 20th to West 26th Street between Tenth & Eleventh
Avenues
Ⓜ 23rd Street (C/E)

7.4 Comme des Garçons

520 West 22nd Street between Tenth & Eleventh Avenues
☎ 212 604-9200
Tuesday-Saturday 11am-7pm; Sunday, Monday noon-6pm

7.5 Printed Matter

535 West 22nd Street between Tenth & Eleventh Avenues
☎ 212 925-0325
Tuesday-Friday 10am-6pm; Saturday 11am-7pm;
closed Sunday, Monday

7.6 Bottino

246 Tenth Avenue between West 24th & West 25th Streets
☎ 212 206-6766
Tuesday-Saturday for lunch and dinner; Sunday, Monday for
dinner only

The largest free show of contemporary art in the world
is at the galleries that fill the blocks from 20th to 26th
Streets between Tenth and Eleventh Avenues in West
Chelsea. Pick up a Gallery Guide—given out free at most
galleries—and plot your course.

If you need a brief respite from art, check out the
uniquely designed Comme des Garçons store on West
22nd Street. And don't miss Printed Matter, a non-profit
arts institution and wonderful bookstore, with some of the
best new, used, and out-of-print artists' books as well as
book-like artworks. Think of great contemporary art in an
affordable, portable format and that's what you'll find
here. Bottino is the art world's restaurant-of-choice in the
neighborhood. The food is quite good and there are always
artists, dealers, and curators there for lunch, early-evening
drinks, and dinner.   ▶

▶

Chelsea galleries between Tenth & Eleventh Avenues:

West 20th Street: Anton Kern, Andrew Kreps

West 21st Street: Paula Cooper, Bonakdar Jancou

West 22nd Street: Matthew Marks, Friedrich Petzel,
                     Marianne Boesky, 303 Gallery,
                     Brent Sikkema

West 24th Street: Gagosian, Luhring Augustine,
                     Andrea Rosen, Matthew Marks,
                     Metro Pictures, Barbara Gladstone

West 25th Street: Feature, PaceWildenstein,
                     Cheim & Read

West 26th Street: Team, Gorney Bravin & Lee

And a few more suggestions just a bit outside Chelsea:

West 14th Street: Casey Kaplan
West 15th Street: Gavin Brown's Enterprise
West 17th Street: Murray Guy

JANELLE REIRING
Owner, Metro Pictures

7.7   Grand Sichuan International

229 Ninth Avenue at West 24th Street, ☎ 212 620-5200
Open daily for lunch and dinner
Ⓜ 23rd Street (C/E)

🍴 What I love about this place is not so much the food—
though it's certainly bountiful and delicious—but the
highly inventive menu, which is a spicy mix of cultural
history, geography, gastronomy, and mythology.

You'll be given two volumes when you're seated at your
table. One is a 27-page explanation of dishes, which
describes the differences in regional cooking (methods,
ingredients, food history), and includes advice for best
appreciating the nuances of spice and temperature. For

instance, the booklet discusses (with no scientific backing) the differences between Chinese and American palates and gullets, and advises Americans on which dishes might please and which might offend. The advice is peppered with other personal insights of the staff and cook, along with practical descriptions of the dishes. It's an earnest attempt by the staff to help diners navigate the complexities of Sichuan cooking. And it's also an entertaining read.

The second volume is the actual menu, which includes the standard dishes. Then there are the specialties of the house such as Mao's Home Cooking, the Prodigal Princess Dishes of the Mandarin Emperor (based upon the Chinese TV series about the Qing Dynasty), special dishes for Halloween and Thanksgiving (seemingly offered all year), and fresh-chicken specials (I've never gotten the details, but have been assured that the chicken is very fresh). These come with lengthy explanations of cultural references and the decision-making process involved in offering these curious dishes.

As for the food, the soup dumplings are delicate, the vegetables fresh, and the sauces—slightly smoky and sublime—transcend the brown spicy goop of so many Chinese kitchens. I've never been here when there hasn't been a line. And I've never had a meal that wasn't worth the wait.

LANA BORTOLOT
Writer

7.8 Dia Center for the Arts
1987, Gluckman Mayner
548 West 22nd Street between Tenth & Eleventh Avenues
☎ 212 989-5566
Wednesday-Sunday noon-6pm; closed Monday, Tuesday
Ⓜ 23rd Street (C/E)

"Rooftop Urban Park Project"
1981, Dan Graham

▶

The Dia Center is unique for its single-artist, long-term exhibitions of contemporary art, many of them large-scale installations by emerging and established artists. Don't miss Dia's rooftop urban park, where sculptor Dan Graham has constructed a striking glass and metal installation that transforms the New York skyline. Relax at the small cafe here or in the center's bright new bookstore on the first floor, while leafing through one of its many volumes on postwar and contemporary art. Dia also hosts monthly contemporary art lectures by scholars and critics.

DANA MICUCCI
Journalist

On the roof of the Dia Center's renovated warehouse is an installation made specifically for the site by Dan Graham in 1981 (installed 1991). The work is a large-scale architectural structure composed of two-way mirrored glass elevated on a wooden floor. In its center stands an inner cylinder that evokes the shape of the roof's own nearby water tower—an iconic New York City shape. The work may be entered and interacted with, as the glass is both translucent and transparent, and the quality of the light and its reflection change constantly, showing and hiding its surroundings—sky, river, and other visitors. The recreated "urban citiscape" is both contemplative and active, providing a type of New York City jungle gym art.

CHRISTINE MOOG
Graphic designer

7.9   General Theological Seminary Garden
175 Ninth Avenue between West 20th & West 21st Streets
☎ 212 243-5150
Monday-Friday noon-3pm; Saturday 11am-3pm; closed Sunday
Ⓜ 23rd Street (C/E/1/2)

Stroll past the bookstore and onto the grounds of the oldest seminary of the Episcopal church in the U.S.

(founded in 1817 and a New York City landmark since 1826). You'll find a central garden or "close," with expansive lawns and towering trees, that is an absolute surprise. Wander in for a bit of Boston in New York. It's beautiful, peaceful, and free.

ERIC STOLTZ
Actor

Skybridges

West 15th Street between Ninth & Tenth Avenues;
Tenth Avenue between West 15th & West 16th Streets;
East 60th Street between Lexington & Third Avenues

The autogyros and skyline freeways of Hugh Ferriss's the Metropolis of Tomorrow never appeared, and dirigibles don't moor at the spire of the Empire State Building. However, these simple bridges cantilevered over Manhattan's streets serve both the prosaic purpose of linking showroom and warehouse and providing a sliver of the romantic comic book city of Gotham amid Manhattan's relentless grid.

SEBASTIAN HARDY
Urban planner

7.10   Chelsea Market

75 Ninth Avenue between West 15th & West 16th Streets
☎ 212 243-6005
Monday-Friday 8am-10pm; Saturday, Sunday 8am-8pm
Ⓜ 14th Street (A/C/E); Eighth Avenue (L)

🍴 The old Nabisco Factory where the original Oreo Cookie was made in 1912 is once again a center for good food. Since 1995, it has housed the Chelsea Market complex of shops. The factory building fills the entire block between Ninth and Tenth Avenues and 15th and 16th Streets. Developer Irwin Cohen drew on the area's history as New York's meatpacking and wholesale produce district at the end of the 19th century and came up with a design that lightheartedly recalls the building's industrial past. A corridor, originally part of the railroad that carried supplies from the Hudson River, runs through the center, lined with shops like the main street of a village. Halfway through, a factory pipe has been made into an indoor waterfall. All along the walk, gears, bits of old brick, and other machinery now serve as sculptures. (There is also, somewhat oddly, a series of stone carvings of various parts of the human body.) The shops do a large part of their business wholesale, using the original loading bays. Each also sells retail from a storefront, offering the same products used at many of New York's most elegant restaurants at excellent prices. In a particularly nice touch, the wholesale kitchens are all on display behind glass, so you can watch huge batches of cookies, breads, and soups being made. The old factory still contains many bakeries, among them the famous Sarabeth's Bakery and Amy's Bread. Other shops offer meat, wine, fresh milk in glass bottles, soups, freshly squeezed fruit juices, Thai food, imported Italian goods, and produce, including some hard-to-find fruits and vegetables. A kitchen supply store sells both new and used kitchen equipment, including some huge professional ovens and restaurant fixtures. There is a flower shop, a hardware store, and a gift basket creator. Several places offer free samples. Many establishments include small restaurant areas, and there are also benches along the central corridor, so you can assemble a picnic and eat it right there. The market and the shops in it sponsor occasional events such as food and wine tastings, and on Saturday evenings there is free tango dancing (Triangulo Tango Salon, ☎ 212 633-6445).

JANET B. PASCAL
Writer and editor

The Renaissance Street Singers
www.streetsingers.org

On a Sunday somewhere in the five boroughs, you may come upon a small semicircle of musicians singing 15th- and 16th-century a cappella motets on the sidewalk. These are the Renaissance Street Singers, a group founded in 1973 by John Hetland. The concerts are always free (and the group returns any donations people try to leave for them), given simply for love of the music and as a gift to the City of New York. For 28 years, the group has sung in any public space they can find (unless someone kicks them out). Some favorite spots are the corner of Christopher and Bleecker Streets in Greenwich Village, Chelsea Market (see p. 167), the corner of Henry and Montague Streets in Brooklyn Heights, and Cleopatra's Needle in Central Park. They perform two or three Sundays a month, usually from 2 p.m. to 4 p.m. If you're interested in tracking them down, the location of the forthcoming Sunday's concert can be found on their web site.

JANET B. PASCAL
Writer and editor

7.11 **Former Port of New York Authority Commerce Building**
1932, Abbott, Merkt & Co
111 Eighth Avenue between West 15th & West 16th Streets
Ⓜ 14th Street (A/C/E); Eighth Avenue (L)

In this full block structure, find an elevator large enough for semitractor trailers, ramps for same, elevator machine room straight out of Charlie Chaplin's *Modern Times*, and circular elevated helicopter landing pad with giant red "X" raised above the roof.

TERENCE RILEY
Chief Curator of Architecture and Design,
The Museum of Modern Art

If you tilted this muscular 1930's Art Moderne behemoth on its end, it would rise as tall as the Woolworth Building. With more than two million sprawling square feet of space, this is the fourth-largest building in New York City. Its enormous footprint (200 by 800 feet) encompasses one of the city's biggest blocks and merits its own subway entrance. This was formerly the Port Authority's headquarters, where six giant elevators once hoisted trucks to 30 loading docks in the sky.

TRACEY HUMMER
Writer

7.12 La Taza de Oro

96 Eighth Avenue between West 14th & West 15th Streets
☎ 212 243-9946
Monday-Saturday 6am-11pm; closed Sunday
Ⓜ 14th Street (A/C/E); Eighth Avenue (L)

🍴 There is really no reason to pay all that money at Starbucks when you can get such a superior product at this popular Puerto Rican diner. A dollar flat will get you a generous cup of café con leche. The brew is foamy and rich, with more than enough caffeine to get you through a morning's worth of Chelsea gallery-hopping or a shopping expedition at Jeffrey. If you need more fuel, sit down to a plate of delectable roast chicken with rice and beans.

MARY CLARKE
Magazine editor

7.13 El Quijote

226 West 23rd Street between Seventh & Eighth Avenues
☎ 212 929-1855
Open daily for lunch and dinner
Ⓜ 23rd Street (C/E/1/2)

🍴 You wouldn't say there's a scene to make at El Quijote, but the place is generally crowded with actual New Yorkers there to eat the excellent lobster and paella, to drink some sangria or Marques de Riscal, and to spend some time in the very cool atmosphere of this handsome and sturdy 60-year-old Spanish restaurant. The Quijote is a survivor, and the better part of its patrons—writers, catalog models, hospital workers, legitimately eccentric denizens of the Chelsea Hotel—appear to be among those who have gone too far down their chosen road to contemplate turning back. The Dulcinea Room and the Cervantes Room are attractive, in a slightly Miss Havishamesque way, but the main dining room, with its terra-cotta walls painted with duotone Quijote murals, is the best spot to take in the underlit defunct elegance of the place. Owner Manny Ramirez says he's a direct descendant of Don Quijote, a claim worthy of the Man of La Mancha himself. Dig into the big portions and the red wine.

CHRISTOPHER CAHILL
Poet and novelist

Most people go to El Quijote, the oldest Spanish lobster palace in the city, for its generous portions of paella, and the staggering surf-and-turf platters. Few go for the bar, which is one of the best spots for revisiting the New York of fedoras, furs, and cigarettes cases. It's one of those places where "old" New York isn't re-created—it simply never left. The bartenders wear uniforms with undersized bow ties and engraved nameplates on their vests. Exceedingly polite and formal, it's clear they consider restaurant service an honorable profession—just one of the many subtleties that places the restaurant in another era. The bar is old-fashioned, too, with its large frosted glass etched with lobsters, and backlit a pale blue. Quixote figures form an odd parade along the bar, filling every space not occupied by bottles. The spirits collection includes crème de menthe, Dubonnet, and sloe gin—things you'd think no one has ordered in years until the night you come in here for a perfect Manhattan and you see a woman of tattered beauty—maybe a 1948 Miss Nassau County or a former showgirl—nursing one of those retro drinks in the curve of her arm. Hemmed into her space by the couples from Jersey or the Island, the guy with slicked-back hair and the well-toned date, and the art types from the Chelsea Hotel, she's a character type that's all but forgotten.

From the bar you have the perfect vantage point from which to see the dining room. Red banquettes line the walls, which in turn are lined with the original black-and-white and burnt-sienna murals depicting Quixote's adventures. Windmills turn slowly along the back wall—the only sluggish element in this bustling place, where waiters hustle at breakneck speed, swooping into the dining room with large trays overhead.

There's no pretension here. There's no kitsch, no irony, and no attitude. It's earnest, authentic, and delicious. And Santoro will make you a perfect Manhattan at an old-fashioned price.

LANA BORTOLOT
Writer

7.14　Capitol Fishing Tackle Co.

218 West 23rd Street between Seventh & Eighth Avenues
☎ 212 929-6132
Monday, Tuesday, Wednesday, Friday 10am-6pm; Thursday 10am-7:30pm; Saturday 10am-5pm; closed Sunday
Ⓜ 23rd Street (C/E/1/2)

🎁 I've attempted to fish only a few unsuccessful times in my life. But when walking down 23rd Street, just past the Chelsea Hotel, I often find myself stopping into Capitol Fishing Tackle to browse the extensive array of fishing paraphernalia and equipment. The beauty, humor, and inventiveness of the vast inventory of lures is astonishing. Their line-up of reels may not rival in diversity the Metropolitan Museum's collection of early weaponry, but it does provide an impressive display of variations on a theme. The theme: a kind of simple mechanical beauty either eliminated or hidden in most current product design. For the avid fisher or anyone who likes cool stuff, it's worth a visit. They also carry a decent collection of T-shirts emblazoned with all kinds of piscine imagery.

BILL KOMOSKI
Artist

7.15 **Biricchino Northern Italian Restaurant**
260 West 29th Street between Seventh & Eighth Avenues
☎ 212 695-6690
Monday-Friday for lunch and dinner; Saturday for dinner only; closed Sunday
Ⓜ 28th Street (1/2); 34th Street-Penn Station (A/C/E)

🍽 Go to Biricchino (don't be put off by the decor) and try
🎁 a sample appetizer of five of their sausages. Made on site since 1925, the sausages and salamis are served at New York's finest restaurants including the Four Seasons, La Caravelle, and Alain Ducasse. When there's a game at Madison Square Garden, people with season tickets also appear to have reservations for tables at the restaurant, until exactly 7:20 p.m. The place stops serving at 9 p.m., so go early. Or, shop for sausages at their deli, Salumeria Biellesse (☎ 212 736-7376), next door.

LIONEL TIGER
Professor of anthropology, Rutgers University

GARMENT DISTRICT

7.16 **The Circle Line**
Departs from Pier 83, West 42nd Street at Twelfth Avenue
☎ 212 563-3200
Three-hour tour (full island) and two-hour tour (half island); schedule varies with season
Ⓜ 42nd Street-Port Authority (A/C/E); Westbound Bus M42

Having the chance to step back and look at something from a little farther away gives you the unique opportunity to see proportions, colors, scale, and relationships between parts. A tour around the island of Manhattan is like a silent movie in slow motion. It gives you a better understanding of the city's architecture, landscape, history, development, and environment by gently showing you all the contrasts, the sudden changes, the overwhelming size of some buildings, and the beautiful and undeveloped areas, all one after the other. You cannot choose what to see and what not to see. It is all there, in front of you. The 32-mile circumnavigation presents an enigma: houses, skyscrapers, deep canyons, parks, forests, bridges, and monasteries don't explain to you how they all came to be built together on this tiny island; it is up to you to figure it out.

MATTEO PERICOLI
Architect and illustrator

7.19 Former Empire Theater, now AMC Empire 25
Facade 1912, Thomas W. Lamb
234 West 42nd Street between Seventh & Eighth Avenues
📞 212 398-7843
Ⓜ 42nd Street-Port Authority (A/C/E); 42nd Street-Times Square (N/Q/R/S/W/1/2/3/7)

How can a vast new 25-screen multiplex on 42nd Street be called a city secret? What makes the AMC worth a careful look is the way the building expresses that it is the largest structure in New York City ever to be physically moved. The remaining signs of that 1998 move are fascinating.

As a boy, I spent happy days on old West 42nd Street, visiting magic shops and Hubert's Flea Circus. The exterior of the new AMC was there then. It was built in 1912 as the Eltinge Theater, named after Julian Eltinge, a famed cross-dressing actor of the era—a work by theater architect

Thomas W. Lamb, who in New York also did the lost
Strand, Ziegfeld, Rialto, Rivoli, Capitol, and Loew's 72nd
Street, and the still extant Cort and Mark Hellinger
theaters. Over the decades, the building's function changed
from comedy playhouse to burlesque theater to cinema,
and its name changed to the Empire in 1954, after it
became a second-run movie house. When 42nd Street was
rebuilt in the last few years, it was decided to transform
the Empire into a multiplex. The single auditorium space
became superfluous, but the building facade and elements
within were thought worth preserving as major historic
constituents of what eventually became an internally
linked, mixed old and new architectural ensemble.

The front of the Eltinge/Empire that in 1998 rolled
170 feet west from its original position weighed 7.4 million
pounds, including its temporary structural reinforcement.
(Though preparations had taken months, the distance was
covered in a single day.) What's architecturally interesting
is how the completed design expresses the assemblage of
parts, the old facade providing an ad hoc component for
the amalgamation. The dome over the lobby, visible behind
exterior glazing, covers a surprisingly kinetic space when
one walks in. Two transparent-sided escalators merrily
penetrate what used to be the old proscenium arch, carrying customers out of the ticketing area into the hinterland
of screened auditoriums and eateries. All this can be visited
and viewed without buying a ticket.

The lobby interior's largely scenographic decoration
includes a restored mural uncovered before the move.
It depicts three muses, probably the likenesses of Julian
Eltinge in drag. A final transformation for you, sir!

NATHAN SILVER
Architect, writer, and educator

7.20 **The New York Public Library**
1911, Carrère & Hastings
Fifth Avenue between 40th & 42nd Streets, ☎ 212 930-0830
Monday, Thursday-Saturday 10am-6pm; Tuesday, Wednesday
11am-7:30pm; closed Sunday

Ⓜ Fifth Avenue (7); 42nd Street (B/D/F/V); Grand Central-42nd
Street (S/4/5/6/7)

Rose Main Reading Room
Restoration 1998, Davis Brody Bond
General Research Division, third floor

Salomon Room
Third Floor

Newly renovated, the Main Reading Room of the New
York Public Library is one of the premier public spaces in
the city. Take a morning to visit the library, perhaps to
order a fine or obscure book from the stacks for perusing
at one of the long reading tables. Then, walk across the
hall to the Salomon Room, where you'll find curious or
arresting exhibits drawn from the library's collection of
books, manuscripts, and papers. Afterwards, lunch or dine
at the Bryant Park Grill behind the library and stroll along
the park path, taking in the sculpture and the people.
PAUL KANE
Poet and scholar

7.21 **Bryant Park**
1871; 1934, redesigned by Lusby Simpson
Sixth Avenue between West 40th & West 42nd Streets
Ⓜ 42nd Street (B/D/F/V); Fifth Avenue (7)

Bryant Park Grill
25 West 40th Street between Fifth & Sixth Avenues
☎ 212 840-6500
Open daily 11:30am-11:30pm, except between 3:30pm-5pm

🍴 One of the best ways to spend an hour in Midtown is in Bryant Park, the oasis behind the New York Public Library—by some miracle restored rather than replaced like its counterparts in London and Paris. Ask about the outdoor roof garden of the Bryant Park Grill. You'll be shown a dark, hidden staircase that takes you to the roof with a wonderful wide view of the elegant park ringed with skyscrapers. Tired from reading, your eyes take in the grassy rectangle below, edged by rows of lush perennials and greenery, partially shaded by rows of tall, graceful trees, and anchored by kiosks selling drinks, tickets, and fresh flowers.

LAURIE LISLE
Author

7.22 **Tinsel Trading**
   47 West 38th Street between Fifth & Sixth Avenues
   📞 212 730-1030
   Monday-Friday 10am-5.30pm, closed Saturday, Sunday
Ⓜ 42nd Street (B/D/F/V); Fifth Avenue (7);
   34th Street-Herald Square (N/Q/R/W)

🎁 The family story of Tinsel Trading is hidden from the casual shopper on this Garment District street. But it's hard to ignore the extraordinary nature of the trims and ribbons sold in this store. Marcia Ceppos inherited this business from her grandfather Arch Bergoffen. In the 1930's, Mr. Bergoffen sold gold trim for military uniforms. He gradually expanded to include many trims using metal thread, handmade raffia flowers from Italy, and straw trims from Switzerland. When things went out of style, he put them away. When Ms. Ceppos found this treasure trove, some of which had not been looked at in 50 years, she decided to keep the business not only going, but in the family.

CHARLES SUISMAN AND CAROL MOLESWORTH
Authors

GRAMERCY,
FLATIRON DISTRICT,
MIDTOWN SOUTH
& MURRAY HILL

8

8

Times Square

Grand Central Terminal

Vanderbilt Avenue

W 42nd St   E 42nd St   E 42nd St
Bryant Park
New York Public Library
E 41st St   E 41st St
E 40th St   E 40th Exit St
Tunnel Exit St
E 39th St   E 39th St
Murray Hill
E 38th St   E 38th St
E 37th St   E 37th St
E 36th St   E 36th St
E 35th St   E 35th St
W 34th St   E 34th St   E 34th St
W 33rd St   E 33rd St   E 33rd St
W 32nd St   E 32nd St   E 32nd St
Penn Station
W 31st St   E 31st St   E 31st St
Midtown South
W 30th St   E 30th St   E 30th St
W 29th St   E 29th St   E 29th St
Flower District
W 28th St   E 28th St   E 28th St
W 27th St   E 27th St   E 27th St
W 26th St   E 26th St   E 26th St
W 25th St   E 25th St   E 25th St
Madison Square
W 24th St   E 24th St   E 24th St
W 23rd St   E 23rd St
Flatiron   Gramercy
W 22nd St   E 22nd St   E 22nd St
W 21st St   E 21st St   E 21st St
Gramercy Park
W 20th St   E 20th St   E 20th St
Gramercy Park S
W 19th St   E 19th St   E 19th St
W 18th St   E 18th St   E 18th St
W 17th St   E 17th St   E 17th St
Stuyvesant Park
W 16th St   E 16th St   E 16th St
Union Square
W 15th St   E 15th St   E 15th St
W 14th St   E 14th St   E 14th St

Seventh Avenue
Sixth Avenue (Avenue of the Americas)
Broadway
Fifth Avenue
Madison Avenue
Park Avenue
Lexington Avenue
Third Avenue
Second Avenue
Park Avenue South
Union Sq W
Union Sq E
Irving Pl
University Pl
Broadway
Fourth Avenue

Greenwich Village

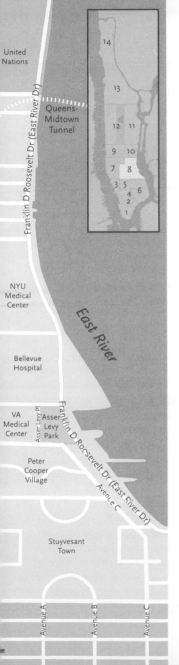

GRAMERCY

1 Gramercy Park Hotel
2 Gramercy Park
3 The National Arts Club
🍴 4 Pete's Tavern
🍴 5 71 Irving
6 80 Irving Place
🍴 7 Yama
🍴 8 Chosi
9 Inn at Irving Place

FLATIRON DISTRICT

10 Arts for Transit
11 Union Square
🏛 11 Union Square Greenmarket
🍴 12 Old Town Bar
🍴 13 Union Square Cafe
🏛 14 Chisholm Gallery
🏛 15 Housing Works
🏛 16 Winter Works on Paper
🍴 17 Eisenberg Sandwich Shop
18 Masonic Hall
🏛 19 Louis Tannen Inc.
🏛 20 The Annex
21 Maintenance Cabin
22 Worth Monument
23 Madison Square Park
24 NYS Supreme Court
🏛 25 Flower District
26 TADA!

MIDTOWN SOUTH

27 Church of St. Francis of Assisi
🏛 28 Brother Sebastian's
🍴 29 I Trulli
🍴 30 Rodeo Bar & Grill
🍴 31 Paddy Reilly's Music Bar
🍴🏛 32 Kalustyan's
33 Della Robbia Bar
34 Empire State Building

MURRAY HILL

35 Pierpont Morgan Library
36 Mid-Manhattan Library
37 Bronze Architectural Plaques
38 Bowery Savings Bank

Gramercy, Flatiron District, Midtown South & Murray Hill

GRAMERCY

8.1 Gramercy Park Hotel

2 Lexington Avenue at East 21st Street, ☎ 212 475-4320

Ⓜ 23rd Street (6)

If I'm not lucky enough to be called across the Atlantic by a publisher willing to foot the SoHo Grand's bill, and the extended shopping mall that is SoHo does not appeal, then the Gramercy Park Hotel is my favoured New York base. I suppose it's partly the sense of anonymity—in a city in which anonymity is prized—and partly the fact that with its leafy green and private garden square, the place feels like home. You might as well be in Bloomsbury as the center of Manhattan. One of the nicest things about staying at the Gramercy Park is that you get access to the square itself (the hotel porter will let you in).

I remember the first time I was admitted to the place and the civilized sense of triumph as I read the Sunday morning papers in the park. Or coming back late at night from the Village or Chelsea, my way guided by fireflies in the undergrowth that seeps out through the park railings. The hotel has gone up in price—I blame Tracey Emin, for staging one of her conceptual art pieces there—but it has still the feel of home about it. I stayed at the Gramercy in the early 90's while researching my biography of Noel Coward, who himself had stayed at the hotel (along with many other thespians) and remember the frisson of excitement that overcame the burly footballer of a receptionist when he handed me a telephone message, telling me in a reverential tone, "Katharine Hepburn called for you." I got pretty good service after that.

PHILIP HOARE
Writer

8.2 Gramercy Park

1831, Samuel Ruggles
East 20th to East 21st Street between Park Avenue South &
Third Avenue
Open to the public only on Gramercy Park Day, an annual
event each spring. Signs will be posted on the park gate
near event time.
Ⓜ 23rd Street (6)

It may look like a London square, but Gramercy Park is a
microcosm of old and new New York. Though most of the
houses that surround it were built in a subdued Greek
Revival style in the 1840's and 50's, most were updated,
enlarged or—on the north and east sides, especially—
replaced over the years, so that today the place is a little
museum of local architectural history up to about 1930.

The red brick house (Number 5, dated 1843), at the
corner of 20th and Gramercy Park West, gives the best
impression of the original type. It would have had a
wrought-iron veranda like that which its elegant neighbors
at Numbers 3 and 4 (dated 1847) still have. The house at
Number 2 later received an additional story, paired
pilasters, and a balustrade. Two houses purchased by
Samuel Tilden at Number 15 were "Victorianized" inside
and out by Vaux & Radford in 1884; they are now home
to the National Arts Club (see p. 184). After the actor
Edwin Booth bought a house with Gothic trim next door
(Number 16) in 1887, Stanford White converted it to a
clubhouse for the Players. The houses at Numbers 13 and
14 were remodeled in the 1930's with large casement windows, but because one is still red brick with its classical
cornice intact, it passes for being older. Their now-
International-Style neighbor—painted white with bright
yellow trim on the windows—had its cornice removed to
emphasize the flat roof. The apartment houses that rose on
the other edges of the park include: the polite Federal-style
tower of duplexes at 24 Gramercy Park; the Gramercy

(Number 34), a Queen Anne fortress dated 1883; the neo-Gothic terra-cotta extravaganza (1910) at Number 36 (complete with metallic-colored knights guarding the door); the collegiate Tudor tower at Number 44; the vaguely Deco building at Number 45; Emery Roth's 1928 New York apartment house with Spanish trim at Number 60; and the massive brick building at 1 Lexington Avenue.
JAYNE MERKEL
Journalist

RECOMMENDED READING
Stephen Garmey, *Gramercy Park, An Illustrated History of a New York Neighborhood*, Balsam Press, 1984.
Andrew Scott Dolkart, *Gramercy, Its Architectural Surroundings: Preserving the Neighborhood's Important Contributing Buildings*, Gramercy Neighborhood Associates, 1996.

8.3 The National Arts Club

1884, Calvert Vaux
15 Gramercy Park South between Park Avenue South
& Irving Place, ☎ 212 475-3424
Galleries open Monday-Friday 9am-5pm; call in advance as
they are sometimes reserved
Ⓜ 23rd Street (6)

This magnificent former residence of Samuel Tilden is now a national landmark and home to the 100-year-old National Arts Club. Overlooking Gramercy Park, the Victorian mansion is a cynosure from a bygone era in one of the city's loveliest neighborhoods. Although the club is private and its finest rooms are open only to members, the space can be rented for functions, and most of the art galleries are open to walk-in visitors. If possible, sneak a peek at the glorious blue-bubble glass ceiling above the bar. It's a jewel by John La Farge, Lewis Comfort Tiffany's great rival.
ALEXANDRA STYRON
Writer

Irving Place Stroll

Ⓜ 14th Street-Union Square (L/N/Q/R/W/4/5/6)

8.4 **Pete's Tavern**
129 East 18th Street at Irving Place, ☎ 212 473-7676
Open daily for lunch and dinner; Thursday-Saturday for late-night meals; Saturday, Sunday for brunch

8.5 **71 Irving Espresso and Tea Bar**
71 Irving Place between East 18th & East 19th Streets
☎ 212 995-5252
Monday-Wednesday 7am-11pm; Thursday, Friday 7am-midnight; Saturday 8am-midnight; Sunday 8am-11pm

8.6 **80 Irving Place**
At East 19th Street

8.2 **Gramercy Park** (also see pp. 183, 188)
1831, Samuel Ruggles
East 20th to East 21st Street between Park Avenue South & Third Avenue

8.7 **Yama**
122 East 17th Street at Irving Place, ☎ 212 475-0969
Monday-Friday for lunch and dinner; Saturday for dinner only; closed Sunday

8.8 **Choshi**
77 Irving Place at East 19th Street, ☎ 212 420-1419
Open daily for lunch and dinner

8.9 **The Inn at Irving Place**
56 Irving Place between East 17th & East 18th Streets
☎ 212 533-4600

🍽 If not for Gramercy Park, Lexington Avenue would storm right down to 14th Street. Luckily, the park deflects Lexington at 21st Street, leaving a six-block oasis in its stead: Irving Place. A tree-lined, quiet, two-way street,   ►

▶

Irving radiates a unique feeling. One senses the absence
of an avenue where an avenue should be, and the particular tranquility created by this vacuum.

Pete's Tavern, at the corner of 18th, is the heart of Irving
Place. Founded in 1864, it is the longest continuously
operating saloon in New York. Two staples of the
American literary canon were created in this corner pub:
O'Henry's "The Gift of the Magi" and Ludwig
Bemelmans's *Madeline*. Bring a pen and maybe you'll get
lucky; clearly something magic is in the beer. Today Pete's
draws mostly young corporate types, but don't let that
scare you off. In the pantheon of old New York gin mills,
it holds a hallowed niche between the dusty Irishness of
McSorley's and the Dylan Thomas romanticism of the
White Horse Tavern.

Across the street percolates a fun little cafe called 71
Irving. They have fresh bread they'll toast and butter for
you, and you can have the satisfaction of buying coffee
from a small-business person rather than a huge multina-
tional. Across, at 19th, stands a wonderful house (Number
80)—home to Sigourney Weaver's character in the movie
Working Girl, but truly triumphant because of its two-car
garage. Living in Manhattan, one gets inured to trappings
of luxury, but a two-car garage still impresses.

At 20th is Gramercy Park, the only private park left in
New York. You can wander around the wrought-iron
gates, looking inside at the kids with their nannies and the
octogenarians on the benches. This is actually the best way
to see Gramercy Park; everything shines brighter when
you're on the outside looking in.

A brick house on the corner of 17th has a plaque
suggesting that Washington Irving once lived there.
Irving, creator of "Rip Van Winkle" and "The Legend
of Sleepy Hollow," certainly gave his name to the street,
but my sources doubt that he ever called that address
home. However, in the basement, the sushi restaurant
Yama serves up fist-sized pieces of yellowtail and toro, so

delicious that the horseman would wish he had a head, so sublime they would wake Rip Van Winkle. So yummy, in fact, that the line is often around the corner. If it is, go up the block to Choshi. Their portions aren't as generous, but they have a pleasant outdoor seating area and I recommend their Kinoko sauté, a delicious blend of Oriental mushrooms in soy sauce and butter.

If you're looking for a place to stay and you don't feel like dealing with the madness of Midtown, try the Inn at Irving Place. The luxuriously cozy bed and breakfast occupies a double-wide town house between 17th and 18th Streets, a perfect base from which to enjoy the charms of Irving.

SAM HOFFMAN
Filmmaker

FLATIRON DISTRICT

8.10 Arts for Transit: *Untitled*

1998, Mary Miss & Lee Pomeroy

Ⓜ 14th Street-Union Square (L/N/Q/R/W/4/5/6)

If you visit the grand outdoor greenmarket at Union Square (see p. 188), spend some time exploring the archaeological layers of the subway station, brilliantly elucidated by artist Mary Miss and architect Lee Pomeroy. Three stations, built in 1904, 1914, and 1930 for now-intersecting lines, are joined and have been recently renovated. Pomeroy and Miss have revealed the layers and history of the site through bright red enameled frames in 115 locations. Framed vertical slits, some with faceted mirrored interiors, indicate the workings of the system (electrical panel boxes, message slots, telephone wiring, ceiling light fixtures, holding cells, mesh and wire grates, concrete arches between the columns, cables), or cut through the walls of one level to another so visitors can view the passage of trains. Red horizontal frames border details that were excavated during construction (particularly bands of patterning and lettering in earlier styles). There are massive hunks of freestanding wall decorated with mosaics and glazed, cast ceramic eagles along an upper-level corridor, outlined with red girders to draw our attention. In fact, this signature red is used throughout on signs, pipes, railings, and poles as a marker, even alternating with white diagonal stripes along the train walls; in this way, infrastructure is highlighted through a contemporary graphic process.

JOYCE KOZLOFF
Artist

Lower Midtown Squares

8.11 **Union Square**
1839; rebuilt 1986
East 14th Street to East 17th Street between Union Square
West (Broadway) & Union Square East (Park Avenue South)
Ⓜ 14th Street-Union Square (L/N/Q/R/W/4/5/6)

8.2 **Gramercy Park**
1831, Samuel Ruggles
East 20th to East 21st Street between Park Avenue
South & Third Avenue
Ⓜ 23rd Street (6)

8.23 **Madison Square Park**
1847, Ignatz Pilat
East 23rd to East 26th Street between Fifth
& Madison Avenues
Ⓜ 23rd Street (N/R/6)

8.11 **Union Square Greenmarket**
North end of Union Square, ☎ 212 477-3220
Monday, Wednesday, Friday, Saturday 8am-6pm
Ⓜ 14th Street-Union Square (L/N/Q/R/W/4/5/6)

I love the "necklace" formed by Union Square, Gramercy, and Madison Square parks so much that I have chosen to conduct my entire personal and professional life around those jewels. It's Manhattan at its most civilized scale, and no neighborhood better combines beautifully preserved historic architecture with a dynamic sense of modern style. One could say that this is where "Ladies' Mile" meets "Silicon Alley." Architects, publishers, and new-media executives commingle with young family residents, green-market farmers, and the city's densest population of excellent restaurants. The trick to any stroll through this zone is to look up. Each building brings an animated story to the streetscape, and many have been lovingly restored and given meaningful, modern uses. The Union Square Greenmarket—open Monday, Wednesday, Friday, and Saturday, but at its abundant and bustling best on Wednesday and Saturday—is New York's closest thing to a vital Italian piazza. It is perhaps the only place in the city where New Yorkers choose to slow down, smell the smells, and talk to each other.

DANNY MEYER
Restaurateur and cookbook author

RECOMMENDED READING
Joyce Mendelsohn, *Touring the Flatiron: Walks in Four Historic Neighborhoods*, New York Landmarks Conservancy, 1998.

8.13 Union Square Cafe

21 East 16th Street between Fifth Avenue & Union Square West
☎ 212 243-4020
Monday-Saturday for lunch and dinner; Sunday for dinner only
Ⓜ 14th Street-Union Square (L/N/Q/R/W/4/5/6)

🍴 Lunch at the bar at Union Square—this is the only bar in the city worth eating at. The combination of the insouciance and professionalism of the staff is a perfect metaphor for what is great about the city—especially after a glass of Sauvignon Blanc and a tuna burger.

ADAM GLICK
President, Jack Parker Corporation

8.14 Chisholm Gallery

55 West 17th Street at Sixth Avenue, sixth floor

☎ 212 243-8834

Tuesday-Friday 11am-6pm; Saturday noon-6pm; closed
Sunday, Monday

Ⓜ 14th Street (F/V); 18th Street (1/2); Sixth Avenue (L)

🎁 Once upon a time, Manhattan and the boroughs had some
great poster and ephemera emporia specializing in antique
advertising paper from the United States and Europe.
Perhaps the natural depletion of original vintage stock
and the advent of eBay has pinched the supply and forced
many of the dealers out of business. Those that have
remained have fewer and fewer gems, but one shop that
has kept the faith—and its stock—is Chisholm Gallery,
owned by Gail Chisholm.

Whenever I feel there's nothing new to be discovered,
I take the elevator to her sixth-floor loft: I'm never disappointed. Chisholm routinely visits the countries where the
best vintage advertising was created in the 1920's and
1930's—France, Italy, Switzerland, although she has very
little stock from pre-Nazi Germany, which is a shame since
there are some excellent specimens from there.

Her holdings go beyond conventional and costly posters.
Among my favorites are advertising fans, point-of-purchase
displays, commercial packages, and enamel signs. But there
are also unclassifiable novelties that can be found as well.
Chisholm Gallery is not a flea market, so if you enjoy dis-
covering cheap, lost treasures, this isn't for you. But come
here if you're looking to fill in the holes in your collection
or for that single curiosity.

STEVEN HELLER

Co-chairman of MFA/Design, The School of Visual Arts

8.15 Housing Works Thrift Shop

143 West 17th Street between Sixth & Seventh Avenues
☎ 212 366-0820
Monday-Saturday 10am-6pm; Sunday noon-5pm
Ⓜ 18th Street (1/2); 14th Street (F/V); Sixth Avenue (L)

A treasure trove in Chelsea. Like thrift shops everywhere, the merchandise is donated, but here the stuff is fabulous. Antiques, furniture, art, collectibles, jewelry, and tchotchkes, often comparable to those found in Madison Avenue antique shops, are to be had at less-than-flea-market prices. There are also racks of gently worn designer and vintage clothing, and from time to time some top-notch designers donate samples. And as if this weren't rewarding enough, all proceeds go to AIDS assistance. Housing Works also operates the terrific used-book store and cafe at 126 Crosby Street (☎ 212 334-3324).
BINNIE KIRSHENBAUM
Writer

8.16 Winter Works on Paper

160 Fifth Avenue at West 21st Street, ☎ 212 352-9013
By appointment
Ⓜ 23rd Street (N/R)

Don't miss this unique gathering of images, the brainchild of dealer David Winter. His collection is favored by contemporary artists and designers—prized as a source of eccentric imagery, vernacular photography, and botanists' specimens. A visit here is reminiscent of browsing the Paris flea markets—you're guaranteed to see something you've never seen before.
PIER CONSAGRA
Artist

8.17 Eisenberg Sandwich Shop

174 Fifth Avenue between 22nd & 23rd Streets
☎ 212 675-5096
Monday-Friday 6am-5pm; Saturday 7am-4pm;
closed Sunday
Ⓜ 23rd Street (N/R)

🍴 Step in the front door here and leave the new millennium behind; inside, it's 1942. To your left, a long row of swiveling stools. To your right, a few tables if you're dining *à deux*. If you're alone, slide onto a stool and peruse the menu, which hangs from wooden plaques on the wall that look like they've been there since, well, 1942. Choose corned beef or pastrami at a fraction of the price of the snob uptown delis, meatloaf (always a special—alas, now served with instant mashed potatoes), or matzoh ball soup bobbing with namesakes bigger than tennis balls. Wash it all down with a Dr. Brown's cream soda. When you're done, there's no check; just tell the cashier what you had. No one running the place seems to be Jewish anymore—the countermen are Hispanic, the cashiers Asian. No matter. In a happy, plastic McDonald's world, Eisenberg's is the real deal.
SUSAN WYLAND
Magazine consultant

8.18 Masonic Hall

1910, Napoleon Le Brun
71 West 23rd Street at Sixth Avenue
Tour information, ☎ 212 337-6602
Monday-Friday 11am-3pm; closed Saturday, Sunday
Ⓜ 23rd Street (F/V)

One of the finest edifices in New York is the Masonic Hall and home of the Grand Lodge of Free and Accepted Masons of the State of New York, as well as Holland Lodge Number 8. Founded in 1787, Holland Lodge's many distinguished members have included Samuel Fraunces (famous tavernkeeper), Baron von Steuben, John Jacob Astor, and F.D.R. The building is of granite and its construction in the early 1900's cost more than a million dollars. Its frontage on 23rd Street is 140 feet, and its height to the capstone is 240 feet. The principal entrance on 23rd Street is through a Doric portico; at the entrances to the lodge rooms are plaster columns of the Egyptian order emblematic of "strength and beauty" and representative of the two great pillars set up at the appointed entrance of King Solomon's Temple at Jerusalem. The inside is also beautifully decorated.

GORDON J. WHITING
Investment banker

8.19 Louis Tannen Inc.

24 West 25th Street between Broadway & Sixth Avenue
☏ 212 929-4500
Monday-Friday 10am-5:30pm; Saturday 10am-4pm; closed Sunday
Ⓜ 23rd Street (F/N/R/V)

🐚 You might never guess that this smallish shop is the largest magic store in the country, but then, nothing here is what it appears to be. You may see a silvery orb float inexplicably through space, a borrowed object vanish… only to reappear in your pocket, or a card you have visualized, rise, slowly and unaided, from its deck. But, of all the tricks—and there are hundreds of them displayed behind glass cases—the most amazing is the transformation of suspicious adults into bewildered children and vociferous children into speechless beings of pure joy.

The salesmen perform their legerdemain with enthusiasm and aplomb and, of course, as a means of selling the illusions. The customers—celebrities and CEOs, teachers and cops—watch in total amazement. The more magically advanced discuss and compare techniques against a learned history of prestidigitation and, maybe, show off their own variations.

Beware: this is a lifelong addiction. You may walk in to pick up some magician's wax or to discuss the "perfect Faro shuffle," when, before you know it, you have purchased all eight volumes of the *Tarbell Course in Magic*, first published in 1927, and presto...your money has vanished.

ROBERT KAHN
Architect

RECOMMENDED READING
Ricky Jay, *Learned Pigs and Fireproof Women*, Farrar, Straus & Giroux, 1998.
Ricky Jay, *Jay's Journal of Anomalies*, Farrar, Straus & Giroux, 2001.
Kenneth Silverman, *Houdini!!!: The Career of Ehrich Weiss*, HarperCollins, 1997.

8.20   **Annex Antiques Fair & Flea Market**
Sixth Avenue between West 24th & West 26th Streets
Saturday, Sunday from sunrise to sunset
Ⓜ 23rd Street (F/V)

The 26th Street Flea Market remains a great source of fun and value in the middle of the city. This cluster of small markets centering around 26th Street and Sixth Avenue has the variety of merchandise and prices that make it worth the trip. If you have the time to browse, give yourself an hour or two to enjoy the entire market. I often see many of the city's top dealers, designers, and decorators buying up tomorrow's ideas. While not everything is inexpensive, you are sure to see things here not seen anywhere else, which really is what a flea market is all about.

LAURIE MCLENDON
Retailer

Rain or shine every weekend, even Christmas! The greatest flea market in the world! I never miss a weekend—I go on Saturday and Sunday both, as each day attracts different vendors. I arrive by 8 a.m and it's open until sunset.

One can find an assortment of antiques and collectibles

here. It's especially good for furniture, vintage clothing, vintage jewelry (fine and costume), paintings, and every other form of antique.

RENEE LEWIS
Designer

I furnished my loft by arriving just as the dealers were packing up and finding great bargains. I bought my green sofa in the dark—I couldn't really see the color, but the dealer said it was "the Cadillac of 50's sofas."

SALLY ORDWAY
Playwright and librettist

8.21 Water Supply Maintenance Cabin
c. 1935, attributed to Aymar Embury II
West 25th Street between Broadway & Fifth Avenue
Ⓜ 23rd Street (N/R)

Just across Fifth Avenue from Madison Square, this gem of a self effacing little black hut is easily mistaken for a disused comfort station. It was erected in 1935 or soon after for the City of New York Department of Water Supply, Gas and Electricity, in order to replace an "eyesore" of a wooden cabin. Short and chunky, flat-roofed as well as flat-faced, this little one-story structure turns its back to downtown and to the adjacent monument of General Worth, with a single bronze window in either short side, while its curved, northerly face bows segmentally out from end to end, inflected only by a central bronze door. The whole, diminutive as it is, is faced with great large rectangles of black granite, with the corner joints sealed by a kind of Chanel-style piping along the seams. Fine materials and radically simple form. This is a stunningly fine, plain little honed box. Upstaged by the general's ho-hum obelisk (1857), it is a little unsung hero.

JOSEPH MASHECK
Art historian and critic

8.22 Worth Monument
1857, James G. Batterson
Fifth Avenue to Broadway between West 24th & West 25th
Streets, on a traffic island facing the Flatiron Building
Ⓜ 23rd Street (N/R)

Researching a novel set in a fictional version of my home-
town of Hudson, New York, I came across a complicated
figure born there, General William Jenkins Worth. He was
born in 1794 and made his name in the War of 1812 (the
Seminole and Mexican wars), specializing in the massacre
of Native Americans. His other claim to fame was as a
dancer; the "General Worth Quickstep" was all the rage in
the early 1830's. But his arrogance defeated him, and he
died of cholera in San Antonio in 1849. Fort Worth and
Lake Worth are named after General Worth, as is Worth
Street in lower Manhattan. He is buried under this obelisk,
which is hard to get close enough to, to really inspect, but
if you dare, you can see all his victorious battles carved on
the stone—Chapultepec, Vera Cruz, Churubusco, Florida,
Lundy's Lane, Puebla, Monterrey, Perote—exotic names,
some barely remembered anymore. *Sic transit gloria*,
although the inscription on the monolith says *Ducit amor
patriae*, "Love of Country."
SAMUEL SHEM
Doctor and author

8.24 Appellate Division, Supreme Court of New York
1899, interior by James Brown Lord
27 Madison Avenue at East 25th Street, ☎ 212 340-0400
Ⓜ 23rd Street (N/R)

The main courtroom has incredible painting and wood-
work. The entire building is a relatively small one so that
the decoration is even more compelling.
ROBERT S. STEINBAUM
Publisher, New Jersey Law Journal

8.25 Flower District

West 28th Street between Sixth & Seventh Avenues
Monday-Saturday from 4:30am to early afternoon;
stores closed Sunday

Ⓜ 28th Street (1/2)

If you are an early riser and want to feel the city hum at
daybreak, jump on the subway and head to 28th Street.
Follow your nose east to New York's sweetest spot, the
wholesale Flower District. (The parking police are unre-
lentingly vigilant on noncommercial vehicles; do not take
your car.) While shops spill a few blocks up and down
Sixth Avenue, the premier vendors are squeezed between
Sixth and Seventh Avenues on 28th Street. Monday
through Saturday, cut-flower vendors open as early as
4:30 a.m., and a bustling business peaks between 5:30 and
7 a.m. French tulips with individual netted caps; Gerber
daisies, their heads arranged like bubble-gum-colored
checkerboards; lotus blossoms plucked from island lagoons
arrive daily from across America and around the world—
California and Canada, South Africa and Holland, New
Zealand and Australia, Israel and Italy. Double-parked
trucks are unloaded and loaded again at a dizzying speed,
while men, shouldering piles of yard-long boxes labeled in
multiple languages, maneuver, hips swaying hula-style,
through the crowded sidewalks. Other men hose the topiary-
lined pavement and sweep up dead flower heads, their fra-
grance ripened into heady perfume. Inside the shops, rub
shoulders—literally, as quarters are notoriously cramped—
with the city's foremost party-meisters, floral designers,
and flower-shop owners and listen as they vie for five-foot,
true-blue delphiniums or tiny nosegays of violets, majestic
Stargazer lilies, or rainbows of sweet peas. While the market is strictly wholesale, carry a little cash in your pocket
and quietly pick up a bouquet of garden roses, fit for
Redouté's brush, for a few dollars.

STARR OCKENGA
Garden writer and photographer

Visiting the flower market is an early-riser must-see and
-smell and -shop. But don't ignore the fake-flower stores—
practically alive-looking trees, plants, and flowers...cheap!
(They also travel better and can spruce up a drab
hotel room.)
DONALD ROBERTSON
Creative director, Glamour

8.26 **TADA!**

120 West 28th Street between Sixth & Seventh Avenues,
☎ 212 627-1732
Ⓜ 28th Street (1/2)

As you walk along West 28th Street, surrounded by the
jungle-like greenery of the wholesale plant district, a bright
red banner flying above might catch your eye. The banner
heralds TADA!, a not-for-profit children's theater company
where talented New York kids perform original musicals.
The performers range in age from 7 to 18 and come from
all different cultural, economic, and social backgrounds.
They work for an intensive six-week rehearsal process, and
the results are often spectacular. The ensemble sparkles, the
songs are catchy, and the performances always seem to
have an energy and freshness that simply comes from the
actors being kids. TADA! puts on a winter, summer, and
spring show; the tickets are cheap and it's easy to make
reservations.
CAITLIN PETRE
Student

MIDTOWN SOUTH

8.27 Church and Friary of St. Francis of Assisi
1892, Henry Erhardt
135 West 31st Street between Sixth & Seventh Avenues
☎ 212 736-8500
Open daily 6am-7pm
Ⓜ 34th Street-Herald Square (B/D/F/N/Q/R/V/W); 34th Street-
Penn Station (1/2/3)

The Great Mosaic
1930, Rudolph Margreiter (design) and Joseph Wild (construction)
Apse

The lovely Church of St. Francis of Assisi is a peaceful
haven in one of the most bustling areas of New York.
The original church, built in 1844, was demolished and
rebuilt in its present form in 1892. Embellished with Italian
marble, the church also incorporates Vermont marble,
Mexican onyx, and white oak into its design. Its most
impressive feature, however, is the huge mosaic in the sanctuary. Unveiled in 1925 and known as the Great Mosaic
because it was the largest mosaic in America at the time
of its execution, it covers more than 1,600 square feet.
It features Mary and includes scenes from the life of Saint
Francis and famous Franciscan saints.

Saint Francis founded an order of friars dedicated to
leading a simple life and to helping the poor. Those ideals
were effectively put into action in Manhattan shortly after
the stock market crash of October 29, 1929. The friars of
St. Francis organized the distribution of bread and alms
to the poor and hungry of New York. The number of
alms-seekers grew as the Depression continued until it
was not unusual for more than 4,000 people to receive
assistance each day.

Today, many New Yorkers and commuters on their way
to and from nearby Penn Station take a short detour from

wherever they are headed and pause in the courtyard of the church to touch the bronze statue of Saint Francis. Kneeling in prayer with head tilted upward, the right heel, hand, and knees of the statue are shiny from rubbing. Practicing the "fingertip ritual," the faithful touch the statue in devotion, to have their prayers answered, or simply for good luck.

JAMES J. BRUCIA AND MARGARET BRUCIA
Justice (retired), New York State Supreme Court and Schoolteacher

Classical Music
September-May, Thursday 1:15pm

A true Midtown surprise: afternoon concerts at the Church of St. Francis of Assisi. Many are performed by the church's early music ensemble in residence, ARTEK, with other concerts from equally outstanding New York City ensembles.

GWENDOLYN TOTH
Music director

8.28 **Brother Sebastian's Leather Craft and Sandal Shop**
139 West 31st Street between Sixth & Seventh Avenues
☎ 212 736-8500
Monday-Friday 10am-noon and 2pm-6pm (best to call ahead); closed Saturday, Sunday

Ⓜ 34th Street-Herald Square (B/D/F/N/Q/R/V/W);
34th Street-Penn Station (1/2/3)

🎁 Visitors to the Church and Friary of St. Francis of Assisi may also want to visit Brother Sebastian's Leather Craft and Sandal Shop, tucked away in a hard-to-find basement corner not far away. Here, high-quality custom handmade footwear —similar to those worn by the Franciscan priests of the church—and other leather articles are available for purchase.

GWENDOLYN TOTH
Music director

8.29 | I Trulli

122 East 27th Street between Park Avenue South & Lexington Avenue, ☎ 212 481-7372
Monday-Friday for lunch and dinner; Saturday for dinner only; closed Sunday

Ⓜ 28th Street (6)

🍴🍷 I Trulli is one of the few restaurants in New York to specialize in the food of Puglia, and Nicola Marzovilla and his family make sure it tastes that way. Nicola's mother comes in every morning to make pasta by hand—not because she has to, but because she "has" to. Unless you're lucky enough to have a mother who makes homemade pasta for you, this shouldn't be missed.

I Trulli is also the only restaurant in New York where you will find a panzerotti. When you translate the southern Italian slang, you'll find it means "busted gut." I won't even try to describe what panzerotti is. You'll have to go find out for yourself.

FRANK PUGLIESE
Playwright and screenwriter

8.30 | Rodeo Bar & Grill

375 Third Avenue at East 27th Street, ☎ 212 683-6500
Open daily 11:30am-2am

Ⓜ 28th Street (6)

🍴🍷 In Gramercy sits a wormhole to the old-style Wild Wild West. Strap on your chaps and 10-gallon Stetson, slim-jim on over to the Rodeo Bar & Grill, and kick up your heels with tattooed truckers and Newport-smoking Upper East Side debutantes. Onstage, you'll find a world-weary Virgil toting a tarnished-steel guitar and backed (frequently) by a world-class band. Five nights out of seven the music's sure to set your brain abuzz, no matter your mood. Rockabilly. Bluegrass. Straight-laced rock 'n' roll with a down-home twist. Calls of "Skynard!" Bowls of unsalted peanuts (which you can hurl stageward, if the tune's not up to par) and no cover make for a raucously good time, even if there's scarce room to dance. Often the performers are among the best in the biz, even though you haven't heard of them, and they last into the early morning hours. Go with Grandma and Grandpa and find out just where you stand, genealogically. Or simply stand in the corner admiring the keyboardist's coiffure. I'm not sure what the restaurant is doing (the food is your straight-up fried variety), but after a long day dodging NYC taxis and tourists aplenty, the stuffed buffalo, poised watchfully over the bar, is a reminder that there's another world out there—west of the Hudson. Thrashabilly (a mix of thrash punk and rockabilly) is also spoken here.

ALEC MICHOD
Writer

8.31 Paddy Reilly's Music Bar

519 Second Avenue at East 29th Street, ☎ 212 686-1210
Open daily 11am-4am

Ⓜ 28th Street (6)

🍴 In much of Manhattan, you can barely stumble down a block without encountering an Irish pub; in some places, several. But not even in Ireland will you find a drinking establishment that serves nothing on its taps but Guinness, as is the case at Paddy Reilly's Music Bar in Murray Hill. In fact, it was only at the urging of the sales reps from Guinness that pub owner Steve Duggan, a former Gaelic footballer, agreed to offer wine, liquor, and even other beer in bottles. But the nine shining taps that stand sentry over his chipped oak landmark bar bleed the bitter only, and thanks to Duggan's care in storing the suds at exactly 41 degrees, I challenge you to find a better cup of it this side of the Atlantic.

But that's only the beginning of what sets Paddy's apart from New York's other Irish pubs (and from the nondescript strip of Second Avenue on which it's located). This relatively small bar—which gets downright cozy at night with its old copper lanterns looming down from the bar ceiling and candles glowing on the tables—is well-known in music circles as an incubator of the finest Irish music talent on the East Coast. Catch it here seven nights a week, starting around 10:30 p.m., when the place fills with locals, music lovers, the occasional celebrity, and the lively sound of the old country.

JULIAN RUBINSTEIN
Writer and journalist

8.32 Kalustyan's

123 Lexington Avenue between East 28th & East 29th Streets
☎ 212 685-3451
Monday-Saturday 10am-8pm; Sunday 11am-7pm
Ⓜ 28th Street (6)

🏛 The best source for ingredients for the cuisines of Greece, Turkey, Indonesia, Morocco, and India—all of Asia and the Middle East, in fact—is Kalustyan's, a souk of sorts tucked away in the aromatic neighborhood of Little India. Enter this bright and orderly store and prepare yourself for the widest and highest-quality array of exotic products in Manhattan.

Upon entering, a shopper spies large, zippered bags of basmati and jasmine rice and, above them, beautifully designed metal tins of saffron, decorated with a 19th-century engraving titled "The Gathering of Saffron." Next, take a look at the piles of delectable dried fruits and nuts, including lemon pistachios, masala cashews, and cinnamon-sugar-honey almonds.

The meticulously organized shelves along the right wall are devoted to condiments. The first section holds chutneys (lime-pickle, mango, lime and ginger, mixed-pickle) as well as several variations on mango chutney. Next, you'll find a stunning array of oils, curry pastes, marinades, and cooking sauces, including fish sauces. Supposedly Cambodia's is the best in the world; a splash enriches almost any soup, as does a dash of the muhamma hot-pepper dip. Four shelves of hot sauces include my personal favorite, Linghams from Malaysia. Harissa, the Moroccan hot sauce, is available in a tube. I consider another item, Zhoug, a Yemenite chili paste with coriander, a magic ingredient when spread on a fish filet.

On a low shelf you'll find three dozen varieties of dried beans with irresistible names, including rattlesnake, European soldier bean, Steuben yellow, Jacob's cattle bean, calypso, Jackson wonder, rice bean, and scarlet runner. Then move into the lentils, couscous, and rices. Something called brown teff is "the smallest grain in the world" according to the label.

There are beverages, too: Arab sorrel tea, which the Bedouins drink to quench their thirst in the desert, as well as the beautiful pink hibiscus flower tea. Then there's the simply named Mountain Tea, a peasant drink from Greece, as well as many varieties of coffee. Some of the syrups here, including flavors such as quince-lemon and sun-baked pure mulberry, can be added to sparkling water for refreshing drinks; I haven't tried Rooh Afza, "the summer drink of the East."

The freezers hold an abundance of fresh frozen items, such as Kafir lime leaves, lemongrass, banana leaves, and galangal, a sort of ginger root, for Thai soups. Preserved lemons, essential for Moroccan cooking, are available here, too. There are delicious samosas and other prepared foods, as well as interesting-sounding ice creams, including fig and saffron pistachio.

In the bakery department is a sweet bread filled with dates, which can be found alongside nan, tahini bread, and Zaatar bread.

The housewares are beautiful objects in themselves. The copper beakers are lovely, as are the brass spice grinders. There are small iron woks with loopy metal handles,

Indian sifters with four interchangeable screens, a rolling pin for chapati, and a wooden hand mixer that looks like a giant champagne aerator. There are strings of dried okra, cosmetics, and many, many more things.

¶ Upstairs, you'll find more housewares as well as a small snack bar with a couple of tables overlooking the street where you can have a delicious lunch of food made on the premises. Order a portion of olives, or wash down a basturma sandwich (air-dried beef in a pita with cumin, pepper, tomatoes, and yogurt hot sauce) with a passionfruit drink or a ginger beer.
HELEN MARDEN
Painter

8.33 Former Della Robbia Bar
1913, Warren & Wetmore
4 Park Avenue at East 33rd Street
Ⓜ 33rd Street (6)

A remarkable space has survived in the former Vanderbilt Hotel. The hotel has a beautiful ceramic rathskeller, which was originally known as The Crypt, and later the Della Robbia Bar. The ceilings are embellished with polychrome terra-cotta ornaments made by the renowned Rookwood Pottery (Cincinnati, Ohio) and surrounded by Guastavino tiled arches. The room was declared a New York City Landmark on April 15, 1994, and is one of the rare restaurant interiors with such a distinction.
SUSAN TUNICK
Artist and writer

Note: At time of publication a new restaurant (Vanderbilt Station, ☏ 212 889-3369) was scheduled to open at this location.

8.34   Empire State Building

1931, Shreve, Lamb & Harmon
350 Fifth Avenue at 34th Street, ☎ 212 736-3100
Observatory open daily from 9am-11:15pm
Ⓜ 34th Street-Herald Square (B/D/F/N/Q/R/V/W);
33rd Street (6)

Yep. It's worth it. Especially right before closing time, at
around 10:30 at night. Take a date, it's stunning.
ERIC STOLTZ
Actor

Viewed from the south at sunset, the parallel lines of stainless steel trim catch the light, gleaming with a red-orange
glow that shimmers along the thousand-foot shaft to the
wings of the crown and television mast above. Surprisingly,
lightning travels *up* the building as well as down, and often
before it hits, a spiral of fire jumps up from the top of the
tower to guide the electric current to the clouds above. The
mysterious Saint Elmo's fire, the hovering light seen on
ships at sea, is also a phenomenon of the upper realms of
the tower, and when it appears, it is accompanied by a
hissing sound. On the 102nd floor, a solid gold rivet tops
off the steel structure, driven in by then-Governor Al Smith.
ALEX GORLIN
Architect

Although the Empire State Building is no secret, there are
secret times to visit. My favorite is in the morning after a
snowstorm, when the air is crisp and clean and all of New
York City's rooftops are covered with snow. The building
creates peculiar wind currents and there are times when it
snows up rather than down. Rain, on the other hand, travels
around the building sideways and sometimes when it is
raining at the top, the street below is completely dry. When
the clouds conceal the city beneath, you feel like you're
floating, weightless, above land.

Back down to earth, try to find out when the fluorescent
lobby lights are scheduled for their yearly cleaning. When the

cleaners remove the translucent panels that cover them, the lobby's original decoratively painted ceiling is exposed and you can see where the original chandeliers once hung. It's like being transported to the great Art Deco days of the 1930's.
RONNETTE RILEY
Architect

City Lights

As New Yorkers, we instinctively chafe at playing second fiddle, gathering our "bests" and "firsts" and "largests" honors as a matter of birthright and taking umbrage when other cities have the temerity to make a claim to fame that we think really ought to be ours. Some distinctions are of little interest: the St. Louis Arch? Don't want it.

Staffordshire thinks of itself as the ceramics capital of the world? Let them have it. Paris's boast, though, that it's the City of Lights, was bound to be seen as a gauntlet thrown, and one advertising executive decided to take it up.

Douglas Leigh was known for masterminding kinetic billboard ads that included the Times Square smoking Camel sign and one for Pepsi with a block-long waterfall. Having spent enough time in Times Square to see the light, he decided to brighten up some of the city beyond the theater district.

Mr. Leigh knew that the Empire State Building, opened in 1931, had remained short of tenants as a result of the Depression. He had the idea of getting Coca-Cola to take the top floors and proposed that the tower have changing lights that would serve as a weather forecast. Coke would package bottles with a small guide to decipher the colors. By late 1941, Coke had agreed, but following Pearl Harbor, the lights of the city were darkened. The government suddenly needed a lot of office space, filling up much of the Empire State Building, and the Coke deal fell by the wayside. After the war, they decided to use a different, simpler lighting scheme. ▶

▶

More immediate success in creating a night skyline is in evidence with his designs for the Crown Building, Citicorp, John Jay College, New York Life, 90 West Street, and 2 Park Avenue. Among his most successful is one for the Helmsley Building at 230 Park Avenue. When the decision was made to illuminate the building, the owners agreed to add plenty of gilding (including the sculptures and the clock) to enhance the effect, and a gold band around the lower part of the pyramid roof. The yellow (high-pressure sodium) light is focused on the tower from beneath and glows through the balustrades and onto the cupola. It gives a spectacular focus to the vista down Park Avenue.

More than three decades passed before Mr. Leigh had another crack at the Empire. In 1976, he was made chairman of City Decor to welcome the Democratic Convention and visitors for the Bicentennial. This time, he suggested to the ESB's owners that the lights be colored red, white, and blue. It was an instant success, and they were left that way until the end of that year. Mr. Leigh then offered the idea of tying the lights to different holidays, rather than the weather, which is the fundamental scheme still in effect today.

The great Broadway lighting designer Abe Feder also made an enormous contribution to the city at night when he was asked to light Rockefeller Center from four sides. He decided to project light up the building (about 850 feet), but the bulbs he used in the theater only projected 80 or so feet. Bulbs used in sports arenas projected greater distances, but they were meant to be on for a shorter period of time and were already big in size. In the end, he took these as a prototype and developed a bulb that had the power wattage increased from 400 watts to 1,500 watts without increasing its size. In all, 342 lights now illuminate Rockefeller Center from many locations, and Mr. Feder focused each one individually. The lighting was unveiled on December 3, 1984, at 5:15 p.m. before the lighting of the Christmas tree.

Bright lights in the big city are also on display at the

Chrysler Building, the Four Seasons Hotel, Park Avenue Tower, Met Life, Con Ed, the Woolworth Building, and American International. For an exhilarating rush of warm light, though, it's hard to beat crossing the street at Fifth Avenue and 55th Street. Two hotels, the St. Regis and the Peninsula, straddle the thoroughfare, so pause as long as you can in the middle of it and look up. The luminosity from both buildings merges mid-avenue in such a great wash that even if New York isn't the City of Lights, its burnished glow stays with you.

CHARLES SUISMAN AND CAROL MOLESWORTH
Authors

The annual lighting schedule of the Empire State Building is as follows:

Red, black, and green:
   Dr. Martin Luther King Jr. Day

Green:
   Saint Patrick's Day, March of Dimes,
   Rainforest Awareness, Earth Day

Red, white, and blue:
   Presidents' Day, Armed Forces Day,
   Memorial Day, Flag Day, Independence Day, Labor Day,
   Veterans Day

Red:
   Saint Valentine's Day, Fire Department Memorial Day,
   Big Apple Circus

Red and blue:
   Equal Parents Day/Children's Rights

Yellow and white:
   Spring/Easter Week

Blue, white, and blue:
   Israel Independence Day, First Night of Hanukkah

Blue:
   Police Memorial Day, Child Abuse Prevention   ▶

►

Purple and white:
  Alzheimer's Awareness

Red, yellow, and green:
  Portugal Day

Lavender and white:
  Stonewall Anniversary/Gay Pride

Purple, teal, and white:
  National Osteoporosis Society

Red and white:
  Pulaski Day, Red Cross

Red, white, and green:
  Columbus Day

Blue and white:
  Greek Independence Day, United Nations Day

Red and yellow:
  Autumn

Black, yellow, and red:
  German Reunification Day

Pink and white:
  "Race for the Cure"/Breast Cancer Awareness

Green, white, and orange:
  India Independence Day

Green and white:
  Pakistan Independence Day

Red and green:
  Holiday Season

Dark/No Lights:
  "Day Without Art/Night Without Lights"
  AIDS Awareness

MURRAY HILL

8.35 **Pierpont Morgan Library**
1906, Charles McKim
29 East 36th Street at Madison Avenue, ☎ 212 685-0610
Tuesday-Thursday 10:30am-5pm; Friday 10:30am-8pm;
Saturday 10:30am-6pm; Sunday noon-6pm; closed Monday
Ⓜ Grand Central-42nd Street (S/4/5/6/7)

I recommend a visit to the Pierpont Morgan Library on a
Friday evening. The galleries are quiet, the crowds have
disappeared, and only a handful of visitors are viewing
some of New York's finest permanent collections and traveling exhibitions of rare books, manuscripts, and Old Master
drawings. After a leisurely walk through the galleries, one
arrives at the garden court to find live piano, harp, or
flute music. Here, enjoy a glass of wine or a superb, chilled
martini and smoked salmon. There's no finer way to pass
an hour or two at the end of a busy Manhattan week.
WILLIAM J. WYER
Rare bookseller

New York constantly rips itself up and puts itself back
together. Yet the Gilded Age still lives, here and there,
and nowhere more than at the Morgan Library.
J. Pierpoint Morgan, the financier, began buying rare
books and autographed manuscripts in the late 19th
century. In 1906, he gave them a home, a dazzling
Renaissance-style palazzo designed by Charles McKim. In
this elegant monument to Western culture, you can find
letters written by Mozart, the journals of Henry David
Thoreau, and not one but three copies of the Gutenberg
Bible. If the abundance of arts and letters becomes too
exhausting, you can stop for tea in the tranquil garden court.
JULIE SALAMON
Author and critic

RECOMMENDED READING
Ron Chernow, *The House of Morgan: An American Banking
Dynasty and the Rise of Modern Finance*, Simon & Schuster, 1991.

8.36 Mid-Manhattan Library

455 Fifth Avenue at 40th Street, ☎ 212 340-0833

Ⓜ Fifth Avenue (7); 42nd Street (B/D/F/V); Grand Central-42nd Street (S/4/5/6/7)

Picture Collection

Third floor, ☎ 212 340-0878

Monday, Wednesday, Thursday 9am-9pm; Tuesday 11am-7pm; Friday, Saturday 10am-6pm; closed Sunday

The Picture Collection at the Mid-Manhattan Library started out in 1915 as a modest collection of pictorial images. Today it is a huge circulating and reference archive containing more than five million images—illustrations clipped from books, magazines, newspapers, catalogs, and pamphlets—as well as postcards, linecuts, prints, and photographs—organized into nearly 12,000 subject categories. In this unique collection, history is served up visually, in images that reflect the constant evolution of popular taste and trends. This archive is an unparalleled resource for research and brainstorming, and it is turned to regularly not only by designers, illustrators, and picture researchers, but also by visual artists, historians, students, writers, and professionals from advertising, interior design, book publishing, theater, fashion, film, and, now, web site development. You can borrow any useful image, and people do, at the rate of half a million pictures loaned out each year.

MUNTADAS
Artist

8.37 Bronze Architectural Plaques

1996, Gregg LeFevre
Block encompassing 41st Street (south side, towards
Lexington), Park Avenue (east side) and 40th Street
(north side, towards Lexington)

Ⓜ Grand Central-42nd Street (S/4/5/6/7)

Few people would think of shifting their gaze downward to
view Midtown's famous towers, but doing so in the block
of Park Avenue bounded by 40th and 41st Streets allows
you to see the rich details of Midtown's skyscrapers without
straining your eyes or craning your neck. Go to the east side
of the Pershing Square overpass and start looking down.
Seventeen bronze plaques are imbedded along the sidewalk,
each depicting a famous building in the immediate vicinity.
Artist Gregg LeFevre, well known for his public art, was
commissioned to create the plaques, which celebrate the
Grand Central area's rich architectural heritage.

The modernist buildings—the Seagram, Pan Am, and
Lever House—don't translate well to the medium; their
geometry is better appreciated when you're standing in
front of them. But the Art Deco jewels—particularly the
Chanin, French, G.E., and the Daily News buildings—are
beautifully rendered in bronze, with details that you can't
see from the street. In particular, note the Egyptian styling
of the French Building, showing mythical animals and
lounging figures in high relief; the decorative detail in the
fiery crown of the G.E. Building; the Aztec geometry of the
Chrysler Building doorway; and the original decorative
elements of the Bowery Savings Bank portal (some of
which have been removed from the building). Some of
these buildings are within a two-minute walk, so after you
see them in bronze, you can see them for real. Or, opt for
a free guided tour with an urban historian, sponsored by
the Grand Central Partnership (☎ 212 883-2468).

LANA BORTOLOT
Writer

Historic Savings Banks

Manhattan:

4.32 **Bowery Savings Bank**
1895, Stanford White of McKim, Mead & White
130 Bowery between Grand & Broome Streets
Ⓜ Bowery (J/M); Canal Street (N/Q/R/W/Z/6)

8.38 **Former Bowery Savings Bank, now Cipriani's 42nd Street**
1923, York & Sawyer
110 East 42nd Street between Park & Lexington Avenues
Ⓜ Grand Central-42nd Street (S/4/5/6/7)

12.31 **Former Central Savings Bank, now Apple Bank for Savings**
1928, York & Sawyer
2100 Broadway at West 73rd Street
Ⓜ 72nd Street (1/2/3)

7.18 **Former Greenwich Savings Bank, now Republic National Bank**
1924, York & Sawyer
1352-1362 Broadway at West 36th Street
Ⓜ 34th Street-Herald Square (B/D/F/N/Q/R/V/W)

Brooklyn:

17.27 **The Dime Savings Bank of New York**
1908, Mowbray & Uffinger; 1932, expanded by Halsey, McCormack & Helmer
9 DeKalb Avenue, off Fulton Street
Ⓜ DeKalb Avenue (M/N/Q/R); Nevins Street (1/2/4/5)

17.31 **Former Williamsburgh Savings Bank Tower, now Republic National Bank**
1929, Halsey, McCormack & Helmer
1 Hanson Place at Ashland Place
Ⓜ Atlantic Avenue (Q/1/2/4/5); Pacific Street (M/N/R/W); Lafayette Avenue (C)

The ATM has made them an endangered species, but from the 1890's to the 1930's the explosion of savings banks eager to house the pennies of New Yorkers created spaces that surpass many of the city's civic buildings and churches in awe-inspiring splendor. Hurry to see them before 3 p.m. closing and before yet another one becomes a Duane Reade drugstore (it happened at the corner of West 96th Street and Amsterdam Avenue) or a Gap (East 85th Street). In most cases the grand but solemn exterior hardly prepares one for the luxury of both space and materials that greets you within. We instinctively become quiet, as if in a church—the only place, it seems, where Americans are hesitant to talk up about money. Moralism and patriotism are also good incentives for squirreling away your cash—be sure and read the inscriptions on the benches provided at my personal favorite, downtown Brooklyn's Dime Savings Bank, before you sit down to wait for your turn at the teller's booth.

BARRY BERGDOLL
Architectural historian and professor, Columbia University

RECOMMENDED READING
Money Matters: A Critical Look at Bank Architecture, McGraw Hill with the Museum of Fine Arts and the Parnassus Foundation, 1990.

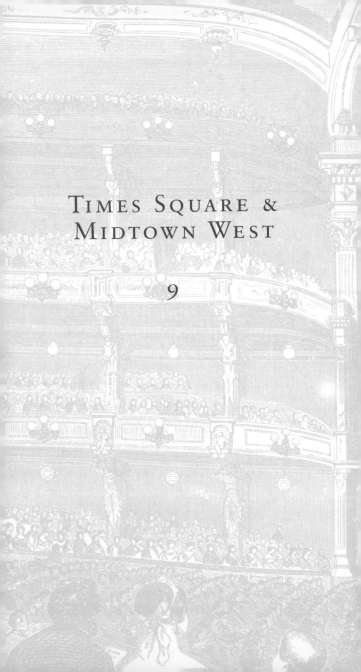

TIMES SQUARE & MIDTOWN WEST

9

Hudson River

Sheep
Meadow

W 66th St

Freedom Pl

West Side Hwy (Joe DiMaggio Hwy)

Broadway

Central
Park

Lincoln
Center

West End Avenue

Amsterdam Avenue

Columbus Avenue

Central Park West

W 60th St

Columbus
Circle

Central Park S

Pier 99   W 59th St

Pier 98   W 58th St

Pier 97   W 57th St   Midtown   ⑬
                                              West

Pier 96   W 56th St

Pier 95   W 55th St

                 W 54th St

Pier 94   W 53rd St

De Witt
Clinton
Park   W 52nd St

                 W 51st St   ⑪⑫

Pier 92   W 50th St   ⑩

Pier 90   W 49th St

Twelfth Avenue

Eleventh Avenue

Tenth Avenue

Ninth Avenue

Eighth Avenue

Seventh Avenue

Broadway

                 W 48th St

Pier 88   W 47th St   ⑤ ④ ③①   ⑦

Pier 86   W 46th St   ②   ⑥   ⑧

                 W 45th St   Times
                                              Square
Pier 84   W 44th St

Pier 83   W 43rd St

Pier 81   W 42nd St

Lincoln
Tunnel

Dyer Avenue

Garment
District

Dyer Avenue

                 W 34th St

Madison   Penn
Square   Station
Garden

Twelfth Avenue

Eleventh Avenue

Tenth Avenue

Ninth Avenue

Eighth Avenue

Seventh Avenue

                 W 28th St

14

13

12   11

9   10

7   8

3 5   6
     4
     2
     1

Times Square & Midtown West

TIMES SQUARE

Restaurant Row

Ⓜ Times Square-42nd Street (N/Q/R/S/W/1/2/3/7);
42nd Street-Port Authority (A/C/E)

9.1   **Barbetta**
321 West 46th Street between Eighth & Ninth Avenues
☎ 212 246-9171
Tuesday-Saturday for lunch and dinner; closed Sunday,
Monday

9.2   **Joe Allen's**
326 West 46th Street between Eighth & Ninth Avenues
☎ 212 581-6464
Open daily for lunch and dinner

9.3   **Becco**
335 West 46th Street between Eighth & Ninth Avenues
☎ 212 397-7597
Open daily for lunch and dinner

9.4   **Lattanzi**
361 West 46th Street between Eighth & Ninth Avenues
☎ 212 315-0980
Monday-Friday for lunch and dinner; Saturday for dinner only;
closed Sunday

9.5   **FireBird Russian Restaurant**
(see next page)

🍴 Before or after the theater, "Restaurant Row," West 46th
Street between Eighth and Ninth Avenues, with almost
every building occupied by a restaurant, offers a wide
choice of cuisines—American, French, Italian, Spanish,

Russian, kosher—at a wide range of prices. My favorites:
Becco for pasta; Joe Allen's for atmosphere; FireBird
for decor; Barbetta for old-fashioned elegant service; and
Lattanzi for the delicacies of the Roman ghetto.
KENNETH SEEMAN GINIGER
Book publisher

9.5 FireBird Russian Restaurant

365 West 46th Street between Eighth & Ninth Avenues
℡ 212 586-0244
Tuesday-Saturday for lunch and dinner; Sunday for dinner
only; closed Monday

For a true elixir, try the honey vodka at the FireBird.
SUSAN KLEINBERG
Artist

9.6 Frankie & Johnnie's Steakhouse

269 West 45th Street between Seventh & Eighth Avenues
℡ 212 997-9494
Tuesday-Saturday for lunch and dinner; Monday for dinner
only; closed Sunday

Ⓜ 42nd Street-Port Authority (A/C/E); Times Square-42nd
Street (N/Q/R/S/W/1/2/3/7)

For a living glimpse of Damon Runyon's Manhattan, that
gin-drinking, hat-wearing, Lucky-smoking town, get yourself seated at the table next to the first full window on the
left as you enter Frankie & Johnnie's, which since 1926
has been feeding Broadway types and theatergoers. The
steak house is on the second floor, and you will be looking
past the ironwork of an artfully placed fire escape down to
a slice of Eighth Avenue that encompasses the half-century-
old neon signage proclaiming the presence of Smith's Bar,
while above the saloon's roof rises the superb 1931 Art
Moderne tower of Raymond Hood's original McGraw-Hill
Building, over on 42nd Street. The view is good at twilight,

wonderful in rainy twilight, and the steak you must have
while taking it in won't disappoint you either.
RICHARD SNOW
Editor-in-chief, American Heritage

9.7 Edison Hotel

228 West 47th Street between Broadway & Eighth Avenue
Ⓜ 49th Street (N/R/W); 50th Street (C/E/1/2)

Edison Coffee Shop
☎ 212 840-5000
Monday-Friday 6am-9pm; Saturday 6am-9:30pm;
Sunday 6am-7:30pm

🍽 This Midtown restaurant is nicknamed "the Polish Tea
Room" (to distinguish from its infinitely snootier Russian
cousin) by the Broadway producers, directors, and actors
who often lunch there. While you eat the classic deli food,
served by that New York rarity, a waitstaff that isn't comprised of actors, you may well overhear what's in the
works for next year's Broadway season.
GREGORY MOSHER
Director and producer

9.8 I. Miller Building

1929, Louis H. Friedland
167 West 46th Street at Seventh Avenue
Ⓜ Times Square-42nd Street (N/Q/R/S/W/1/2/3/7);
49th Street (N/R/W); 50th Street (C/E)

As you stroll down Broadway after your matinee, stop and
glance at the inscription on the facade of 167 West 46th
Street (close to the northeast corner of Seventh Avenue and
46th Street), the site of the I. Miller shoe shop that served
New Yorkers from 1929 into the 1970's. The words "The
Show Folks Shoe Shop Dedicated to Beauty in Footwear"
describe I. Miller's two passions—shoes and stars. As an
added attraction, four statues by Alexander Stirling Calder

(father of Alexander Calder of mobile fame) appear in niches below the inscription. Miller invited the public to vote for their favorite actresses as models. The winners were Ethel Barrymore as Ophelia, Mary Pickford as Little Lord Fauntleroy, Marilyn Miller as Sunny, and Rosa Ponselle as Norma.

THERESA CRAIG
Writer and editor

9.9 Church of St. Mary the Virgin

1895, Napoleon Le Brun & Sons
145 West 46th Street between Sixth & Seventh Avenues
☎ 212 869-5830
Ⓜ Times Square-42nd Street (N/Q/R/S/W/1/2/3/7);
47th-50th Streets-Rockefeller Center (B/D/F/V)

Established in 1868 as the first Episcopal church in America to combine the Roman Catholic liturgical tradition with the Protestant tenets of the Anglican church, St. Mary's is a bastion of the "high church" ceremonial tradition in America. The church is famous for its use of incense, which hangs particularly heavy on humid days, and enjoys the nickname "Smoky Mary's." The second and current building, completed in 1895, has the distinction of being the first church facade in New York City to be adorned with religious statues, counter to the prevailing Puritan tradition eschewing religious iconography—a climate that would change dramatically in fewer than 40 years. This "new" building is one of the surprises of New York's grid of streets, which hides some of the city's best assets. Located mid-block on 46th Street between Sixth and Seventh Avenues, just steps from Times Square, the building, with its 80-foot nave, was once the tallest and most prominent structure in the neighborhood. Now the church lies virtually buried in the skyscrapers of the last century. Ironically, it was the skyscraper technology that allowed this impressive complex of church, mission house, and rectory to be constructed in fewer than two years. New visitors and the many pilgrims who find their way here each day are agape at the splendid interior, decorated in the French Gothic taste with a sky-blue ceiling and gold stars. This combination is steep competition to the nexus of neon and bright lights less than a block away. No single work of art dominates the space; instead it is the sum of its parts, the four marble altars, probably a hundred statues, and the exceptional late-Victorian metal, glass, and wood-work. The Aeolian-Skinner organ is one of the most famous church organs in the world and is particularly well suited to the building. These elements combine to enhance the most ceremonious celebration of the Mass. The services, especially High Mass at 11 a.m. on Sunday, have particular style and dignity. While the social tradition of the church has progressed (there are women priests, and gays and les-bians are welcomed) the service has a decidedly old-fashioned air. After the 11 a.m. service there is coffee hour where a great cross section of the city is present. Over homemade cakes and cookies, you are just as likely to meet a visiting bishop, a homeless person, or a Park Avenue matron.

THOMAS JAYNE
Decorator

Cherished Churches

9.16 **St. Thomas Church**
1914, Cram, Goodhue & Ferguson
1 West 53rd Street at Fifth Avenue, ☎ 212 757-7013
Ⓜ Fifth Avenue-53rd Street (E/V); Fifth Avenue–59th Street (N/R/W)

12.29 **Christ and St. Stephen's Church**
1880, William H. Day
120 West 69th Street between Broadway & Columbus Avenue
☎ 212 787-2755

Ⓜ 66th Street-Lincoln Center (1/2)

9.10 **St. Malachy's Roman Catholic Church**
1903, Joseph H. McGuire
239 West 49th Street between Broadway & Eighth Avenue
☎ 212 489-1340
Ⓜ 50th Street (C/E/1/2); 49th Street (N/R/W)

5.3 **Church of the Ascension**
*1841, Richard Upjohn; 1889, interior renovated by McKim,
Mead & White*
36-38 Fifth Avenue at West 10th Street, ☎ 212 254-8620
Ⓜ 14th Street (F/V); 8th Street-NYU (N/R); Sixth Avenue (L)

New York, unlike European capitals, is not too faithful
to her treasures. Paris wouldn't have let the wrecking ball
get anywhere near the Empire Theatre (see p. 174),
that elegant little jewel box, or the marvelous, stately
Metropolitan Opera House (the old one, not the Lincoln
Center World's Fair-ish one).

But God and the Chamber of Commerce willing, some
of my favorite icons are still around. To start with, I'm a
church junkie—not so much for the grandiose cathedrals
like St. John the Divine and St. Pat's. But I love St. Thomas;
its stained-glass rose window is hard to beat.

Christ and St. Stephen's Church has wonderful windows,
too. They were designed by Sir Edward Burne-Jones, a
19th-century painter.

The actors' chapel in St. Malachy's Roman Catholic
Church is beloved, of course, by all us showbiz types
who appreciate their staying open late so that those who
work in Broadway shows can worship after the curtains
come down.

I have a sentimental spot in my heart for Church of the
Ascension. It's not at all grand, but in the halcyon days
of the 1930's when I first attempted to storm Manhattan's
bastions, it was open all night. I shed many a tear on its
altar as I asked God please to let me find work so I ▶

▶

could stay in this glittering, improbable city and not have to retreat in defeat to Alabama.

HUGH MARTIN
Songwriter

MIDTOWN WEST

9.11 The Russian Samovar

256 West 52nd Street between Broadway & Eighth Avenue
☎ 212 757-0168
Tuesday-Saturday for lunch and dinner; Sunday, Monday for dinner only
Ⓜ 50th Street (C/E/1/2); 49th Street (N/R/W)

🍴 When Joseph Brodsky was alive, he and I would often go to the Russian Samovar to drink and talk about poetry. It was always vodka—many flavors of it. Joseph would usually have cilantro. I would have cranberry. We talked and talked, stopping now and then to take large bites of smoked salmon, smoked sturgeon, pickled herring, usually with black bread. And the caviar we consumed! The food, like the vodka, was excellent. But what made the Russian Samovar special was its owner, Roman Kaplan, who knew Joseph before he came to this country. He is one of the warmest and most generous men that I have ever known. Whenever I go to New York, I go to the Russian Samovar, sit down, have some vodka, and talk with Roman. A gifted pianist plays sad Russian songs. Almost everyone in the restaurant is speaking Russian. Mikhail Baryshnikov, who is a part owner, is a frequent patron. Joseph hovers nearby.

MARK STRAND
Poet

9.12 Gallagher's Steak House

228 West 52nd Street between Broadway & Eighth Avenue
☎ 212 245-5336
Open daily for lunch and dinner
Ⓜ 50th Street (C/E/1/2); 49th Street (N/R/W)

🍴 This sprawling speakeasy-turned-restaurant has been here since 1927 when Helen Gallagher (a former Ziegfield girl) and Jack Solomon opened the place. Take a peek at the meat from the street—the front window offers a prime view of the walk-in locker loaded with aging marbleized beef at this classic steak house just off the Great White Way. The wood-paneled walls are covered with portraits of celebrities, sports heroes, and legendary racehorses— from Jackie O to Joe DiMaggio to Man O'War. Sit "under the bull" (one of the best seats in the house) or perhaps at Marilyn Monroe's table (Number 83), where one night she was thrilled when the mutually starstruck Myrna Loy, and then Henry Fonda, paid calls to her corner banquette. Joe DiMaggio (Number 84) was a regular, too. When a young boy requested his autograph, "Broadway" Joe Namath responded by grabbing a roll from the bread basket and telling the kid he'd sign only if he ran deep for a pass. Liza Minelli and her mom, Judy Garland, considered Gallagher's a real New York joint. The red-and-white checkered table-cloths attest to its zero-pretension, comfortable comfort-food attitude.

Gallagher's legendary late owner, Jerome Brody, was the founder of Restaurant Associates and at one time also owned the Four Seasons, the Oyster Bar, and the Rainbow Room. The friendly waiters and bartenders have been here for years and along with the gregarious general manager, Bryan Reidy, treat everyone like a celebrity. The oval racetrack of a bar is its centerpiece. Down a couple of rounds pre-theatre and come back for a great steak after the show.

TRACEY HUMMER AND FREDERIC SCHWARTZ
Writer and Architect

Classic Coffee Shops

9.13   **Cosmic Restaurant**
1775 Broadway at West 57th Street, ☏ 212 245-5948
Open daily 6am-9:45pm
Ⓜ 59th Street-Columbus Circle (A/B/C/D/1/2)

5.5   **Joe Junior**
482 Sixth Avenue at West 12th Street, ☏ 212 924-5220
Open daily 6am-1am
Ⓜ 14th Street (F/V/1/2/3); Sixth Avenue (L)

⊪ Every visitor should have a meal at one of the city's
classic coffee shops. The food is reasonably priced and
there is great people-watching; every kind of New
Yorker shows up at one hour or another. Choose to sit
at a booth (comfy!) or at the counter (friendly!).

Two favorites: Cosmic (good egg-white omelets) and
Joe Junior (famous for their tuna sandwiches).
MARY CLARKE
Magazine editor

9.14   **Henri Bendel (former Coty Building)**
1909, facade by Woodruff Leeming
714 Fifth Avenue between 55th & 56th Streets
Ⓜ Fifth Avenue-53rd Street (E/V); Fifth Avenue-59th Street
(N/R/W)

Lalique windows
1912, René Lalique

While you're window-shopping at Henri Bendel, look up
to the top three floors to see René Lalique's lead-crystal
Art Nouveau windows, the only example of his architectural glass in New York, and one of few examples in the
United States.

Go to the back of the store and up the winding staircase
to each mezzanine, where you can see the etchings up

close. Merchandise sometimes obscures the view, but you can still get a good look at the tulips and vines crisscrossing gracefully through the panes. Lalique also designed the original interior, commissioned by the French perfumer Coty, for whom the building was built. Messieurs Coty and Lalique had neighboring businesses on Place Vendôme in Paris and, as a designer for the perfume labels and bottles, Lalique was the natural choice for Coty's flagship store in the United States. Though the Lalique interior no longer exists—the entire store was renovated in the 1990's—the windows (also recently restored) are a sparkling piece of Belle Epoque Paris in Midtown Manhattan.

LANA BORTOLOT
Writer

9.15 The Museum of Modern Art
1939, Philip Goodwin & Edward Durrell Stone
11 West 53rd Street between Fifth & Sixth Avenues
☎ 212 708-9480
Ⓜ Fifth Avenue-53rd Street (E/V); 47-50th Streets-
Rockefeller Center (B/D/F)

Note: In 2002, MoMA will temporarily relocate to its Queens location (MoMA QNS, see p. 503) while the 53rd Street building undergoes renovation. The renovation is scheduled for completion in 2005.

9.16 St. Thomas Church
1 West 53rd Street at Fifth Avenue, ☎ 212 757-7013
Ⓜ Fifth Avenue-53rd Street (E/V); Fifth Avenue-59th Street
(N/R/W)

The St. Thomas Choir of Men and Boys
Choral Eucharist: Sunday 11am, Wednesday 12:10pm
Choral Evensong: Sunday 4pm
Choral Evensong and Eucharist: Tuesday, Thursday 5:30pm

The St. Thomas Choir of Men and Boys is recognized as the premiere choral ensemble of the Anglican musical tradition in the United States today, and as one of the world's finest choral groups. Patterned after the Continental and English cathedral and collegiate chapel choir models, and comprised of men and boys, it consists of 12 professionals from the New York City metropolitan region singing countertenor, tenor, and bass parts, while 18 boys from the St. Thomas Choir School provide the soprano section. The school is the only church-related residential choir school in the country, and one of only four schools of this type remaining worldwide.

Go for Handel's *Messiah* just before Christmas, one of three major concerts yearly with accompanying orchestra. On a wintry evening, New Yorkers can pretend they are climbing the steps of the Imperial Chapel in Vienna. Or go for one of the numerous occasions between mid-September and May, on which you can hear this choir's large and beautiful repertory of mass settings, canticles, anthems, cantatas, and oratorios at services. The combination of voice, music, and magical Gothic setting is uplifting.

JANE FISHER
Independent consultant

9.18 Donnell Library Center

20 West 53rd Street between Fifth & Sixth Avenues
☎ 212 621-0618
Central Children's Room: Monday, Wednesday, Friday
noon-6pm; Tuesday 10am-6pm; Thursday noon-8pm;
Saturday, Sunday noon-5pm; closed Sunday in summer
Ⓜ Fifth Avenue-53rd Street (E/V); 47-50th Streets-Rockefeller
Center (B/D/F)

Central Children's Room
Second floor

Stop at the Central Children's Room on the second floor

of the Donnell Library Center. There you'll discover an old
friend in a glass case (they say it's bulletproof). It's the
world's most famous teddy bear, Winnie-the-Pooh. Given
to the New York Public Library in 1987 and part of
a *cause célèbre* when a member of the British Parliament
tried unsuccessfully to extradite him in 1998, he waits
for fans old and young to pay homage. Not on view, but
available for the asking, is the copy of *Peter Parley* that
belonged to Robert Louis Stevenson when he was a child.
Your mother probably told you not to write or color in
your books. RLS went ahead and did it anyhow, and that
makes this old book all the more interesting to look at.
JOHANNA HURWITZ
Children's book writer

9.19 The Museum of Television & Radio

1991, John Burgee and Philip Johnson
25 West 52nd Street between Fifth & Sixth Avenues
☏ 212 621-6600
Tuesday, Wednesday, Saturday, Sunday noon-6pm;
Thursday noon-8pm; Friday noon-9pm; closed Monday
Ⓜ Fifth Avenue-53rd Street (E/V); 47-50th Streets-
Rockefeller Center (B/D/F)

John Burgee and Philip Johnson's building attempts to
discipline the 20th century's unruly mass media inside
a tight little tower of respectability and historic allusion,
exemplified by a grand country house window above a
Romanesque doorway. Fat chance. Everyone has a favorite
treasure in this seductive archive of history and entertainment—Roosevelt, HUAC, Bankhead, Benny, *I Love Lucy*,
The War of the Worlds—but respectability has little to do
with it. More like a need to connect with the lost anarchies
of showbiz and the compulsiveness of the filmed past.

My first choice is always Imogene Coca, sublime
clown and stooge to Sid Caesar in *Your Show of Shows*

(1950-54), the benchmark series from America's heroic age of television comedy, when programs went out live and scary. Pop-eyed, toothy, and built like a collapsible bird, Coca is the token girl in a Manhattan boys' town— the gagsters joining Caesar in the famous room above City Center included Carl Reiner, Mel Brooks, Neil Simon, and Woody Allen—and when she is on screen you don't even look at the star. Caesar is brilliant but very aggressive; Coca distills an air of eagerness, gentility, and incompetence that would be funny with no script at all. I never tire of "The Clock," in which C and C run amok as malign, desynchronised figures on a Mittel-European timepiece; or "The Lorelei," in which our heroine acquires a tutu and falls over the scenery while trying to stay out of sight. *Swan Lake* was never the same after that.

Reserve your viewings from the catalog in the lobby as you arrive; you will then be allotted a booth in a viewing room. There are also public showings from the collection of more than 50,000 items every day. One drawback: no cafe, but here in Midtown you'll hardly go short, and MoMA (see p. 229) is on the next block.

MICHAEL RATCLIFFE
Critic and writer

9.21 Rockefeller Center

1932-1940, The Associated Architects: Reinhard & Hofmeister, Corbett, Harrison, and MacMurray; Hood, Godley & Fouilhoux
West 48th Street to West 51st Street between Fifth & Sixth Avenues, ✆ 212 632-3975
Ⓜ 47-50th Streets-Rockefeller Center (B/D/F/V)

New York State has many architecturally notable venues. Given the variety of scale, use, and context, it is extremely difficult to single out just a few projects. Some of the indigenous styles, like the rhythmical Manhattan brownstones, the rich expressions of the cast-iron district, the glorious skyscrapers, the parks, and many cultural centers, are wonderments in themselves. But on the basis of enrichment to the human experience, I would have to rank Rockefeller Center at the top. This complex of buildings, larger than some cities, is a marvel of urban design, enduring architecture, and integrated art.

The composition of massing and open space has made Rockefeller Center the most powerful and dramatic man-made environment in the world. Upon entering the complex from Fifth Avenue between 49th and 50th Streets, one is immediately struck by the intimacy of the axial allée with its refined low-scaled flanking buildings, central gardens, and restrained storefronts. As the gardens gently slope toward the delightful, oasis-like central plaza with its sunken courtyard, they form a perfectly proportioned forecourt for the soaring 60-story RCA Building (now the G.E. Building). Beyond the face of this multiple-slab tower, form immediately draws the eye up and marks the focal point of the center.

Each building in the ensemble is beautifully scaled and balanced to support the overall composition. While the components forming the central axis are symmetrical, the remainder of the buildings vary in height and bulk, thereby blending naturally into the surrounding urban fabric. Remarkably, there is no clear demarcation of Rockefeller Center. Except for the sunken plaza area and an unusual sense of visual order with a consistently high quality of architectural expression in a similar vocabulary, the streetscape does not dramatically change from adjoining neighborhoods.

The architectural vocabulary, a unique blend of Art Deco and vertical modern, consists primarily of naturally cleft limestone, refined bronze storefronts, and metal spandrel panels. The lower elevations are solid stone with elegantly balanced combinations of ribbon glass and punched retail windows. As the buildings rise, the facades turn to exquis-itely composed vertical bands of limestone, alternating with windows and recessed limestone or rippled cast-aluminum spandrels that create a dramatic soaring effect. These vertical elements continue to the top of each wall plane, building energy as they rise and meet the sky.

Each building has a unique entry that creates visual interest and identity at the pedestrian level. The Fifth Avenue buildings have nicely scaled, recessed courtyards that appropriately relieve the congestion on the crowded sidewalk and create dramatic settings for the huge bronze sculptures. Most entries are marked by polychrome reliefs above the openings, each with its own theme relating to the original tenancy of the respective buildings. The lobbies—all different—have their own ambience, with large wall murals, black granite Deco motifs, terrazzo floors, and wainscot. Some are more successful than others, but all are executed with an artistic flair and sense of permanence. The underground network of shopping concourses, subway access and service corridors, linking the buildings to the sunken plaza as well as to each other, is a marvel in itself.

No aspect was overlooked in the design of this remarkable complex, and it works just as well today as it did when it opened 70 years ago! This is urban design at its finest—holistic, timeless, futuristic, culturally enriching, uplifting, pedestrian-oriented, and economically viable. It may never be matched.

BRUCE S. FOWLE
Architect

Rock's Paper, Scissors

Ⓜ 47-50th Streets-Rockefeller Center (B/D/F/V); 49th Street (N/R/W)

9.22 **Kinokuniya Bookstores**
10 West 49th Street between Fifth & Sixth Avenues
☎ 212 765-7766
Open daily 10am-7:30pm

9.23 Minamoto Kitchoan

608 Fifth Avenue at West 49th Street, ☎ 212 489-3747
Sunday-Thursday 10am-7:30pm; Friday, Saturday 10am-8pm

🍽 A visit to the Japanese bookstore Kinokuniya, often
🏯 overlooked because of its location on a side street in
Rockefeller Center, makes an exhilarating field trip
for those interested in books, graphics, and the visual
refreshment of the Eastern aesthetic. The store specializes
in Japanese books, magazines, and English books on
Japan (check out the collection of Japanese cookbooks in
English). Although those not fluent in Japanese can only
appreciate the graphics, anyone should be able to follow
the diagrams in the sophisticated and specialized assortment of origami manuals. For a lovely inventory of origami
paper, walk upstairs to the mezzanine level—and
if you are someone who has been known to lust after
a beautifully engineered and designed notebook, buckle
your seat belt. You will find a sublime assortment here,
along with an irresistible array of stationery, paper goods,
and all manner of related items. Several of the binders here
can be customized by choosing from a wide array of
inserts: dividers, clear envelopes, paper with different colors, lines, and grids, and more. Even the staple removers
are a delight, as are many of the pens, clips, drawing
pads, notebooks, and blank books. The discriminating
calligrapher will appreciate the wide selection of paints,
inks, and brushes. There are clipboards, erasers, and pencil
cases for the design-forward student. Stickers for kids. Chic
aluminum containers as well as cardboard drawers and
nesting boxes. This is the place to find the gift you won't
find elsewhere: sachets wrapped in printed silk and tucked
in a beautiful wooden box; or metal, ceramic, and lacquer
paperweights and desk accessories, which will be appreciated by an executive or an aesthete. Wrap it up in one of
the decorative papers, available by the sheet, printed with
traditional Japanese designs.

There is a small snack counter on the main floor   ▶

►

of Kinokuniya that serves teas, coffees, soft drinks, sandwiches, and cakes. For more elaborate fare, walk down the block to Minamoto Kitchoan, a Japanese confectionery filled with exotic sweet delicacies artfully displayed.

ANGELA HEDERMAN
Editor and publisher

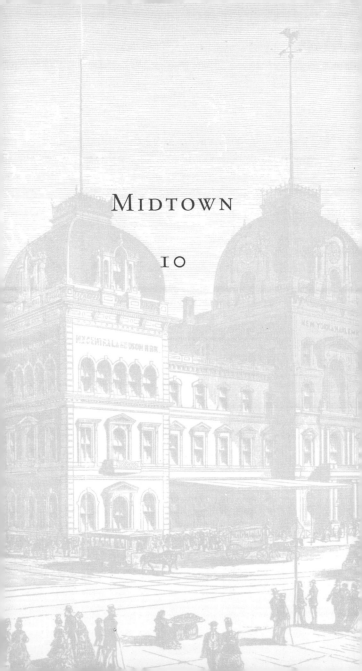

MIDTOWN

10

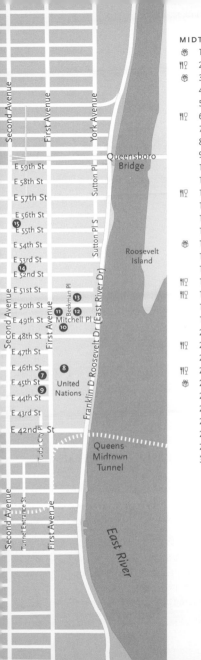

MIDTOWN

MIDTOWN

10.1 Gotham Book Mart

41 West 47th Street between Fifth & Sixth Avenues

☎ 212 719-4448

Monday-Friday 9:30am-6:30pm; Saturday 9:30am-6pm;
closed Sunday

Ⓜ 47th-50th Streets-Rockefeller Center (B/D/F/V)

🎁 New York's greatest literary bookstore, quaint and
crowded with photos.

ROBERT PHILLIPS
Author and editor

RECOMMENDED READING
W. G Rogers, *Wise Men Fish Here: The Story of Frances Steloff
and the Gotham Book Mart*, Booksellers Publishing Inc., 1994.

*Note: At press time, the Gotham Book Mart had plans to
relocate the store, pending sale of the building.*

Three Bookstores

10.1 Gotham Book Mart
(see above)

7.18 Drama Book Shop

250 West 40th Street between Seventh & Eighth Avenues

☎ 212 944-0595

Monday-Saturday 10am-8pm; Sunday noon-6pm

Ⓜ 42nd Street-Port Authority (A/C/E); Times Square-42nd Street
(N/Q/R/S/W/1/2/3/7)

5.1 Strand Book Store

828 Broadway at East 12th Street, ☎ 212 473-1452

Monday-Saturday 9:30am-10:30pm; Sunday 11am-10:30pm;
rare book room closes daily at 6:20pm

Ⓜ 14th Street-Union Square (L/N/Q/R/W/4/5/6)

🎁 By the time this book comes out, the Gotham Book Mart

on West 47th Street, between Fifth and Sixth in the heart of the Diamond District, might be gone. Andreas Brown, the owner, has it up for sale but vows to relocate. I hope the ghosts of Tennessee Williams and W.H. Auden and Edward Gorey that haunt the store currently make the transfer.

If you're interested in the theater, don't miss the Drama Book Shop, which recently relocated to West 40th Street. You'll see stars of tomorrow stretched out in chairs and on the floor, reading scripts for auditions and not buying. The management doesn't mind.

And then there is mecca, the Strand Book Store, advertised as eight miles of books, and that's being modest. Every new book is here for half-price. Every out-of-print book seems to be here. The rare book room on the third floor is a paradise of treasures.

JOHN GUARE
Playwright

10.2 Diamond Dairy Kosher Luncheonette

4 West 47th Street between Fifth & Sixth Avenues,
mezzanine level, ☎ 212 719-2694
Monday-Thursday 7:30am-5pm; Friday 7:30am-2pm;
closed Saturday, Sunday

Ⓜ 47th-50th Streets-Rockefeller Center (B/D/F/V)

🍴 Everyone knows you go to the Diamond District to buy precious stones, but not everyone knows you can find there the best cheese blintzes in the city. Climb the stairs at the back of the Jewelers Exchange at 4 West 47th Street and take a seat at one of the Formica tables at the window. Watch the haggling in the shops below, and when your waitress finally decides she has a moment for you, if you're really hungry, order the gefilte fish with cold cooked vegetables as a main course and the cheese blintzes with applesauce for dessert. The counter is where the Chassidic Jews from the street eat lunch—chatting into their cell phones without removing their hats or long coats.

Everyone's welcome, but you'll feel more comfortable if you bring a kippah or a baseball cap, and if you drop some change in the pushkas at the register as you leave. Oh, and they daven mincha at 4 p.m. in the room on the other side of the stairs.

RICHARD HYLAND
Professor of law

10.3 H.P. Kraus Books

16 East 46th Street between Fifth & Madison Avenues
☎ 212 687-4808
Monday-Friday 9:30am-5pm; closed Saturday, Sunday
Ⓜ 47th-50th Streets-Rockefeller Center (B/D/F/V);
Fifth Avenue (7)

The premier rare book and manuscript emporium, H.P. Kraus, opened its New York headquarters to the public in 1946. The serious collector can find works from some of history's leading thinkers, writers, and artists—Plato, Descartes, Machiavelli—and books containing woodcuts by Dürer and Holbein. Or you may discover the writings of, say, Cesare Lombroso, who as director of a lunatic asylum in Pesaro, Italy, revolutionized the study of forensic and criminal psychiatry at the turn of the 20th century. Civilians are welcome to browse the shelves of the first floor without an appointment. There can be found affordable treasures such as an exquisitely decorated single leaf from a medieval illuminated manuscript.

BILL KOMOSKI
Artist

10.4 The New York Yacht Club

1900, Warren & Wetmore
37 West 44th Street between Fifth & Sixth Avenues
☎ 212 382-1000
Interior not open to the public
Ⓜ 42nd Street (B/D/F/V); Fifth Avenue (7)

The architects of Grand Central Terminal, Warren &
Wetmore, humored their sea-faring Gilded Age clients with
this outrageous 1900 Beaux Arts facade. Among the
building's stately columns and arches are fantastic nautical
motifs pirated from the designs of High Renaissance
galleons and grottoes. Into each tall clubhouse window, an
old ship appears to have just sailed, trailing sea foam in its
wake which pretends to pour over the stone ledges and
into the street.

COLTA IVES
Curator of drawings and prints, The Metropolitan Museum of Art

RECOMMENDED READING
Norval White & Elliot Willensky, *AIA Guide to New York City,*
Fourth Edition, Three Rivers Press, 2000.

10.5 Grand Central Terminal

1913, Reed & Stem and Warren & Wetmore
East 42nd Street at Park Avenue
Ⓜ Grand Central-42nd Street (S/4/5/6/7)

As Sun Tzu, author of *The Art of War*, might have put it,
"Never stand between a commuter and his train." The vast
marble floor of Grand Central Terminal is the prime
vantage point for observing the remarkable sight of New
Yorkers walking. Unlike out-of-towners, who walk four
abreast, arms swinging widely or who stand stolidly
unmoving when you try to get past, New Yorkers walk
sleekly, rapidly as surgeons on rounds. They dodge and
shift, adjusting shoulders and briefcases to allow one
another to pass with minute precision. You can see them
on any New York street, their shoulders drawn in, arms
barely swinging, advancing with long strides. You can see
them inching into traffic, jockeying on corners, waiting
for their moment of opportunity. They juggle coffee cups,
cigarettes, briefcases, groceries, and gym bags and still
manage to have a hand free to hail a cab or gesticulate to
their companion. But the newly scrubbed Grand Central

is the best place to watch New Yorkers walk. Stand on the
steps leading to Vanderbilt Avenue and look down at
the wonderful ballet. Each person is on an urgent mission,
each must take the shortest path to their train or office or
shrink; they cannot yield, but none collide. It is the essence
of New York's grace.

DAVID HELLERSTEIN
Writer and psychiatrist

RECOMMENDED READING
Alfred Kazin, *A Walker in the City*, Fine Communications, 1997.

The Whispering Gallery
In Grand Central Terminal, East 42nd Street & Vanderbilt
Avenue entrance

When I was a boy, it seemed to me that this acoustical
oddity was pretty well known, but in recent years nobody
I've mentioned it to has heard of it. The Whispering
Gallery offers another reason (not that one is needed) to
visit the magnificently restored Grand Central Terminal.
Once in the station, go to the Oyster Bar and at the main
entrance, which is on the ramp to the lower level, turn
your back to the restaurant, look up, and you'll see a
tawny, supple Guastavino tile dome riding on four piers.
Go to one of these piers and stand with your face close
into the corner; send a companion to the one diagonally
across the way. Then speak softly; your voices will sound
in each others' ears, as close, intimate, and audible as if
you were sitting together in a small car rather than mur-
muring across a broad concourse full of urgent clatter.

RICHARD SNOW
Editor-in-chief, American Heritage

In the bowels of the bustling terminal, not far from the
Oyster Bar, is a remarkable corner best visited in the dead
of night. A crossing pair of vaulted arches creates an

acoustically perfect spot. Two lovers may stand at opposite ends of the cavern, whisper sweet nothings, and be heard only by each other.
JOHN JILER
Writer

Oyster Bar
In Grand Central Terminal
East 42nd Street & Vanderbilt Avenue, 📞 212 490-6650
Monday-Saturday for lunch and dinner; closed Sunday
Ⓜ Grand Central-42nd Street (S/4/5/6/7)

🍴 A pearl, a treasure, this vast, bustling 88-year-old classic is tucked under Guastavino's vaulted tiled ceilings at the foot of Grand Central Terminal's great ramps. Not exactly a secret, this New York institution serves the freshest and widest range of seafood in the city. Choose from more than two dozen different types of oysters and more than two dozen types of fish. A real New Yorker will skip the dining room, sit at the lunch counter and ask Charlotte for a half-dozen briny, luscious cherrystones, followed by the creamy, plump oyster pan roast. You'll be back tomorrow for more.
TRACEY HUMMER AND FREDERIC SCHWARTZ
Writer and Architect

10.6   Sakagura
211 East 43rd Street between Second & Third Avenues
📞 212 953-7253
Open daily for dinner
Ⓜ Grand Central-42nd Street (S/4/5/6/7)

🍴 I was always told to eat in a Japanese restaurant that catered to Japanese customers living in New York, but I could never find one. This place, located in the basement of an office building, requires that you walk by the night porter and down a metal staircase, where you'll find the best sushi in

New York, along with an extensive sake list. It helps to speak Japanese for a good table—my kind of sushi bar.

ALEXANDER DUFF
Restaurateur

RECOMMENDED READING
Yasuo Yoshida, et al., *Japanese for Beginners*, Barron's Educational Series, 1992.

10.7 Edward J. Kaufmann Conference Rooms

1965, Alvar Aalto
In the Institute of International Education
809 United Nations Plaza (First Avenue) between East 45th & East 46th Streets
☎ 212 883-8200
Ⓜ Grand Central-42nd Street (S/4/5/6/7)

Alvar Aalto (1898-1976) was one of the most important and influential Modernist masters of the 20th century. Frank Lloyd Wright briefly put his ego in the backseat to praise him as a genius and, with this endorsement, architectural historian Edgar J. Kaufmann Jr. (of Fallingwater family fame) commissioned Aalto to design the 12th-floor conference room in 1965. Located in the Institute of International Education, the space overlooks the United Nations and the East River. The only place in New York where one can experience the Finnish architect's work, his convertible, blond-on-blond interior seamlessly combines fluidity and sensuousness with practical and functional details. The undulating walls include Aalto's signature hockey stick-like birchwood slat sculpture and sedate ash panels. For a splash of color, Aalto framed openings in the entry hall with cobalt blue tiles. Jump at the chance to see this somewhat secret spot, recently "saved" by the Municipal Art Society.

TRACEY HUMMER AND FREDERIC SCHWARTZ
Writer and Architect

10.8   United Nations Headquarters

1953, International Committee of Architects; Wallace K. Harrison, chairman

United Nations Plaza (First Avenue) between East 42nd & East 48th Streets; not all areas are open to the public

Guided tours, ☎ 212 963-8687

Ⓜ Grand Central-42nd Street (S/4/5/6/7)

A world unto itself stretching six blocks, from 42nd to 48th Streets along First Avenue and the East River, the U.N. Headquarters complex is the architectural apotheosis of modern functionalism and the embodiment of post-World War II optimism. On land given to the U.N. by John D. Rockefeller, the buildings we see today include the Secretariat, a 39-story glass-and-aluminum curtain-wall skyscraper, the low-slung profile of the General Assembly with its awkward dome, the Conference Building overlooking the river, and a library. Given the geopolitical structure of the U.N., perhaps it is not surprising that the buildings are the result of design by committee. In 1947, New York architect Wallace Harrison chaired an international board of design comprised of 10 architects from various member countries, including Le Corbusier from France and Oscar Niemeyer from Brazil, whose ideas were seminal to the final outcome. Harrison hoped that the "workshop for peace," an economical, functional, and efficient modern design, would symbolize the rational ideals of the member nations. The unfortunate addition of the dome over the Assembly chamber had been requested by the American Representative to the U.N., Senator Warren Austin, because he believed this traditional architectural element was a necessary symbol for a new world capitol.

The interior is well worth a tour, as much to observe the ambitious, complex work of the organization as to enjoy the art (such as the Fernand Léger murals in the Assembly chamber), interior design, and views from the dining room overlooking the river, from which see the southern tip of Roosevelt Island (which still awaits its presidential memorial), and the giant, decades-old Pepsi sign in Queens. Near the visitors' entrance, one can also mail cards and letters with unique U.N. stamps from the post office on the lower level. Take note of the three council chambers, each designed by a Scandinavian at the time when the concept of "Scandinavian design" was born. Finn Juhl (Denmark) designed the Trusteeship Council, Sven Markelius (Sweden) designed the Economic and Social Council, and Arnstein Arneberg (Norway) the Security Council. As any student of modern architecture must realize, the renowned Alvar Aalto of Finland, who was at the peak of his career, is absent from this architectural constellation—this, for the simple and unfortunate reason that Finland was not yet a member country of the U.N. Interestingly, some years later, in 1965, this omission was corrected when Aalto was given an opportunity to design his surrogate council chamber across from the U.N. atop the former Institute of International Education. Believing that New York deserved a work by the Finnish master, Edgar Kaufmann Jr. commissioned Aalto to design the Edgar J. Kaufmann Conference Rooms (see p. 246), to be named after his father. The elder Kaufmann was a Pittsburgh merchant who also had a strong design sensibility: he commissioned Frank Lloyd Wright for his home, Fallingwater. The Kaufmann Conference Rooms are one of only three works by Aalto in the United States.

PETER REED
Curator, The Museum of Modern Art

RECOMMENDED READING
Robert A.M. Stern, Thomas Mellins and David Fishman, *New York 1960: Architecture and Urbanism Between the Second World War and the Bicentennial*, Monacelli Press, 1995.
Adam Bartos and Christopher Hitchens, *International Territory: The United Nations 1945-95*, Verso, 1994.

Peace Bell
1952, Chiyoji Nakagawa
In the Garden of Peace, northwest of the Secretariat

A grand Shinto bell gong of 256 pounds is sheltered in a shrine on the grounds of the United Nations. Cast in Japan of tinkling coins from more than 60 countries, its history is magical.

In 1952, 60 United Nations officials at a Paris conference table dreamed aloud, searching for a symbol whose language people of the world would understand. Discussion led to each tossing coins from his pocket onto the table. An observer delegate from Japan offered to have an esteemed bell foundry cast them into a giant bell, adding pennies from the children of Japan. Famous throughout history, Oriental bells have been forged of molten metal, often including donated coins to add to the sentiment and tone of the bells. This one is inscribed "Long Live Absolute World Peace" in Japanese.

Each September, there is a celebrated ringing of the bell to open the General Assembly of the U.N. It also rings for Earth Day in the spring and other special occasions.

TERRY MAYER
Jeweler and bellologist

53rd Street Stroll

10.9 **United Nations Plaza Apartments**
First Avenue at 44th Street
Ⓜ Grand Central-42nd Street (S/4/5/6/7)

10.10 **Mitchell Place**
East 49th Street between First Avenue & Beekman Place
Ⓜ 51st Street (6); Lexington Avenue-53rd Street (E/V)   ►

▶

10.11   Beekman Tower
1928, John Mead Howells
3 Mitchell Place, 49th Street east of First Avenue
Ⓜ 51st Street (6); Lexington Avenue-53rd Street (E/V)

10.11   Top of the Tower Restaurant
3 Mitchell Place, 26th floor, ☎ 212 980-4796
Open daily for dinner and late-night meals
Ⓜ 51st Street (6); Lexington Avenue-53rd Street (E/V)

10.12   Luxembourg Mission to the United Nations
17 Beekman Place at East 50th Street, ☎ 212 935-3589
Ⓜ 51st Street (6); Lexington Avenue-53rd Street (E/V)

10.13   Former Home of Paul Rudolph
1987, Paul Rudolph
23 Beekman Place at East 50th Street
Ⓜ 51st Street (6); Lexington Avenue-53rd Street (E/V)

10.14   Wood Frame Houses
312 & 314 East 53rd Street between First & Second Avenues
Ⓜ 51st Street (6); Lexington Avenue-53rd Street (E/V)

10.17   Seagram Building
*1958, Ludwig Mies van der Rohe, with Philip Johnson;
Kahn & Jacobs*
375 Park Avenue between East 52nd & East 53rd Streets
Ⓜ 51st Street (6); Lexington Avenue-53rd Street (E/V)

10.17   Brasserie
100 East 53rd Street between Park & Lexington Avenues
☎ 212 751-4840
Monday-Friday for breakfast, lunch and dinner; Saturday,
Sunday for brunch, lunch and dinner; Monday-Saturday for
late-night meals
Ⓜ 51st Street (6); Lexington Avenue-53rd Street (E/V)

10.17 The Four Seasons
1959, Philip Johnson & Associates
99 East 52nd Street
In the Seagram Building, ☎ 212 754-9494
Monday-Friday for lunch and dinner; Saturday for dinner only;
closed Sunday
Ⓜ 51st Street (6); Lexington Avenue-53rd Street (E/V)

10.19 Lever House
1952, Gordon Bunshaft of Skidmore, Owings & Merrill
390 Park Avenue between East 53rd & East 54th Streets
Ⓜ 51st Street (6); Lexington Avenue-53rd Street (E/V)

10.20 Racquet and Tennis Club
1918, McKim, Mead & White
370 Park Avenue between East 52nd & East 53rd Streets
☎ 212 753-9700
Not open to the public
Ⓜ 51st Street (6); Lexington Avenue-53rd Street (E/V)

10.22 Segment of Berlin Wall
On East 53rd Street between Fifth & Madison Avenues,
east of Samuel Paley Plaza
Ⓜ Fifth Avenue-53rd Street (E/V); 51st Street (6)

10.23 Samuel Paley Plaza
*1967, Robert Zion and Harold Breen in association
with Albert Preston Moore*
3 East 53rd Street between Fifth & Madison Avenues
Ⓜ Fifth Avenue-53rd Street (E/V); 51st Street (6)

9.16 St. Thomas Church and Parish House
1914, Cram, Goodhue & Ferguson
1 West 53rd Street at Fifth Avenue, ☎ 212 757-7013
Ⓜ Fifth Avenue-53rd Street (E/V); Fifth Avenue-59th
Street (N/R/W)

►

►

9.20 **Former Tishman Building**
666 Fifth Avenue between 52nd & 53rd Streets
Ⓜ Fifth Avenue-53rd Street (E/V)

9.15 **The Museum of Modern Art**
(see p. 229)

9.17 **CBS Building**
1965, Eero Saarinen & Associates
51 West 52nd Street at Sixth Avenue
Ⓜ 47-50th Streets-Rockefeller Center (B/D/F);
Fifth Avenue-53rd Street (E/V)

A walk west across 53rd Street from Beekman Place
to Sixth Avenue offers an unrivaled concentration of
architectural gems.

Start at the monolithic United Nations Plaza Apartments
at 44th Street and First Avenue, home to Truman Capote in
the last years of his life, and the residence Robert Kennedy
established when he ran for the U.S. Senate in 1964.

Walk north to 49th Street and cross the avenue to a little
one-block street, Mitchell Place, named for a distinguished
19th-century jurist. The major structure on this small,
inclined street (corner of First and Mitchell) is Beekman
Tower. Originally the Panhellenic Hotel, built as a proper
residence for college alumnae who were sorority members,
some of the bricks in this 1930's modern building bear the
Greek letters of prominent college sororities.

Occupying the crown of the 26-story suite hotel is the
🍽 aggressively Art Moderne Top of the Tower Restaurant
and cocktail lounge. Its architectural furniture, wrought-
iron and obsidian-glass tabletops, and grand piano allow
me to close my eyes and see William Powell and Myrna
Loy bobbing for olives, or Ginger Rogers dancing back-
ward with Fred Astaire.

Continue up the street to the understated luxury
of Beekman Place. The toponymic street was part of

the Beekman family farm during the Colonial and Revolutionary War eras. Young Nathan Hale, Yale graduate, schoolteacher, and America's first spy, was allegedly hanged on the "north 40" of Beekman's farm (see p. 276).

On the east side of this cul-de-sac (corner of 50th Street, Number 17), is an elegant townhouse that now bears the coat of arms of the Grand Duchy of Luxembourg, a relatively new tenant in the large limestone structure with its splendid East River view. This newly minted consulate was the home of American composer and lyricist Irving Berlin for the last 42 years of his life.

Born in Russia as Izzy Ballin, Berlin died at age 101 (1888-1989), outliving the copyrights on a number of his songs. He wrote "White Christmas" and "God Bless America," as well as the music and lyrics to such Broadway classics as *Annie Get Your Gun*. After his death, his daughters sold the house to the Grand Duchy. It was fitting, since Berlin's last major Broadway hit, *Call Me Madam*, was set in that tiny nation.

After this medley of memories and an envious look at the late architect Paul Rudolph's house on the northeast corner of 50th Street and Beekman Place and the wrought-iron balconies on the adjoining townhouses, briskly make your way to 53rd Street. Find there an anachronistic pair—the last two wood frame houses in Midtown Manhattan. These well maintained Federal-era dwellings are on the south side of 53rd Street between First and Second Avenues (Numbers 314 and 312).

On the left side of 53rd Street as we approach Park Avenue is New York's only Mies van der Rohe—the Seagram Building. This bronze and bronze-glass tower brought the plaza back to New York. Its two reflecting pools are coolly inviting in the warm weather, and when the illuminated Christmas trees are set afloat on them during the holiday season, who the hell needs tickets to *The Nutcracker*? If this monument to the International School and the geniuses of the Bauhaus wasn't enough   ▶

▶

🍴 as an edifice, it also houses two unique restaurants, the newly reopened Brasserie on the 53rd Street side of the building, and on the 52nd Street side the remarkably consistent and glorious 43-year-old Four Seasons (see p. 259). The latter has a liberal sprinkling of Van der Rohe's Barcelona chairs, a well-placed Picasso or two, and interiors so striking that the restaurant has its own designation as an official landmark.

Catercorner to the Seagram Building is another icon of the International Style, Lever House. Designed by Gordon Bunshaft of Skidmore, Owings & Merrill, it has been designated a landmark by the New York City Landmarks Preservation Commission. Lever House was the first glass-and-steel curtain-wall building erected on Park Avenue (1952). The Anglo-Dutch firm sacrificed certain economies of scale by letting Mr. Bunshaft open up the site as much as possible. The office tower itself is offset to the right on top of a windowed and landscaped one-story pavilion. Between the columns of the pavilion sits a plaza area and interior spaces fit for art exhibitions and, at Christmas-time, the joyful Lever House carousel.

In 1952, Lever House was a jolt of emerald glass and stainless steel on neo-Renaissance Park Avenue. This L-shaped new resident was particularly striking as it reflected the heavy stonework of that bastion of the Brahmins, the Racquet and Tennis Club, designed by McKim, Mead & White. The Racquet and Tennis Club sold its air rights and, in 1981, a dense application of the floor-area ratio was used with brutal effectiveness by Skidmore, Owings & Merrill in its design of that 44-story giant that runs from 52nd to 53rd Streets.

At 520 Madison Avenue, a segment of the Berlin Wall is mounted by a fountain in a well-hidden plaza at the south-west end of the building between Madison and Fifth. The side of the wall that faced West Berlin is filled with graffiti in an Abstract Expressionist mode, while the side that faced east is pristine concrete, with the exception of some pockmarks approximately nine millimeters in diameter.

It is time for an island of elegant tranquility—Samuel Paley Plaza (also see p. 263), also known as Paley Park, just west of 520 Madison. The gentle cascades of the waterfall running down the back wall of New York's first vest pocket park are not only visually relaxing, but also provide a baffle against the cacophony of a busy crosstown street. Conveniently placed Bertoia chairs and a discreet snack bar make Paley Park a perfect urban oasis.

Refreshed in a literal sense at Paley Park, cross Fifth Avenue and gratify your spiritual sense at Cram, Goodhue & Ferguson's superb French Gothic St. Thomas Church and Parish House. Although its exterior and interior designs are of the French style, St. Thomas keeps its Anglican connection with windows by Whitefriars of London. St. Thomas is noted for its superb male choir (see p. 229), and it is fitting that a magnificent choir should have a majestic reredos (choir screen). Bertram Goodhue designed the reredos with sculptures by Lee Lawrie.

The one-million-square-foot embossed aluminum-clad siding on the southwest corner of 53rd and Fifth, 666 Fifth Avenue, formerly known as the Tishman Building, has its own hidden treasure—a lobby waterfall by the late Isamu Noguchi (enter from 53rd Street).

Press onward to view the Museum of Modern Art, currently under renovation. Its original structure, plus its expansions and additions, were done by an all-star team of architects: Edward Durell Stone, Philip Johnson, Philip Goodwin, and Cesar Pelli. Pelli's sleek and subtle Museum Tower Apartments, overlooking Johnson's spectacular sculpture garden, will be more visible when the expansion of the Museum of Modern Art is completed.

Your walk ends on the southeast corner of 53rd Street and Sixth Avenue, at the only high-rise building designed by Eero Saarinen. Its honed and beveled columns of gray granite have earned it the sobriquet Black Rock. The CBS Building, commissioned by company founder, the late William Paley, has been designated an official ►

▶

New York City landmark.

Saarinen designed the building inside and out, with a lot of input from art connoisseur Paley and the vice president for corporate design, Louis Dorfsman (Dorfsman's signature typeface, CBS News, abounds throughout the building). The Finnish-American master even specified the ashtrays in the reception areas on each floor. True to his Northern European roots, Saarinen chose the late lamented Scandinavian retailer Bonniers to supply the ashtrays. This masterpiece of creativity and entrepreneurship stands in its recessed plaza like an elegant maître d'hotel in a classic temple of haute cuisine.

LEE GELBER
Director of training and tour development,
Gray Line New York Tours

10.15 **Paul J. Bosco**
1050 Second Avenue between East 55th & East 56th Streets, in the Manhattan Art & Antique Center, Store 89
📞 212 758-2646
Wednesday-Saturday 10:30am-6pm; or by appointment
Ⓜ Lexington Avenue-53rd Street (E/V); 59th Street (4/5/6); Lexington Avenue-59th Street (N/R/W)

🎁 This subterranean cubbyhole is a treasure trove—literally. The owner, Paul Bosco, has been collecting coins and medallions for more than 40 years. The currency spans ancient coins to modern subway tokens. The medallions (struck to commemorate people and events) range from the Renaissance to present day. Here you can find a portrait of an Italian noble by the early Renaissance artist Pisanello—the first and finest of the medallists—or perhaps the official medal from the 1925 Exposition des Arts Décoratifs from Pierre Turin, the Art Deco master. Although Mr. Bosco caters to serious collectors, including museums, there is plenty here for the rest of us. It is possible to find a coin or medallion covering almost any

subject—actually, the place is "organizationally chal-
lenged," so that it is almost impossible to find anything
without Mr. Bosco's help. Among the hundreds of themes
covered are world fairs and world wars, bridges and bunny
rabbits, cemeteries and cathedrals, magic and mythology.
I have bought subject-specific gifts for architects and doctors as well as playwrights and actors (although in the last
instance, any shiny object with a reflective surface would
have done the trick). Mr. Bosco also has an assortment
of objets d'art, mostly acquired because he just couldn't
say No. The last time I was there, he handed me an old
letter opener with a decorative handle and asked if I knew
what it was. After a few minutes, I answered that it
looked as if the entire object was made from a single piece
of carefully twisted metal. He then handed me its leather
case, which read, "Compliments of John A. Roebling's
Sons Company"; it was a 19th-century "giveaway" from
the inventors of the steel cable and designers of the
Brooklyn Bridge.

ROBERT KAHN
Architect

10.16 **St. Peter's Lutheran Church**
1977, Hugh Stubbins & Associates
619 Lexington Avenue at East 54th Street, in the Citicorp
Center, ✆ 212 935-2200
Ⓜ Lexington Avenue-53rd Street (E/V); 51st Street (6)

"Environment"
1977, Louise Nevelson
Erol Beker Chapel of the Good Shepherd

Enter the still space of St. Peter's Church. Concerts are
given here; art exhibits change. But I come to seek out
a permanent installation—the painted-wood sculpted
environmental mystery by Louise Nevelson. It is designed
to be entered, wandered into, stayed with. The structure

waits like a building with an address, yet you must come upon its door by accident. Passageways are walled by constructions of boxes, dowels, some recognizable as drawer handles or newel posts, perhaps, but no part is any longer an object apart, with any name or function separate from the whole. Inner spaces contain opposites, as though shadow and light were equal and the same; surfaces simultaneously invite touch and warn against probe.

I go back to this space as to a recurrent dream of a place familiar and fascinating.

CHARLOTTE MANDEL
Poet

Black and White

10.17 **Seagram Building**
(see next page)

9.17 **CBS Building**
1965, Eero Saarinen & Associates
51 West 52nd Street at Sixth Avenue
Ⓜ 47-50th Streets-Rockefeller Center (B/D/F);
Fifth Avenue-53rd Street (E/V)

1.13 **Marine Midland Bank**
1967, Skidmore, Owings & Merrill
140 Broadway between Liberty & Cedar Streets
Ⓜ Fulton Street-Broadway Nassau (A/C/J/M/Z/1/2/4/5)

I used to think that, with the exception of Frank Lloyd Wright's Guggenheim, the best works of architecture built in New York City during the last half of the 20th century were the black buildings: the Seagram Building designed by Mies van der Rohe, the CBS (Black Rock) building designed by Eero Saarinen, and the Marine Midland Bank designed by Skidmore, Owings & Merrill.

But as the world we live in has grown more ominous,

I think it will be the white buildings that will stand out,
adding their much-needed light to the third millennium.
RICHARD MEIER
Architect

10.17 **Seagram Building**
1958, Ludwig Mies van der Rohe, with Philip Johnson;
Kahn & Jacobs
375 Park Avenue between East 52nd & East 53rd Streets
Ⓜ 51st Street (6); Lexington Avenue-53rd Street (E/V)

It happens that this great building contributed to my
becoming an art historian. While it was under construction, the Museum of Modern Art installed in one of their
regular galleries a full-size mockup of a stretch of the
bronze facing, with I-beam moldings between the bays.
How vividly I remember the amazing way this was mirrored on floor and ceiling. I was still in school, but looking
back, this and Mondrian really did it for me.

Pay attention to certain, perhaps underappreciated,
features: the unfussy disposition and lofty but unintimidat-
ing proportions of the lobby as a space of transition from
the terrace, and the relation of the tower to the shorter
block behind. My single favorite view is looking up from
the south side entrance on 52nd Street at the asymmetrical,
rectilinear composition framing the sky.
JOSEPH MASHECK
Art historian and critic

10.17 **The Four Seasons**
1959, Philip Johnson & Associates
99 East 52nd Street between Park and Lexington Avenues
In the Seagram Building
☎ 212 754-9494
Monday-Friday for lunch and dinner; Saturday for dinner only;
closed Sunday
Ⓜ 51st Street (6); Lexington Avenue-53rd Street (F/V)

🍴 I still love the Four Seasons restaurant in the Seagram
Building. At first, Mies and I weren't sure what would go
in those spaces. At one point we considered a car showroom. Fortunately, the final decision was for a restaurant. I
got to do the interiors since Mies was eager to get back to
Chicago.

The Grill Room and the Pool Room are different in
feel, but they are two of the prettiest rooms in New York.
More than 40 years later, these designs still please me
greatly. One of the more amusing elements is the chain
window coverings. Have you seen how they move with the
air currents? I can't take credit for that effect; it's just the
way it turned out. Those types of things often just happen
in architecture. The entire project was an architect's
dream—I was working with not only Mies van der Rohe,
but Phyllis Bronfman Lambert.
PHILIP JOHNSON
Architect

For only a fraction of the cost of a trip to one of the two
main dining rooms, I recommend a drink at the bar of the
Four Seasons restaurant, the quintessential New York
power scene for more than 40 years. From Marie Nichols's
fluttering, gold-anodized aluminum curtains (a happy
accident of the ventilation system) to Richard Lippold's
perilously perched sculpture over the bar, this Philip
Johnson-designed space is an appropriate counterpart to
the building in which it sits, Ludwig Mies van der Rohe's
bronze masterpiece, the Seagram Building.
DAVID FISHMAN
Writer

You are walking down the street in Midtown Manhattan
when you realize you need a bathroom. This is not a problem. Head directly to the Seagram Building and the Four
Seasons restaurant. Go to the bar on the second floor of
this wondrous example of modernist architecture, order a
drink and the crab cakes, sit back for 30 seconds and take

in the real magic of Mies van der Rohe and Philip Johnson's brilliance, then walk briskly down the stairs to the men's room. There you will encounter the most lush, extravagant, and completely perfect combination of marble and wood man has ever envisioned.

After this Zen-like experience, return to the bar, sip your drink, and marvel at the golden beaded window treatment, pulsing at something roughly equivalent to your new, reduced heart rate. (That Mies and Johnson did not know warm air currents would facilitate this visual effect when they designed the space only proves there is an architectural god out there somewhere.) Finish your crab cakes, have another drink—or not—and now, more slowly than you entered, walk out the middle door leading to the Grill Room and toward Park Avenue.

As you exit, directly in front of and around and above you is Roy Lichtenstein's 32-foot-high black-and-white *Brush Stroke*. Humorous, huge, wonderful, it's a big sculpture—as good as sculpture gets—by a painter. For me, it's the sweetest dessert.

And so there you have it. A Midtown imperative turned into an aesthetic, spiritual, and culinary vacation—all in about 30 minutes.

DENNIS ASHBAUGH
Artist

10.18 Villard Houses

1884, Joseph Wells, facades; Stanford White, interiors;
1981, restored by James Rhodes
451-455 Madison Avenue between East 50th & 51st Streets
Ⓜ Fifth Avenue-53rd Street (E/V); 51st Street (6)

The architectural historian Henry Russell-Hitchcock applauded the Renaissance detailing of the houses. For me, however, they are much more, both urbanistically and architecturally. The entry court is New York's first, and perhaps finest, vest pocket park. The use of brownstone is at once majestic and recalls common row houses. Careful scaling can be seen in the entrance porches, in the conglomeration of six houses—two of which are not entered off the courtyard—in the deflection of the main house to the sunny south, and in the bisection of the main axis into two houses (now lost). All this brings to mind precedents much more varied than the detailing of a simple Renaissance palazzo. Pay no attention to the Palace Hotel except to note that it pretty much leaves the original facades intact.

ROBERT LIVESEY
Architect

10.21 St. Regis-Sheraton Hotel

2 East 55th Street at Fifth Avenue
Ⓜ Fifth Avenue-53rd Street (E/V); Fifth Avenue-59th Street (N/R/W)

King Cole Bar and Lounge
1906, Maxfield Parrish
☎ 212 753-4500
Monday-Thursday 11:30am-1am, Friday, Saturday 11:30am-2am, Sunday noon-midnight

🍽 Stop for a drink at the King Cole Bar and Lounge and admire the magnificent 28-foot mural by (Frederick) Maxfield Parrish (1870-1966), whose studio was not far away at 49 East 63rd Street. This spectacular painting illustrates the eponymous nursery rhyme. Commissioned in 1905 by Nicholas Biddle for Colonel Astor, it was originally installed in the Hotel Knickerbocker on Times Square. Astor also owned the St. Regis, and the mural was moved to its present site in the 1930's.

MARGARET A. BRUCIA
Latin teacher and scholar

10.23 Samuel Paley Plaza

*1967, Robert Zion and Harold Breen in association
with Albert Preston Moore*
3 East 53rd Street between Fifth & Madison Avenues
Ⓜ Fifth Avenue-53rd Street (E/V); 51st Street (6)

This little vest pocket park is a lovely spot that easily takes
one away from the surrounding bustle of Midtown
Manhattan. Replete with waterfall, this park offers a
bonus during summer months by serving from its tiny food
stand the best hot dog in New York. Grilled and served on
a buttered bun, it is made even better by the surroundings.
JIM CODDINGTON
Chief conservator, The Museum of Modern Art

A civilized oasis in one of the most congested parts of the
city, landscape architects Robert Zion and Harold Breen's
Samuel Paley Plaza was the first and by far the best of the
city's vest pocket parks. Located on a tight, 42-by-100-foot
site, Zion & Breen expertly manipulated just a few key
ingredients—12 honey locust trees, roughly hewn granite
pavers, ivy-covered gray brick side walls, chairs by Harry
Bertoia, tables by Eero Saarinen, and a rear wall of cascad-
ing water tumbling over stone that fortuitously whites out
just enough of Midtown's din—to create a remarkably
restrained and sophisticated outdoor room suitable for
contemplation, conversation, a quick snack (there's a discreet kiosk just to the side of the entrance), or simply a
refreshing rest. Built and maintained with private funds,
Paley Park is the prototype that has unfortunately either
been ignored or poorly imitated. The good news is that the
original one-tenth-of-an-acre parklet looks—and works—
just like new.
DAVID FISHMAN
Writer

Paley Park has been a favorite spot of mine since I was
a child. It is an utterly urban landscape that cannot help

but suit New York. The space is serene, elegant, and modern. The water wall is a particularly welcome element in Midtown. The architect, Robert Zion, worked on landscapes with Philip Johnson, which may explain why I feel such an affinity for the design. How wonderful that a private source, in this case William Paley, could create such a gem of public space.

HILARY LEWIS
Urban planner and architectural historian

10.24 **Steven Salen Tailors**
18 East 53rd Street between Fifth & Madison Avenues
☎ 212 755-5665
Monday-Friday 10am-5pm; closed Saturday, Sunday
Ⓜ Fifth Avenue-53rd Street (E/V)

🎁 Several years ago I purchased a handsome suit from a noted emporium of high fashion (subsequently brought to bankruptcy by arrant hubris), where seemingly simple alterations turned out to be an utter botch. Trouser lengths were uneven, the collar gaped, and lapels ballooned. And worse, no amount of adjusting could put it right. From this grim experience I launched upon a new course: all my tailoring would be done by an experienced independent practitioner. For advice in the selection I turned to a dapper friend who had been advised by his Savile Row fabricators to engage the services of Steven Salen Tailors.

Both affable and no-nonsense, Mr. Salen presides over a suite of venerable wood-paneled rooms, where one can obtain an entire wardrobe or request just a minor alteration. Regardless of the task, it is completed to perfection. But clearly this has always been the case with this firm; when Ernest Hemingway, in 1937, wrote to Gerald Murphy requesting advice in the selection of a tailor, Murphy replied, "The name of the tailor is Gray and Lampel, 18 E. 53rd Street, I have spoken to them about you. Very good reliable old New York house, no chi-chi..." Except for a name change, the rest of the information is still current.

The always sartorially precise actor Adolph Menjou titled his autobiography *It Took Nine Tailors*. Had he visited Steven Salen, Menjou would have needed only one.
RICHARD LAVENSTEIN
Architect

Horological Stroll

Ⓜ Fifth Avenue-53rd Street (E/V); Fifth Avenue-59th Street (N/R/W)

10.25 **Cartier**
653 Fifth Avenue at 52nd Street

10.26 **Fifth Avenue Presbyterian Church**
7 West 55th Street at Fifth Avenue

10.27 **Tiffany & Co.**
727 Fifth Avenue at 57th Street

10.28 **F.A.O. Schwarz**
767 Fifth Avenue between 58th & 59th Streets

10.29 **Sherry Netherland Clock**
Fifth Avenue at 59th Street

12.4 **Delacorte Clock**
Located near the Arsenal in the southeast corner of Central Park

Watch the clock as you take a leisurely stroll up Fifth Avenue to the southern end of Central Park. Begin at 653 Fifth Avenue (the southeast corner of 52nd Street) and note the time on the ornate clock between the windows of Cartier's second and third floors. As you proceed uptown, notice the golden hands and numerals of the clock on the Fifth Avenue Presbyterian Church at 55th Street. Continue north for two blocks and admire the Tiffany clock, ▶

▶

supported by a nine-foot-tall Atlas. At the northeast corner of 58th Street is F.A.O. Schwarz's colorful street clock, topped by a drum major. At 59th Street, take a moment to look at the elegant Sherry Netherland street clock, one of seven clocks designated as landmarks by the city's Landmarks Preservation Commission. Cross the street and enter Central Park at the corner of 60th Street and head north on the walkway to the zoo. Located above the walkway at 64th Street near the Arsenal is one of my favorite clocks—the musical Delacorte Clock. Its clock-tower houses two clockfaces on its north and south sides. Sitting on top of the tower are two bronze monkeys with hammers who appear to strike a large bell to sound the hours of the day, while six musical animals revolve around the tower to nursery rhyme tunes. The animals give a shorter performance on the half-hour. The best show, of course, is at noon.

BETTY KEIM
Editor, writer, and musicologist

10.30 **Former Pepsi-Cola Building, now ABN-Amro Bank Building**
1960, Gordon Bunshaft and Natalie DuBois of Skidmore, Owings & Merrill
500 Park Avenue at East 59th Street
Ⓜ Lexington Avenue-59th Street (N/R/W/4/5/6)

Anybody who doubts that a simple modernist grid of aluminum and glass can amount to a composition that is somehow more than just a grid of aluminum and glass, should get a load of this. Superbly proportioned, the building is at once earthbound and light. Each single window unit consists of a broad, horizontal rectangle of plate glass above a narrower aluminum parapet-like panel, with two elements together comprising, to the eye, an approximate square. And these "horizontals-and-a-half" in turn stack up vertically in regular bays. Between are vertical mullions of an astute slenderness, on the scale not of a skyscraper but of an urbane mansion. Here is perhaps a hint of Russian avant-garde suprematism, as well as of the Italian Renaissance.

JOSEPH MASHECK
Art historian and critic

MTA Self-guided Tour

To obtain a free copy of *Art en Route*, write to MTA Arts for Transit, 347 Madison Avenue, New York, NY 10017.

Take the MTA self-guided tour by using *Art en Route: Your Guide to Art in the MTA Network*. The guide will lead you to over 100 works of art in the transit system, including works in the subway, Grand Central Terminal, and Penn Station. The tour includes mosaics, sculptures and faceted glass installations by such internationally known artists as Elizabeth Murray, Maya Lin, and Donald Lipski, as well as works by other well-known and emerging artists. Art en Route is organized according to rail and subway lines.

SANDRA BLOODWORTH
Artist and director of Metropolitan Transportation Authority Arts for Transit

UPPER EAST SIDE

II

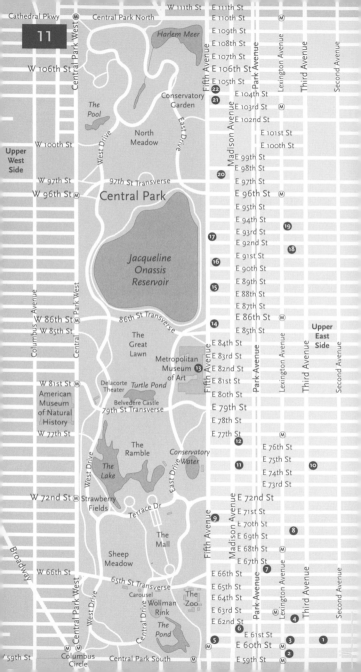

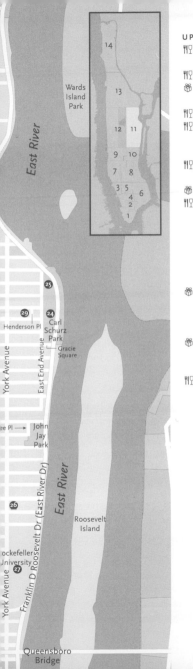

Upper East Side

11.1 **Serendipity 3**
225 East 60th Street between Second & Third Avenues
☎ 212 838-3531
Open daily for lunch and dinner
Ⓜ Lexington Avenue-59th Street (N/R/W/4/5/6); Lexington
Avenue-63rd Street (F)

🍴 While Holly Golightly was eating breakfast at Tiffany's,
all the cool kids in New York City were having frozen
hot chocolates at Serendipity. The sandwiches and sodas,
which are quite good, are mere obstacles to amazing
desserts. The ambience is cozy and fun. Children's treasures,
miniature tea sets, stuffed animals, and marbles are sold
at the front of the shop. While hectic city life persists
on just the other side of the door, this little haven promises
nourishment and fun. My particular favorite—grilled
cheese and a Coke and a caramel sundae for dessert.
DEBORAH SKELLY
Writer and editor

If you have kids, bring them here and let them gorge on
the giant sundaes. Then take them to Central Park so they
can run around for eight hours 'til they come down.
ERIC STOLTZ
Actor

11.2 **Arts for Transit: *Blooming***
1996, Elizabeth Murray
59th Street subway station between 4/5/6 and N/R lines
Ⓜ Lexington Avenue-59th Street (N/R/W/4/5/6); Lexington
Avenue-63rd Street (F)

The best way to experience artist Elizabeth Murray's
surreal metropolitan masterpiece is to stumble upon
it (or rather, into it) by accident—preferably when
half-asleep. Change subway trains at 59th Street, and

you will pass through a work of contemporary art that
is also a playful visual pun. In *Blooming*, Murray has con-
jured a subterranean world of dreamy, evocative images.
Gigantic trees with serpentine branches form a blooming
dale—a witty allusion to the department store above.
Along one wall towers a fantastic high-heeled slipper trailing
long golden laces—a lost Manolo Blahnik, possibly? In
ribbons of steam, fat yellow coffee cups spill poetic apho-
risms: "In dreams begin responsibility," by Delmore
Schwartz, and "Conduct your blooming in the noise and
whip of the whirlwind," by Gwendolyn Brooks.

A long-time subway rider herself, Elizabeth Murray has
said that she created her monumental mosaic for workers
on their daily commute from Queens into Manhattan. For
the price of a subway token and the willingness to climb
a few stairs, you can see it, too. Take the trip. It will wake
you up. It will make you smile.

ANN BANKS
Journalist

11.3 Subway Inn

143 East 60th Street at Lexington Avenue
☎ 212 223-8929
Open daily 8am-4am
Ⓜ Lexington Avenue-59th Street (N/R/W/4/5/6); Lexington
Avenue-63rd Street (F)

🍴🍷 This is the end of the line and the last great dive in Midtown.
Up and running since 1933, its great neon SUBWAY INN sign
has survived outside, as has its original Art Moderne
glass-block storefront. Between takes of *The Seven Year
Itch*, Marilyn Monroe stepped off the grate and dropped in
to throw a few back with fellow straphangers. Photos and
paintings of the blonde bombshell line the smoky walls.
Once through the doors, you realize that this grimy broken-
down joint is for the serious rider and regulars board at
noon. When you're down and out, pop some quarters into

the great jukebox and down a double Johnnie Walker on the rocks.

TRACEY HUMMER AND FREDERIC SCHWARTZ
Writer and Architect

Go to the Subway Inn on 60th Street and Lexington Avenue, and order a whisky and a draught beer to back it up, then sit there and soak up one of the last authentic bars in New York. If you have two rounds the tab won't surpass 10 bucks.

When you're done, walk outside and look diagonally across Lexington Avenue at the tiny brownstone that seems to be stuck into the enormous skyscraper that surrounds it. The story goes that an old Italian lady lived in the top-floor apartment for decades. When developers wanted to build the skyscraper, they offered her a buyout of her lease—and she refused. They doubled their offer, she still refused. After she turned down a million dollars, they decided to build the thing around her, which they figured would drive her out. It didn't. When I think about the beautiful stubbornness of New Yorkers, I think about this lady. For years she lived there, keeping her window boxes filled with fresh flowers through the spring, summer, and fall.

DAN ALGRANT
Film director

11.4　**Tender Buttons**

143 East 62nd Street between Lexington & Third Avenues
☎ 212 758-7004
Monday-Friday 10:30am-6pm; Saturday 10:30am-5:30pm; closed Sunday

Ⓜ Lexington Avenue-59th Street (N/R/W/4/5/6); Lexington Avenue-63rd Street (F)

🎁 Whether you're trying to replace a missing button, looking for the perfect buttons for a homemade sweater, or just in a browsing mood, come to this little button boutique. You may not have thought of buttons as interesting or noteworthy, but step inside this quaint shop (here since 1967) and you'll marvel at the selection. Organized in small self-serve boxes, you can find buttons in every style made from horn, vegetable ivory, silver, leather, crystal, wood, Bakelite, and ranging in price from 50 cents to a few hundred dollars. Framed on the wall and just for show are rare, antique buttons that give the store more of a museum feel. The friendly staff can help find a particular button or make inspired suggestions.

SARAH CAPLAN
Designer and graphic artist

11.5 The Metropolitan Club
1894, McKim, Mead & White
1 East 60th Street at Fifth Avenue, ☎ 212 838-7400
Not open to the public
Ⓜ Fifth Avenue-59th Street (N/R/W)

My vote for the prettiest room in the city just might be the main room of the Metropolitan Club; you might have trouble getting in, but just go up the stairs and gaze in at a McKim, Mead & White marble, soaring-ceilinged treasure.

JOHN GUARE
Playwright

11.6 Vland
673 Madison Avenue between East 61st & East 62nd Streets
☎ 212 751-6622
Open daily 6am-10pm
Ⓜ Lexington Avenue-63rd Street (F); Fifth Avenue-59th Street (N/R/W); Lexington Avenue-59th Street (4/5/6)

🍴 If you are looking for a quick bite in Midtown, pop into Viand for a classic New York coffee shop experience. Established in 1976, this miracle of Manhattan real estate caters to a wide cross section of New Yorkers—from the Upper East Side matron dripping in furs to the neighborhood cop on the beat.

Waiters call out orders like "jack with tommy" (grilled cheese with tomato), "full house" (grilled cheese with tomato and bacon), "short stack bac" (two pancakes with bacon), and "42 whiskey down" (four eggs, two plates, rye toast). Viand is famous for its fresh turkey sandwiches, delicious cheeseburgers, and a great tuna salad. The hospitable owner, Georgou Kontoziannis, oversees his galleyesque eatery like a captain on his ship in a storm.

ROBERT KAHN
Architect

Nathan Hale Was Here

While Nathan Hale may have said he had "but one life to lose" for his country, there are four places in Manhattan that claim to be where he lost it.

The most visible site is his statue in City Hall Park, placed there on the probably mistaken presumption that that's where the British hanged him as a spy in 1776.

The most invisible site was marked by a plaque in a slaughterhouse on First Avenue in the East 40's, since razed to make way for the United Nations. The plaque was saved and reproduced at the Yale Club at the corner of Vanderbilt Avenue and East 44th Street, across from Grand Central Terminal. It must have seemed logical since Hale was a Yale man (class of 1773). No matter that the plaque says he was hanged "near this site" and the Yale Club is nowhere near any of the alleged sites.

The slaughterhouse claim was nearer, because most historians now seem to agree that the heroic 21-year-old was hanged from a tree in the British encampment at what is now the intersection of Third Avenue and East 66th Street. A new plaque at the entrance to the Banana Republic at Third and 65th indicates that the dastardly deed was probably done near the 66th Street corner. The Dove Tavern stood there in 1776. It's a Starbucks now.

RICHARD MOONEY
Journalist

11.7 Seventh Regiment Armory
1879, Charles W. Clinton
640 Park Avenue between East 66th & East 67th Streets
Ⓜ 68th Street-Hunter College (6); Lexington
Avenue-63rd Street (F)

The Park Avenue Armory (Seventh Regiment Armory), host to numerous art fairs throughout the year, is a fascinating building to explore. At one end of the ground floor is the Tiffany Room, covered top to bottom with decoration—stained glass, mosaic, and metalwork. On the top floor is the restaurant that feels like a time capsule from the 1950's (Seventh Regiment Mess and Lounge, ☎ 212 744-4107).

NADINE ORENSTEIN
Associate curator, The Metropolitan Museum of Art

11.8 Urasenke Chanoyu Center
153 East 69th Street between Third & Lexington Avenues
☎ 212 988-6161
Call to register for monthly classes
Ⓜ 68th Street-Hunter College (6)

Housed in Mark Rothko's old studio is the Urasenke Chanoyu Center, a non-profit society that cultivates an appreciation of the Japanese tea ceremony. Membership is not required to attend one of the monthly classes, presided over by a kindly older gentleman. The transformation of the space is quite incredible, and the devotion of the staff is touching as they set about educating you about the ceremony, emphasizing the role of the guest as well as that of the host.

Certainly the experience depends on the group you attend with, but the force with which it demands you stop your day and experience the beauty of the ceremony itself, both deliberate and simple, is great. Before and after the actual ceremony there are short lessons about the aesthetics as well as general philosophy of tea and life. While it sometimes stays on a less-than-profound level, it is always pleasant. *Wabi-sabi*, the Japanese aesthetic of imperfect and impermanent beauty, is among the discussions, and guests are encouraged to participate.

LAURIE MCLENDON
Retailer

11.9 The Frick Collection

1914, Carrère & Hastings; 1935, renovated as a museum by John Russell Pope
1 East 70th Street at Fifth Avenue, ☎ 212 288-0700
Tuesday-Thursday, Saturday 10am-6pm; Friday 10am-9pm;
Sunday 1pm-6pm; closed Monday
Ⓜ 68th Street-Hunter College (6)

It's easy to love the Frick, not only because of its great works of art and sumptuous rooms, gardens and fountains, but because it is relatively small and intimate for a museum. One can go there for half an hour or 45 minutes and see the entire collection briefly. The Frick very seldom loans art and rarely moves pictures; and it is this consistency that allows one to retain its artworks so indelibly in one's mind.

AGNES GUND
President, The Museum of Modern Art

The price of bliss in New York City is 10 dollars. This is the admission fee to the Frick Collection, a once-private house just steps off Fifth Avenue, where you may enter the enchanted interior garden court. Beneath the vaulted glass ceiling, supported by paired columns, is a grand Roman atrium with year-round plantings of exotic palms, orchids and ferns. You may want to sit a while among the carved stone benches and listen to the water-music of the enormous fountain with its squatting frogs. You would certainly want to experience the incredible sense of serenity by gazing at Jean Barbet's *Angel* (1475), whose beautiful face and gently closed wings seem to whisper, "Rest, rest." And when you have recovered your ability to see with

fresh eyes, you are ready to stroll along the outer corridors
and into the great room to view some of the best-known
paintings by the greatest European artists.
JEAN RATHER
Painter

This is the smallest, densest, and finest collection of art per
square yard in New York. For an exceptional afternoon
in New York City, visit the Frick. With its few rooms, this
is an incredibly manageable experience. The collection
mirrors the weight, substance, and gravitas of Frick himself
and contains remarkable paintings by Hans Holbein the
Younger (*Sir Thomas More*), Bellini (*Saint Francis in the
Desert*), Ingres (*The Comtesse d'Hausonville*), as well as
beauties by Vermeer, Rembrandt, and Georges de la Tour.
As I tell my students, the only reason Frick is remembered
(despite his power, wealth, and "robber baron" status) is
because of this magnificent art collection.
SIMON DINNERSTEIN
Artist

The Frick is exquisite, especially the Whistlers.
HUGH MARTIN
Songwriter

"Saint Francis in the Desert"
c. 1480, Giovanni Bollini
In the Living Hall

One of the more unusual masterpieces of Venetian art from
the late 15th century, Giovanni Bellini's *Saint Francis in
the Desert* (also see p. 280) is a celebration of God through
landscape. Standing on an outcropping of rock outside his
cave, Saint Francis curves his spine backwards toward the
makeshift study behind him, greeting warm sunlight as it
falls over his body. Barefoot, lips parted, and with his
palms exposed (perhaps a reference to his receiving the
stigmata, although his wounds are already visible),
Francis's thin body is dwarfed and humbled by the beauty
of his natural surroundings. An olive tree bends toward him,

grapevines fall over his study, water spills from a spout in the rock, and a shepherd tends his flock (all details that carry Christian symbolism). With painstaking attention to detail, Bellini has infused his composition with brilliant color, enticing us to feel the same spiritual ecstasy that Francis found in his own backyard.

KATEY BROWN
Art historian

11.10 Candle Cafe

1307 Third Avenue between East 74th & East 75th Streets
☎ 212 472-0970
Open daily for lunch and dinner
Ⓜ 77th Street (6)

🍴 The best vegan restaurant in the city, in a neighborhood where you'd never expect to find such a thing. The staff is wonderful and the dishes are tasty as well as inventive.

KATHARINE RISTICH
Editor

Three Paintings

9.15 "Broadway Boogie Woogie"

1943, Piet Mondrian
The Museum of Modern Art (see p. 229)

11.9 "Saint Francis in the Desert"

c. 1480, Giovanni Bellini
The Frick Collection (see p. 278)
Living room

11.13 "Juan de Pareja"

1650, Diego Velázquez
The Metropolitan Museum of Art (see p. 287)
Second floor, Gallery 16, The Old Masters Gallery

May I present a walk comprised of paintings, which, at points in my life, were destinations of sustenance and in which I identified various New York City aspects. Go straight to the mentioned paintings, and try not to be distracted by the other beauties calling for attention. Keep the enterprise clean.

At the Museum of Modern Art, go to Piet Mondrian's great *Broadway Boogie Woogie*, painted in homage to his adopted city in reverence for its ongoing energies, movements, sounds, rhythms, and intensities. Give the painting at least five minutes of concentration. Leave.

Go to the Frick Collection and straight to its Bellini, *Saint Francis in the Desert*. New York City is a teeming place (remember *Boogie Woogie*), but it is made up of millions of pure individuals. Here is Saint Francis, surrounded by beings, a golden light, his town, but he is alone in communion with an energy directed only to him (see the wind in the olive tree) in an otherwise still environment. He is alone, inspired, and fully conscious of his greater self.

It's on up to the Met for a visit with Diego Velázquez's *Juan de Pareja*. Stand in awe of Velázquez's total mastery of the illusion achieved through the workings of the eye, the hand, and the paint. Be reminded by Pareja, an obviously proud man of color, of our own city's ethnic diversity and how much that adds to our power and beauty.

BRICE MARDEN
Painter

11.11 Whitney Museum of American Art

1966, Marcel Breuer & Associates; 1998, addition by Gluckman Mayner
945 Madison Avenue at East 75th Street, ☎ 212 570-3676
Tuesday-Thursday, Saturday, Sunday 11am-6pm;
Friday 1pm-9pm; closed Monday
Ⓜ 77th Street (6)

"Dwellings"
1981, Charles Simonds
In the stairwell between the second and third floors

The mysterious ruins of a lost nomadic civilization can
be seen on a second-floor window ledge of a palatial
neo-Classical building at 940 Madison Avenue, across the
street from the Whitney Museum. Seldom noticed by
passers-by, the diminutive clay dwellings and ritual towers
are the abandoned habitations of the Little People,
a vanished urban tribe that has been fully imagined,
chronicled, mythologized, and architecturally contextual-
ized by the artist Charles Simonds. *Dwellings*, a three-part
site-specific piece, was commissioned by the Whitney
Museum and installed in 1981. A second part of *Dwellings*
is perched on a chimney at the right back corner of the
building and is also visible to pedestrians from across
the avenue (field glasses helpful here). The principal component of the work is permanently installed inside the
Whitney, above a window in the airshaft of the main
stairwell, between the second and third floors. From that
window, all three parts of *Dwellings* are visible, although
the label describing the piece in the museum fails to
mention that there are two more parts of the work. If you
don't know about the outdoor pieces and don't, by chance,
spot the one on the far right window ledge, you will miss
seeing these extraordinary and beguiling works of art.

Starting in the early 1970's, Simonds constructed nearly
300 outdoor pieces representing the abandoned settlements
that marked the passage of the Little People. They were
deliberately impermanent works, made of unfired clay,
sand, twigs, bits of cloth, and other materials that would
eventually decay outdoors. Simonds sited the pieces chiefly
in the slums of the Lower East Side, half-hidden in the
earth and litter of vacant lots, or tucked into crevices
of crumbling brick walls. He expected these street pieces
would be stolen, destroyed by neglect and weather, or
otherwise lost to sight. And they were. The physical
traces of these tiny primitivistic villages are gone now,
though recorded on film and in photographs. Simonds
made similar works on wooden platforms, for indoor

viewing, and for keeping. The only outdoor ruins that remain are on pricey Madison Avenue on a building used as a bank until mid-1999, an irony most likely intended by Simonds.

Simonds's constructions strongly evoke the archaeological ruins of the cliff-dwelling Anasazi, who lived in the Four Corners region of the American Southwest from roughly 600 A.D. to 1300 A.D. The Anasazi, precursors of the Pueblo culture, vanished as enigmatically as Simonds's mythical Little People. His invented civilization and its vestigial settlements hint at a nostalgia for a simpler child-like past, but there is nothing sentimental about Simonds's art. His work challenges conventional perceptions of scale, of artwork as precious collectible, of historical record as reliable. What's more, it has powerful narrative appeal. Looking at *Dwellings*, we can't help wondering about the daily lives and dreams and social realities of the Little People, can't help thinking about how and if they differ from us, ordinary folks wandering the canyons of vast and difficult cities. These provocative ruins are small in size only, and certainly worth seeing.

LUCIENNE S. BLOCH
Writer

The Stair at the Whitney

Of all the museums in the city, the Whitney captures the vibe of the local and national art scene the best. The collection is sophisticated yet accessible, raw but accomplished. And Breuer's 1966 building, an idiosyncratic landmark, well reflects the strength, fluidity, and independence of the art inside, even as it complements the staid brownstone fabric of the surrounding neighborhood.

As a visitor moves between floors, the stair becomes a showcase for the structure's finessed tectonics. The massive elements of the museum's construction are delicately assembled and organized in a way that communicates eloquently the various scales at work within the building. In a very confined area, the stair combines poured-in-place concrete walls (with the aggregate carefully exposed), stone slab stair treads suspended from those walls, oversized, elegant bronze balustrades, and wooden handrails and benches, and sets them off a stepped pane of glass that recalls the inverted ziggurat form of the structure and brings in the light of the city.

Take a break between floors, sit on a bench at one of the landings and talk about the art, feel the building, and watch the crazy cross section of people walking up and down the stairs.

SCOTT GLASS
Architect

11.12 **Ursus Rare Books Ltd.**

981 Madison Avenue between East 76th & East 77th Streets; mezzanine of the Carlyle hotel, ☎ 212 772-8787
Monday-Friday 10am-6pm; Saturday 11am-5pm; closed Sunday

Ⓜ 77th Street (6)

🎁 Located in the Carlyle hotel, Ursus offers a vast selection of rare books, fine bindings, and first editions covering a broad range of subjects. Here, you will find manifestos from Marx to Marx, literature from Shakespeare to Joyce, and illustrated books by artists Dürer to Picasso. In the B's alone, Ursus has had the elusive first edition of *En Attendant Godot*, the Complutensian Polyglot Bible, and a 12-volume first-edition Babar collection. To experience perfect symmetry, locate a first edition of Bemelmans's *Madeline*, then head down to the lobby for a drink in Bemelmans Bar to celebrate your good fortune. Book-loving tourists and book-reading former presidents can be found browsing through the shelves. Ursus also offers a superior selection of art books and a room of decorative prints from the 17th through the 19th centuries.

ROBERT KAHN
Architect

11.12 Bemelmans Bar

1947, murals by Ludwig Bemelmans
35 East 76th Street between Madison and Park Avenues;
ground floor of the Carlyle hotel, ☎ 212 744-1600
Open daily for breakfast, lunch, and dinner
Ⓜ 68th Street-Hunter College (6)

🍴 Legend has it Bemelmans Bar in the Carlyle hotel was one
of the late Jackie O's favorite haunts, and that her protests,
along with cries from others, helped save this landmark
from being remodeled into just another Madison Avenue
piano lounge *ordinaire*. Classy, but not fussy, Bemelmans is
so elegantly dim that the most shimmering celebrity can be
rendered inconspicuous in the shadows of the deep leather
booths. Fine, since sighting the rich and famous isn't the
appeal here—people come to see the walls. Four walls of
murals, once vibrant and now perfectly subdued by half a
century of nicotine fumes, teem with characters you will
immediately recognize unless you spent your childhood in
a culvert. Ludwig Bemelmans, author, artist, and restaurateur, was best remembered as the creator of the *Madeline*
books. In 1947 Bemelmans brought his characters in out of
the rain and painted them to life among seasonal views of
Central Park. Ever since, 12 little girls in two straight lines,
and tweed-clad, shotgun packing rabbits welcome regulars
famous and not.

For a half-century a self-portrait of Bemelmans near the
bar has overseen the preparation of countless thousands of
perfect martinis by the white-tuxed, black-tied bartenders.
The bartenders are no-nonsense veterans, and while only
a few could possibly remember Bemelmans himself, they
speak of him as if this good friend has just stepped from
the room.

I try to visit whenever I'm in New York. One afternoon
when I was either dressed well enough or the lights were
low enough that I might be mistaken for an Upper
Eastsider, the barman headed to my booth with a phone

in his hand, just like the movies, bowing from the waist—
I swear he clicked his heels—and offered me the receiver,
inquiring, "Miss Colgate?"

I was tempted by the mischievous Madeline perched just
over my shoulder: Take the call, take the call!

"Miss Colgate?"

But gumption failed and I could only reply, "I wish."
The barkeep and I had a good laugh, and a few moments
later I was delivered a potent something on the house,
which is exactly the type of hospitality Bemelmans himself
was loved for.

SARAH STONICH
Writer

A great place to stop for a drink and a smoke (as in
cigars). This oasis has a timeless feel and never seems
to be crowded. Plus, the walls are covered in Ludwig
Bemelmans's lyrical illustrations. I like to take the Sunday
paper there for an afternoon beer and smoke.

ROB MORROW
Actor and filmmaker

For me, an evening at Bemelmans Bar has always been
both fanciful and familiar. When I was a young editor just
getting started in New York, a visit to Bemelmans meant
slowly savored martinis and a meal of homemade chips,
rosemary marinated olives, and divine mixed nuts. I would
float through the front door, past the tastefully dressed
giraffe with the yellow handbag that graces the wall near
the entry, and casually settle in for a cocktail and conversation. Tommy, the friendly Irishman who has been tending
the bar for more than 40 years, made me feel right at
home. I would slip into a tufted leather banquette and slip
back in time. By the end of the evening, I felt as though I
had stepped out of a Noël Coward play. Today, the experience of turning back the elegant clock at Bemelmans is
every bit as transporting. The refined service and urbane
pianist, along with the warm glow of the room and

Ludwig Bemelmans's amazing wall murals, have endured and I expect always will.

KATE SPADE
Fashion designer

11.13 The Metropolitan Museum of Art

Fifth Avenue at 82nd Street, ✆ 212 535-7710
Tuesday-Thursday, Sunday 9:30am-5:15pm; Friday, Saturday
9:30am-8:45pm; closed Monday

Ⓜ 86th Street (4/5/6)

For me, the best expenditure of two hours' recreation in New York City is a visit to the Metropolitan Museum of Art. In fact, I enjoy my trips to the museum so much that I go about every two weeks. There is always a new exhibition to be seen or an old collection to be revisited in order to learn even more about it. The permanent collections that draw me to visit again and again are the Egyptian Art collection and Arms and Armor.

I have been a frequent visitor to the museum for many years. When I became a Member of Congress in 1969, I compared life in New York City to Washington, D.C. New York came out way ahead for a host of reasons, of which the museum is only one.

EDWARD I. KOCH
Former Mayor of New York City

Greek and Roman Art
First floor

Cubiculum from Boscoreale
40-30 B.C.

Walking along the sidewalks of New York we sometimes want to know what lies behind the anonymous walls of urban structures. Where are the brilliant salons of Cole Porter where beautiful people chat wittily over cocktails? The period rooms at the Metropolitan Museum of Art allow us to enter elite environments from different periods in history. My favorite is the richly painted cubiculum (small bedroom) excavated from the villa of P. Fannius Synister at Boscoreale (just north of Pompeii), now installed in the Greek and Roman Galleries.

It is decorated in what art historians term the Second Style of Roman painting, a system of complex perspectives that may derive from architectural stage backdrops (*frontes scaenarum*). These views appear to open behind the actual wall plane, which is reinforced by painted columns and piers. The ancient viewer would move about the room and imaginatively escape into three different worlds: the courts of urban sanctuaries, cityscapes of jostling buildings, and a rocky landscape. Modern visitors can also suspend belief and project themselves back into the middle of the first century B.C. Elsewhere in the galleries are other paintings from the same villa. These feature near-life-size figured scenes (megalography) that derive from the decorations found in Hellenistic royal courts. The paintings, together with some of the statuary and luxury items displayed in the galleries, provide an *Architectural Digest*-like glimpse into the opulent private lives of wealthy Romans.

PETER J. HOLLIDAY
Historian of classical art and archaeology

RECOMMENDED READING
P.W. Lehmann, *Roman Wall Paintings from Boscoreale in the Metropolitan Museum of Art*, Archaeological Institute of America, 1953, o.p.

Metropolitan Museum Figure Tour

The most omnipresent image in the history of art is the figure. At the Metropolitan Museum, you can follow the figure through thousands of years. Unique in this part of the world in offering such a sweeping reach in a single location, the museum provides visitors a view of this entire arc in one of the finest collections anywhere. The striking similarity between the "beginning" and the "present"—between the Cycladic and Brancusi—is a marvelous paradox, which we have the good fortune to witness here.

Key stops along the way:

Third millennium B.C.
Cycladic art
Greek and Roman Art Galleries, first floor

With only crude tools at hand, our forebears created splendid frontal images of themselves in kind. They would have a lasting effect on the making of sculpture into the 20th century.

Fourteenth century B.C.
"Fragment of the Face of a Queen"
1353-1336 B.C.
Egyptian Art Galleries, first floor

In a glass case near the entrance to the Temple of Dendur, find this piece composed from yellow jasper, the second hardest stone known to man after the diamond. Note the little stand with the metal pin, required when this piece came to the Met in 1926 because there was no drill strong enough to pierce the jasper. Ponder, then, how the contour line of the lip was carved in 1350 B.C.

Fourteenth century B.C.
"Haremhab as a Scribe of the King"
1336-1323 B.C.
Egyptian Art Galleries, first floor

Find it, also, near the entrance to the Temple of Dendur. This king worked his way up to sovereign without the usual bloodline requirement. This portrayal of him seems to keep that crucial fact in mind, juxtaposing refined elegance and mass, and seeming to say that power can be achieved only through intelligence. It is one of the museum's finest works.

Sixth century B.C.
"Kouros" (Statue of a Youth)
590-580 B.C.
Greek and Roman Art Galleries, first floor

▶

We've returned to the Greeks and Romans. The only tool
in Attica at this time was the bull-nose chisel, which
limited the ability to achieve a rounded naturalism. Still,
look at the way the artist handled the hair, and pushed
the chisel to create lifelike anatomy. This is a work of
amazing intelligence and liveliness.

Fifth century B.C.
Marble Statue of a Diadoumenor
430 B.C., Polykleitos (copy, 69-96 A.D.)
Greek and Roman Art Galleries, first floor

This youth tying a fillet around his head is attributed
to Polykleitos, the man who put the class in classical.
Polykleitos invented the Classical canon: seven and
one-half heads. This canon measures anatomical length
in the following fashion: Squint with one eye closed and
extend your arm. Using the thumb and index finger of
the extended hand, measure the height of the head of the
youth. This measurement equals one head. It is then one
head again to the nipples. One head to the belly button.
Half a head to the pelvic bone. Two heads to the knee.
Two heads to the plinth. Total? Seven and one-half. Try
it. This method of rendering the figure has lasted until
the present day.

Third-second century B.C.
"Veiled and Masked Dancer"
Greek and Roman Art Galleries, first floor

Look at this little miracle—so miraculous in fact, so modern, the detailing so perfect, that some believe it is a phony.
It's impossible to stay in one place when viewing it; one is
forced to walk around it.

First century
"Old Market Woman"
Greek and Roman Art Galleries, first floor

Here, genre and type supersede ideal beauty. The result

is a startling, lifelike presence. Now leave the ancients and head for the roots of modern Europe.

Twelfth century
"Dancing Celestial"
Irving Galleries for the Arts of South and Southeast Asia, second floor

The apotheosis of figure as decoration. Near the Jain Temple, find this jewel wearing jewels in a pose of unabashed sexuality.

Thirteenth century
"Golden Boy"
Charlotte C. Weber Galleries for the Arts of Ancient China, second floor

This wooden masterpiece hovers between stasis and movement and stands in charmed vibration between the two.

Fifteenth century
"Enthroned Virgin and Child"
c.1420, attributed to Claux de Werve
Medieval Art Galleries, first floor

Take note of the rear view. Compare and contrast it with *Haremhab as a Scribe of the King*.

Fifteenth century
"Adam"
1490-95, Tullio Lombardo
Vélez Blanco Patio, first floor

A masterpiece of sexual sublimation. Here is a startling union: Modern Man's fig leaf on an ancient monumental sculpture, for the first time. Compare with Polykleitos's *Diadoumenor*.

Seventeenth century
"A Faun Teased by Children"
1616-17, Gian Lorenzo Bernini
European Sculpture and Decorative Arts Galleries, first floor ►

▶

The prodigy at work, at age 19. This piece shows you the
master who will soon emerge.

Eighteenth century
Jack and Belle Linsky Galleries
European Sculpture and Decorative Arts Galleries, first floor

Now you are at the Rococo. Despite the leap of 2,000
years, you can find the *Old Market Woman* in these porce-
lains, on a different scale.

Nineteenth century
New Hebrides Slit-Gongs
Arts of Africa, Oceania, and the Americas Galleries, first floor

These amazing structures are part functional—serving as
drums—and part fertility figures; both male and female
gender in one giddy form. Spiritual, too.

Nineteenth century
"Perseus with the Head of Medusa"
1804-06, Antonio Canova
Balcony above the Great Hall, second floor

We're neo-Classical now and you have two precedents to
consider: Polykleitos's *Diadoumenor* and Tullio
Lombardo's *Adam.*

Nineteenth century
"Ugolino and His Sons"
1865-1867, Jean-Baptiste Carpeaux

"Burghers of Calais"
1884-95, Auguste Rodin (cast in 1985)
European Sculpture and Decorative Arts Galleries,
Sculpture Court, first floor

Back downstairs to the Carroll & Milton Petrie Sculpture
Court. Carpeaux gives us Dante's most harrowing canto
brought to life. Rodin's sculpture of the doomed burghers
as they make their way to the gallows, hints at modernism's
dialectic between collective suffering and personal growth.

Twentieth century
"Sleeping Muse"
1920, Constantin Brancusi
Modern Art Galleries, first floor

Brancusi's polished simplicity completes the arc. You've not only journeyed some 5,000 years, you have, in significant ways, traveled full circle back to the Cycladic. One can quibble with this mix of work, but you'll see that the startling parallels overwhelm the inherent differences.
It's the most convincing case under one roof for the notion of progress as inconsequential to art-making. Brancusi may have been a happy man when the electric sander was invented, but it didn't make him a better artist.
PIER CONSAGRA
Artist

Arts of Africa, Oceania, and the Americas
First floor

Michael C. Rockefeller Wing

The most internationally renowned collection of non-Western art on display is a series of treasures that includes a 16th-century ivory pendant mask depicting a queen mother from the kingdom of Benin, a primordial couple by a Dogon master, and a majestic series of monumental Bamana allegorical figures from present-day Mali.
ALISA LAGAMMA
Associate curator, African art, The Metropolitan Museum of Art

European Sculpture and Decorative Arts
First floor

The Studiolo from the Palace of Duke Federico da Montefeltro at Gubbio
c.1478-1483, Francesco di Giorgio Martini

Among the many treasures in the Metropolitan Museum, one worth spending some time with is the Gubbio studiolo. Created in Gubbio, central Italy, for the 15th-century humanist scholar and soldier Federico da Montefeltro, Duke of Urbino, this small private study embodies the diverse interests of a true Renaissance man. Federico was renowned for his love of books, art, and learning—he employed 40 scribes in his library and five men to read him the classics during meals. His studiolo is an irregularly shaped room decorated entirely in perspective intarsia— wood inlay. The benches jutting into the room; the shelves and cabinets overflowing with artifacts symbolizing learning, art, and power; the half-opened cabinets; the organ; the birdcage—all are created with astonishing realism from thousands of minute slivers of different colored woods. The room repays careful study, as it is full of delightful tiny details. You can discover distinct strings on the musical instruments, legible text from Virgil's *Aeneid* on an open book, convincingly rendered shadows, a pair of eyeglasses neatly folded in their case, an hourglass full of sand. All the views are calculated for a person about five feet tall. If you crouch, you can see how the perspective works, particularly by watching as the circular headdress casually laid on the bench becomes, from the wrong point of view, a distorted ring with shadows in the wrong places, and then falls back into place as you stand up again. The Met completed its meticulous renovation of this friendly little room in 1996. The museum trustingly put up no barriers in front of the walls, and the light streaming in through the small window convincingly simulates sunlight. Although the studiolo was opened with great fanfare, it is now often empty for long stretches. You can easily spend a quarter of an hour there without seeing anyone except the guard, who checks periodically to make sure you don't touch anything.

JANET B. PASCAL
Writer and editor

One of the gems of the Medieval Department is the studiolo (or private study) of Federico da Montefeltro, Duke of Urbino, formerly located in his palace at Gubbio (a hilltown in the Umbria region of Italy). A masterwork of 15th-century craftsmanship, this intimate room— approximately 16 feet by 12 feet—exhibits the illusionistic qualities of intarsia, or wood inlay technique. Thousands of tiny pieces of wood act like a painter's palette: the multiple varieties, cuts, and grains of wood create the *trompe l'oeil* appearance of cabinet doors slightly ajar, revealing inside objects dear to a humanist's intellect and curiosity. Books are casually stacked or left open, as if someone has just thumbed through their pages. A parrot sits patiently on a perch in a cage. Lutes, candles, scientific instruments, a portable pipe organ, lectern, sand hourglass, convex mirror, hunting horn, and helmet are all displayed as cherished belongings of perhaps the most renowned *condottiere* (soldier of fortune) of his time. Among the visual rewards for feasting one's eyes in this room are the latticework designs that incorporate the effects of natural light from the window, as well as the use of perspective that invites our eyes to question the two-dimensionality of the flat wall.

KATEY BROWN
Art historian

Sienese Paintings

"The Creation of the World and the Expulsion from Paradise"
1445, Giovanni di Paolo
The Robert Lehman Collection, first floor

"St. Anthony in the Wilderness"
("Saint Anthony the Abbot Tempted by a Heap of Gold")
c.1420, The Osservanza Master
The Robert Lehman Collection, first floor

"The Journey of the Magi"
c.1420, Sassetta
European Paintings Galleries, second floor

Sienese painting has always been overshadowed by its more famous cousin, Florentine painting, which broke through to the full-on science of rational representation. By contrast, Sienese paintings are illogical and medieval—but that's exactly what modern viewers love about them. These paintings have spaces more absurd than Cézanne, colors right out of the comics, and images that tamp down academic space and accentuate the expressive. Candy-colored castles! Giant people walking through miniature worlds! Mystical experiences in improbable architectures! If you want to make a little pilgrimage to this uncanny world, there are some great Sienese paintings that you can visit at the Met. They are not presented with much fanfare and can be missed easily.

Go directly to the back of the ground floor of the museum to the Robert Lehman Collection, walk through the glass doors and along the wall on the left with paintings by Degas, Renoir, Cézanne, and Vuillard (some of the Vuillards alone make this worth the trip). Go back around the wall to the left to find the Sienese room, the first of a suite of semi-hidden rooms containing Lehman's collection of older paintings, all fitted out in red velvet and gilded wood to imply a 15th-century Italian environment. Hanging here are two outstanding examples of Sienese painting: *Saint Anthony the Abbot Tempted by a Heap of Gold* by the Osservanza Master, and *The Creation of the World and the Expulsion from Paradise* by Giovanni di Paolo. Both artists were active in the second quarter of the 15th century in Siena. You will probably find the di Paolo first because it is marked for the Museum's headphone audio tour. This heavily cracked painting shows Adam and Eve's expulsion from the garden set against a chart-like mini-universe that includes the prime mover himself presiding over everything from the circles of hell to the four great drainage ditches of the world.

Across the room is the extraordinary *Saint Anthony the Abbot Tempted by a Heap of Gold (St. Anthony in the Wilderness)* by the Osservanza Master, a small tempera-and-gold painting hanging modestly amidst a wall of more conventional Madonna paintings. In it, a startled-looking Saint Anthony gestures toward a little gray bunny crouching at the base of a bare tree. There is an almost minimalist space and silence between the man and the animal, as though some phantom thing between them has been painted out. What's going on in the background is even weirder. The Osservanza Master seems to have had a background man who was either new at the job or a brilliant pre-Van Gogh hallucinator, 400 years before his time. Saint Anthony and the mute bunny live in a wild and crazy pink and green world inhabited only by listing and hunkering animals. The action twists back along a pebbled path to a variety of green Mister Softee hills, some stuck with what look like cloves. The earth is orange, the castles are hot pink, the sea is bright green with a thrift-store-looking boat in it and, above it all, crows fly in a flaming sky lit up with crimson clouds.

For a comparison, visit the more polished Sassetta in the Met's regular Italian painting collection. Take the main staircase to the second floor, through the doorway ►

▶

straight ahead of you on the right side, into the first room
of the corridor of 14th- to 16th-century Italian paintings.
On the right side and behind glass, you will find the truly
amazing *Journey of the Magi* by Sassetta, painted in tempera
and gold on wood, c.1420. Here's the ubiquitous speckled
path, but in this tiny painting all the townspeople march
down a hill in a frieze-like procession, which disappears
out of the painting as though it were stage left, leaving a
lone horse's leg in view as it exits. As the people walk off,
swallows pose, storks graze on mottled hills, stars bleed
gold, trees lose their branches, and leaves and buildings
glow in the distance, all in a painting the size of a piece
of typing paper.

AMY SILLMAN
Artist

Islamic Art
Second floor

Deep inside the labyrinthine corridors of the Metropolitan
Museum of Art are a series of galleries devoted to the
museum's superb collection of Islamic art. These galleries
are among the most serene and pleasant spaces within the
museum—oases of repose and contemplation where you
can see and enjoy works of art of incomparable beauty and
power. Located in the southeast corner of the second floor,
the galleries were designed in 1975 and they remain among
the most intelligent and compelling displays of Islamic art
anywhere in the world. They're home to more than 12,000
works of art from almost every corner of the Islamic
world—from Spain to India—that date from the eighth
to the 18th century. Among my favorite objects, which
have fascinated me since I was a graduate student and first
encountered them, are the reconstruction of Núr ad-Dín's
room from a wealthy Syrian home of the early 18th century; the great 12th-century Seljuk incense burner in the
shape of a lion; the dazzling tile mihrab (or prayer niche)

from the mid-14th century madrasa (school) of Imami in
Isfahan; the majestic early 16th-century "Simonetti" carpet
from Mamluk, Egypt; and the illustrated pages from the
Shahnama or *Book of Kings* commissioned by the Safavid
ruler Shah Tahmasp (1514-76), one of the Islamic world's
most ardent bibliophiles.

What distinguishes all these works is a precision of line,
complexity of design, and a level of craftsmanship and
detail that is not only breathtaking, but awe-inspiring.
The weave of the "Simonetti" carpet, for instance, is a
staggering 100 asymmetrical knots per square inch. Many
of the colors used in the painting of the *Shahnama* are
made from semiprecious ground minerals such as lapis
lazuli and malachite. The lustrous gold backgrounds are,
in fact, a thinly applied layer of gold leaf.

GLENN LOWRY
Director, The Museum of Modern Art

European Paintings
Second floor

"The View of Toledo"
c.1597, El Greco

After you have viewed the city, climb the steps at the
Metropolitan Museum, head to the second floor (European
Paintings), and be transported by El Greco's *The View
of Toledo*.

This is not a painting of the state of grace already fully
realized, like Bellini's wondrous *Saint Francis in the Desert*
at the Frick Museum. Instead, we are in the middle of
a hallucination, in the anxious peripheries of revelation.
The sky is doubt, the landscape ambiguity, and the source
of light a riddle.

As you travel through the painting, sweeping past the
architecture, you are at once pulled by the weight of
weather, human events, botany, history, a familiar world—
time-bound, color-bound, language-bound—up to the

prospect of the skyline that is Toledo. Here the painting abruptly stops. The skyline is a horizon. There is no beyond. There is only the above, leading the eye by way of the church spire to the light that creates the scene. Is it nighttime or day, twilight or dawn? All you really know is that a supernatural illumination is eclipsing the scene.

In this spot of time, the world of weather and human events stops. You have reached the terminus of earthly experience. There is no beyond, even though there is a potential for beyond. El Greco takes the scene, arrests it, holds it. Then, through a series of silvery gleams of light, he abstracts you from real time to the realm of timelessness. The entire painting unfolds within a shadow—which confesses to the mystery of spiritual illumination—toward the opening in the sky, an oculus in the celestial dome. You are in the exact spot where the ordinary is about to reach beyond itself to immanence.

This hallucination in light and dark releases the gradations of secular time and distance into a supernatural hilltop and sublimity, heaving upward and pointing, sky beyond sky, to receive God in an instant. As Thoreau would say, it is a light to behold but to dwell not in.

JACK BARTH
Artist

"Madonna and Child"
c.1480, Carlo Crivelli

Hidden among the many blockbusters in the Metropolitan Museum of Art are some wonderful little jewels that are, unfortunately, often overlooked by the average visitor. Carlo Crivelli's *Madonna and Child* is one of these.

Crivelli originally lived in Venice but left the city after serving a short prison term in 1457 for seducing a married woman. From that time forward he painted in the Provincia di Ancona. While Giovanni Bellini painted with oils in the new Renaissance manner, Crivelli, using egg tempera, created masterpieces more visually aligned with the Gothic painting tradition. The word best used to describe his paintings is sumptuous. His pensive Madonnas are cloaked in fabrics that are gilded and tooled so as to reflect, almost kinetically, a warm golden glow back to the viewer. During the early Renaissance this sheen was believed to be heavenly light.

This particular painting has the Virgin surrounded by a beautiful garland similar to those Andrea Mantegna used to adorn his Madonnas. However, unlike Mantegna, who used exotic assortments of fruits and flowers to construct his garlands, Crivelli preferred everyday fruits and mundane vegetables.

The Madonna has long, elegant, and slightly spidery fingers, a characteristic often found in Crivelli's paintings. She stands before a hanging drapery in Belliniesque fashion while slivers of the local landscape appear on either side of the cloth. The baby Jesus sits on a bumpy lavender cushion that looks as if it could have been tailored from a hunk of dyed ostrich skin and ponders a housefly (a symbol of evil) the size of his foot. He simultaneously clutches a goldfinch, which, like the giant cuke, symbolizes redemption.

The juxtaposition of these wonderfully strange objects, the impact of the tooled gold, the peaceful, meditative Virgin, and the magnificent use of color, make this a jewel of a painting not to be missed.

FRED WESSEL
Artist

"The Triumph of Marius"
1729, Giovanni Battista Tiepolo

"Elizabeth Farren, Later Countess of Derby"
1790, Sir Thomas Lawrence

A brimstone-yellow banner flutters against a hot Italian sky and compels the eye and mind up the great staircase of the Metropolitan and into the collection of European paintings. The dazzling half-smile of an actress out for a walk on a breezy spring day makes further exploration of the English rooms hard to resist. Both these superb paintings display the particular genius of the Metropolitan for leading us effortlessly from one room of the enormous building into the next. Their appeal is immediate and obvious, but they are also about aspirations, both extinct and alive. Tiepolo's rich, shadowed procession of a Roman victory over the Moors reminded Venetians of their claimed—if phony—descent from ancient Rome, and of the political power they had just relinquished. There's a vintage, sulky-lipped Tiepolo matron in the bottom right-hand corner, but basically this is a great painting of a brimstone-yellow banner.

Known as "The Queen of Comedy" at London's Haymarket and Drury Lane theaters, Elizabeth Farren was so furious when Lawrence first catalogued her portrait as *An Actress* that she demanded (and received) an apology. He claimed his original title had been *Portrait of a Lady*. Farren also wanted him to make her look fatter—Regency times were just around the corner and gentlemen's tastes were running to the zaftig. Happily, he declined, and gave us the best of everything: Portrait of an Actress Classy Enough to be a Lady. Dressed in oyster satin and furs, her face turning just long enough for the painter to capture its candour, she's gorgeous. The Earl of Derby had been potty about her for years and, Reader, she married him.

MICHAEL RATCLIFFE
Critic and writer

Asian Art
Second floor

The Astor Court
1981

You don't know serenity until you visit the Chinese Scholar's Garden in the Metropolitan Museum, a classi-cally simple space that you are unlikely to find unless you ask directions. Ask for the Astor Court, named for the philanthropic Brooke (Mrs. Vincent) Astor, whose foundation paid for it. Tucked among the Asian Galleries on the second floor, this island of tranquility is modeled on a Ming dynasty courtyard—in the "Garden of the Master of the Fishing Nets"—in Suzhou, China, a city near Shanghai once renowned for its culture and elegance.

In those ancient times, a learned man had a scrupulously sculptured garden to which he might repair for composing poetic thoughts, maybe for tea and conversation, or just for quiet contemplation. In the Met, you might go to the garden to wonder at the delicacy of its design, to take a break from the hubbub, or even to compose your own verse. Others may be resting there when you enter, never many and always hushed.

The principal entrance is a moon gate—a big round hole in the wall, flanked by lions, under a motto that reveals the garden's secret in archaic script: "In search of quietude." The space inside measures about 60 by 40 feet. A sheltered walkway lines two sides, with low walls to sit on. A graceful pavilion stands opposite, beside a spring trickling through rocks into a goldfish pond. Windows, cut out in lattice patterns, frame living bamboo and Oriental grasses, while a large skylight bathes the scene in sunshine (on a good day). Everything about this lovely space came from China: the tile from an old imperial kiln reactivated for just this purpose; eroded rock formations from the bottom of Lake Tai, near Suzhou; timber from gingko, camphor and fir trees, and the rare nan evergreen. The garden and the fine paneled room that opens onto it were installed by 27 Chinese craftsmen in 1980.

They created a secret gem.

RICHARD MOONEY
Journalist

Viewing the Met's magnificent art collections is a usual experience in New York. But for the unusual, come to the

Met early, when it opens, go to the Asian Galleries and ask directions to the hidden Astor Court—named because the Astor family financed it—but, in reality, the re-creation of a 17th-century courtyard from Suzhou, China. If you're really early, you may have the court all to yourself. The ambience of tranquility is pervasive here. Another world, another time: enclosed, silent, serene. Cool stone floors, a rock pond with fish, and a gentle waterfall washing the stones. Sit on benches at the back and watch the bamboo sway and listen to the water. Time to be at peace, to reflect, to dream a little, before you go back to thronging, clattering, 21st-century Manhattan.

SHIRLEY LAURO
Playwright and novelist

Iris and B. Gerald Cantor Roof Garden

1987, Kevin Roche, John Dinkeloo & Associates
Rooftop of Lila Acheson Wallace Wing
Open May–October

After living in New York and visiting for many years, I face the challenge—how to see all those old friends and professional contacts when I'm only in town for a few days? Answer: arrange a collective rendezvous at 6 p.m. on Friday on the rooftop terrace of the Metropolitan Museum (open until 9 p.m. Friday and Saturday). Cocktails, superb sculpture, views over Central Park of the capital of capitalism—the apotheosis of civilization.

FENTON JOHNSON
Writer

For a sense of the scale and uniqueness of Central Park, for the western skyscape, and for the astonishing vibrancy of northeastern foliage, this is the place to visit in late October.

ROSLYN SCHLOSS
Editor

🍴 Lunch on the roof of the Metropolitan Museum—the fourth-floor Sculpture Garden—great view of Central Park

and the Midtown and Central Park West skylines.
JEAN PARKER PHIFER
President of the Art Commission of the City of New York

Museum Evenings

A city's best-kept secrets are often in plain sight. As any
tour book will tell you in its listing of hours, most of the
major museums in New York are open late on Friday and
Saturday evenings. As many longtime aficionados of art
in the city know, this is the time when tourists head downtown for dinner and the theater, and you can view the art
undisturbed.
ELIZABETH WINTHROP
Writer

11.9 **The Frick Collection** (see p. 278)
Friday until 9pm

11.11 **Whitney Museum of American Art** (see p. 281)
Friday until 9pm

11.13 **The Metropolitan Museum of Art** (see p. 287)
Friday, Saturday until 8:45pm

11.15 **Solomon R. Guggenheim Museum** (see p. 307)
Friday, Saturday until 8pm

11.16 **Smithsonian's Cooper-Hewitt, National Design Museum**
(see p. 308)
Tuesday until 9pm

11.17 **The Jewish Museum** (see p. 309)
Thursday until 8pm

12.34 **American Museum of Natural History** (see p. 351)
Rose Center for Earth & Science only
Friday, Saturday until 8:45pm

▶

▶

13.10 The Studio Museum in Harlem (see p. 379)
Friday until 8pm

16.12 Brooklyn Museum of Art (see p. 434)
First Saturday of the month until 11pm

11.14 Neue Galerie New York
1914, Carrère & Hastings
1048 Fifth Avenue at 86th Street, ✆ 212 628-6200
Open Friday, Saturday, Monday 11am-7pm; Sunday 1pm-
6pm; closed Tuesday-Thursday
Ⓜ 86th Street (4/5/6)

If you ever wished for an art museum with an excellent
collection that you could survey in its entirety in one visit,
the Neue Galerie is for you. This small museum is housed
in an elegant former mansion, dating from 1914. Originally
designed as a private residence by Carrère & Hastings
(who also designed the New York Public Library), it was
occupied at one time by Mrs. Cornelius Vanderbilt III.
More recently, it was home to the YIVO Institute for
Jewish Research.

The collection focuses on German and Austrian fine art
and decorative art of the early 20th century. It is derived
from the holdings of Serge Sabarsky and Ronald Lauder, an
art dealer and businessman respectively, who share an abid-
ing interest in this field. They purchased the building in
1994. You may or may not be familiar with the several
German schools represented, namely, die Brücke, der Blaue
Reiter, Neue Sachlichkeit, Bauhaus, and Werkbund. You
will, however, recognize many of the artists they included,
such as Klee, Schiele, Kandinsky, Klimt, Hoffmann, Van der
Rohe, and many others who are shown at their very best.
LAWRENCE KAHN
Professor emeritus of pediatrics, Washington University

11.15 Solomon R. Guggenheim Museum

1959, Frank Lloyd Wright; 1992, addition by Gwathmey Siegel
& Associates
1071 Fifth Avenue between 88th & 89th Streets
☎ 212 423-3500
Sunday-Wednesday 9am-6pm, Friday & Saturday 9am-8pm;
closed Thursday
Ⓜ 86th Street (4/5/6)

Frank Lloyd Wright chose the location for the Guggenheim
Museum for its proximity to Central Park, and his design
encourages the visitor to communicate with nature,
particularly from the vantage point of the small rotunda,
or "Monitor Building," as he called it. Here, two glass-
enclosed mini-rotundas are inscribed in wide terraces,
one rectangular and one round. Although visitors are not
allowed access onto these terraces, the new Gwathmey
Siegel tower building, completed in 1992, includes
a marvelous jewel of a sculpture terrace, which is open
to the public. Access is through the fifth-level tower gallery.
From this perch, the visitor has a superb view of Central
Park and the Reservoir. An added bonus is a sculpture or
group of sculptures from the Guggenheim's collection.
Go at sunset and enjoy the silhouetted skyline of Central
Park West. This is the view of only the privileged few who
live on Fifth Avenue overlooking the park. An added
attraction is reduced museum admission on Fridays after
6 p.m., with music from the museum's acclaimed jazz
program filling the rotunda.

After the Guggenheim, explore the charming residential
neighborhood of Carnegie Hill and the Guggenheim's
neighboring museums, including the Smithsonian's Cooper-
Hewitt, National Design Museum (see p. 308) and the
Jewish Museum (see p. 309). Pick up a picnic lunch from
the museum cafe or any of the take-out shops on Madison,
such as Petak's (between 89th and 90th Streets) or Yura &
Company (at 92nd Street) and dine in the park. The most

beautiful spot is the Conservatory Garden on Fifth Avenue and 104th Street (see p. 337).

LISA DENNISON
Deputy director and chief curator, Solomon R. Guggenheim Museum

11.16 Former Carnegie Mansion, now Smithsonian's Cooper-Hewitt, National Design Museum

1903, Babb, Cook & Willard
2 East 91st Street at Fifth Avenue, ☎ 212 849-8400
Tuesday 10am-9pm; Wednesday-Saturday 10am-5pm;
Sunday noon-5pm; closed Monday
Ⓜ 86th Street (4/5/6)

Arthur Ross Terrace and Garden

Andrew Carnegie left us a legacy of public libraries across the country, but one of the best places to read is the garden in what was his own backyard. Now the Arthur Ross Terrace and Garden behind the Cooper-Hewitt, this plot of land is a well-kept oasis at the highest elevation on Fifth Avenue, located between 90th and 91st Streets. Descending the steps from Carnegie's former home, one enters a central lawn set among lovely plantings, with the original wisteria still flowering. Along a picturesque path winding around the circumference are welcoming benches, ideal for spending a bucolic afternoon outside while in the city. Looking through the enclosing wrought-iron fence (the only flaw in the view), west to Central Park and south to apartment buildings and the Church of the Heavenly Rest, it is hard to imagine that for the first 15 years the Carnegies were in residence, the plot across the street held a decrepit wooden shack that sold lemonade, peanuts, ginger cakes, and other snacks. Now, the perfect afternoon in the garden includes a treat from one of Carnegie Hill's nearby gourmet food shops and an absorbing book—Mr. Carnegie no doubt would approve.

While neighbors used to be privileged with private keys,

now all visitors access the garden through the Carnegie
mansion, which Andrew and his wife, Louise, built for his
retirement, intended as "the most modest, plainest and
most roomy house in New York." (Along the way, take
time to look for the charming period details adorning the
interior of the house or view the exhibitions featuring
objects from the extraordinary collections amassed by the
Hewitt sisters.) Daydreaming in the garden, while looking
at the southwest corner of the back limestone-and-brick
facade, one can imagine Carnegie in his office within his
private suite of rooms. Visitors would come seeking
donations from Carnegie, who devoted the end of his life
to dispensing his wealth for the benefit of society. To get
to the philanthropist, supplicants had to pass through a
small vestibule with a dropped ceiling then duck through
a low doorway (Carnegie was only 5'2") to enter a library
dominated by a painted frieze of inspirational quotations,
where they would await the small, but powerful man.

LISA PODOS
Arts educator

RECOMMENDED READING
Andrew Carnegie, *The Gospel of Wealth*, Applewood Books, 1998.
Joseph Frazier Wall, *Andrew Carnegie*, University of Pittsburgh
Press, 1989.

11.17 The Jewish Museum
1908, C. P. H. Gilbert; 1993, addition by Kevin Roche
1109 Fifth Avenue at 92nd Street, ☎ 212 423-3200
Sunday 10am-5:45pm; Monday-Wednesday 11am-5:45pm;
Thursday 11am-8pm; Friday 11am-3pm; closed Saturday
Ⓜ 86th Street (4/5); 96th Street (6)

In the heart of New York City there is a piece of ancient
Jerusalem—a foundation stone from a wall that protected
the city in the first century that tells a story of desperation,
disaster, and transformation. In 66 C.E., the Jews of
ancient Israel rebelled against their Roman overlords and
hastily completed the city wall as a part of their defense

system. The wall did not hold, however; the Roman army breached it, going on to destroy Jerusalem and the Temple, the focus of ancient sacrificial worship. The Jews were exiled from the city and were forced to devise an alternative form of worship, based on prayer in the synagogue and the study of the sacred texts. This new form of worship became the mainstay of Judaism thereafter. All this can be read from a single stone!

The foundation stone is one of more than 800 works of art and artifacts on view in the Jewish Museum's permanent exhibition, "Culture and Continuity: The Jewish Journey." Each tells a part of the dramatic story of the Jewish people's artistic and cultural creativity in response to the challenges of preserving and defining their identity over four millennia. I have many favorite objects in the show in addition to the foundation stone. One is a 19th-century Hanukkah lamp from Australia, decorated with kangaroos and emus. It started out as a souvenir from Down Under, with an emu egg hanging in the center. When the egg eventually broke, someone decided to convert it into a Hanukkah lamp. It is a marvelous example of Jewish adaptation of art styles and traditions from the cultures among which they lived. Another favorite, also from the 19th century, is a painting by the German artist Moritz Oppenheim titled *The Return of the Jewish Volunteer*. It reflects both the opportunities and conflicts Jews experienced after the Emancipation, when they were allowed for the first time to participate as citizens in the activities of their adopted homeland. In the painting, the soldier has just arrived home from his unit, interrupting his family's Sabbath observance. While he is now free to serve his country, he has broken with his religious tradition by traveling on the Sabbath.

After viewing the permanent exhibition, the visitor might take a rest by examining the museum building itself, which is a gem. It was designed by Charles Prendergast H. Gilbert in the style of a François Premier French Gothic château. The second floor of the museum retains many of the original details of the rooms from the first half of the 20th century, when the mansion was occupied by Felix and Frieda Schiff Warburg. In 1993, an addition was made to the building and the interior of the original mansion renovated. Architect Kevin Roche chose to extend the French Gothic facade and interior decoration, and the visitor will be hard-pressed to distinguish the original parts of the mansion from the more recent addition.

SUSAN L. BRAUNSTEIN
Curator of archaeology and Judaica, The Jewish Museum

11.18 Clapboard House

1852, attributed to Albro Howell
160 East 92nd Street between Lexington & Third Avenues
Not open to the public
Ⓜ 96th Street (6)

This 1852 two-and-a-half-story residence is one of only a handful of wood frame houses remaining on the Upper East Side. In 1915, it was purchased by Willard Straight and his wife to serve as servants' quarters for their Fifth Avenue mansion on the corner of 94th Street.

The charming house has classical fluted columns on the first-floor porch and the upper stories have wooden shutters at their windows. Although it's a designated New York City Landmark, this romantic and evocative orphan has received too little loving care in recent years.

MARGOT GAYLE
Writer and preservationist

11.19 Kitchen Arts & Letters

1435 Lexington Avenue between East 93rd & East 94th Streets
☎ 212 876-5550
Monday 1pm-6pm; Tuesday-Friday 10am-6:30pm;
Saturday 11am-6pm; closed Sunday; July-August:
closed Saturday, Sunday
Ⓜ 96th Street (6)

🕮 Proprietor Nach Waxman carries a marvelous assortment
of books on food and wine, culinary history, and food
ephemera. It's absolutely top drawer. He sells one food
product, which happens to be my favorite olive oil—Alziari,
in the beautiful blue can with stars on it. It's from Nice
and is suave and full-flavored.

JANE DANIELS LEAR
Senior editor, Gourmet

11.20 St. Nicholas Russian Orthodox Cathedral

1902, John Bergesen
15 East 97th Street between Fifth & Madison Avenues
📞 212 289-1915
Ⓜ 96th Street (6)

St. Nicholas Russian Orthodox Cathedral of New York is
the only example of Moscow Baroque in the United States,
and a particularly splendid one. It is reminiscent of the
world-famous Church of Protection in the historic Russian
village of Fili (constructed in 1693), St. Nicholas-the-Great-
Cross in Moscow, and several others. The cathedral is
decorated with frescoes by the renowned Russian artist
Sokolov, and in 1973 was declared a landmark by the City
of New York. Few are aware, however, that this building
is something of a monument to entirely different Russian-
American relations that are today difficult to imagine. These
could be characterized as the relations, if not between
friends, then between close acquaintances, and span from
the cultural to the military. The initial contributions toward
the construction of the cathedral were made by the sailors
of the Russian warship *Retvizan,* on which could be seen the
mark "Made in Philadelphia." The *Retvizan* was sunk in
the Russo-Japanese war and a cross from the ship's chapel
was saved. Today this cross hangs in the cathedral.

The construction of the cathedral is connected with the
then-head of the mission of the Russian Church in the
United States, Bishop Tikhon (Belavin). Bishop Tikhon was

fluent in English and was able to establish strong and useful contacts in New York when he moved his headquarters here from San Francisco. He was to be the famous Moscow Patriarch, elected after Russia's February Revolution, who died in 1925, most likely with the participation of the Bolshevik administration. From 1924 to 1960, St. Nicholas Russian Orthodox Cathedral, in the heart of Manhattan, was the subject of a protracted legal battle over ownership of this remarkable example of Moscow Baroque.

YURI MILOSLAVSKY
Writer

11.21 Museum of the City of New York

1930, Joseph H. Freedlander
1220 Fifth Avenue at 103rd Street
☎ 212 534-1672
Wednesday-Saturday 10am-5pm; Sunday noon-5pm;
Tuesday 10am-2pm, preregistered tours only; closed Monday
Ⓜ 103rd Street (6)

On Fifth Avenue, a stone's throw away from the magnificent Conservatory Garden in Central Park, is the Museum of the City of New York, home to a wonderful toy collection that tells the story of growing up in New York over the last three centuries. Particularly thrilling is a quiet room filled with antique doll houses dating back to 1769. As you contemplate these miniature universes filled with dolls dressed by long-forgotten children, a lost world begins to shimmer in your mind's eye. The crown jewel of the collection is the Stettheimer Doll House, created in the 1920's by Carrie Walter Stettheimer, hostess to New York City's avant-garde artists and writers. This extraordinarily detailed evocation of the Stettheimers's home and life has its own art gallery, which houses such works as Marcel Duchamp's miniature version of his *Nude Descending a Staircase*, an alabaster *Venus* by Gaston Lachaise, and other works of art by Albert Gleizes, and Marguerite and William Zorach.

Before you leave, take a look at Elizabeth Yandell's treasure box, circa 1885. Elizabeth, orphaned when she was six years old, kept this special box throughout her life, bringing it out on occasion to amuse her own children when they were ill. It's filled with mementos—a piece of rope from a trip to Europe, an autograph album, a favorite wax doll resplendent in a red-tasseled hat and gold-buttoned jacket, an assortment of shells and stones, a stuffed cat and dog, their fur rubbed smooth. Elizabeth's sadnesses and joys come vividly to life, although the child has

...grown up and gone away,
And it is but a child of air
That lingers in the garden there.
—R.L. Stevenson, "To Any Reader."
ANNE LANDSMAN
Novelist

11.22   El Museo del Barrio

1230 Fifth Avenue at 104th Street
☎ 212 831-7952
Wednesday-Sunday 11am-5pm; closed Monday, Tuesday
Ⓜ 103rd Street (6)

At El Museo del Barrio you will find a permanent exhibit of works by the Taino, a pre-Colombian Caribbean culture, as well as temporary exhibitions that might include such renowned Hispano-American artists as Frida Kahlo and Diego Rivera (Mexico), Francisco Oller (Puerto Rico), Fernando Botero (Colombia), Amelia Paez (Cuba), and other Latin American masters of the arts. Through their paintings one gets to know the passions, the imagination, the originality, the devotion, and the fascinating sense of style that has propelled these artists to become international figures in the art world.
ANITA VELEZ-MITCHELL
Writer

East River Promenade

11.23 **Eli's Vinegar Factory**
431 East 91st Street at York Avenue
☎ 212 987-0885
Open daily 7am-9pm
Ⓜ 86th Street (4/5/6)

11.24 **Carl Schurz Park**
Along the East River from East 90th Street to Gracie Square
Ⓜ 86th Street (4/5/6)

🐞 Start by paying a visit to Eli's Vinegar Factory, a food store
with fabulous cheeses, meats, and breads. Get enough delicacies for a picnic and walk north to 96th Street, then one
block east to the promenade that runs along FDR Drive
and the East River. Farther north you'll encounter men
fishing, often with great success. If you're lucky, you'll be
around when a 30-inch bluefish is pulled in. With your
appetite whetted, head back south where the promenade
rises above the Drive and widens to become Carl Schurz
Park (from 90th to 84th Street). You can peek through
the fence at Gracie Mansion, the mayor's residence, and
then find a bench to enjoy a great river view. Here, the
turbulent waters helped protect the city from attack from
the north; prior to powerboats, this confluence of water-
ways was difficult to navigate under sail.
DEBORAH BERKE
Architect

11.25 Gracie Mansion

1804, attributed to Ezra Weeks

In Carl Schurz Park, enter at East 88th Street & East End
Avenue, ☎ 212 570-4751

March-November, preregistered tours only: Wednesdays
10am, 11am, 1pm, and 2pm

Ⓜ 86th Street (4/5/6)

Most Gracie Mansion visitors are drawn by the prospect
of seeing the Federal period house and its collection of
fine and decorative art, or by the possibility of catching a
glimpse of New York's mayor. However, three lesser-
known features reveal traces of previous residents.

Elegant floor-to-ceiling windows in the Mayor's Library
overlook the East River. On one windowpane is etched in
script, "Millie, 1875," and beneath in a bold scrawl
"Margie, 1965." Amalia Hermione Wheaton (Millie) was
born at the mansion, and as a young girl scratched her
name and birthdate on the window. Almost a century later,
the young daughter of newly elected Mayor John Lindsay
spotted the window. Her mother, pleased to have Margie
bond with her new home, permitted her to write her own
name on the glass.

The mansion's front door is framed by a finely carved
Adam-style surround. Sharp-eyed guests note an odd,
angled notch cut into the right side of the doorjamb.
During the mayoralty of Edward I. Koch, the notch held
a traditional Jewish mezuzah, a small case containing a
piece of parchment. Written on the parchment is the Shema
prayer, which reminds Jews of their obligations toward
God. It is customary to kiss the mezuzah in passing. The
mezuzah was removed at the end of Mr. Koch's term.

During early 20th-century construction projects, workers
unearthed remains of narrow stone-lined tunnels leading
from the mansion's basement to the riverbank. Historians
identified the tunnels either as an escape route built during
the American Revolution or as a stop on the Underground

Railroad during the Civil War period. Visitors ask about the rumor that Mayor William O'Dwyer stashed money missing from city coffers in the tunnels before abruptly departing for Mexico in 1950. These stories are not true; modern archaeology has revealed instead that the tunnels, of the same vintage as the 1799 house, provided drainage for the basement, which tended to flood. The real secret is that the basement still floods.

DAVID L. REESE
Curator, Gracie Mansion

11.26 Sotheby's

1334 York Avenue at East 72nd Street
Ⓜ 68th Street-Hunter College (6)

Sotheby's Cafe

Tenth floor of Sotheby's, ☎ 212 606-7070
Monday-Friday for breakfast and lunch; Saturday,
Sunday for lunch during viewings

Bid

First floor of Sotheby's, ☎ 212 988-7730
Monday-Friday for lunch and dinner; Saturday for dinner;
closed Sunday

🍴 Enter the new Sotheby's building, proceed directly to the 10th floor, grab a hot panino or a salad in the cafe, and head outside to the terrace. Linger and enjoy the great city feel. When you've had enough, walk back inside to the best new gallery space in New York City...some say in America. Or wander among French furniture, antiques, fab jewels, or very affordable prints, all on view in the approximately 75,000 square feet of exhibition space.

As a more serious alternative to the cafe, try Bid on the ground floor of Sotheby's: a wonderful "multi-starred" new American restaurant.

GERALDINE NAGER
Senior vice president, Sotheby's

11.27 Rockefeller University

1910, York & Sawyer

1270 York Avenue between East 63rd & East 68th Streets

Ⓜ 68th Street-Hunter College (6)

Caspary Auditorium

1957, Harrison & Abramovitz

☎ 212 327-7007

Open to the public for events only

Harrison & Abramovitz's dreamy, hemispherical dome could have floated over from a World's Fair. This colossal sunken sphere, a 40-foot-high, 90-foot-diameter bubble, was once covered with beautiful blue tiles. Slide into an aisle seat to gaze at the convex circles bulging everywhere. Imagine being inside a giant golf ball.

TRACEY HUMMER AND FREDERIC SCHWARTZ
Writer and Architect

11.28 Mount Vernon Hotel Museum & Garden, formerly the Abigail Adams Smith Museum

421 East 61st Street between First & York Avenues

☎ 212 838-6878

Tuesday-Sunday 11am-4pm; closed Monday; closed August

Ⓜ Lexington Avenue-59th Street (N/R/W/4/5/6);
Lexington-63rd (F)

This is great fun—an 18th-century carriage house hidden in the middle of the city.

In 1796, William Stephens Smith and his wife Abigail Adams Smith, daughter of President John Adams, began construction of an estate on 23 acres of Manhattan's Upper East Side, at the time a rural area and a refuge from the congested city to the south. They named it Mount Vernon in honor of George Washington's Virginia home. Unfortunately, beset by financial troubles, the couple had to sell their unfinished property just a year later. By the turn of the century, under a different owner, the main house and stone carriage house (now housing the museum) were completed. In 1826, the main house was destroyed by fire and the carriage house was converted into a posh day resort called the Mount Vernon Hotel. The hotel operated there until 1833 and today is New York City's only surviving day hotel—one of only a handful of sites in the United States affording a window on hotel life in the early 19th century. It also contains a beautiful decorative arts collection, along with furniture, costumes, quilts and textiles, and historical documents.

LAURA LINNEY
Actress

CENTRAL PARK &
UPPER WEST SIDE

12

Hudson River

Central Park North

Harlem Meer

Cathedral Pkwy
W 109th St
W 108th St
W 107th St
W 106th St
W 105th St
W 104th St
W 103rd St
W 102nd St
W 101st St
W 100th St
W 99th St
W 98th St

B'way
Riverside Dr
Amsterdam Avenue
Columbus Avenue
Manhattan Avenue
Central Park West

46 45 47 44 43 42 41 40 39

The Pool

North Meadow

West Drive

W 97th St
W 96th St
W 95th St
W 94th St
W 93rd St
W 92nd St
W 91st St
W 90th St
W 89th St
W 88th St
W 87th St
W 86th St
W 85th St
W 84th St
W 83rd St
W 82nd St
W 81st St

97th St Transverse
Central Park

Riverside Park

Upper West Side

West End Avenue
Broadway
Amsterdam Avenue
Columbus Avenue
Central Park West

38 37 36

Jacqueline Onassis Reservoir

86th St Transverse

The Great Lawn

West Side Hwy (Henry Hudson Pkwy)
Riverside Drive

Delacorte Theater
Turtle Pond

14 16 13 15 17
Belvedere Castle
79th St Transverse

W 80th St
W 79th St
W 78th St
W 77th St
W 76th St

American Museum of Natural History

35 34

33

9

11

W 75th St
W 74th St
W 73rd St
W 72nd St
W 71st St
W 70th St
W 69th St
W 68th St
W 67th St
W 66th St
W 65th St
W 64th St
W 63rd St
W 62nd St
W 61st St
W 60th St
W 59th St

32
31
30

The Lake
The Ramble

10

West Drive

12
Strawberry Fields

7
Terrace Dr

29
28 27 26 24
25
23
22
Lincoln Center
21

Amsterdam Avenue
Columbus Avenue
Central Park West

Sheep Meadow

The Mall

65th St Transverse

1
Carousel

2
Wollman Rink

The Pond

Joe Dimaggio Hwy
Freedom Pl
West End Avenue

Columbus Circle
Central Park South

Central Drive
West Drive

19

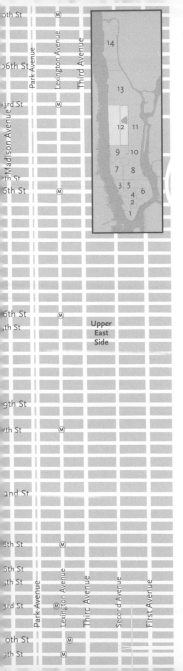

CENTRAL PARK

1. The Ballfield's Cafe
2. Wollman Memorial Rink
3. Central Park Zoo
4. Delacorte Clock
5. Balto
6. Central Park Tour
7. Bethesda Terrace
8. Conservatory Water
9. The Still Hunt
10. The Butterfly Habitat
11. The Ramble
12. Strawberry Fields
13. Marionette Theater
14. Bird-watching in Central Park
15. The Shakespeare Garden
16. Delacorte Theater
17. Belvedere Castle
18. Conservatory Garden
19. Andrew H. Green Bench
20. The Pumpkin Float

UPPER WEST SIDE

21. West Side Y.M.C.A.
22. Lincoln Center
23. Arts for Transit
24. Hotel des Artistes
24. Café des Artistes
25. 2 West 67th Street
26. Central Park Studios
27. Atelier Building
28. 39 West 67th Street
29. Christ & St. Stephen's Church
30. Dakota Apartments
31. Central Savings Bank
32. Steps on Broadway
33. New-York Historical Society
34. Museum of Natural History
35. Balloon Blowup
36. Riverside Park
37. Drip Cafe
38. Barney Greengrass
39. Murder Ink.
40. Pomander Walk
41. Tennis Courts
42. Manhattan Table Tennis
43. Firemen's Memorial
44. Hudson Beach Cafe
45. Nicholas Roerich Museum
46. Riverside Park Above 96th St.
47. Awash

Central Park & Upper West Side

CENTRAL PARK
1876, Frederick Law Olmsted & Calvert Vaux
Central Park South (59th Street) to Central Park North
(110th Street) between Fifth Avenue & Central Park West
Open from dawn to 1am

12.1 ### The Ballfield's Cafe
Mid-park near the 65th Street Transverse, ☎ 212 717-5940
May-October: open daily 8am-8pm

Ⓜ Fifth Avenue-59th Street (N/R/W);
66th Street-Lincoln Center (1/2)

🍽 The Ballfield's Cafe just west of the carousel, south of the
65th Street transverse, has an amazing view of Midtown
Manhattan up close with the ballfields in the foreground.
JEAN PARKER PHIFER
President of the Art Commission of the City of New York

12.2 ### Wollman Memorial Rink
1950, rebuilt early 1980's
Southeast corner of park, enter at Fifth Avenue &
60th Street, ☎ 212 439-6900
Mid-October through the first week of April: Monday,
Tuesday 10am-3pm; Wednesday, Thursday 10am-10pm; Friday,
Saturday 10am-11pm; Sunday 10am-9pm

Ⓜ Fifth Avenue-59th Street(N/R/W)

New York City has several outdoor ice skating rinks,
but skating at the Wollman Rink in Central Park, especially at night, is a transcendent experience. I always think
of the opening sequence of Woody Allen's *Manhattan*—you
can almost hear Gershwin playing as you stare at the illuminated skyline of Central Park South. In the early evening
when the kids go home, you can skate to Sinatra, Ella

Fitzgerald, Fred Astaire, and Duke Ellington. There's a sense of continuity as you imagine the New Yorkers who skated on this spot a hundred years ago, when this part of New York was so far uptown it was considered "the country." They were dressed more formally—long skirts, bonnets, and fur muffs for the women, suits and overcoats for the gentlemen. But the delightful feeling of gliding, the shared silliness, the thrill of being outdoors on a cold night—these things don't change with the times. Go on "Cheap Skate" nights, when the admission fee is discounted and there's usually enough room to fall without taking anyone down with you. Bring your own skates if you can—the hard green plastic rental skates with frayed laces do not inspire gracefulness. Every hour or so the ice is cleared and it's time for a cup of the most delicious hot chocolate in the city. I don't know if it's really tastier than any other, but it seems that way when you are warming your frigid fingers with the heat from the paper cup and watching the Zamboni machine sweep the ice to a glassy smoothness. As the hot liquid travels through you, and the smell of chocolate fills you up, everything seems right with the world.

GINA ROGAK
Director of special events, Solomon R. Guggenheim Museum

12.3 Central Park Zoo

Redesigned 1988, Kevin Roche, John Dinkeloo & Associates
Enter at Fifth Avenue & 64th Street, ☎ 212 439-6500
November-March: daily 10am-4:30pm; April-October:
Monday-Friday 10am-5pm; Saturday, Sunday 10am-5:30pm
Ⓜ Fifth Avenue-59th Street (N/R/W); Lexington-63rd Street (F)

Go to the Central Park Zoo and pay tribute to the seals, then check in with the penguins, and then the polar bears, and your head will be screwed back on properly.

JOHN GUARE
Playwright

Madagascar Giant Day Gecko
Tropic Zone

In this city of egos where everyone's clamoring, "Look at me! Look at me!" there is one exquisite creature who makes a point of invisibility. Its beauty is so shocking that people cry out in surprise when they see it. That is, if they can see it.

It's displayed behind a floodlit window like a priceless piece of jewelry, but finding it amidst the tangle of ferns can take a good 20 minutes. It's not only a master of camouflage, but like the silver mime who works the subway, it rarely moves, clinging to the wall like a wad of chewed gum. Parents tend to spot it first—the electric-green Madagascar giant day gecko that lives in the Tropic Zone of the Central Park Zoo, along with two motionless tomato frogs.

Waiting for this shy and dainty soul to reveal itself takes time. A lot of time. Many don't have the patience and move on to the frolicking penguins and polar bears. But for those who adjust their vision to this miniature stage set, the rewards are exhilarating.

Suddenly, there it is! Glued to the wall beneath a fern! An intensely green lizard with a sprinkling of orange spots on its head and back. It's about a foot long with four hilarious cartoon toes on each foot. Its shiny black eyes are lidless and never flicker. Its only sign of life is a slight pulsing of the stomach. Avert your gaze for a moment, and it's gone. All you see are ferns and the two orange tomato frogs miserably trying to conceal themselves on the leafy green floor.

So there you stand, waiting for just one more glimpse. Now you see it, now you don't—the most ravishing peep show in all of New York City.

TINA HOWE
Playwright

12.5 Balto

1925, Frederick G.R. Roth
Near East Drive at 67th Street
Ⓜ Lexington Avenue-63rd Street (F); 68th Street-Hunter
College (6)

One of the statues in Central Park is a bronze of an
Alaskan sled dog, a husky named Balto. The big dog seems
a little out of place in New York, and his story involves
a largely forgotten event in a faraway place.

January 1925, in the depths of an exceptionally bitter
winter, an epidemic of diphtheria broke out in Nome,
on Alaska's west coast. The supply of antitoxin serum was
soon used up, and with the coast ice-bound and no planes
available, it was decided that the best way to get more
serum was by dogsled. Twenty teams would be used in
a relay that would start from the nearest point reachable
by rail—almost 700 miles from Nome.

The serum was poured into a cylinder wrapped in a
quilt. Each village along the route dispatched its best musher,
teamed with the best dogs, to carry the cylinder through
its territory. Along the way, temperatures dropped to more
than 60 below, wind blew up to 80 miles per hour, and
blizzard after blizzard rendered the crude trail invisible.
One team was almost stranded on an ice floe. Two dogs
froze to death.

The trip took seven days, and when the serum arrived
safely in Nome, the story of "the great race of mercy" was
widely reported. Nome's best-known dogsled racer, a man
named Leonhard Seppala, had carried the serum more
than 90 miles—twice as far as any other musher—and his
daring wilderness exploits made him a hero to newspaper
readers around the country.

In recent years, the success of the Iditarod race, which
retraces much of the original route of the serum run, has
revived the Seppala legend, and many people assume that
Balto was Seppala's lead dog. In fact, Seppala passed

over the black husky when he picked his team, preferring a faster dog named Togo. Balto, left behind, was then chosen by Gunnar Kaasen, the musher who wound up completing the final leg of the journey. Thus Balto, not Togo, was around for the photo op when Kassen handed the serum to Nome's doctor.

So visit Balto (in the winter, it's better that way), being sure to check for the ironic grin on his bronze mouth.

And take your pooch.

SAM POSEY
Racecar driver, artist, and designer

12.6 Central Park Tour

Fifth Avenue at 67th Street

Ⓜ Fifth Avenue-59th Street(N/R/W); 68th Street-Hunter College (6); Lexington Avenue-63rd Street (F)

Throughout Western civilization, public parks have been designed to provide an array of recreational opportunities, and Central Park may be viewed as the pinnacle of this achievement. My favorite walk through this park takes into account the use New Yorkers make of it, in addition to its finest views, its historical highlights, its natural charms, and some of its dramatic twists.

Enter the park from Fifth Avenue at 67th Street, and walk west to the statue of Balto (see p. 327). The statue honors the sled dog that saved Alaska from diphtheria and it has been sat upon by every kid passing by. Proceed westward through the tunnel until you come up onto Literary Walk. Pass Shakespeare and Burns, turn right and head north. This famous walk is lined with a spectacular collection of elm trees and is Frederick Law Olmsted's quintessential Victorian strolling promenade. Cross over 72nd Street, down the magnificent stairs, around Bethesda

Fountain, and then bear slightly left to cross Bow Bridge, one of the two finest of the five original cast-iron bridges remaining in the park. Swans, boats, and lovers abound. Once across the bridge, head into the Ramble (see p. 332). Perhaps one of the greatest stopover points for migratory birds, the Ramble also plays host to meandering streams, Adirondack-style rustic benches, and all sorts of people.

Wend your way due north until you come out at Belvedere Castle with its medieval parapets and breathtaking views of the Great Lawn. Check out the Nature Center and ask the rangers some questions. Look carefully 50 yards to the east of the castle on the north side of the transverse: these secret stairs have taken many of the famous and notable—Paul Simon and a president or two—to and from great events. Stroll down around Turtle Pond and the Great Lawn if you have the time. Turn south now and find your way into and through the Shakespeare Garden (see p. 335) and past the Swedish Cottage (see p. 333). If you want to pop out of the park and visit the American Museum of Natural History (my favorite place in New York City), then do so here at 81st Street. Otherwise, stroll down along the west side of the lake, up into Yoko Ono's Strawberry Fields (see p. 332) and pause at the "Imagine" mosaic. Candles and hippies are always here. Continue down past the Sheep Meadow, where city residents get their tan and youngsters meet, and past the glitter of Tavern on the Green. See the lights, the topiary, and the limos. Your tour is now complete. Exit at Columbus Circle or head back east if you care to dally at the Central Park Zoo (see p. 325), with its resplendent tropical birds, awesome penguin display, and idiosyncratic polar bears.

ALEXANDER R. BRASH
Chief Park Ranger

12.7 Bethesda Terrace
1862, Calvert Vaux, designer; Jacob Wrey Mould, sculptor
Mid-park at 72nd Street
72nd Street (B/C)

The stonework at Bethesda Terrace at 72nd Street merits
a close look. Moving east to west, the hand-carved
sandstone piers and balustrades flanking the stairs both
north and south of the road represent 1) spring, youth,
dawn; 2) summer, adolescence, noon; 3) fall, adulthood,
afternoon; 4) winter, old age, evening.
JEAN PARKER PHIFER
President of the Art Commission of the City of New York

Walk east through the park, past Bethesda Terrace. Look
down the steps toward the lake. On weekend afternoons,
drummers and dancers gather by the fountain, and near
the steps you can often catch the Crowtations, a wonderfully strange group of puppeteers and their dancing
puppets.
MARGOT ADLER
Correspondent, National Public Radio

12.8 Conservatory Water (Model Boat Pond)
North of the Fifth Avenue & 72nd Street entrance
Ⓜ 77th Street (6)

Red-tailed hawks

In late spring and early summer, between May and July,
the best show in town is at the Model Boat Pond. Along
its west shore, facing Fifth Avenue, you'll find people with
serious telescopes on tripods aimed up at the 12th story
of a building facing the park just north of 72nd Street.
What's up there is a massive, sprawling nest of twigs that
tops a long classical arch on the building's facade. The

nest—huge and messy, and under the official protection
of the National Fish and Wildlife Department—is the
home of the red-tailed hawks who have made Central Park
their unlikely home. Any of the telescope owners will let
you have a look, and you can home in on this beautiful
feral family, fierce-eyed, preening, and unbelievably wild.
By June the chicks will be clearly visible in the nest,
stalking stiffly back and forth, peering out across the park
like sentries, waiting for dinner, leading their own unknow-
able lives before you. Suddenly, into your field of vision,
a parent arrives; silent, a rush of reddish feathers, vast
smothering wings beating backwards. The chicks make
a swarming rush forward, there is a voracious flurry of
attention, and dinner is over. The parent moves regally
to the edge of the great nest, swivels its neck, gives a
pitiless stare out into the park, and sails off again, gliding
smoothly out into the upper air. The hawkwatchers cheer.
ROXANA ROBINSON
Writer and biographer

RECOMMENDED READING
Marie Winn, *The Red-Tails in Love: A Wildlife Drama in Central
Park*, Pantheon Books, 1999.

12.9 The Still Hunt

1883, Edward Kemeys
East Drive at 77th Street
Ⓜ 77th Street (6)

Walk down East Drive. On an overhang, find a bronze,
life-size statue of a mountain lion, crouched ready to
pounce. This Central Park reminder of the wilderness
from which Manhattan was carved can have a startling
effect on passers-by who happen to glance up.
KASSY WILSON
Museum professional

12.10 The Butterfly Habitat

Mid-park at 74th Street

Ⓜ 68th Street-Hunter College (6)

To the left of the Boathouse restaurant, near where bicycles are rented, is a fenced-in area with flowering wild plants. This is a butterfly habitat, a garden created specifically to attract the winged creatures. Beyond and to your left, up the pathway and then down, is "the point," a place where you can see Bethesda Fountain from the other side of the lake.

MARGOT ADLER
Correspondent, National Public Radio

12.11 The Ramble

East Drive to West Drive between the 79th Street
Transverse & The Lake

Ⓜ 81st Street-Museum of Natural History (B/C)

Shunned by many due to its reputation as a furtive and dangerous place by night, the Ramble is Frederick Law Olmsted's vision of primeval New York. Park thickets, untrimmed trees, and apparently unintended streams belie the skilled artfulness of this romantic pre-Gotham fantasy. Rustic stonework and a few ruins are the only hint that this place, like everything else in Manhattan, has been willfully shaped by man.

WALTER CHATHAM
Architect

12.12 Strawberry Fields

Near the Central Park West & West 72nd Street entrance

Ⓜ 72nd Street (B/C)

Enter the park at West 72nd Street and find Strawberry Fields, the oasis planted by Yoko Ono in memory of John Lennon. You can be one of the thousands who have stood for a meditative moment by the Italian mosaic circle inscribed with the word "Imagine." Every year on the night of the anniversary of John Lennon's death (December 8, 1980), several hundred people gather here, holding candles and flowers. They sing every Beatles song they can remember until about one o'clock in the morning, when the police insist that they leave. Strawberry Fields has lovely grass to lie on, luxurious plantings of trees and foliage, and a sense of peace that is extraordinary in New York City.

MARGOT ADLER
Correspondent, National Public Radio

12.13 Swedish Cottage Marionette Theater

1876, Manneus Isaeus
Between Delacorte Theater & 79th Street Transverse
Reservations required for performances, ✆ 212 988-9093
July-August: Monday-Friday 10:30am and noon
September: Saturday, Sunday 1pm
October-June: Tuesday-Friday 10:30am and noon;
Saturday 1pm
Ⓜ 81st Street-Museum of Natural History (B/C)

Central Park as a haven from the noise and the intensity of everyday city life, is no secret. However, the park does contain little-known features, one of which is the Swedish Cottage Marionette Theater. Just south of the Delacorte Theater, at the base of the Shakespeare Garden, one discovers a 19th-century Swedish cottage designed originally as a one-room schoolhouse exhibit by prominent Swedish architect Manneus Isaeus for the 1876 Centennial Exposition at Philadelphia. Frederick Law Olmsted was so taken with it that he paid 1,500 dollars to have it shipped and rebuilt in 1877 in the new park he co-designed in New York.

Subsequently utilized as public restrooms, a nature study, and civil-defense headquarters during World War II, in 1947 it became the headquarters and workshop of the Central Park Marionette Theater, which produced touring shows. Budget cuts eradicated funding for touring, and the interior was redesigned in 1973 to include a permanent theater.

Decades of neglect and disrepair threatened the

building with demolition by the early 1990's. The long
and distinguished history of delightful productions of
children's classics, in conjunction with the City Parks
Foundation, proved its saving grace. A coalition of
private and public interests raised funds for a $1.5 million
renovation in 1997. Besides a beautiful and historically
faithful restoration of the exterior details, a new
proscenium stage and modern technical facilities now
enable the talented staff and visiting artists to produce
what is arguably the finest marionette theater for children
in the United States.

In May 1998, the Swedish Cottage Marionette Theater
reopened to the public with a glorious production of
Gulliver's Travels, followed by equally magnificent
presentations of *Jack and the Beanstalk* and *Sleeping
Beauty*. At a ticket price of 5 dollars, it's one of the true
bargains and secret treasures of New York.
KEVIN JOSEPH ROACH
Set designer

12.14 Bird-watching in Central Park

West 81st Street and Central Park West
For information about bird-watching: New York City
Audubon Society, ☎ 212 691-7483; Linnaean Society,
☎ 212 252-2668; Parks Department, ☎ 866 NYC-PARK;
Starr Saphir, ☎ 212 304-3808
Ⓜ 81st Street-Museum of Natural History (B/C)

Birding is one of Central Park's best secrets. Indeed, it's
considered one of the 15 most extraordinary birding sites
in the United States during spring and fall migrations.
That's because birds—more than 270 species—come to the
park as they cross the Atlantic flyway. Most New Yorkers
believe the park belongs only to people, pigeons, rats, and
squirrels, but it turns out that suburbs do not provide

migrating birds with enough cover from predatory hawks, so Central Park, with its seed-bearing trees and forested areas, has become a haven for hundreds of thousands of birds to rest and feed during their long migratory flights.

A host of organizations, including the Audubon Society, the Linnaean Society, and the Parks Department, lead bird walks, and this is the best way to get a feel for birding in the park, especially since the best birding site, the Ramble, is a maze of complex paths in which it is easy to get lost. My favorite guide is Starr Saphir, who has been doing these walks for years, and even the total amateur, armed with a pair of binoculars, will see miraculous things in a couple of hours. I've lived near the park for 52 years, yet before I met Saphir, I had never seen a scarlet tanager, or a green heron, or 20 species of warblers.

The birding log, a diary in which expert birders record what they've seen in the park that day, can be found at the Boathouse restaurant (where you can also get your morning coffee). Other animals and flowers are often included as well, and if you read back through the year's entries, you'll be amazed at the exuberant life of the park.

MARGOT ADLER
Correspondent, National Public Radio

12.15 The Shakespeare Garden

c. 1915
79th Street Transverse near Belvedere Castle
Ⓜ 81st Street-Museum of Natural History (B/C)

Each flower of this literary maze is mentioned in one of Shakespeare's poems or plays. The medley of herbs and flowers brings the Bard's works into a very beautiful and amazing tangle of winding green and varicolored swirls. This small garden offers lovely benches to sit amidst the poetry of posies and read Shakespeare's sonnets.

KAREN MOODY TOMPKINS
Artist

12.16 Delacorte Theater
1962, Eldon Elder
Mid-park, enter at Central Park West & 81st Street or Fifth
Avenue & 79th Street, ☎ 212 539-8750; www.publictheater.org
Ⓜ 81st Street-Museum of Natural History (B/C); 77th Street (6)

In 1962, after a contentious dispute with Robert Moses—
the undisputed czar of public construction in New York
City for about 30 years—the enterprising theatrical
producer Joseph Papp obtained permission to perform
Shakespeare plays in the middle of Central Park. He set up
a group of bleachers and established free "Shakespeare in
the Park," which soon became a desirable summer attraction in New York (June through August). The unbeatable
Mr. Papp secured the promise of a check from George
Delacorte for the construction of a real amphitheater
to be built in lieu of the bleacher arrangement.

Unfortunately, a new mayor, less prone to cultural
fantasies than his predecessor, turned down the proposal
for a structure that would have remained through the ages,
though the design had already been approved by his own
commissioner of parks. Joe Papp's persistence eventually
forced the mayor to permit the creation of a 2,000-seat
amphitheatre, provided its wood appearance and main
platform construction marked it as a "temporary"
structure. The amphitheater has now stood for 24 years,
and though it requires yearly repairs, it is much enjoyed
by the community.

If one is willing to queue for them, free tickets are
available only on the day of performance at either the
Delacorte Theater or the Public Theater (425 Lafayette
Street). Senior citizens have a less crowded queue of their
own in front of the Delacorte box office.

GIORGIO CAVAGLIERI
Architect

RECOMMENDED READING
Helen Epstein, *Joe Papp: An American Life*, Da Capo Press, 1996.

North End of Central Park
Above the 96th Street Transverse

Most people vaunt the pleasures of Central Park, but few have ventured to its northern end. Once feared as a haven of crime, now the only thrills that await visitors (during the daytime) are the *mise en scène* of raw rock, tight crevices, rushing water, and ruins of a fort that served in the War of 1812. Olmsted's attempts to make a veritable portrait of the natural world, running the gamut from the pastoral to the sublime, can only be fully savored by those who push into the undercrofts of the bridges and passages he created in the "wild" northern end above 100th Street. Calm your nerves afterwards in the refinements of the Conservatory Garden.

BARRY BERGDOLL
Architectural historian and professor, Columbia University

12.18 Conservatory Garden
1936, Gilmore D. Clarke, Thomas D. Price & M. Betty Sprout;
1983, redesigned by Lynden B. Miller
Enter at Fifth Avenue between 104th & 105th Streets
☎ 212 360-2766
Open daily 8am-dusk
Ⓜ 103rd Street (6)

Central Park offers many pleasures, but none so unexpectedly delightful as the Conservatory Garden. Perhaps because most visitors frequent the southern end of the park, it comes as a complete surprise to walk through the ornate iron gate that once guarded Cornelius Vanderbilt's mansion on Fifth Avenue and 58th Street, and find yourself in this elegant time warp. There are three gardens, each in a different style. The south garden (my favorite) is done in informal English, themed to Frances Hodgson Burnett's children's classic *The Secret Garden*. Narrow slate paths bordered by exquisite plantings draw you to the center, where a tree-shaded lily pond, watched over by a bronze pair of children, attracts many birds.

The center garden is classic Italian, with its long manicured lawn leading to a dramatic, unadorned fountain
spouting its single, geyser-like spray. In the background, a
terrace of yew and spiraea lead upward to an arbor covered
in Chinese wisteria, most beautiful in spring when it is
overrun by purple blossoms.

The North Garden, with its shallow pool featuring a
trio of dancing nymphs in its center, is French. Enter from
one of its four arbors, covered with white-and-pink-tinted
roses. This garden offers dazzling displays of tulips in
spring and chrysanthemums in the fall. Come on a beautiful
day and be prepared to stay a while.
LORRAINE B. DIEHL
Writer

I treasure the formal, symmetrical walks of the
Conservatory Garden at 105th Street in Central Park.
The fountains and their quiet, enclosed surroundings are
a sheer joy, especially the fountain in the North Garden,
where nymphs combine innocence and hedonism in a
perfect, idiosyncratic picture of happy youth in motion.
MARIA ARRILLAGA
Writer and professor

Amidst the magnitude of the city, you can sit in relative
quiet, hearing only the drips of water from the garden's
nymph fountain. For its breadth of flora and generous and
strategically placed benches, the garden still feels like an
undiscovered treasure. It is the perfect afternoon spot
and a great gateway to the newly restored Harlem Meer
(see p. 340).
CLARE BELL
Director of exhibitions, PaceWildenstein

Andrew Haswell Green

`12.19` **Andrew H. Green Bench**
1929, John H. Van Pelt & Margaret Van Pelt
Near East Drive at 105th Street
Ⓜ 103rd Street (6)

`2.14` **"The Consolidation of Greater New York"**
1904, Albert Weinert
In Surrogate's Court/Hall of Records (see p. 47)

Andrew Haswell Green is a personal—and utterly forgotten—hero of mine. He's sometimes described as the Robert Moses of the 19th century, yet hardly anyone knows his name. He supervised the creation of Central Park, rescued the city from bankruptcy after the Boss Tweed scandals, and helped create the Metropolitan Museum of Art, the Bronx Zoo, the Museum of Natural History, Riverside Park, and the New York Public Library. But most importantly, he was the man who championed the 1898 consolidation of the five boroughs into the New York City that exists today. That triumph earned him the title "The Father of Greater New York." After nearly five decades of selfless public service, the 83-year-old Green was shot dead on the front steps of his home in a case of mistaken identity.

All that exists in the city to honor his memory is a forlorn stone bench in Central Park that's not even listed on most park maps. The original five trees that surrounded the bench—each one representing a borough—succumbed to Dutch elm disease decades ago, so in 1998 the Parks Department rededicated the bench and planted new saplings.

Green's greatest accomplishment, the consolidation, is almost as forgotten as he is. But just inside the entranceway of the Surrogate's Court building you'll find a monument that marks the event, a sculpture titled *The Consolidation of Greater New York*. Allegorical ▶

▶

Ms. Brooklyn is shown reaching out to allegorical Ms.
New York, a union that, I can assure you, was easier to
render in marble than in real life.
MICHAEL MISCIONE
Writer

12.20 **The Pumpkin Float at Harlem Meer**
Northeast corner of park
Ⓜ Central Park North-110th Street (2/3)

On most days at the Harlem Meer you can find children
fishing with long poles and bread dough. But if you come
on a Sunday shortly before Halloween, you can watch as
hundreds of children bring carved pumpkins with candles
inside and float them on wooden rafts on the Meer—a
magical site as darkness falls.
MARGOT ADLER
Correspondent, National Public Radio

UPPER WEST SIDE

12.21 **West Side Y.M.C.A.**
1930, Dwight James Baum
5 West 63rd Street between Central Park West & Broadway
☎ 212 875-4100
Open daily
Ⓜ 66th Street-Lincoln Center (1/2)

Felicitously sited between Central Park and Lincoln Center
is the largest freestanding Y.M.C.A. in the United States.
Decorative Tuscan towers top the 14-story building.
Opened in 1929, this Mozarabic-style Y was designed by
Dwight James Baum, architect of many buildings in
Riverdale. But this Y.M.C.A. contains hidden treasure in
its interior—hand-painted decorative tiles, a gift from the
Spanish government. They make one swimming pool an

azure fantasy—Neptune stands guard in a decorative panel—and adorn other rooms as well. The second pool, called the Pompeiian Pool, features marine-blue and gold Italian tilework, and balconies with stained-glass windows. This fanciful Y.M.C.A. building, which also houses a ship's cabin and a log cabin, is undergoing extensive renovation and boasts a new 11-story annex behind a preserved historic facade in its landmarked district.

PAMELA BAYLESS
Writer and communications consultant

12.22 Lincoln Center for the Performing Arts
West 62nd to West 66th Street between Columbus & Amsterdam Avenues

Ⓜ 66th Street-Lincoln Center (1/2)

Sit on the rim of the plaza fountain and feast your eyes and mind on the monumental cluster of buildings devoted to the performing arts. Next, move to the North Plaza and contemplate the glorious Henry Moore in a reflecting pool.

GEORGE WEISSMAN
Chairman emeritus, Lincoln Center for the Performing Arts

North Plaza
1965, Dan Kiley

One of the most restful places in the Upper West Side is the little park, designed by the legendary landscape architect Dan Kiley, in front of the Vivian Beaumont Theater at Lincoln Center. Shade trees and a large reflecting pool set off two Henry Moore sculptures, and the three huge glass walls that appear to support Eero Saarinen's simple and graceful theater building shimmer with the light off the pool. From early morning until the crowds pour out from the various Lincoln Center attractions, it's a fine place to bring a snack or just sit and collect your thoughts.

GREGORY MOSHER
Director and producer

12.23 **Arts for Transit: *Artemis, Acrobats,***
Divas, and Dancers
1998, Nancy Spero
Ⓜ 66th Street-Lincoln Center (1/2)

My current favorite piece of subway art is Nancy Spero's
Artemis, Acrobats, Divas, and Dancers, 22 multicolored
glass mosaic panels on either side of the train tracks at
Lincoln Center. All the figures are women—diving,
dancing, running, playing musical instruments, performing
acrobatic feats, rollerskating. They are culled from
classical and contemporary sources and are the perfect
introduction to the performing arts center directly above.
On the downtown platform, the mythological figure Diva
repeats, sometimes large, sometimes smaller, but always
sheathed in royal golds and crimsons and attended by
other, more delicate goddesses and warriors. The mosaicist,
Peter Colombo, who worked on this project for three
years, possibly has cut the finest, most detailed smalti
since ancient times. His mixes of tiny colored glass tesserae
sparkle brilliantly among the surrounding stretches of
larger, more solidly colored glazed ceramic mosaic tiles.
Thin bands of Naples yellow, Etruscan red, and cobalt blue
cleverly flow from section to section, uniting them while
elucidating individual passages.
JOYCE KOZLOFF
Artist

West 67th Street Studios

Ⓜ 66th Street-Lincoln Center (1/2)

12.24 **Hotel des Artistes**

1918, George Mort Pollard
1 West 67th Street between Columbus Avenue
& Central Park West
Not open to the public

12.24 **Café des Artistes**

(see p. 344)

12.25 **2 West 67th Street**

1919, Rich & Mathesius
2 West 67th Street between Columbus Avenue
& Central Park West

12.26 **Central Park Studios**

1905, B.H. Simonson and Pollard & Steinam
15 West 67th Street between Columbus Avenue
& Central Park West

12.27 **Atelier Building**

1905, B.H. Simonson and Pollard & Steinam
33 West 67th Street between Columbus Avenue
& Central Park West

12.28 **39 West 67th Street**

1907, Pollard & Steinam
39-41 West 67th Street between Columbus Avenue
& Central Park West

West 67th Street, just off Central Park West, harbors one
of the most remarkable urban environments in Manhattan.
The high facades lining the narrow street primarily belong
to apartment buildings, many created as artists' studios.
George Mort Pollard designed the finest of them,
particularly the neo-Gothic Hotel des Artistes (Number 1).
The windows of its facade, like Number 2 across the   ▶

▶

street, reveal the double-height spaces inside intended for painters. The Hotel des Artistes was built by a syndicate of artists as a studio and apartment building; the artists rented half the building to nonartists and realized enough of a profit that there was a rush to erect similar buildings. Among them were: the Central Park Studios (Number 15); the Atelier Building (Number 33), whose lobby features some of the finest period Gothic detailing; and 39-41 West 67th, which has a stack of bay windows on the street facade made of sheet metal, rather than masonry. On the first floor of Number 1 is one of New York's most

🍴 venerable restaurants, the Café des Artistes. Howard Chandler Christy, a tenant of the hotel in its early days who specialized in pin-ups, decorated the walls with vividly spirited murals. Among the tenants of the lavish spaces above were Isadora Duncan, Norman Rockwell, Alexander Woolcott, Noël Coward, Fannie Hurst, and John V. Lindsay.

Fortunately, recent additions to the street, including two studios for ABC Television (149 Columbus Avenue) designed by Kohn Pederson Fox in 1978, respect the scale of their neighbors and maintain the tight environment.

PETER J. HOLLIDAY
Historian of classical art and archaeology

12.24 Café des Artistes

1979, redecorated by Judith Stockman & Associates
1 West 67th Street between Columbus Avenue
& Central Park West, 📞 212 877-3500
Monday-Friday for lunch and dinner; Saturday, Sunday
for brunch and dinner
Ⓜ 66th Street-Lincoln Center (1/2)

"To ourselves, to each other, and to the happiness of us all!"
—Noël Coward

🍴 George and Jenifer Lang serve delicious classic fare at this romantic Old World beauty. Thirty-six seductive, naughty

nude nymphs frolic in naturalistic murals by Howard
Chandler Christy (a student of William Merrit Chase) and
envelop the dining rooms. Among the many writers, artists,
musicians, actors, and celebrities frequenting the cafe since
the early 1900's, regulars have included the likes of Al
Jolson, Beverly Sills, Zasu Pitts, Noël Coward, Norman
Rockwell, Isadora Duncan, Rudolf Valentino, Paul
Newman, Rudolf Nureyev, and Mayor Fiorello La Guardia.
In dead of winter following the opera, I prefer a cozy
banquette in the quiet wood-paneled bar hidden in the
back for a late night pot-au-feu.

FREDERIC SCHWARTZ
Architect

12.30 Dakota Apartments

1884, Henry J. Hardenbergh
1 West 72nd Street at Central Park West
Not open to the public
Ⓜ 72nd Street (B/C)

When I was kid trying to escape the monotony of Flatbush,
I'd take the D train across the bridge each Saturday to
the place I really belonged: Manhattan. Despite all the
mysteries and glories I discovered, I remember the rush
I got walking up Central Park West and coming upon
that behemoth of a building for the first time, that German
Gothic/French Renaissance/English Victorian cacophony
called the Dakota. Of course, I didn't know the architectural styles when I was 15. I only knew this wasn't Brooklyn.
This wasn't Flatbush. This was glamour. This was sophisti-
cation. This was Manhattan. Although half-shutters mask
the first-floor windows, you can still peer into an apartment
or two, now as then; I was dazzled by the enormous rooms,
and the spectacular architectural details. I remember
wondering, "Who lives here? What kind of people can
be surrounded by this luxury?"

Of course, this was before December 8, 1980, when

John Lennon was killed outside the building. Now, tourists come by the score to pay their respects or gawk. But when I first discovered the building, its pop-culture claim to fame was that it was where *Rosemary's Baby* was filmed.

The Dakota was designed by Henry Hardenbergh, who also designed the Plaza Hotel. Legend has it that it was called the Dakota because it was so distant from the then-urban hub. About 10 years ago the grime of New York City was sandblasted away and now, instead of the black sooty color I remember, it's a camel-hair tan. It seemed more gothic, more foreboding with the dirt, but I still can look at it for hours in amazement: the moldings, the terra-cotta panels, the corner pavilions, and the storybook gables and roofing.

Don't try to penetrate its courtyard. The ever-present guard knows exactly who should be there and who shouldn't. The apartments are for Yoko, Betty, Rex and their friends. But we mortals can still marvel at the magnificence. I've lived on the Upper West Side for more than 25 years, but every time I walk down 72nd Street, I become the 15-year-old from Brooklyn, gazing up in amazement at my favorite building in New York.

GLEN ROVEN
Composer

12.32 Steps on Broadway

2121 Broadway at West 74th Street, ✆ 212 874-2410
Open daily 9am-9pm
Ⓜ 72nd Street (1/2/3)

While most New Yorkers and visitors find the ballet at Lincoln Center the finest in spectator sports, I prefer to participate in this incredible art form. On any given day there are numerous marvelous classes to take at Steps, a dance studio fortuitously located upstairs from Fairway Market at 74th Street and Broadway. There is no more heavenly spot in New York; upstairs the sounds of *Don Q* or *Swan Lake* or *La Bayadère* treat your ears, and downstairs there is the heady symphonic perfume of basil and figs and olives. At Steps, anyone who is qualified and has training may pay for a ticket and take a class.

Classes are taught by seasoned ballet masters from all parts of the globe, and in many classes, the positions, steps, and instructions are given in French, the universal language of ballet. On any given day, the higher-level classes might include visiting professionals and hopefuls. The reward after an hour and a half of focused class is the last exercise, when the dancers leap across the floor to a selection of the pianist's choice. Afterwards, everyone runs down the stairs to Fairway to pick up dinner before going home or to the ballet or back out into the streets of the city.

JANE TUCKER VASILIOU
Scholar

12.33 New-York Historical Society

1908, York & Sawyer; 1938, addition of north and south wings by Walker & Gillette; 1990's, restoration by Beyer Blinder Belle
2 West 77th Street at Central Park West, ☎ 212 873-3400
Exhibit open Tuesday-Sunday 10am-5pm; library open
Tuesday-Saturday 10am-5pm; closed Monday
Ⓜ 81st Street-Museum of Natural History (B/C); 79th Street (1/2)

Henry Luce III Center for the Study of American Culture

2000, Beyer Blinder Belle
Fourth floor
Open Tuesday-Sunday 10am-5pm

This is an institution that has been overlooked and eclipsed by other New York institutions such as the Museum of the City of New York and the Met. It has recently been brought back to new life by former New York City Parks Commissioner Betsy Gotbaum. She has gone through their many collections of artworks related to old New York families and furnishings—including paintings, sculpture,

furniture, household tools, and decorative objects, much
of it stored and unseen for many years but now on display
in the wonderful new Henry Luce III Center for the Study
of American Culture—and also found the funding so that
this great institution could be ready for the 21st century.
MARIO BUATTA
Interior designer

Although many residents and visitors to New York City
may be familiar with the New-York Historical Society and
its various exhibitions, few seem to know about the Luce
Center on the building's fourth floor. It's like the city's
attic, with an amazing collection of Americana, including
a piece of George Washington's coffin, a barrel used for the
opening ceremonies of the Erie Canal in 1825, Duncan
Phyfe's tool chest, a collection of 132 Tiffany lamps, and
thousands of other objects and artworks. While much of
the material has little more than an accession number,
there are wall displays with more information and computer stations set up throughout the gallery where visitors
can search through a database of the museum's collection
for greater detail. It is a pleasure just to walk around and
look at the things that catch your eye and, best of all, you
can pick up an engaging audio guide that is offered for
free. Anyone interested in American history will find this
a treasure trove.
THORIN TRITTER
Historian

Reading Room
Second floor

The Reading Room of the New-York Historical Society is
the portal to one of the great institutional repositories for
the city's secrets. The library's marvelous collections of
broadsides, newspapers, sheet music, and documentation
about the history of New York City hotels have been
assembled over the course of nearly 200 years, and capture
the textures of everyday existence now hidden under the

strata of New York's various past lives. These, too, are represented and preserved in the society's stacks and drawers: the turbulent geological prehistory, the Dutch, English, and Revolutionary periods, the great fires, the slave trade and brutal repression of African-American revolts, mercantile expansion and the Civil War, the influx of immigrants and the consolidation of Greater New York at the end of the 19th century, and the whole history of the 20th. Little known to the general public—to which it is open—or even to those who tour the galleries on the first and second floors, or the Henry Luce III Center on the fourth, the library is a mecca, and a home away from home for scholars who return day after day to mine its archives of books, letters, manuscripts, maps, prints, drawings, and photographs.

BARNET SCHECTER
Writer

RECOMMENDED READING
Edwin G. Burrows and Mike Wallace, *Gotham: A History of New York City to 1898*, Oxford University Press, 1998.
Elizabeth Blackmar and Roy Rosenzweig, *The Park and the People: A History of Central Park*, Cornell University Press, 1998.

New York's Royal Governor

12.33 **New-York Historical Society**
(see p. 347)

1.3 **Former Governors House**
1708
Governors Island
Not open to the public

1.11 **Trinity Church**
1846, Richard Upjohn
Broadway at Wall Street, ☎ 212 602-0800
Ⓜ Wall Street (1/2/4/5); Rector Street (N/R);
Broad Street (J/M/Z)

►

▶

Edward Hyde, Lord Cornbury, first cousin to England's Queen Anne, whom he "mightily resembled," was New York's royal governor from 1702-1708. Although the occasional historian will dismiss this as vile anti-Royalist gossip, he was also fond of showing up—at work and at play—in women's clothing. Reputedly, after nights of drinking, he would stumble onto the wooden ramparts of the colony's fort and accost soldiers, who mistook him for a tipsy wench. He would give them a tug on the ear (apparently his favorite body part) and rush off shrieking. Among Cornbury's many achievements during his stay here was the introduction of horseracing to America. Here, for your amusement and instruction, are city landmarks trodden, in an elegant pair of pink slippers, by His Lordship.

The New-York Historical Society owns a portrait, reputedly of Cornbury, wearing a low-necked blue silk dress with a hoopskirt and fitted bodice. The canvas is in the style of itinerant painters of the day, who would bring "blanks"—ready-made portraits lacking only the head— to the homes of prospective customers.

Cornbury's arms and hands—swanlike and ivory—are an ill match to his face with its heavy jowls, protruding lower lip, and self-satisfied expression. The society also owns an agonized letter, on parchment, that Cornbury wrote to his father while still in England, begging him to liquidate his debts.

Governors Island, in New York Harbor, contains Lord Cornbury's second great achievement, after horseracing. He persuaded the colonial legislature to grant him the huge sum of 1,500 English pounds to fortify the harbor against "French privateers." Two years went by without the appearance of the proposed battlements. People did notice, however, that much of the primeval timber on the northeast end of Nutten's Island had been felled, and a grand mansion of imported brick—a fabulously expensive material in 17th-century America—was going up. From its description in the annals of the New York legislature, one expects something the size of the New York Public Library's 42nd Street branch, but to our standards, the house is disappointingly small, and looks to have been resurfaced by Garden State brickface.

City Hall Park was the site of Debtor's Prison, an unheated plank structure in back of the tavern that then served as City Hall. Cornbury found his way into this accommodation in 1708 when, upon the death of Queen Anne, the colonial legislature and an army of other creditors descended upon him. He did not emerge until 1709 when his father's death simultaneously made him the Third Earl of Clarendon and economically solvent.

Trinity Church, on lower Broadway facing Wall Street, received its land (and the contiguous parcels on which many of the houses of commerce now rest) as a royal grant from Cornbury. Burned by the British during the Revolutionary War, it, too, has been rebuilt. Cornbury's wife, a wealthy Irish heiress named Katharine O'Brian (to whose funeral Lord Cornbury is reputed to have worn a dress), is still buried there, apparently forgotten.

KATHRYN NOCERINO
Poet and fiction writer

12.34 American Museum of Natural History

Central Park West at West 79th Street, ☎ 212 769-5100
Open daily 10am-5:45pm
Ⓜ 81st Street-Museum of Natural History (B/C);
79th Street (1/2)

Holden Caulfield's Tour of the Museum of Natural History

Ask any child in New York City. Whether it's the girl with the skates in J.D. Salinger's 1945 novel *The Catcher in the Rye* or a contemporary kid whizzing by on Rollerblades, the answer will be the same: "the museum" means the American Museum of Natural History. Tracing the history of life and matter from the very beginning of time, the museum also contains the personal history of countless children, some of whose earliest memories have been formed in its shadowy halls.

One such child was Holden Caulfield himself. In Miss Aigletinger's fourth grade, he used to visit the museum "damn near every Saturday." "I knew that whole museum routine like a book," he tells us, recollecting with great nostalgia.

A teacher myself, I imitate Miss Aigletinger. Every year, when my seventh graders read *The Catcher in the Rye*, I take them to the Museum of Natural History to retrace Holden's path. We steer clear of the newer exhibits—the Hall of Biodiversity, the glassy new Rose Center—and explore the older, dustier recesses of the museum that seem never to change. As if on a treasure hunt, the kids try to find the same Indians, the same dioramas, the same glass cases that Holden describes in such vivid detail. Take this tour with us, guided by Holden's voice, and see how you score on the quiz that follows.

What to bring:

- J.D. Salinger, *The Catcher in the Rye*. (Remember, this is a literary pilgrimage and the book is our map.)
- A pen or pencil
- A handful of marbles
- Candy or gum for optional smuggling into the Imax theater. Just don't get caught.

Start at the main entrance on Central Park West, where the building sprawls like a fortress across from the trees. Passing the triumphal statue of Theodore Roosevelt, go up the stairs and into the rotunda, where the lofty ceiling echoes with the shouts and shrieks of school groups, tourists, and disgruntled babies. Read the four inscriptions on the walls.

Go down the stairs to the first floor, make a left and walk through the museum shop to the Imax theater. Built in 1995, it is not the same auditorium that Holden remembers, but with its huge screen, squeaky chairs, and enveloping darkness, it still feels like you are in "the only nice, dry, cosy place in the world." If you like, you can chew on some squashed gumdrops you've kept hidden in your pocket.

Proceed to the Hall of Northwest Coast Indians that Holden remembers as "a long, long room, and you were only supposed to whisper." No such rule is instituted today, but it doesn't need to be. Full of monstrous, huge-eyed totem poles, cruel spears, life-size dioramas of bear dances and shamans, the room is so vast with mystery and shadow that speaking aloud feels disrespectful. If you have dramatic flair, however, drop your handful of marbles on the stone-and-mosaic floor so that they make "a helluva racket."

Look carefully at the first display case on your left. Various members of the Kwakiutl tribe are performing domestic tasks, and near the corner is the source of one of Holden's earliest erotic memories. There was "a squaw weaving a blanket," he confides, who was "sort of bending over, and you could see her bosom and all. We all used to sneak a good look at it.... " She is, in actuality, not weaving a blanket, but her bosom is indeed showing if you sneak a good look at it.

Exit the Northwest Coast Indians and you'll be confronted by the gigantic Haida Indian canoe. Holden is right when he says it's "about as long as three goddam Cadillacs in a row, with about twenty Indians in it.... " Circle the canoe a couple of times to take in its size—the entire boat was carved out of a single red cedar—and to appreciate all the poses, masks, and weapons of the chief, oarsmen, and attending medicine men. At the center of the prow, find the "witch doctor," or shaman, in the wolf-headed mask; he is Holden's favorite.

Unfortunately, some of the exhibits have been removed since Salinger's time. The lone Eskimo that Holden describes fishing so intently at his ice hole no longer exists, nor do some of the dioramas with the birds flying south.

But you can still find a few, painted in illusionistic perspective, as well as deer "with their pretty antlers and their pretty, skinny legs..." Spend some time in the great mammal exhibits on the first and second floors (just retrace your steps back to the staircase) and wander through the forests and veldts with their flora and fauna captured in place and time. "You could go there a hundred thousand times, and...Nobody'd be different. The only thing that would be different would be *you*."

Quiz:

1. What are the titles of each of Teddy Roosevelt's inscriptions?
2. In which inscription does Roosevelt mention "game boys"?
3. In Miss Aigletinger's class, you were supposed to hold hands with your partner. What was the name of Holden's partner and why didn't he like holding hands with her?
4. What does Holden remember about candy and gum in the auditorium?
5. What was the Kwakiutl Indian really doing?
6. Holden calls the Haida Indian canoe a "war canoe," but the craft is actually built for a ceremonial feast. What is the feast called?
7. How many Indians are in the canoe exactly?
8. How many fish has the Eskimo caught?
9. What happens when you look upside down at the birds flying south?
10. After speaking to the little girl, what part of the museum does Holden visit?

Answer Key:

1. Youth, Manhood, Nature, and the State	5 points
2. Youth	5 points
3. Gertrude Levine. Her hands were sweaty or sticky.	10 points
4. They made the auditorium smell nice, like it was raining outside.	10 points
5. She is shaving cedar bark for a paddle.	10 points

6. A potlach	10 points
7. Seventeen	10 points
8. Two	10 points
9. They look like they're in an even bigger hurry to fly south.	10 points
10. Trick question. He changes his mind and decides not to go in.	20 points

Scoring Guide:

0-35   You are a worse student than Holden. Reread the book at once!

40-65   Mediocre at best. Go hang out with Ackley, or even worse, Stradlater.

70-85   Not bad. Take a break and listen to "Little Shirley Beans."

90-100 You are an expert! Treat yourself to Holden Caulfield's tour of the "toons" at the Metropolitan Museum of Art.

JANE AVRICH
Writer and teacher

RECOMMENDED READING
J.D. Salinger, *The Catcher in the Rye*, Little, Brown & Co., 1991.

12.35 Thanksgiving Parade Balloon Blowup

West 81st Street & Central Park West

Ⓜ 81st Street-Museum of Natural History (B/C)

On the eve of Thanksgiving, after dark, head for West 81st Street and Central Park West. You'll find the street strewn with your favorite characters, who will be billowing overhead the next morning. It's much more fun than the parade itself.

ERIC STOLTZ
Actor

12.36 Riverside Park

1873, original design by Frederick Law Olmsted
Riverside Drive to the Hudson River between West 72nd
& West 153rd Streets
Open from dawn to dusk

It is little recognized among tourists that Riverside Park is
the gateway to one of the most spectacular views in New
York City. Enter the park at 90th Street. Proceed down the
hill, past the playground with the hippo. Straight ahead,
down a seemingly neglected set of steps, through the tunnel
(the traffic from the West Side Highway exit is on your
right), and there you have an incredible Hudson riverside
view. On your right stands the George Washington Bridge
and on your left is downtown Manhattan, accessible now
via a bicycle path that runs along the Hudson River. Before
you stretches the river, and past that, New Jersey.
NADINE ORENSTEIN
Associate curator, The Metropolitan Museum of Art

A good place to enter is at 72nd Street, which forms the
southern end of the park. Standing sentry here is a statue
of Eleanor Roosevelt, a patron saint of the liberal Upper
West Side. Walk west through the arch that leads under
the West Side Highway and you'll find yourself facing the
majestic Hudson River. The walk along the river is one of
the most bracing in the city, and the view north toward
the George Washington Bridge is stunning. A short stroll
will bring you to the 79th Street Boat Basin, home to an
eccentric community of houseboats. During summer
months, you can watch the sun set over a beer and burger
at the Boat Basin Cafe (seasonal, ☎ 212 496-5542), though
be warned that in the evening the place becomes a singles
zoo. Walking farther north, you'll find a path leading back
under the highway and into the park proper, where joggers, dog walkers, parents with strollers, and other Upper
West Side types abound.
MICHAEL MASSING
Writer

12.37 Drip Cafe

489 Amsterdam Avenue between West 83rd & West 84th
Streets, ☎ 212 875-1032
Sunday-Thursday 8am-1am; Friday, Saturday 9am-2am

Ⓜ 86th Street (1/2); 81st Street-Museum of Natural History
(B/C)

🍴 Have a seat. Look over the selection. And order up a
Milky Way latte with a nice Jewish doctor from SoHo
on the side. You see, Drip Cafe, an Upper West Side coffee
and alcohol bar, runs an in-house matchmaking service.
Profiles of available singles fill the many binders that clutter
up the perky, lounge-cum-rumpus-room decor. The binders
come in categories: Men-for-Women, Women-for-Men and,
yes, Men-for-Men, and Women-for-Women.

Munch and sip; browse and flip. If someone strikes your
fancy, tell the counterperson. For three bucks they'll call
the object of your desire and try to arrange a future date
for you—at Drip, of course. For 20 bucks you can fill
out a profile of yourself to go in one of the binders. Even
if you never meet Mr. or Ms. Right, it's still lots of
wholesome, amusing, flirty fun and certainly more titillat-
ing than any Starbucks.

MICHAEL MISCIONE
Writer

12.38 Barney Greengrass "The Sturgeon King"

541 Amsterdam Avenue between West 86th & West 87th
Streets, ☎ 212 724-4707
Tuesday-Sunday for breakfast and lunch (take-out until 6pm);
closed Monday

Ⓜ 86th Street (C/1/2)

🍴 An Upper West Side landmark, Barney Greengrass looks
much as it did when it moved here from Harlem in 1929,
and the Greengrass family still runs it. Here you can get
oversized platters of bagels, cream cheese, lox, and whitefish; the specialty is eggs scrambled with nova and onions.

At weekend brunch, the place is packed, so be prepared to wait, but it's worth it for a taste (literally) of the old Jewish Upper West Side. (The giant apartment building across the street, the Belnord, was once home to Isaac Bashevis Singer, the Yiddish writer.)

MICHAEL MASSING
Writer

A genuine New York fixture—three generations, 90-plus years in business, more than 70 in the same location—Barney Greengrass is the place to experience one of New York's ur-cuisines: the salty-sweet-smooth salmon, sturgeon, and whitefish that are the product of the long Jewish love affair with smoked fish. Who eats at Barney's? Mavens, old-timers, Upper West Side families, returnees from the huge New York diaspora, Philip Roth characters (see *Operation Shylock*), Philip Roth himself, and now, you. A good—and traditional—place to start is the scrambled eggs with lox and onions, but for my money, true perfection lies in the lox and kippered salmon with onion, tomato, and scallion cream cheese. I recommend having it on a toasted everything bagel, but no matter what bagel you choose, you'll be in smoked-fish heaven.

MARTHA SCHULMAN
Writer and teacher

12.39 Murder Ink.

2486 Broadway between West 92nd & West 93rd Streets
☎ 212 362-8905
Monday-Saturday 10am-10pm; Sunday 11am-7pm
Ⓜ 96th Street (1/2/3)

🎁 The next rainy evening that you find yourself stuck inside, staring out your window at steam rising from the subway grates, when the streets are black and wet, and lonely siren wails crescendo and die down abandoned alleys, shake the mothballs out of your trenchcoat, yank your fedora down to hide your eyes, and head out along Broadway. Hunch your shoulders as you walk past darkened shopfronts. Make sure that dark sedan slinking around the corner isn't trailing you, then duck into the doorway of Number 2486, underneath the silhouette of a .45-caliber revolver. As the door swings shut behind you, look up in the sudden blaze of light to find yourself in a room full of goons, girls, petty thieves, spies, and the pockmarked faces of cops gone wrong.

Don't worry, you aren't in danger—you're in Murder Ink., the oldest murder-mystery bookstore in the world, where all the customers look like Lew Archer or Sam Spade. Murder Ink. stocks classic detective novels and hard-boiled detective fiction. There is also a true crime section. Many of the books are autographed, and vintage editions from as far back as the 1930's stand behind glass cases. If you're looking for a liaison with the ruthless Brigid O'Shaughnessy, or are trying to discover who left the millionaire lying face down in the swimming pool, the staff at Murder Ink. will help direct you, as will the customers, all of whom are die-hard murder-mystery buffs.

Until Murder Ink. moved to its present location 10 years ago, it held a St. Valentine's Day Massacre reenactment on the old premises, in a tiny room overrun with cats, sandwiched between a garage and a grocery store off West End Avenue. The new store is larger, and adjoins Ivy's Books and Curiosities, whose cream and green shelves and selection of literary fiction and whimsical writing paper is a peculiar neighbor to the blood-red shelves and floors of Murder Ink.

When you've finished browsing through Murder Ink., make your way back through the dark streets and, secure in your apartment, crack open your new mystery, the rain sliding down your windowpanes and the sound of a pair of running footsteps echoing on the street below.

NADIA AGUIAR
Writer

London Mimicry

12.40 **Pomander Walk**
1921, King & Campbell
West 94th Street to West 95th Street between Broadway
& West End Avenue
Ⓜ 96th Street (1/2/3)

11.29 **Henderson Place**
1882, Lamb & Rich
North side of East 86th Street between York & East End Avenues
Ⓜ 86th Street (4/5/6)

New York's signature architectural style is the imaginative towers of the skyscrapers built during the first third of the 20th century. At ground level, you have either the very plain brownstone Edith Wharton so detested, or buildings that echo the cities of Europe, most often London.

My favorite bit of this architectural mimicry is Pomander Walk, built in 1921 and named for a popular Broadway play of the time. This easy-to-miss thoroughfare, which runs parallel to Broadway and West End Avenue between 94th and 95th Streets, was, like the play, named for a tiny street in the London suburb of Chiswick.

Although the gates have been closed since 1986, on a recent sunny morning it took literally no more than two minutes before a resident, on her way back from shopping, let me in. Up a flight of a dozen steps is an enchanted streetlet, its scaled-down Tudor houses apparently modeled after the sets of the long-forgotten play. In front of each house is a well-tended garden in the English country style. Looking up, you see window boxes with hanging flowers that enhance the overall theatricality.

New York is a much more sociable city than it is given credit for being, but Pomander Walk seems incredibly like some small town where everybody knows everybody else.

It has an architectural cousin across town on East

86th Street, just around the corner from Gracie Mansion. Henderson Place, which runs only half a block, has a row of red brick townhouses in Queen Anne style. What distinguishes them from so many other imitations of London is the fact that they do not seem full size. The miniaturization gives them a sweet theatricality. (Not surprisingly, the Lunts lived here for many years.)

These elegant houses face an undistinguished modern apartment building, so they do not have the enveloping enchantment of Pomander Walk. But they are a reminder of the kind of imagination New York developers used before their only consideration was how high, and thus, how lucrative.

HOWARD KISSEL
Journalist

12.42 Manhattan Table Tennis

2628 Broadway between West 99th & West 100th Streets
☎ 212 864-7253
Monday-Friday 3pm-midnight; Saturday, Sunday
noon-midnight
Ⓜ 96th Street (1/2/3); 103rd Street-Broadway (1)

On the east side of Broadway between 99th and 100th Streets, there is a bargain bazaar that sells everything from soap to sundresses. The items overflow into a presumably unofficial annex of tables and clothing racks on the pavement in front of the store. One flight above the bazaar is the Home Grown Theater Company and one flight above the theater is Manhattan Table Tennis.

Manhattan Table Tennis proudly claims to be the only place in Manhattan where one can play the "official" version of table tennis. Walk in and the differences between the official version of the game and the ping-pong of your youth immediately become apparent. The official-sized tables are considerably smaller than the ping-pong tables in basements and frat houses across America. The players of the official game bend at the waist and hold their arms at seemingly painful, crooked angles in their quest for the perfect spin with which to launch the balls across the net. As a result, the best players look like extraordinarily well-muscled marionettes as they lurch forwards and back, hitting balls to each other.

Go during the day and you may see Nigerian businessmen conducting deals in the Yoruba language over games of table tennis, or the associates from a major New York investment bank on a corporate outing.

Go in the evening and you may be able to watch Renata Pulochova, who once played on the Czech national table tennis team and is now the Number 5 female table tennis player in the United States; Wang Chen, once the Number 4 female table tennis player in the world and who is now working her way up through the U.S. Table Tennis Association rankings; George Brathwaite, who was one of the "ping-pong diplomats" to China in 1971 and is now both the Number 1 male "50 and over" and Number 1 male "60 and over" table tennis champion in the United States; and Wally Green, a New York Parks Department in-line skating instructor and up-and-coming table tennis star (complete with corporate sponsorships).

Try to corner Brathwaite and ask him about his dreams for table tennis in the United States. Or sign up for a lesson with Atenda Musa, the eight-time All-African champion and one-time coach to the Saudi Arabian royal family and national team. Musa is willing and able to teach students of all levels. (He spent much of my lesson asking me to "move, please move" praising me on those rare occasions when I actually did move with, "Thank you. Very good!" My friend, considerably more energetic than I on that particular evening, actually received instruction on how to spin the ball.)

Or simply go and play a game or two, while steeping yourself in the table tennis subculture surrounding you. Or if you don't want to play, go to watch anyway.

KATE HARTNICK
Marketing consultant

A Summer Evening in Riverside Park

12.41 **Riverside Park Tennis Courts**
Riverside Park at West 96th Street, ☎ 212 978-0277
Open April-November
Ⓜ 96th Street (1/2/3)

12.44 **Hudson Beach Cafe**
Riverside Park at West 105th Street, ☎ 917 567-2743
Seasonal hours
Ⓜ 103rd Street-Broadway (1)

Take a stroll along the promenade. Stop at the community gardens at 89th Street, and enjoy the Upper West Side's interpretation of an English country garden. Drop down to the river's edge at 95th Street, and continue to the public tennis courts on 96th Street. Play here at sunset, with a river breeze. When your game is finished, follow the sounds of salsa music to the Hudson Beach Cafe on 105th Street in Riverside Park, where Puerto Rican and American flags are displayed proudly above the bar. Dance, have a margarita, and toast the city for nights like this.
GEORGIA O'NEAL
Designer

17.41 **Firemen's Memorial**
1913, Attilio Piccirilli, sculptor; H. Van Buren Magonigle, architect
Riverside Drive at West 100th Street
Ⓜ 96th Street (1/2/3); 103rd Street-Broadway (1)

At the funeral service for Deputy Chief Kruger in 1908 (he died at a fire on Canal Street), Episcopal Bishop Henry Potter called for the erection of a monument to honor the heroism of New York City firefighters. Newspapers throughout the city took up the bishop's plea, and a few years later the Firemen's Memorial was dedicated, high on top of Riverside Drive, in beautiful park-like surroundings: a quiet, somber setting amidst the hustle of Broadway and near Columbia University only a few blocks away. The inscription on the monument reads, "To the men of the Fire Department of the City of New York who died in the line of duty, soldiers in a war that never ends, this memorial is dedicated by the people of a grateful city." Each October, memorial services are held here by the department. Completely refurbished in 1991, this monument is for firefighters a sacred and honored place, and for New Yorkers, a reminder of the price paid for their safety.

THOMAS VON ESSEN
Former New York City Fire Commissioner

12.45 Nicholas Roerich Museum

1898, Clarence F. True
319 West 107th Street between Broadway & Riverside Drive
☎ 212 864-7752
Tuesday-Sunday 2pm-5pm; closed Monday
Ⓜ 103rd Street-Broadway (1); Cathedral Parkway-110th Street (1)

This is a fabulous museum in a charming townhouse displaying the work of the rather mystical Russian artist Nicholas Roerich. Many of the paintings reflect his intense spirituality and deep passion for art.

KAREN MOODY TOMPKINS
Artist

12.46 Riverside Park Above West 96th Street

There is, of course, that pesky problem of the West Side Highway directly to one side, but the beauty of this particular unsung river path is that it maintains a distinctly nonlandscaped feel. There are no railings, no gardens, no restaurants—only a straight shot up the west side of Manhattan along the river, the George Washington Bridge ahead in the distance, and the rocky coastline of New Jersey to espy on the other side. If you're a serious runner— as, say, in training for the New York City Marathon (which

everyone should do at least once)—you can run over the
bridge for a truly magnificent view.
KATHLEEN DEMARCO
Writer and film producer

12.47 Awash
947 Amsterdam Avenue between West 106th & West 107th
Streets, ☎ 212 961-1416
Open daily for lunch and dinner
Ⓜ 103rd Street-Broadway(1); Cathedral Parkway-110th Street (1)

🍽 Whatever exists in the rest of the world, some portion of
it exists in New York. So when I'm in the mood to revisit
Ethiopia, my favorite country in Africa, I seek out her
many restaurants here. My favorite is Awash on Amsterdam
Avenue. The interior walls are covered with paintings of
the country's last four emperors. There are restaurant and
traditional Ethiopian basket tables, called messobs. But the
real treat here is the food that comes out of the kitchen of
Bogalech, the cook and co-owner. Most nights when she
cooks, she'll visit your table and see how you are enjoying
her food. Her fare includes beef and chicken, but I prefer
the vegetarian dishes. My wife and I often start out with an
order of Yetimatim fitfit—an appetizer with tomatoes, hot
peppers, onions mixed with injera (the national pancake-
like bread that is made here with teff, an Ethiopian grain)
and moistened with olive oil and lemon. Then we have
one of the vegetarian combos. My wife washes her meal
down with an African beer, but I prefer a cup of chai, a tea
flavored with cloves and cardamom.
CHESTER HIGGINS JR.
Photographer, The New York Times

MORNINGSIDE
HEIGHTS & HARLEM

13

MORNINGSIDE HEIGHTS

1. Hungarian Pastry Shop
2. St. John the Divine
3. Columbia University
4. Riverside Church
5. Sakura Park
6. Grant's Tomb
7. Grave of St. Clair Pollock
8. Riverside Drive Viaduct

HARLEM

9. Lenox Lounge
10. Studio Museum in Harlem
11. Sylvia's Soul Food Restaurant
12. The Schomburg Center
13. Harlem Y.M.C.A.
14. Countee Cullen Library
15. Strivers' Row
16. Abyssinian Baptist Church
17. Mother A.M.E. Zion Church
18. St. Nicholas Park
19. Riverbank State Park

Morningside Heights & Harlem

MORNINGSIDE HEIGHTS

13.1 **Hungarian Pastry Shop**
1030 Amsterdam Avenue between Cathedral Parkway
& West 111th Street, ☎ 212 866-4230
Monday-Friday 7:30am-11:30pm; Saturday 8:30am-11:30pm;
Sunday 8:30am-10:30pm
Ⓜ Cathedral Parkway-110th Street (1)

🍴 Slotted into the ground floor of an anonymous apartment
building on Amsterdam Avenue just below 111th Street,
the Hungarian Pastry Shop is one of the sweetest retreats
in the city. Despite its generic name, and with no decor
to speak of, it's been a bastion of the Columbia University
neighborhood for at least a quarter of a century. You give
your order at the front counter along with your first name,
which a waitress then circulates about five minutes later.
Usually she misreads her own handwriting, so whose order
she has is always a matter of interpretation (Mel? Bill?
Cal?). This is neatly appropriate for a place in which the
table reading is as likely to be Derrida as *The New York
Post*. But the real secret to the Hungarian Pastry Shop's
success is the pots of mediocre coffee with which you can
refill your initial overpriced order as frequently as you
wish—for hours or, as seems the case of some perennial
students, decades. Thus the place has probably fueled more
Ph.D.'s than any institution in the hemisphere.

One fringe benefit of the Hungarian Pastry Shop is
its view across the avenue to the gardens of the Cathedral
of St. John the Divine and especially the so-called Peace
Fountain. Hands down the ugliest public sculpture in
New York, it rises massively from a placid marble pool
to a bulging man-in-the-moon face from which a gigantic
winged figure, who appears to be strangling a gazelle,

emerges while huge bronze crab claws drip over the edge.
Local rumor has it that the sculptor donated a million
dollars to the cathedral—in the days when that was
real money—in return for the permanent display of his
well-intended statement of universal amity gone grotes-
quely awry. So be it; the thing is so awful you can't help
but admire it as you pour a cup of coffee and return to
your reading.

MELVIN JULES BUKIET
Novelist and professor

13.2 Cathedral Church of St. John the Divine

1892-1911, Heins & La Farge; 1911-1942, Cram & Ferguson
Amsterdam Avenue at West 112th Street, ☎ 212 316-7540
Ⓜ Cathedral Parkway-110th Street (1)

On the hillside of Morningside Heights stands the
Cathedral of St. John the Divine, unfinished more than
100 years after the first stone foundations were laid in
1892. The Episcopal diocese purchased this lot north of
110th Street in the 1880's and began planning a cathedral
that would rise above the city and be visible throughout
the island of Manhattan. It was to be like Paris's Sacré
Coeur. That was before skyscrapers began to sprout on
the city's grid. Today, the cathedral is largely hidden from
view, unless you're right in front of it, but it's well worth
a visit. Even incomplete, it's the largest church in America
and one of the largest cathedrals in the world. Its main
vault, standing 124 feet high, is more than 600 feet long
and could hold two football fields in a row. Along the edge
of this expanse, individual niches filled with sculptures,
stained glass, and historical artifacts catch the eye.

After viewing the interior, walk around the outside to see
the results of changing architectural tastes. The Episcopal
diocese initially chose a Romanesque and Byzantine plan
by Heins & La Farge, which was used for the sanctuary
and choir. In 1911, however, the church, concerned with

changing tastes, chose Ralph Adams Cram as its new architect and adopted a Gothic Revival design to complete the building. This shift is visible inside the building, but even more from the street along the north side, where you can see the rounded Romanesque choir next to Gothic flying buttresses.

To get the full experience of the cathedral, take advantage of the Vertical Tour, which is offered periodically. This guided walk takes you 124 feet up stone spiral staircases onto the roof of the cathedral. As you ascend through the walls of the building, you get close-up views of gargoyles, and other ornamentation, that are barely visible from the floor below. At the "summit," there are spectacular views down to the city below. From there you get a sense of the geography that made the site so attractive to its planners.

THORIN TRITTER
Historian

The guidebooks will tell you that it is the largest Gothic cathedral in the world, that the Statue of Liberty could stand upright in the nave, that the figure of Christ in the rose window is six feet tall, but more telling for me is that at most times of the day you can't see the ceiling. It's that far away. The impression is that heaven has somehow been included in the congregation.

CYNTHIA ZARIN
Poet and writer

Believe it or not, one of the largest cathedrals in the world sits across from a funky Hungarian coffee shop (see p. 370) at the edge of Harlem. Pass through St. John's Portals of Paradise under the gaze of Moses, John the Baptist, and 30 other limestone figures from the Old and New Testaments and feel the transformation take place as you enter sacred space. Though the cornerstone was set in 1892, like much of New York, the cathedral is still a construction site—its scaffolded stone towers are not yet finished. But the magnificent breadth of the room inside inspires a sense of utter completeness and can convince even the faithless to believe. The first time I walked the length of the vaulted nave to the great choir and looked up at the dome 177 feet above, I got weak in the knees. The Statue of Liberty could stand on her toes and still fit underneath. Built as a sanctuary for faiths of all nations, the cathedral has seen the Dalai Lama, as well as Sufi masters, Zen roshis, and rabbis, lead prayer services. This is the place to surrender to your higher power or to the simple need for refuge from the chaos of urban life.

RENEE SHAFRANSKY
Writer

13.3 Columbia University
1897, McKim, Mead & White
West 114th Street to West 120th Street between Broadway & Amsterdam Avenue; entrance at West 116th Street & Broadway, ☎ 212 854-4900
Columbia offers regularly scheduled tours of the campus and its buildings. Call for information.
Ⓜ 116th Street-Columbia University (1)

Buell Hall/Maison Française
1885, Ralph Townsend
Central campus, south of St. Paul's Chapel

Low Memorial Library
1897, Charles McKim of McKim, Mead & White
Central campus, north of West 116th Street (College Walk)

St. Paul's Chapel
1907, Howells & Stokes
North campus, east of Low Library

Avery Hall
1912, McKim, Mead & White
North of St. Paul's Chapel

Alma Mater
1903, Daniel Chester French
Central Campus, on the steps in front of Low Library

Columbia University is one of the oldest and largest institutions of higher education in America. Its Morningside Heights campus, designed by McKim, Mead & White, is one of the great urban spaces in New York and complements the university's prestige.

The history of the university's founding and expansion reflects the growth of the city. Chartered in 1754 as King's College, the fledgling institution quickly outgrew its original home on a site adjacent to Trinity Church. In 1760, it moved to a three-acre site near Park Place (then named College Place). By 1810, the city had begun to close in on the openness and greenery of that site: there were concerns about the noise from the city's nearby port, and the area was gaining notoriety for prostitution. Columbia College (patriotically rechristened after the Revolution) therefore acquired the failed Elgin Botanical Gardens, about 20 acres just north of 47th Street and fronting Fifth Avenue. As the city continued to expand northward, this landholding proved to be one of Columbia's most profitable investments, leased after 1929 to Rockefeller Center until it was sold in 1987.

In 1857, the trustees applied the proceeds of the sale of the College Place property to acquiring the grounds of the Deaf and Dumb Asylum located at 49th Street between Madison and Fourth (Park) Avenues. That institution's buildings were to serve as temporary quarters until a new campus could be built on the Botanical Garden site, just a block away, but the Civil War and volatile economy in its aftermath delayed such plans. After 40 more years, the phenomenal growth of Manhattan above 42nd Street, especially the arrival of the railroad into Grand Central and the northern push of speculative residences and commerce, made the conditions at 49th Street increasingly

untenable. In addition, Columbia determined to expand
along the model of a Germanic research university, as several other American institutions did during the 19th century.
In 1891, the newly constituted Columbia University
acquired the grounds of the Bloomingdale Insane Asylum in
Morningside Heights (an irony generations of students and
professors have relished). Construction began in 1897.
PETER J. HOLLIDAY
Historian of classical art and archaeology

One of the few great contributions of City Beautiful
planning to New York City, the Columbia University campus is a permanent testimony to the impact of Chicago's
ephemeral White City of 1893 (the World's Columbian
Exhibition), from which master planner Charles Follen
McKim was freshly graduated. At the same time, it is a
place richly suggestive of the inherent tension between the
Beaux Arts processional planning that captured the
American civic imagination in the late 19th century and the
nearly relentless grid of the Commissioner's Plan of 1811,
which was laid out to the northern tip of the island even
before building had reached the island's frontier.

When Columbia acquired the pastoral site of the old
Bloomingdale Asylum (the quaint brick villa known today
as Buell Hall/Maison Française just to the east of Low
Library is the only remnant), McKim seized the opportunity to build on the four blocks uninterrupted by cross
streets to compose in brick, limestone, and granite a vision
of the American research university as a grand forum.
Though he dreamed of an axial approach to its great
central axis, and even a vista from the upper terrace of this
academic sanctuary of the city to the south, neither the
grid nor the city's vertical drive allowed that. Rather, we
come obliquely upon the Pantheonesque centerpiece of it
all, Low Library (1895-97). Approached across a grand
forecourt paved with deep-red bricks laid in a herringbone
pattern to recall the floor of the Roman Forum, McKim's

great outdoor room comes alive on warm fall or spring days, when the stairs become the bleachers for this civic stage. Students, faculty, and neighbors of all ages chat, distribute pamphlets, exchange footballs, or hurry upward to the grand plateau on which McKim arranged a backdrop of red brick classroom buildings, accented by a trio of cupolas of the library, the student center, and the chapel. Be sure to go before 5 p.m., when the great bronze doors of Low Library close, for the interior, even without its grand central desk and concentric reading tables reminiscent of the old British Museum and the Library of Congress, is one of the most solemn Beaux Arts interiors in New York.

For decorative subtlety and even technological innovation, McKim's former employees, Howells and Stokes, outdid the master in St. Paul's Chapel (1903-05). In their use of the recently patented thin-tile vaults of the Guastavino system (you saw some in the IRT subway as you arrived), they elevated this new technology to new aesthetic heights in the dome, vaults, galleries, and even stairways of this richly textured sanctuary. The small spiraling stair, visible by entering the right side door off the narthex porch of the chapel, is a veritable primer in how this medieval Spanish technique revolutionized American building circa 1900. Take a peek into Avery Library, one of the great repositories of architectural books anywhere in the world. And maybe before you leave school you'll discover Columbia's most famous secret—as hundreds of first-year students do each autumn—by gazing between the folds of the statue of Alma Mater, Daniel Chester French's great enthroned matron who presides over the whole scene.

BARRY BERGDOLL
Architectural historian and professor, Columbia University

RECOMMENDED READING
Andrew S. Dolkart, *Morningside Heights: A History of Its Architecture and Development*, Columbia University Press, 2001.
Barry Bergdoll, Janet Parks and Hollee Haswell, *Mastering McKim's Plan: Columbia's First Century on Morningside Heights*, Columbia University Press, 1997.

13.4 Riverside Church

1930, Allen & Collens and Henry C. Pelton
490 Riverside Drive between West 120th & West 122nd
Streets, ☎ 212 870-6700
Ⓜ 116th Street-Columbia University (1)

Laura Spelman Rockefeller Memorial Carillon

Unconcerned with the liability insurance that transformed
the Empire State Building observation deck into a rat cage,
the carillon at Riverside Church provides the best chance
to ascend one of the city's spires and gaze out over the city.
An ecclesiastical office building disguised as a cathedral,
the tower offers a bank of elevators in place of the winding
spiral stair.

SEBASTIAN HARDY
Urban planner

13.5 Sakura Park

1934, Olmsted Landscape Architecture Firm
West 122nd Street between Riverside Drive
& Claremont Avenue
Open from dawn to dusk
Ⓜ 125th Street (1)

Sakura Park, one of New York's prettiest and least-known
parks, at first seems little more than an annex of Riverside
Park, which it adjoins at the northern tip of Morningside
Heights. But spend a few minutes here and you'll realize
that it has a peaceful, melancholy charm all its own.
Situated directly across Riverside Drive from Grant's
Tomb, elevated slightly from the street, filled with benches,
big trees, and a gazebo, it's a perfect place to rest your feet,
eat your lunch, or simply contemplate the teeming city that
lies beyond.

RACHEL WETZSTEON
Poet

13.6 Grant's Tomb/General Grant National Memorial
1897, John H. Duncan
Riverside Drive at West 122nd Street, ☎ 212 666-1640
Open daily 9am-5pm
Ⓜ 125th Street (1)

General Grant National Memorial Bench
1973, Pedro Silva and Cityarts Workshop, with Phillip Danzig

These colorful, tile-covered benches stretch 450 feet along
both sides and the rear of the solemn mausoleum to the
general and president, and his wife. They were completed in
1973 as a community folk art appreciation of Grant's role
in preserving the nation in 1865. More than 2,000 people
volunteered to complete the benches. The tiles are reminiscent of the work of Antonio Gaudì in Barcelona, Spain.
PHILLIP DANZIG
Architect

13.7 Grave of St. Clair Pollock
1797
North of Grant's Tomb, across Riverside Drive (southbound)

Just north of Grant's Tomb, on the edge of Riverside Park,
is a fenced enclosure surrounding a stone urn, "Erected to
the Memory of an Amiable Child, St. Clair Pollock, a 5-year-
old who fell to his death from these rocks on July 15, 1797."
GERALD WEALES
Writer and critic

13.8 Riverside Drive Viaduct
1901, F. Stewart Williamson, engineer; rebuilt 1987
West 125th Street & the Hudson River
Ⓜ 125th Street (1)

The viaduct at 125th Street at the Hudson River is a little-
known but elegant metal bridge structure.
M. PAUL FRIEDBERG
Landscape architect

HARLEM

13.9 Lenox Lounge

288 Lenox Avenue (Malcolm X Boulevard) between
West 124th & West 125th Streets, ☎ 212 427-0253
Open daily noon-4am

Ⓜ 125th Street (2/3)

The Cotton Club and Savoy are long gone, but this
legendary lounge remains and has played host to Bird
and Billie (Holiday), Miles Davis (with Malcolm X
watching), and a thousand other jazz journeymen. This
joint is living history and I get the chills just thinking
about what went down here. The famous back room is
where you can hear some young cats wail, while the hard,
loud, long front bar is jammed with a rainbow coalition
of locals mixed with up- and downtowners. The original
Art Deco decor, complete with zebra-striped walls and
padded leather ceiling, was recently over-restored. I miss
the 60-year-old nicotine-blackened ceiling and the sconces
falling off the walls.
FREDERIC SCHWARTZ
Architect

13.10 The Studio Museum in Harlem

144 West 125th Street between Lenox Avenue (Malcolm X
Boulevard) & Adam Clayton Powell Jr. Boulevard
☎ 212 864-4500
Wednesday-Friday noon-6pm; Saturday 10am-6pm; Sunday
noon-6pm; closed Monday, Tuesday; closed between
exhibitions

Ⓜ 125th Street (2/3)

The least ivory-tower museum in town, the Studio
Museum in Harlem has both serious historical exhibitions
and contemporary artists at work in studio areas of the
building. There is an outdoor space for art and a sense of

interaction and porousness between the museum and the community. After visiting the Studio Museum, have lunch at Sylvia's.

REBECCA SMITH
Artist

13.11 Sylvia's Soul Food Restaurant
328 Lenox Avenue (Malcolm X Boulevard) between
West 126th & West 127th Streets, ☎ 212 996-0660
Open daily for breakfast, lunch, and dinner
Ⓜ 125th Street (2/3)

🍴 In the heart of Harlem, Sylvia's (now seating and serving 450) has been a soul food institution since 1962. Sylvia and her husband, Herbert Wood, met in a beanfield when they were kids and they've been together ever since. Stick to the basics like the ribs, fried chicken, collard greens, and sweet potato pie. Go late at night to bypass the tour buses or try the gospel brunch after Sunday services at the Abyssinian Baptist Church (see p. 383).

TRACEY HUMMER AND FREDERIC SCHWARTZ
Writer and Architect

Harlem Stroll

13.12 The Schomburg Center for Research in Black Culture, The New York Public Library
1980, Bond Ryder Associates
515 Lenox Avenue (Malcolm X Boulevard) at West 135th Street
☎ 212 491-2200
Monday-Wednesday noon-8pm; Thursday-Saturday
10am-6pm; Sunday 1pm-5pm, exhibition area only
Ⓜ 135th Street (2/3)

13.13 Harlem Y.M.C.A.
(see p. 382)

13.14 **Countee Cullen Branch, The New York Public Library**
1942, Louis Allen Abramson
104 West 136th Street between Adam Clayton Powell Jr.
Boulevard & Lenox Avenue (Malcolm X Boulevard)
☎ 212 491-2070
Monday-Tuesday 10am-6pm; Wednesday noon-8pm;
Thursday, Friday noon-6pm; Saturday 10am-5pm; closed
Sunday
Ⓜ 135th Street (2/3)

13.15 **Strivers' Row**
West 138th & West 139th Streets between Frederick Douglass
& Adam Clayton Powell Jr. Boulevards
Ⓜ 135th Street (B/C)

13.16 **Abyssinian Baptist Church**
(see p. 383)

Near the geographic center of Harlem stands the New
York Public Library's Schomburg Center, one of the world's
great research facilities for studying African-American and
African life and culture, and a mecca for the curious about
Harlem and the fabled 1920's Harlem Renaissance. A
modern three-story complex, it incorporates a landmark
building as well as the Countee Cullen Library, the site of
heiress A'Lelia Walker's mansion and literary salon known
as the Dark Tower. One half-block west on 135th Street is
the Harlem Y.M.C.A., temporary home of Langston Hughes
and Claude McKay. Walk three blocks north on the west
side of Seventh Avenue and you come to Strivers' Row, two
streets of elegant turn-of-the-century Italianate houses
designed by architect Stanford White. Half a block east,
down 138th Street, is the historic Abyssinian Baptist Church.

If you are less adventurous, a few steps from the IRT
Seventh Avenue express subway exit at 135th Street will
put you inside the lobby of the Schomburg Center. Sign
the visitor's register and, comfortably indoors, you can
begin to satisfy an hour's curiosity or a lifetime's   ►

▶

scholarly interest. For the sightseer, a tour is recommended
before a leisurely visit to the several exhibition galleries.
One can also attend a lecture, film screening (some are
free), or performance in either of two theaters. Peek into
the sculpture garden on your way to browse in the gift
shop for that hard-to-find book. A walk through the large,
sunlit lobby of the Langston Hughes Auditorium is essential. Its terrazzo and brass-strip floor, designed by Houston
Conwill, illuminates the Langston Hughes poem "The
Negro Speaks of Rivers." Beneath the center of the floor
rests the poet's ashes. Before you leave, stand at that spot
in the center of Harlem and read the inscription: "My soul
has grown deep like the rivers."

RAYMOND R. PATTERSON (1929-2001)
Poet and English professor, City College of New York

RECOMMENDED READING
David Levering Lewis, *When Harlem Was in Vogue*, Penguin, 1997.

13.13 **Harlem Y.M.C.A.**
1932, James C. Mackenzie Jr.
180 West 135th Street between Lenox Avenue (Malcolm X
Boulevard) & Adam Clayton Powell Jr. Boulevard
📞 212 281-4100
Monday-Friday 6am-11pm; Saturday 6am-8pm; closed Sunday
Ⓜ 135th Street (2/3)

On this important thoroughfare stands a proud institution
that has been a beacon for the community since the first
Harlem Renaissance. Opened in 1933, the 11-story neo-
Georgian Harlem Y.M.C.A. received landmark status
in 1999. As one of the country's major African-American
Y.M.C.A.'s, its handsome halls and rooms, with their original tiles, wooden doors, and carved ceiling beams, have
embraced countless children and adults, nurtured great
talents, and sheltered many aspiring souls. Renowned
writer Langston Hughes stayed in its residence; Paul
Robeson, Harry Belafonte, Ossie Davis, and Ruby Dee,

among others, graced its Little Theater program for more than 40 years; major artist Aaron Davis painted a still-extant wall mural, *The Evolution of Negro Dance*, during the Great Depression; and revered baseball hero and one-time Y member Jackie Robinson lives on in the youth center named for him opposite the main Y.M.C.A. building.

Sharing the block with two other major community institutions—Harlem Hospital and the Schomburg Center for Research in Black Culture (see p. 380)—the Y.M.C.A. is a key player in the second Harlem Renaissance, now underway.

PAMELA BAYLESS
Writer and communications consultant

13.16 Abyssinian Baptist Church

1923, Charles W. Bolton & Son
132 Odell Clark Place (West 138th Street) between Adam Clayton Powell Jr. Boulevard & Lenox Avenue (Malcolm X Boulevard), ☎ 212 862-7474
Open to the public for services only; Sunday 9am and 11am
Ⓜ 135th Street (2/3)

The ashlar neo-Gothic stone church became famous for its prominent ministers, notably Adam Clayton Powell Sr. and his son Adam Clayton Powell Jr., the first black congressman from New York City. Founded in 1808 by black worshippers who wanted independence from the First Baptist Church, the congregation took a name associated with ancient Ethiopia. The city's second-oldest black church took more than a century to move north to Harlem, as did the city's downtown "Little Africa" population.

CHRISTOPHER PAUL MOORE
Author and historian

13.17 Mother African Methodist Episcopal Zion Church

1925, George W. Foster Jr.
140 West 137th Street between Adam Clayton Powell Jr.
Boulevard & Lenox Avenue (Malcolm X Boulevard)
📞 212 234-1545
Open to the public for services only; Tuesday 8pm;
Sunday 11am (July, August at 10am)
Ⓜ 135th Street (2/3)

Organized in 1796 by black worshippers who withdrew
from the John Street Methodist Church in lower
Manhattan, the Mother A.M.E. Zion Church is the city's
oldest African-American church and, as its name implies,
the "mother" church of the international A.M.E. Zion
denomination. Designed by George W. Foster Jr., one of
the first black architects in the United States, the neo-
Gothic stone church is the sixth edifice and location for
the congregation, which started in a house neighboring the
18th-century African Burial Ground (see p. 48) and moved
gradually up to Harlem in the 1900's.
CHRISTOPHER PAUL MOORE
Author and historian

13.18 St. Nicholas Park

West 127th to West 141st Street between St. Nicholas Avenue
& St. Nicholas Terrace
Open 6am-sunset
Ⓜ 135th Street (B/C)

Commemorating colonial New Amsterdam's patron Saint
Nicholas, who through local writers Washington Irving
and Clement Clarke Moore and local artist Thomas Nast
became our beloved Santa Claus, the frontier-like park
is my family's favorite Christmas holiday spot. Built in
1906 to the designs of landscape architect Samuel Parsons
on a massive, rocky outcrop following the rugged and
hilly topography of northern Manhattan, the park's
development and the construction of the elevated rapid

transit line made this section of Harlem a fashionable residential district at the turn of the century. In the park is "The Point of Rocks," where George Washington commanded and observed the Battle of Harlem Heights in 1776. During the 17th century, the steeple of Manhattan's first permanent church (built in 1642 and popularly called the St. Nicholas Church by the children of the Roosevelts, Stuyvesants, and my grandcestor Nicholas Manuel) could be seen from the point nine miles south in downtown Fort Amsterdam. New York City may not look like the North Pole, but it is the birthplace of Santa Claus!

CHRISTOPHER PAUL MOORE
Author and historian

13.19 Riverbank State Park

1991, Richard Dattner & Associates
West 137th to West 145th Street, west of the Henry Hudson Parkway; entrance at West 145th Street
☎ 212 694-3600 (park), ☎ 212 694-3666 (pool)
Open daily 6:30am-11pm; hours vary for the pool
Ⓜ 145th Street (1)

My favorite pool in New York is the splendid 50-meter pool at Riverbank, over the Hudson River at 145th Street in Harlem. This is part of an extraordinary recreational and cultural complex that is virtually unknown to most New Yorkers.

OLIVER SACKS
Neurologist and author

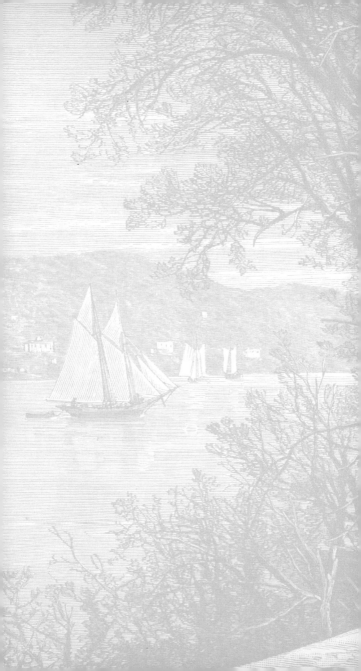

Upper Manhattan

14

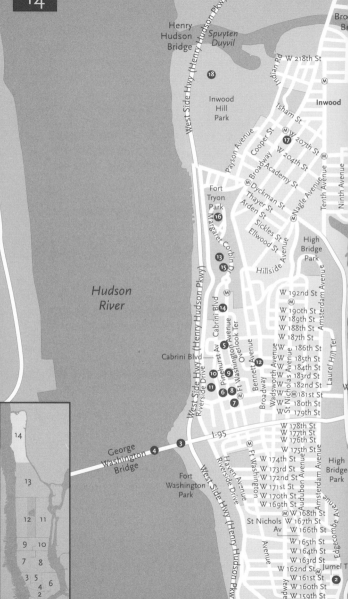

INWOOD, FORT GEORGE, WASHINGTON HEIGHTS & AUDUBON

Inwood, Fort George, Washington Heights & Audubon

14.1　Hispanic Society of America

1908, Charles Pratt Huntington
Audubon Terrace: Broadway between West 155th & West 156th
Streets, ☎ 212 926-2234
Tuesday-Saturday 10am-4:30pm; Sunday 1pm-4pm;
closed Monday
Ⓜ 157th Street (1)

I work at the Hispanic Society, but all institutional pride
aside, we have by far and away the best museum and
library in this country for the study of Spanish culture. The
fact that the society is in one of the most culturally vibrant
cities in the world, in a neighborhood that is almost entirely
Spanish-speaking, and yet is largely unknown, simply
makes it more intriguing. The grand Beaux Arts terrace that
it occupies on Broadway between 155th and 156th Streets
serves as a reminder of how swiftly this part of Manhattan
evolved over the 20th century.

WILLIAM AMBLER
Curator, Hispanic Society of America

The Hispanic Society of America was hugely popular
at first. In 1909, when it opened a big show devoted to
Valencian Impressionist Joaquín Sorolla, it obliged a total
of 150,000 visitors by staying open until 11 p.m. At the
time, *ARTnews* reported that the exhibit "won the most
emphatic popular success ever known in the history of art
in New York." Today, however, you might feel as though
you're in a dark ducal home in a Spanish province, about
50 years ago.

The Hispanic Society sits in a recessed courtyard off
Broadway between 155th and 156th Streets in a bustling,
mostly Dominican neighborhood. It has changed very little
since it was founded in 1904 by Archer Milton Huntington,

who used the family fortune (shipbuilding and the Central Pacific Railroad) to acquire the best collection of Spanish art, books, and manuscripts in the United States.

He bought objects chronicling the panorama of Spanish history, from paleolithic stone tools to modern Catalan porcelain, rare Roman glass vessels and ivory combs, silken textiles woven in Moorish patterns, intricately illuminated medieval Bibles, and some of the best lusterware you will see anywhere. And he amassed paintings by masters including El Greco, Velázquez, and Zurbarán. Principal among the major works is Goya's portrait of his alleged mistress, the Duchess of Alba, who flaunts a ring with the artist's name on it.

Huntington also bought a parcel of farmland from the naturalist John James Audubon, with the intention of creating an acropolis on the Upper West Side. Known as the Audubon Terrace Historic District, it includes buildings for the American Numismatic Society, the American Academy of Arts and Letters, and one for George Gustave Heye, whose great collection of Native American art has since been transplanted downtown to the Smithsonian's National Museum of the American Indian (see p. 17). The inner court of the Hispanic Society, in the style of the Spanish Renaissance, looks like a palace and was, in fact, inspired by the Vélez Blanco Castle in the province of Almería. Sculptures of El Cid, Don Quixote, and Boabdil, the last Moorish king of Granada, by Huntington's wife, Anna Hyatt Huntington, adorn the outdoor space.

ROBIN CEMBALEST
Executive editor, ARTnews

This is a neglected museum with some fine Old Master paintings.
VICTORIA NEWHOUSE
Writer

14.2 Morris-Jumel Mansion

1765
65 Jumel Terrace between West 160th & West 162nd Streets
📞 212 923-8008
Wednesday-Sunday 10am-4pm; closed Monday, Tuesday
Ⓜ 163rd Street-Amsterdam Avenue (C)

This house, on a rise overlooking Harlem Valley, was built
in 1765 for Roger Morris, an English colonel. During the
American Revolution it was used as General George
Washington's headquarters. In 1810 it became the residence
of Stephen and Eliza Jumel, who decorated it in the French
Empire style. After the death of her husband, Eliza married
former Vice President Aaron Burr, the man who had shot
Alexander Hamilton in a duel years before. Eliza had been
a prostitute in her youth and had amassed a fortune that
Burr managed to squander in bad investments. She sought
a divorce from Burr in 1834, and he died two years later,
on the day the divorce was granted. Eliza remained in the
house until her death in 1865.

   Today the house is open to the public as a museum,
with period furniture in all the rooms. Entering the house
is like stepping back into the 19th century. It is a true
part of American history, with ties to President George
Washington and Vice President Aaron Burr.
CELEDONIA JONES
Manhattan Borough Historian

Women Who Soared the Heights

14.13 Fort Tryon Park

1935, Frederick Law Olmsted Jr.
West 192nd Street to Dyckman Street between Broadway
& Riverside Drive
Park closes at 1am; park road closes at 10pm
Ⓜ 190th Street (A)

14.14 **St. Frances Cabrini Shrine**
701 Fort Washington Avenue at West 190th Street
☎ 212 923-3536
Open daily 9am-4:30pm
Ⓜ 190th Street (A)

14.15 **New Leaf Cafe**
1 Margaret Corbin Drive in the Heather Garden
☎ 212 568-5323
Tuesday-Saturday for lunch and dinner; Sunday for brunch
and dinner; closed Monday
Ⓜ 190th Street (A)

14.5 **Cafe Santiago**
589 Fort Washington Avenue at West 187th Street
☎ 212 543-9888
Open daily for breakfast, lunch, and dinner
Ⓜ 190th Street (A)

14.6 **Emilou's Cafe**
829 West 181st Street between Cabrini Boulevard
& Pinehurst Avenue
☎ 212 795-9312
Open daily for breakfast, lunch, and dinner
Ⓜ 181st Street (A)

14.7 **Jesse's Place**
812 West 181st Street between Fort Washington & Pinehurst
Avenues, ☎ 212 795-4168
Monday-Friday for lunch and dinner; Saturday, Sunday
for brunch, lunch, and dinner
Ⓜ 181st Street (A)

14.8 **Smart Choice**
805 West 181st Street at Fort Washington Avenue
☎ 212 740-7397
Open daily for breakfast, lunch, and dinner
Ⓜ 181st Street (A)   ►

▶

14.9 Bennett Park

West 183rd to West 185th Street between Fort Washington & Pinehurst Avenues

Ⓜ 181st Street (A)

The rock layer of Manhattan schist that forms the solid foundation for the city's famous skyscrapers runs the full length of the island and is highest at the northern end. Motorists on the George Washington Bridge and Henry Hudson Parkway will notice the sheer faces of cliffs in the section of upper Manhattan called Hudson Heights. Possibly inspired by its geological supremacy as the highest point in the city, Hudson Heights has long been home to women who soared to great heights themselves.

At the time of the American Revolution, upper Manhattan was the home of farmers who were mostly Tory sympathizers. Our boys lost big time at the battle of Fort Washington in 1776, fought in what is now Bennett Park. (The site is bordered by Hudson View Gardens, New York City's first cooperative apartments.)

The ramparts of the fort are outlined in granite blocks, and include the site of the highest natural point in Manhattan (268 feet above sea level). A plaque on Fort Washington Avenue relates the details of the battle, but not the story that a turncoat informed the British of the placement of patriot guns. George Washington watched the capture of 2,800 troops from the New Jersey side of the Hudson. The captured patriots were marched to lower Manhattan and placed in the notorious prison ships in the harbor downtown.

Among the wounded from the Battle of Fort Washington was Margaret "Captain Molly" Corbin, a camp follower who had accompanied her husband, John, who served in the patriot army as a matross, loading and swabbing the cannon. When John was killed, Molly took his place. Left for dead after suffering severe wounds to her arm and face, Molly was found and transported by the patriots to

Philadelphia. She survived, but never fully recovered from her wounds. In 1779, she was made part of the Invalid Corps—soldiers who had been disabled fighting for freedom—and received a lifetime half-pension for the wounds she suffered. But her lifestyle did not inspire D.A.R. types to promote her as a figure of feminine patriotism as they did her more genteel Revolutionary sister, Molly Hays McCauley (Molly Pitcher), with whom she often is confused. It appears that our Molly was a hard-drinking girl.

Molly Corbin, first heroine of the American Revolution, is buried in West Point, just up the Hudson River, but she is commemorated by various sites in upper Manhattan. Going uptown a few blocks, you'll come to a traffic circle before the park entrance—Margaret Corbin Plaza. The spot from which her statue was stolen years ago by some enterprising New Yorkers now has a carved wood sign announcing the entrance to Fort Tryon Park.

Fort Tryon Park is named after the last English civil governor of New York—a bit of a kick in the face for our guys and Molly. But pro-British feelings were at a high in 1935, when park renovations were completed and Rockefeller gave the land to the city. A plaque along the paved road near the site of the battle attests to Molly Corbin's contribution to the Revolution.

Just south of Margaret Corbin Plaza is the St. Frances Cabrini Shrine. The shrine, adjacent to Mother Cabrini High School, houses the relics of the saint known commonly as Mother Cabrini. In the chapel is a large mosaic relating the story of Mother Cabrini's life and works. She was born in Italy on July 15, 1850, and originally wished to become a missionary in China, choosing the name Frances Xavier for the martyred saint. After visiting Rome to request permission to travel to China, she was instructed by Pope Leo XIII, "Not to the East, but to the West." Mother Cabrini was sent to America. Here she cared for the immigrants flooding into New York who had neither social services nor access to the sacraments. She ▶

▶

established schools, hospitals, orphanages, and nursing homes throughout the city. Mother Cabrini became an American citizen in 1909 and was canonized as "Mother of the American Immigrant" in 1946—the first American saint.

Mother Cabrini's relics are housed in a crystal coffin directly under the altar. It is a bit startling to see the relics of this pint-sized nun close up. Mother Cabrini is wearing the black habit of the nuns of her order, the Missionary Sisters of the Sacred Heart of Jesus. The chapel is crammed full of votive offerings and plaques thanking the saint for her intercession in granting miracles, and mementos from her life are displayed in the glass cases lining the gift shop. There are photos, medals, articles of clothing, and even the springs from her dentures. The nuns can be persuaded to open the cases to allow the faithful direct access to the saint's ribbons. Saint Cabrini's feast is November 13. Every year the chapel celebrates with eight masses in five languages. An annual birthday celebration on July 15 includes masses in English, Spanish, and Creole, as well as a children's carnival to which all Hudson Heights children are invited.

St. Frances Cabrini Shrine is located on a cliff overlooking the Hudson River at a site chosen by Mother Cabrini herself. As she drove her buggy to what was then a remote corner of New York City, she stopped there to rest her horses and enjoy the view. Much like those who visit here today, Mother Cabrini found great peace of mind in contemplating the magnificent view over the Hudson River and the Palisades. She purchased the property and opened Sacred Heart Villa, a boarding school for girls. Now known as Mother Cabrini High School, the school continues to educate young Catholic women and was named a Blue Ribbon School by President Clinton in the year 2000, 100 years after its founding.

World War II brought such an influx of German Jews to Hudson Heights that it became known as "Frankfurt on the Hudson." Today it is one of Manhattan's nicest residential neighborhoods, attracting families with small children as well as sizable Polish and Russian immigrant populations. It is not unusual to visit the famous Heather Garden of Fort Tryon Park and find young mothers who speak Spanish, Russian, or Polish seated beside older ladies chatting in German and Yiddish. Each may have a tale of courage to relate.

Visitors to Hudson Heights should be on the lookout for families of yellow hawks, which can occasionally be seen resting after their return from hunting in the thick woods of Fort Tryon Park. Human visitors looking for a place to rest and a bite to eat should head for New Leaf Cafe in the Heather Garden, or Cafe Santiago on Fort Washington Avenue. On 181st Street, stop at Emilou's Cafe for sandwiches and fruit shakes or Jesse's Place for Moroccan fare, soups, and salads. If the day is fine, drop in at Smart Choice, a Russian delicatessen. You can purchase prepared food and sit at the chess tables in Bennett Park. Here, you can indulge in a picnic of marinated mushrooms, pickled herring, and Russian pastries, while enjoying the views and contemplating the scene where Molly Corbin made history as America's first heroine of the Revolution.

KIM DRAMER
Art historian

14.3 Little Red Lighthouse, originally Jeffrey's Hook Lighthouse

1880
West 178th Street & the Hudson River under the east tower of the George Washington Bridge
Tours only, ☎ 212 304-2365

Ⓜ 175th Street (A)

The cast-iron Little Red Lighthouse was originally the North Hook Beacon from 1880 to 1917 in Sandy Hook, New Jersey. In 1921, 10 years before the George Washington Bridge was built, it was moved to this spot,

known at the time as Jeffrey's Hook. After the erection
of the bridge, the lighthouse's beacon was no longer
required, but it was saved from auction by letters from
young readers who loved the classic children's book
The Little Red Lighthouse and the Great Gray Bridge.
JAMES BOORSTEIN
Architectural conservator and artist

RECOMMENDED READING
Hildegarde Hoyt Swift and Lynd Ward, *The Little Red Lighthouse
and the Great Gray Bridge*, Harcourt, 1983.

14.4 **George Washington Bridge**
1931, O.H. Ammann (engineer) & Cass Gilbert (architect)
West 178th Street & Fort Washington Avenue (Manhattan)
to Fort Lee (New Jersey)
Ⓜ 175th Street (A)

Wear your sneakers, walking shoes, or hiking boots.
Whatever your walking pleasure, New York has myriad
unique places—parks, gardens, bridges, and boardwalks
in which, on which, and over which to walk. And well
within an hour of the city you can hike through wilderness
and sand dunes or even climb stone faces.

One of the most exciting city walks is crossing the
George Washington Bridge into New Jersey. From the
bridge's north walk you can see upstream to the mountains
along the Hudson River and watch the river's swift tidal
current rush below your feet. Behind you are cars, buses,
and trucks, and beyond them, the city's towers, but for
a few moments in mid-span, you feel as free as the seagulls
above you.
ESTELLE GILSON
Writer and translator

If your time in New York has not humbled you, then a trip to the base of the George Washington Bridge might. Rising 604 feet above the water, the most influential 20th-century suspension bridge was completed in 1931; the lower level was added 30 years later, making it the world's only 14-lane suspension bridge. Le Corbusier famously described it as "the most beautiful bridge in the world."

To understand why, try examining its underbelly. There is a perfect point, directly under the roadway, where the lines of the span and the towers converge and everything falls—abstractly, serenely—into place.

When you get there, notice the two granite abutments that project well beyond the metal structure, just a few feet from the water. These were designed as the pedestals for the granite cladding designed by Cass Gilbert. The stone covering was abandoned, however, during the Depression, leaving the bridge's intended skeleton exposed. The commissioners and the public came to appreciate the modernist view of the bridge's elegant structure, and over the years, it achieved iconic status. Beginning in 2001, the steel towers were illuminated for special occasions.

Before you leave, take some time to enjoy the Hudson River views. To the south, Manhattan arcs toward the east, allowing a view of the tall Riverside Church tower, seemingly nestled beside the Statue of Liberty and the skyscrapers of downtown. To the north are Manhattan's northern tip, the great Palisades, and the majestic, lazy Hudson, all looking amazingly rural.

JAMES BOORSTEIN
Architectural conservator and artist

RECOMMENDED READING
Le Corbusier, *When the Cathedrals Were White*, 1947, o.p.

Hudson Heights Stroll

14.10 **Hudson View Gardens**
1925, George F. Pelham
116 Pinehurst Avenue between West 183rd
& West 185th Streets
Ⓜ 181st Street (A)

14.11 **Castle Village**
1939, George F. Pelham II
120-200 Cabrini Boulevard between West 181st
& West 186th Streets
Ⓜ 181st Street (A)

14.12 **Birthplace of Maria Callas**
689 West 184th Street between Broadway & Bennett Avenue
Ⓜ 181st Street (A/1)

14.13 **Fort Tryon Park**
West 192nd Street to Dyckman Street between Broadway
& Riverside Drive
Ⓜ 190th Street (A); Dyckman Street (A)

Upper Fort Washington Avenue begins at the George
Washington Bridge in Manhattan. As you proceed north,
you'll see Hudson View Gardens, a Tudor-style co-op
apartment complex built in the 1920's. One street over
is Castle Village, another co-op built over the Hudson in
the 1930's. Beginning at 184th Street, several 1930's Art
Deco-style apartment buildings remain. The brick
Romanesque building at Number 689, now a co-op, was
once a hospital where it's said that Maria Callas was born.
Fort Washington Avenue ends at Fort Tryon Park, one of
the city's most beautiful, with gorgeous views of the
Hudson and the George Washington Bridge. The Cloisters,
which houses part of the Metropolitan Museum's medieval
collection, is located there.
ALFRED CORN
Author and educator

14.16 The Cloisters, The Metropolitan Museum of Art

1939, Allen, Collens & Willis

Fort Tryon Park, ☏ 212 923-3700

March-October: Tuesday-Sunday 9:30am-5:15pm

November-February: Tuesday-Sunday 9:30am-4:45pm;

closed Monday year-round

Ⓜ 190th Street (A)

The Cloisters, an extraordinary branch of the Metropolitan Museum at Fort Tryon Park, is a time machine that takes us back to medieval days. It is rich in its collection of tapestries, windows, statues, and icons from before the Renaissance, and the music playing softly throughout is authentic and reverent.

HUGH MARTIN
Songwriter

Unicorn Tapestries

c. 1500

Unicorn Tapestries Room

The Cloisters houses the celebrated Unicorn Tapestries, a series of late medieval tapestries depicting The Hunt of the Unicorn. The medieval legend, an allegory of both human love and the Incarnation of Christ, relates that only a virgin can tame the swift and powerful unicorn. An ivory tusk from a narwhale, once thought to be that of a unicorn, stands in one corner of the tapestry room.

KIM DRAMER
Art historian

The Cloisters' Gardens

1938, Margaret Freeman and James J. Rorimer

There are three different gardens: the Trie Cloister and the Bonnefont Cloister Herb Garden are located on the lower level; the Cuxa Cloister is located near the entrance on the upper level.

Three cloisters in the building have gardens planted

according to horticultural information gathered from medieval art and literature. This place is relatively tourist-free and there are magnificent views of the Hudson from the terraces. All this, along with the smell of the flowers and herbs, makes you feel as if you're in an old palazzo in Tuscany, even though the building itself is constructed from various buildings from France.

KATHARINE RISTICH
Editor

RECOMMENDED READING
Bonnie Young, Malcolm Varon and the Metropolitan Museum of Art, *A Walk Through the Cloisters*, Harry N. Abrams Inc., 1990.

In the spring and summer visit the outdoor, early-14th-century-style herb garden, located in the Bonnefont Cloister. The enchanting smells of 250 species of flowers, plants, and herbs include those used for medicinal purposes, for painting illuminated manuscripts, for poison, and for cooking.

CHRISTINE MOOG
Graphic designer

14.17 Arts for Transit: *At the Start . . . At Long Last . . .*
1999, Sheila Levrant de Bretteville
Ⓜ Inwood-207th Street (A)

Traveling north to Fort Tryon Park or the Cloisters at the last (or first) stop on the A train in Inwood, one passes through Sheila Levrant de Bretteville's multifaceted oral history project at 207th Street and Broadway. *At the Start . . . At Long Last . . .* includes on the walls of the mezzanines scores of reminiscences about the neighborhood by community members past and present, representing several waves of immigration. The words and notes of the jazz classic "Take the A Train" are etched into the railings, and long, leggy mosaic Caribbean festival dancers descend or ascend the elevator with you from the street to the station.

JOYCE KOZLOFF
Artist

14.18 Inwood Hill Park

Entrance on West 215th Street & Indian Road

Ⓜ Inwood-207th Street (A)

> Inwood Hill Park is virgin forest, not chopped down
> since the days of the Dutch.
>
> PETE SEEGER
> *Musician*

Take the A train to 207th Street and walk a few blocks west
to Inwood Hill Park. The park, bounded on the west by the
Hudson River, on the north by the Harlem River and on the
south by Dyckman Street, occupies the northernmost tip of
Manhattan Island. From the entrance on Seaman Avenue,
wide paths wind along the edge of acres of ballfields. The
fields descend to a broad tidal marsh tucked into a cove of
the Harlem River. Covered by mud and reeds at low tide,
and shallow water at high tide, the marsh attracts legions of
birds. On the south side of the open fields are dense woods
and soaring ridges of stone, and at the opening of a narrow
valley between two ridges is a small boulder bearing a
bronze plaque that reads. *Shorakkupoch*.

According to legend, on this site of the principal
Manhattan Indian village, Peter Minuit in 1626 purchased
Manhattan Island for trinkets and beads worth about 60
guilders. This boulder also marks the spot where a tulip
tree (*Liriodendron tulipifera*) grew to a height of 165 feet
and a girth of 20 feet. It was until its death in 1933, at the
age of 280 years, the last living link to the Reckgawawanc
Indians who lived here.

Beyond the boulder, paths snake through thick woods
up the face of the western ridge. The trails pass alongside
tall cliffs and through groves of ancient, towering tulip-
poplar trees, perhaps the last vestige of primeval forest on
the island. At the summit of the ridge, the foliage opens to
reveal panoramic views of the Hudson. There are expansive vistas across to the New Jersey Palisades, south to the

George Washington Bridge, and many miles upriver to the Tappan Zee. The serenity of the spot is only slightly undercut by the sounds of traffic on the West Side Highway far below.

Peter Minuit's meeting with Native Americans at their village may be apocryphal. Historians have proposed other locations for the exchange, or suggested that an official purchase never took place. Native people had no conception of the private ownership of land, so even if the "purchase" occurred, it had little meaning for them. Still, there is a palpable sense of history here. It is easy to imagine Indians living in this valley. Fish and small game would have been abundant in the tidal marsh, and patches of corn or squash would have grown nicely in the low fields. A scout could run quickly up the western ridge, and from its peak observe anyone approaching from the Hudson. The proximity of two rivers made the village easily accessible, yet the high ridge hid and protected the valley behind it. Stone caves in the cliffs provided convenient shelter, as confirmed by Indian artifacts discovered there and removed in 1909.

The undisturbed landscape of Inwood Hill Park and the presence of a Native American past join to convey an impression of what Manhattan was like before being reshaped by Europeans.

DAVID L. REESE
Curator, Gracie Mansion

THE BRONX

15

New Jersey

Yonkers

Hudson River

College of Mt St Vincent

Riverdale Av

Palisade Av

Saw Mill River Pkwy

12

Wave Hill

E 241st St

Van Cortlandt Park

W 249th St

Riverdale

W 239th St

Broadway

Major Deegan Expressway

Woodlawn Cemetery

E 233rd St

Baychester Avenue

Bronx River Pkwy

11

Palisade Avenue

Independence Av

Henry Hudson Pkwy

Van Cortlandt Village

13

E 222nd St

Bainbridge Av

Mosholu Parkway

W Gun Hill Rd

Jerome Avenue Expressway

Webster Avenue

Boston Rd

E Gun Hill Rd

Eastchester Rd

Spuyten Duyvil

Jerome Park Reservoir

Inwood Hill Park

Broadway

E Kingsbridge Rd

Concourse Blvd

200th St

Kazimiroff Blvd

9

New York Botanical Garden

Willamsbridge Rd

Astor Avenue

W Fordham Rd

5

6

Manhattan

Grand Concourse (University Avenue)

E Fordham Rd

Belmont Av

Bronx and Pelham

Hall of Fame Ter

4

Arthur Av

8

W 180th St

187th St

Crescent Av

10

Lydig Av

Third Av

7

186th St

Bronx Zoo

White Plains Rd

Morris Park Avenue

E Tremont Avenue

Cross Bronx Expwy

E Tremont Avenue

Claremont Park

Crotona Park

Sheridan Expwy

Bronx River Av

Cross Bronx Expwy

Castle Hill Avenue

Hutchinson River Pkwy

Jerome Avenue

Concourse Blvd

Webster Avenue

Third Avenue

Boston Road

E 167th St

3

E 164th St

2

Grand Concourse

E 161st St

Joyce Kilmer Park

E 163rd St

1

Bruckner Expwy

River Av

E 149th St

Westchester Av

Sound View Park

Soundview Avenue

Pugsley's Creek Park

Major Deegan Expwy

E 138th St

St Mary's Park

Bruckner Expwy

Hunts Point Market

Third Avenue Bridge

Willis Av Bridge

Port Morris

North Brother Island

East

River

Triborough Bridge

Randalls Island

South Brother Island

Riker's Island

Flushing Bay

Wards Island

Queens

La Guardia Airport

THE BRONX

The Bronx, City Island
& Hart Island

THE BRONX

15.1 **ABC Warehouse Outlet**
1055 Bronx River Avenue at Bruckner Boulevard
☏ 718 842-8770
Monday-Friday 10am-7pm; Saturday 9am-7pm;
Sunday 11am-6pm
Ⓜ Whitlock Station (6)

🎁 Christmas shop for your trendiest friends—exactly like the
Manhattan version, just bigger, cheaper, and top-secret.
DONALD ROBERTSON
Creative director, Glamour

15.2 **Yankee Stadium**
*1923, Osborn Engineering Co.; 1976, rebuilt by
Praeger-Kavanagh-Waterbury*
River Avenue & East 161st Street, ☏ 718 293-6000
For schedule information: www.yankees.com
Ⓜ 161st Street-Yankee Stadium (B/D/4)

After admiring the superb restoration of Grand Central
Station (see p. 243), go below and take the Number 4
subway north to one of New York's most accessible
pleasure palaces, Yankee Stadium. As the elevated train
approaches the 161st Street station, high in the air over the
bars and souvenir shops of River Avenue, there is, from
the left side of the train, a tantalizing millisecond view of the
brilliantly lit field through a slot in the right field bleachers,
only 80 feet away. This profound moment prepares you
for the most stylized, secular procession in all sports...
a descent to the street, along the walkway around

the building, past the ticket windows and T-shirt vendors, through the jammed entry gates, up the ramp, across the concourse, and through the narrow, dark vomitory—and then, there it is: one of the most heart-stopping views in all New York. The shape of the house directs everyone's attention to the 60 feet between the pitcher's mound and home plate. The triple decks are steeply stacked so that the sense of intimacy is never lost. And the simplicity of materials and colors underscores the classical, traditional values of the architectural organization—the incomprehensibly deep green of the natural grass field, the wall of Yankee blue on the tiered seats, and the white icing of the surrounding cornice over which no ball has ever been hit. And then there are, of course, those uniforms with pinstripes, since 1912. There can be, arguably, no more memorable moment for a New Yorker than the joyous experience, by day or by night, of Yankee Stadium. And don't ignore the hot dogs and beer...

ALEXANDER COOPER
Architect

Yankee Clipper

Ferry stops along the East River at the South Street Seaport, East 34th Street, and East 90th Street

☎ 800 53-FERRY or www.nywaterway.com

You don't have to be a fan of the Yankees, or even of baseball, to enjoy the ferry trip up the East and Harlem rivers to Yankee Stadium. On the trip up, the ferry is animated by the intensity of the crowd in anticipation of the game. The return trip is full of awe: the night is cool, the passengers are happy, and the extraordinary lights of Manhattan dazzle and amaze.

DEBORAH BERKE
Architect

15.3 Lorelei Fountain

1899, Ernst Herter
East 164th Street at the Grand Concourse, northeast corner
of Joyce Kilmer Park
Ⓜ 161st Street-Yankee Stadium (B/D/4)

Not far from where a legendary baseball team captured 26
World Series titles, the legendary "Lorelei" peers into
Yankee Stadium, linking myths across an immense cultural
divide. The Lorelei Fountain (also called the Heinrich
Heine Fountain) honors the German poet (1797-1856)
who is lionized in his homeland as the most famous writer
of the generation after Goethe. The monument evokes
"Die Lorelei" from the poem immortalizing the siren
whose bewitching song lured sailors to their deaths.
Perhaps she now casts her sorcery upon those sportsmen
who deign to tinker with the mythological status of the
New York Yankees. The marble sculptural group depicts
Lorelei sitting among mermaids, dolphins, and seashells
on a rock above the Rhine River.

A successful campaign by German writers and scholars
helped convince Empress Elizabeth of Austria to procure
financing for a monument commemorating the poet, and
in 1888, the sculptor Ernst Herter received the commission. Slated for the poet's home city of Düsseldorf, the
monument was met by intensely negative political pressure
and ultimately rejected. The fountain was purchased by
the German-American singing society, Arion, in 1893 and
dedicated on the Grand Concourse Plaza (as it was then
known) on July 8, 1899. It was moved to the park's north
end in 1940.

Years of neglect and vandalism took their toll. The
figure's arms, legs, and heads were damaged and, in the
1980's, Lorelei was painted black—making the statue,
again, a statement of the times. In 1999, private and public

funding through the Adopt-A-Monument program restored the sculpture, and returned it to its original site in a newly landscaped setting that links Old World grandeur with the 21st century.

PHYLLIS SAMITZ COHEN
Director, Adopt-A-Monument and Mural programs, The Municipal Art Society of New York

15.4 Bronx Community College

1912, original buildings by McKim, Mead & White and Calvert Vaux
University Avenue between West 180th Street & Hall of Fame Terrace, ☎ 718 289-5100
Ⓜ 183rd Street (4); 182nd-183rd Street (B/D)

The Hall of Fame for Great Americans and National Landmark Shrine

1900, McKim, Mead & White
Entrance on Hall of Fame Terrace on western periphery of Bronx Community College campus, ☎ 718 289-5973
Open daily 10am-4pm

Hardly anybody but Regis Philbin knows that Sylvanus Thayer was the first superintendent of West Point. Among the busts of military geniuses, scientists, physicians, teachers, and leaders featured at the Hall of Fame for Great Americans are some of the most well-known—and, sadly, least-known—names to all Americans. This Stanford White-designed colonnade, on a bluff overlooking the beautiful Palisades at the highest point of the Bronx, has been an inspiration to historians, educators, students, and world visitors over the last century. An award-winning national landmark and the country's original hall of fame, it's a quiet, noble, and important corner of New York and its history.

FERNANDO FERRER
Former Bronx Borough President

The Hall of Fame at Bronx Community College contains the DNA of our nation's roots. Described by Norman Mailer as "The People's Palace," this national landmark stands as a reminder that America's strength derives ultimately from its people.

The Hall of Fame opened in 1900, one year before the Nobel Prizes were established, and for a while "Hall of Famer" carried greater cachet in American life than "Nobel Laureate." Even popular culture followed suit: in *The Wizard of Oz*, the munchkins sing of Dorothy, "She'll be a bust, be a bust, be a bust in the Hall of Fame!"

The Hall of Fame is the quintessential democratic institution. Candidates are chosen by a board of electors of 100 distinguished citizens nationwide. Four honorees still wait in the wings to join their peers: Supreme Court Justice Louis Dembitz Brandeis, elected in 1973; Clara Barton, organizer of the American Red Cross; Luther Burbank, horticulturalist; and Andrew Carnegie, industrialist and philanthropist. All elected in 1976, they are American legends on hold. Meanwhile, one visible result of the recent revitalization project is the restoration of the portrait bronzes. Suddenly, there's a fresh, bright gleam in the Bronx.

RALPH M. ROURKE
Director, Hall of Fame for Great Americans

15.5 Jimmy's Bronx Cafe

281 West Fordham Road off the Major Deegan Expressway
☎ 718 329-2000
Open daily for brunch, lunch, dinner, and late-night meals
Ⓜ Fordham Road (4)

🍴 I spent a few years in the 1990's working in one of those on-the-rebound-but-not-quite-there-yet Bronx neighborhoods. I watched with interest as an entire nearby block of derelict buildings was rebuilt into a flashy incarnation called Jimmy's Bronx Cafe. Don't let the homespun name fool you. Jimmy's is an elegant full-menu restaurant by day and a sizzling Latin dance club—complete with a bandstand for live acts—by night. The expansive dining room looks out onto the University Heights Bridge spanning the Harlem River—not quite a match for the view at the River Cafe, but give it points for trying.

From the looks of his anteroom wall, the proprietor, Jimmy Rodriguez, is one of those go-getter New York restaurateurs who strives to be everybody's friend; photos of him posing with local and national powerbrokers of every political leaning—left, right, and in between—abound. I didn't quite appreciate how irrepressible Jimmy was until I heard a news story that made me smile. In 1995, the United Nations marked its 50th anniversary. They held a celebration in New York and invited the leaders of all the member nations to attend the event. For a week the city was awash in presidents, prime ministers, and kings. Naturally they took advantage of the best dining and entertainment New York had to offer: five-star restaurants, Broadway shows, and the Metropolitan Opera. But not Fidel Castro; he went to Jimmy's Bronx Cafe.

MICHAEL MISCIONE
Writer

15.6 Poe Cottage

c. 1812

In Poe Park at East Kingsbridge Road & the Grand Concourse

☎ 718 881-8900

Saturday 10am 4pm; Sunday 1pm-5pm; closed Monday-Friday except for prearranged group tours

Ⓜ Kingsbridge Road (B/D/4)

It was always there, for as long as anyone could remember, at the end of a city park: the last home of Edgar Allan Poe. For Bronx schoolchildren, when it came time to learn about Poe, the material took on a special buzz; the man once lived in the neighborhood.

Poe Cottage is a lovely little museum dedicated to the poet as well as the place where he wrote "Annabel Lee" and "The Bells." Poe lived there from 1846 to 1849, the year of his death. The small rooms, the steep stairs, tell of his less-than-opulent life. In a spare upstairs room, a video recording, wildly anachronistic in this setting but informative, recounts his years in the Bronx.

About 10,000 visitors a year come to Poe Cottage—substantial, but less than would fill the lower stands of Yankee Stadium on a bad weather day. Yet for the adventurous tourist, there is a Bronx beyond Yankee Stadium. Poe Cottage is 10 minutes north on the same subway lines that run to the ballpark and then a five-minute walk from the subway station. A few blocks east are entrances to both the New York Botanical Garden (see p. 416) and the Bronx Zoo. (Growing up in the Bronx, we were familiar with the zoo downtown in Central Park and sometimes we went there, but we knew ours was the real zoo, and it is the largest city zoo in America.)

A short ride away on the eastbound Number 12 bus at Fordham Road, which also stops at the zoo and botanical gardens, is the Arthur Avenue section of Italian specialty stores and restaurants. A colorful place for lunch, it is called with quaint civic pride, "Little Italy in the Bronx."

AVERY CORMAN
Author

Ferragosto di Belmont

15.7   **Roberto's**
(see next page)

15.8   **Ann & Tony's**
2407 Arthur Avenue at 187th Street, ☎ 718 933-1469
Tuesday-Sunday for lunch and dinner; closed Monday
Ⓜ Fordham Road (B/D), or Pelham Parkway (2/5), to BX12 bus

🍽 Belmont's annual Ferragosto takes place on the second
Sunday in August and celebrates Italian culture in a century-
old Italian neighborhood dense with cafes, markets,
bakeries, clam bars, and shops. Running along Arthur
Avenue between 187th Street and Crescent Avenue, the
festival includes opera, Italian folk songs, and, of course,
food. One year, my young daughter and I watched a
cheesemaker (who happened to be Bolivian) sculpt pigs,
giraffes, and elephants out of mozzarella cheese. We ate
until we could eat no more.

On quieter days, Belmont is a great area for shopping
and wandering. My favorite restaurants are Ann & Tony's,
which has been in the neighborhood for something like
40 years, and gives discounts if you have a Yankees game
ticket, and Roberto's, a relative newcomer slightly off the
beaten track (it's around the corner from Arthur Avenue
and often looks likes it's closed, when it's not) which has
some of the most original cuisine in the area (check out the
ricotta cheesecake).

Belmont is making a comeback as a cultural venue,
and the Bronx Dance Company relocated its studio to the
neighborhood in 2000.
MYRA ALPERSON
Editor and publisher, NoshNews

15.7 **Roberto's**
632 Crescent Avenue at 186th Street & Belmont Avenue
☎ 718 733-9503
Tuesday-Friday for lunch and dinner; Saturday, Sunday
for dinner; closed Monday
Ⓜ Fordham Road (B/D), or Pelham Parkway (2/5), to BX12 bus

🍽 The best restaurant in New York City is in the Bronx—the
only borough with "the" in front of it. And Roberto's is
"the" best. The restaurant is two blocks over from Arthur
Avenue, but walking into the dining room, it feels more
like Italy. You can smell the food in the wood of it...in
the tables...the chairs.

There are rumors about Roberto's. Some say deliveries

are literally unpacked and cleaned on the sidewalk out front so as to prevent small, unwanted guests. Another rumor has the kitchen on wheels, so that every night, everything can be rolled out to keep the corners spotless, which they are. But these are rumors. There is only one fact: the food in your mouth.

My advice is to let Roberto order for you. There are only about 20 tables in the restaurant and at some point he'll come out in his white chef's coat, cruise the tables, and stop to say hello. Before he leaves you he'll ask you in a nonchalant way if you'd like him to choose for you.

It would be a mistake to say no.

FRANK PUGLIESE
Playwright and screenwriter

This restaurant's out-of-the-way location hasn't discouraged customers, who wait in line nightly (no reservations) to sample Roberto's out-of-this-world meats, fish, and fresh vegetables. The homemade sauces are worthy of the unsurpassed fresh pastas, made daily *a mano* on the premises by Roberto's own mother.

FISHER STEVENS
Actor, director, and co-owner of GreeneStreet Films

15.9 New York Botanical Garden

200th Street & Kazimiroff Boulevard, ☏ 718 817-8700
April-October: Tuesday-Sunday 10am-6pm, closed Monday, except Monday holidays; November-March: Tuesday-Sunday 10am-4pm, closed Monday, except Monday holidays
Ⓜ Bedford Park Boulevard (B/D); Bedford Park Boulevard-Lehman College (4); or Metro-North Railroad (Harlem Local) to New York Botanical Garden

Being a plant lover, the first places I look up in any new city are the botanical gardens. And since my hospital (Beth Abraham Hospital, where *Awakenings* occurred in 1969) is right opposite the New York Botanical Garden in the Bronx, I am lucky enough to be able to wander through this every day. Though I have been doing this for more than 30 years, I still find freshness and surprises and new enchantments on every walk. Often I go there after I have seen my patients in the morning, to let my thoughts distill themselves while I am striding round the garden visiting my favorite plants.

OLIVER SACKS
Neurologist and author

15.10 Bronx Zoo

Fordam Road & the Bronx River Parkway, ☎ 718 367-1010
Ⓜ Pelham Parkway (2), walk west to the Bronxdale entrance

Holiday Lights Exhibit
Friday of Thanksgiving weekend through December 15th,
Friday-Sunday 5pm-9pm; December 16th-January 6th,
open daily 5pm-9pm; closed December 24th

Want to see magic? Go to the Holiday Lights exhibit at the Bronx Zoo. Against bare branches and the crisp, night sky, white lights twinkle away. The trees along the zoo's paths are strung with lights to guide you. Monkeys and birds hang in the trees, pink flamingos flank a bridge, frogs leap from lily pads, a spider spins her web—all created from lights that shimmer in the cold air.

Happily you find hot chocolate and popcorn vendors stationed throughout the zoo—then you discover the open flame pit where you can buy a skewer of marshmallows that you toast yourself. Can it possibly get any better than this? Yes—they sell graham crackers and chocolate, too.

Ice sculptors create works of art. Carolers stroll the zoo's paths. You marvel at the surreal beauty and the fantasy, made all the more amazing when you remember you're in New York City... breathtaking.

ELISSA STEIN
Graphic designer and writer

15.11 **Palisade Avenue, Riverdale**
Bounded on the south by Spuyten Duyvil and on the north
by the College of Mount St. Vincent
Ⓜ Metro-North Railroad, Spuyten Duyvil Station

A walk on Palisade Avenue in the Riverdale section of the
Bronx gives startling vistas of wooded country homes (and
a few large estates) that have survived modern urban
development. Despite a few contemporary eyesores and
some nearby high-rise construction, most of it conveniently
blocked by towering trees, much of Palisade Avenue is bordered by late 19th- and early 20th-century manor houses
that had or still have great river views. Start in Spuyten
Duyvil, near the Metro-North railroad station, and wander
north alongside forests and streams, past the Wave Hill
gardens, and on toward the College of Mount St. Vincent,
where one can see Fonthill, the Macbeth-like Scottish
castle (now a library) built by legendary American actor
Edwin Forrest in the mid-1800's. This surprising area has
more in common with upstate Hudson River villas than
anything in New York City.
ROBERT MARX
Essayist, producer, and foundation executive

15.12 **Wave Hill**
Begun 1843 with later additions; 1975, renovated by Stephen Lapp
Entrance on Independence Avenue at West 249th Street
☎ 718 549-3200
April 15-October 14: Tuesday-Sunday 9am-5:30pm, closed
Monday; October 15-April 14: Tuesday-Sunday 9am-4:30pm,
closed Monday
Metro-North Railroad to Riverdale Station, walk east on
254th Street to Independence Avenue, turn right to Wave Hill
Ⓜ 231st Street (1), to BX7 or BX10 bus to 252nd Street

I feel at home amongst the splendor of Wave Hill's sprawling vegetation and transcendent beauty. It is a fabulously
well-kept and vibrant series of gardens with a variety

of places in which to wander about or sit. Though it has
a great deal of energy, it is also a very quiet and peaceful
place. The nearby river adds to this calm. Wave Hill
embodies the drama and history of the Palisades, and I am
especially fond of its touch of history, including the house
on the grounds where Toscanini once lived.

Most beautiful are the gardens, so carefully tended and
groomed. Many trees are labeled and there are greenhouses
filled with tropical plants, as well as a wonderfully
eclectic herb garden. The various greenhouse plants change
throughout the seasons to include a lovely array of orchids,
succulents, South African bulbs, and cacti.

AGNES GUND
President, The Museum of Modern Art

15.13 Woodlawn Cemetery

1863
Enter at Jerome Avenue north of Bainbridge Avenue, or
at the southwest corner of 233rd Street & Webster Avenue
☎ 718 920-0500
Open daily 8:30am–5pm
Ⓜ Woodlawn (4)

Cemeteries are an integral component of any city and
should not be overlooked. On an elevated site in the Bronx
where Washington's troops kept a lookout for the advancing British Army, Woodlawn Cemetery was created in the
latter half of the 19th century. In reality, it is a beautifully
landscaped, English-style, 400-acre park (half the size of
Central Park) that is the setting for impressive mausoleums
and monuments. The cemetery is an oasis that contains
roughly 3,000 magnificent trees and is the final resting
place of many wealthy industrialists and notables. The
trees include specimens of weeping pendant silver linden,
European cut-leaf beech, and umbrella pine. The industrialists, buried in veritable tombs, include members of the
Armour, Belmont, Borden, Gould, Macy, Westinghouse,

Whitney, and Woolworth families. The notables include
George M. Cohan, Admiral Farragut, Fiorello La Guardia,
Herman Melville, and Elizabeth Cady Stanton. Duke
Ellington and Miles Davis lie alongside each other.

The Belmont mausoleum is a replica of the Chapel of
St. Hubert at Château d'Amboise in France, where
Leonardo da Vinci is buried. There is a monument in the
shape of an Egyptian funeral barge for department store
owners Isidor and Ida Straus, who went down on the
Titanic together after she refused to leave his side.

A final interesting anecdote about Woodlawn is that
the ransom money in the Lindbergh baby case was handed
over to the kidnapper just outside one of the gates.

WILLIAM MUIR MANGER JR.
Chairman, Director's Council of the Museum
of the City of New York

RECOMMENDED READING
Judi Culbertson & Tom Randall, *Permanent New Yorkers: A
Biographical Guide to the Cemeteries of New York*, Chelsea Green
Publishing, 1987.

15.14 Bartow-Pell Mansion Museum

1675; 1842, alterations by Minard Lafever; 1914, restoration
by Delano & Aldrich
895 Shore Road, Pelham Bay Park, ☎ 718 885-1461
Wednesday, Saturday, Sunday noon-4pm; closed Monday,
Tuesday, Thursday, Friday and the last three weeks of August;
gardens are open Tuesday-Sunday 8:30am-4:30pm
Ⓜ Pelham Bay Park (6), then change to Westchester Bee-line
bus No. 45 to Bartow-Pell (bus does not run on Sunday)

This Federal mansion, the sole survivor of more than a
dozen grand manor houses that once overlooked Long
Island Sound, is a favorite place for film, TV, and fashion
shoots, as well as settings for wedding pictures.

Nevertheless, it remains relatively undiscovered by
tourists. In fact, it's possible to be the only visitor enjoying
the mansion's Greek Revival interiors, the freestanding

elliptical staircase, period furniture and paintings. The grounds have a lovely garden as well as a wonderful view of Long Island Sound. The mansion can be reserved for "breakfast, luncheon, or tea tours," in case you have a sudden urge to play the country squire.

KATHARINE RISTICH
Editor

CITY ISLAND

15.16 **Johnny's Reef Restaurant**
2 City Island Avenue, City Island, ☎ 718 885-2086
March-November: daily for lunch and dinner;
closed December-February

Ⓜ Pelham Bay Park (6), then take Bx29 bus to the last stop and walk two blocks south

🍽 The waterfront community of City Island is, stem to stern, a gem on the Long Island Sound—from its waterfront park to its quaint art and antique shops to more seafood restaurants than you could ever hope to see in your life along its mile-long main and side streets. If you explore City Island Avenue, follow it to its end. At the tip of the island is Johnny's Reef Restaurant. It's a cross section of humanity: internationally renowned musicians, artists, business owners, clergy, and dads and moms taking their kids to a really great old-fashioned fish fry. The lines are long but manageable. The cocktail sauce is the best this side of heaven and the fish is fried by the tractor-trailer load.

FERNANDO FERRER
Former Bronx Borough President

HART ISLAND

15.17 **Abandoned NIKE Missile Base and Potter's Field**
Not open to the public

Most visitors to City Island never wander past the oyster bars and seafood joints that line the main drag, City Island Avenue. But if you stroll north on Fordham Street, past the quaintly shabby City Island Museum (well worth a visit, ☎ 718 885-0008) you'll wind up at the foot of a Department of Corrections ferry slip. Across the water you can glimpse one of New York City's most peculiar historical sites, Hart Island.

During the Civil War, Hart Island served as a training facility for New York State's African-American troops and later as a prison camp to hold captured Confederate soldiers. In 1868 the city purchased the island to create a Potter's Field—a cemetery for its indigent and unclaimed dead. The island still serves this purpose today. It is supervised by the Department of Corrections, whose inmates perform the burials and maintenance.

Less known is that from 1955 to 1961, the U.S. Army established a NIKE surface-to-air missile base on the island. This facility was one of several NIKE sites around the metropolitan region that was built as a last line of defense against a Cold War Soviet bomb attack.

Though Hart Island is not accessible to the public, I was fortunate enough to attend an official tour once. (No, not as a prisoner!) What remained of the NIKE site—the main reason I went—wasn't much to see: a ground-level concrete slab, a couple of empty, covered-over underground missile pits—each about as big as a city bus—and lots and lots of weeds. But just knowing that a nuclear missile was cranked and ready to go somewhere inside the city limits couldn't help but get your heart racing a bit. Elsewhere on the island, the Potter's Field, with its white grave markers and little brick storage sheds, was more photogenic but undeniably depressing.

The realization that these two unrelated institutions—one, the product of war, the other, the product of charity—both coexist on the same lonely piece of New York real estate always gives me pause.

MICHAEL MISCIONE
Writer

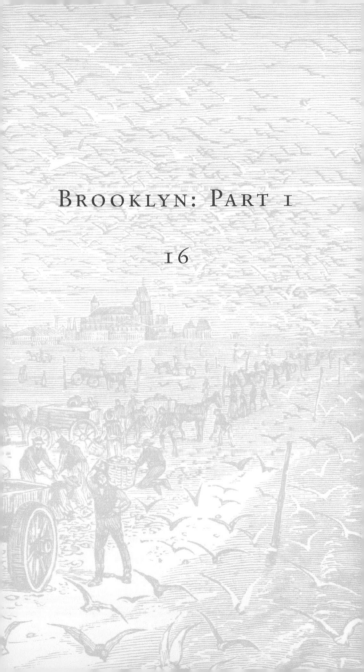

Brooklyn: Part 1

16

Red Hook, Park Slope,
Prospect Park, Institute Park,
Crown Heights, Sunset Park,
Dyker Heights & Gravesend,
Coney Island, Brighton Beach &
Sheepshead Bay

RED HOOK

Red Hook Stroll

16.1 **Visitation of the Blessed Virgin Mary**
98 Richards Street between Visitation Place & Verona Street
Ⓜ Carroll Street (F/G)

16.2 **Balzano's (aka Sunny's)**
253 Conover Street at Reed Street
Ⓜ Carroll Street (F/G)

To the uninitiated, the tough and gritty neighborhood
of Red Hook, home of New York's only container port,
may seem like an unlikely place for a Saturday afternoon
stroll, but in fact it is one of the most engaging. Away
from the giant cranes of the port, the hulking presence of
a housing project and some ragged blocks, the village is a
wonderful relic of the old-time working waterfront from
the days when New York had the busiest harbor in the
world. It's where Arthur Miller did his research for *A View
from the Bridge* and where *On the Waterfront* might have
been shot. The horizon is low except for the steeple of
the Visitation Parish, which has windows by Tiffany and
a vaulted wooden ceiling, ribbed like the inside of a clipper
ship. (The church is open during regularly scheduled
services.) The rowhouses are mid-19th century and lined
up around Van Brunt, a single main street named for the

town's Dutch colonial heritage. Here, one-time seamen still swap stories at the American Legion Hall and several local artists have opened galleries.

Forty-two longshoremen's bars once lined the water; 🍴 now Balzano's, also called Sunny's, is the only one that remains, still displaying in the window the big coffee urn that once served thousands of cups a morning. All along the shore, shapes of the prosperous past—the Romanesque Revival New York shipyards, the grain terminal, and the upside-down funnel-shaped Revere sugar refinery—stand like dramatic pieces of sculpture, now all empty. Walk out onto Pier 41 or the Beard Street pier—two long wharves that are occupied by rosy brick Civil War-era warehouses, the finest in the country. They've recently been renovated to house small businesses and a popular art show each spring. Breathe in the surrounding New York Bay and enjoy an uncommon view. Governors Island seems to be a stone's throw away; it was wading distance at low tide for the early settlers. The Statue of Liberty is so close that it could be the patron saint of Red Hook.

ELIZABETH HAWES
Writer

PARK SLOPE

16.3   **Coco Roco**

   392 Fifth Avenue between 6th & 7th Streets

   ☎ 212 965-3376

   Monday-Friday for lunch and dinner; Saturday, Sunday for brunch and dinner

   Ⓜ 4th Avenue-9th Street (M/N/R/F)

🍴 Authentic Peruvian cuisine. My friend, a total food snob who lives on the Upper East Side, will actually take the long subway trip on the F train to the "outer borough" just for the Argentine steak stir-fry—a bargain at less than 10 dollars.

JON MADOF
Musician

The Battle of Brooklyn

16.4   **Old Stone House**
336 3rd Street between Fourth & Fifth Avenues,
in James J. Byrne Memorial Playground, ☎ 718 768-3195
Call for hours
Ⓜ 4th Avenue-9th Street (M/N/R/F)

16.5   **William Alexander Middle School**
350 Fifth Avenue between 4th & 5th Streets
☎ 718 369-7603
Ⓜ 4th Avenue-9th Street (M/N/R/F)

16.6   **The Maryland 400 Monument**
1895, McKim, Mead & White
Near Lookout Hill, off Well House Drive in Prospect Park
Ⓜ Grand Army Plaza (1/2)

No less than the fate of the American Revolution—and in turn, the fledgling United States—hung in balance when British forces engaged George Washington's army on an improbable Brooklyn battlefield in August 1776. The fight, the largest military encounter of the American Revolution, is known as the Battle of Brooklyn. (Some call it the Battle of Long Island. Bah on them!)

It did not begin well for the ill-equipped Americans, who were outnumbered four-to-one by the Crown's 33,000 newly landed British regulars and Hessian mercenaries. After a stealthy nighttime flanking maneuver, the British Army trapped and attacked the American forces near present-day Prospect Park. Soon, the American ranks broke. Those who managed to survive the ensuing slaughter fled toward the American lines in Brooklyn Heights with the British in pursuit. The Colonial Army needed to retreat and regroup so it could live to fight another day; otherwise, it would be snuffed out and the Revolution likely would be lost there and then. To stem the rout, one of Washington's commanders, General

William Alexander, led a force of 400 Maryland volunteers to engage and delay the enemy at the Old Stone House. Nearly three-quarters of the Marylanders were killed or wounded in the fighting, but their heroic efforts were not in vain. The delay bought General Washington the time he needed to gather his army and escape across the East River to Manhattan.

The Old Stone House had a bittersweet fate. It passed from one landowner to another. For a while it even served as the clubhouse for the Brooklyn baseball team that would one day become the Dodgers. It was demolished in the 1890's. Then, in the 1930's, it was rebuilt by the Parks Department using the original stones. Today it houses a museum that recounts the details of the battle.

Across the street is William Alexander Middle School, named for the fearless commander of the doomed Marylanders, who, incidentally, survived the battle. A mural depicting the engagement can be seen in the vestibule of the Fifth Avenue entrance nearest 4th Street.

In 1895 the Maryland Society and the then-city of Brooklyn erected a Monument to the Maryland 400 inside Prospect Park. Vandalized and ignored, it has not weathered the years well. But the inscription, quoting George Washington as he watched the carnage from afar, has lost none of its poignancy: "Good God! What brave fellows I must this day lose."

MICHAEL MISCIONE
Writer

PROSPECT PARK & INSTITUTE PARK

16.7 The Soldiers' and Sailors' Memorial Arch
1892, John H. Duncan
Grand Army Plaza
Exhibits in the spring and fall, ☎ 718 965-8999
Ⓜ Grand Army Plaza (1/2)

I've always seen the Soldiers' and Sailors' Monument at Grand Army Plaza as a long-forgotten but magnificent landmark to pass by as you wheel around it on your way to the Brooklyn Museum or Prospect Park. I never thought of it as a destination until someone reminded me that the base of the arch held some of the most exquisite bas-reliefs of Civil War scenes, executed by Thomas Eakins and William O'Donovan. The sculpture above the arch facing Prospect Park is heroic and a must-see. But the surprise was my discovery of a door on the outer side of the arch opening to a small lobby and set of stairs that wind their way up to a good-sized rectangular gallery with a vaulted ceiling and skylight.

My curiosity and a healthy sense of creative trespassing helped me find the viewing roof, officially accessible to the public twice a year when the gallery mounts exhibitions.

If you find yourself there during an exhibition, make your way to this spot, which overlooks the treetops of Prospect Park—a magnificent and triumphal destination!
FRANK LUPO
Architect

16.8 Prospect Park
1873, Frederick Law Olmsted & Calvert Vaux
📞 718 965-8999
Open from dawn to dusk
Ⓜ Grand Army Plaza (1/2); Eastern Parkway-Brooklyn Museum (1/2); Prospect Park (Q/S); Parkside Avenue (Q)

16.9 Meadow Port Arch
Frederick Law Olmsted
Northwest of Long Meadow

A brief walk on the pedestrian path at the northwest entrance to Brooklyn's Prospect Park leads to the simple yet graceful Meadow Port Arch, a short tunnel of approximately 60 feet that runs under the Park Drive (originally the park's carriageway). As one passes through the arch, a double opening frames the view of the Long Meadow and the sense of unfolding space beyond. Here is a modest entrance to the green expanse of space and mystery that is the centerpiece of Olmsted's creative genius. Here too, the architect's arrangements of paths and berms serve as invitations to explore the edges of this centerpiece—to discover what our senses tell us is yet to be experienced.

JOSEPH G. MERZ
Architect

16.10 **Long Meadow**
West side of Prospect Park

Olmsted and Vaux's vision of bucolic urbanity is all very nice; a stroll through the dusky woods, a view of a distant waterfall, a picnic under ancient trees, are just fine. But the truly great experience of Brooklyn's Prospect Park is to be had on a weekend morning before nine o'clock. There, on the wide spill of greensward known as the Long Meadow, is the revivifying sight of hundreds of dogs of every description—unleashed! Running, leaping, mounting one another; chasing balls, sticks, and the occasional jogger; communicating, cavorting, and generally engaging in the companionable chaos that to a dog is the very essence of life. Here is a hint of the wild-yet-tamed attitude intended by its designers for this same ground. Here is a rebuke to those who believe dogs were made for solitary confinement in suburban backyards; for here, obviously, they are in their true element. And here is a sight that can, briefly, make the human observer as happy as a dog.

MELISSA HOLBROOK PIERSON
Writer

16.11 **Prospect Park Carousel**
Empire Boulevard & Flatbush Avenue, Willink Entrance

A pure joy. The carousel dates from 1912 (primarily the work of noted horse carver Charles Carmel, a

►

▶

Russian-born immigrant who was a keen observer of the
horses at the Prospect Park stables) and came to the park
from its original Coney Island home in 1952. It features a
pipe organ, 51 glorious carved wooden horses, a lion, a
giraffe, a deer, and two chariots with dragons spewing fire
and flowers. Rivals any packaged playland thrill.
JOHN PENOTTI
President, GreeneStreet Films

16.12 Brooklyn Museum of Art

1915, McKim, Mead & White
200 Eastern Parkway at Washington Avenue
☎ 718 638-5000
Wednesday-Friday 10am-5pm; Saturday, Sunday 11am-6pm;
first Saturday of each month 11am-11pm; closed Monday,
Tuesday
Ⓜ Eastern Parkway-Brooklyn Museum (1/2)

Fourth-most-important museum collection in the nation,
though it languishes in the shadow of the most important
museum collection in the world, at the Metropolitan
Museum of Art.
CHRISTOPHER FORBES
Vice chairman, Forbes

Worgelt Study
Fourth floor

For knowledgeable New Yorkers, the treasures of the
Brooklyn Museum are a poorly kept secret. The Brooklyn's
Egyptian and African sculpture and 19th-century American
paintings would be exceptional in any museum. But has
anyone singled out that ravishing gem, the Worgelt Study?
You go to the fourth floor, and ask a guard to direct you
to the period rooms. This one is 1930 Art Deco, perfectly
preserved, an entrée into a world of dark elegance,
ingeniously simple in all its forms, yet the opposite of
high-keyed Bauhaus modern and the expensive chastity

of the International Style.

With a token library and discreet bar, the space discloses itself as an enclave for conversation, in soft tones, perhaps accompanied by a schnapps. It was done by a Parisian firm, Alavoine, the name itself somehow resonant of Art Deco styling. You're greeted by a warm palette of palisander and olive woods with intarsia designs, and painted lacquer panels illuminated by sconces and a chandelier of frosted Lalique glass. The furniture consists of nubby textured armchairs and a settee upholstered in chevron patterns. What I love about this worldly room for a Park Avenue apartment is the muted, coppery light that bathes it in an atmosphere of quiet and really enchanting meditation. A few steps away, in a vitrine that displays Deco appliances, do not miss the 1930 radio by the Air-King Products Company of Brooklyn, the one in a startling permanent green plastic. Its embossed tuning knob and its modified ziggurat shape contribute to a charm that its unforgettable color enhances with a panache that is as democratic as the Worgelt Study is aristocratic.

MAX KOZLOFF
Art and photography critic

16.12 Brooklyn Botanic Garden

1000 Washington Avenue between Empire Boulevard & Eastern Parkway, ☎ 718 623-7200

October-March: Tuesday-Friday 8am-4:30pm; Saturday, Sunday, holidays 10am-4:30pm; closed Monday, except Monday holidays

April-September: Tuesday-Friday 8am-6pm; Saturday, Sunday, holidays 10am-6pm; closed Monday, except Monday holidays

Ⓜ Prospect Park (Q/S); Eastern Parkway-Brooklyn Museum (1/2)

I often go to the Brooklyn Botanic Garden, for its scale is large enough to be satisfying without tiring you out. The variety of spaces and levels, the writer's walk, the Japanese garden, aromatic plantings, bonsai, and water lilies make it interesting and comforting in any weather. I particularly like the dogwood and lilacs in the spring. Napping under the cherry blossoms in bloom will make you feel like you have entered a private fantasy. This is a good place for all sorts of encounters, including amorous ones. The food in the outdoor cafe is quite good and well priced. I had a very respectable broiled salmon and salad for a fraction of what it would cost anywhere else in the city.

MARIA ARRILLAGA
Writer and professor

16.13 Arts for Transit: *Garden Stops*
1994 and 1996, Patsy Norvell
Ⓜ Beverley Road (Q); Cortelyou Road (Q)

If you're going to Prospect Park, take a look at the exquisite, hand-etched glass ivy on the windows and curved, wrought-iron railings with their Victorian floral detailing by Patsy Norvell in the twin stations at Beverley and Cortelyou Roads. These outdoor stations are built on bridges over the tracks and look like small stucco gingerbread bungalows with mint-green trim and orange-tiled roofs. Ivy and other hanging plants grow down adjacent walls along the tracks, spilling over from the backyard gardens of local residents. The scene's charm and nostalgia are lovingly reflected in Norvell's art, an unexpected oasis in Brooklyn.

JOYCE KOZLOFF
Artist

CROWN HEIGHTS

16.14 Hunterfly Road Houses of Weeksville

1840-1883; restoration begun 1990's
1698 Bergen Street between Rochester & Buffalo Avenues
☎ 718 623-0600, by appointment only
Ⓜ Utica Avenue (A/C); Crown Heights-Utica Avenue (1/4)

Weeksville was a 19th-century African-American community, the present traces of which are the restored houses
on Bergen Street in the Bedford-Stuyvesant area. Originally
built on the now vestigial Hunterfly Road, the houses were
rediscovered by aerial photographers in 1968, and
a restoration effort was launched. The restored houses
are now open to the public; one contains the offices
of the Society for the Preservation of Weeksville and
Bedford-Stuyvesant History.

THOMAS HEFFERNAN
Professor of English, Adelphi University

RECOMMENDED READING
Joan Maynard and Gwen Cottman, *Weeksville Then and Now,*
Society for the Preservation of Weeksville and Bedford-Stuyvesant
History, 1983.

These modest, 19th-century structures represent some essence
of the millions of African descendents who have populated
and benefited New York since the 17th century. This community is generally not represented with structures of stone,
brick, or steel, but these wood frame houses can be visited by
inquiring minds to learn the earliest history of our city.

The full restoration and public use of these landmarks
is a truly elegant use of historic preservation: to help save
and restore an underserved community. These cottages
provide a venue for preservation, education, economic development, and tourism that can benefit present and future
generations of this community, as well as all of New York
City and beyond.

JOAN BACCHUS MAYNARD
Preservation activist

RECOMMENDED READING

Beth L. Savage, ed., *African American Historic Places*,
John Wiley & Sons, 1994.

Ellen M. Snyder-Grenier, *Brooklyn! An Illustrated History*,
Brooklyn Historical Society, Temple University Press, 1996.

Howard Dodson, Christopher Moore & Roberta Yancy,
The Black New Yorkers: The Schomburg Illustrated Chronology,
John Wiley & Sons, 2001.

SUNSET PARK

16.15 Sunset Park

To some folks, Sunset Park is a sprawling immigrant neighborhood in Brooklyn. On one side—Fifth Avenue, from 38th to 60th Streets—it's Latin American, mostly Mexican and Ecuadorian. On the other—40th to 62nd Streets—it's mostly Chinese. The texture and rhythm of these two sides is dynamic and fascinating, enhanced by other countries in the mix: a strong residue of earlier Irish communities, a touch of the Middle East (with Turkish and Palestinian influences), and newer arrivals from Vietnam and Malaysia.

To others, Sunset Park is a stretch of land from Fifth to Seventh Avenues, and from 41st to 44th Streets—the park itself, which has a magical setting. There are several ways to enter it, but I most like going in at the corner of Seventh Avenue and 44th Street.

People bring a picnic lunch, either from Ranchero las Tinajas (☎ 718 686-0800), a Mexican restaurant a few blocks south on Seventh Avenue between 47th and 48th Streets, or a selection of Chinese, Malaysian, or Turkish foods from the markets on Eighth Avenue in the 50's. Food and beverage in hand, enter the park and take a look at the attractive W.P.A. recreation facility, then walk northwest, past a beautiful new playground. Here, neighborhood families enjoy the park according to their customs: Chasidic Jews take a quiet Sabbath stroll, while loads of

Chinese, Mexican, and other Latino families crowd the park, patronizing stands of food and fresh tropical fruit juices. There may even be mariachi bands. Continuing the walk, you'll soon arrive at a slight dip in the park, before a more dramatic dip overlooking one of the most brilliant vistas in all of New York City: the Manhattan skyline and the Statue of Liberty, with New Jersey in the distance.

MYRA ALPERSON
Editor and publisher, NoshNews

DYKER HEIGHTS & GRAVESEND

16.16 **Dyker Heights Christmas Lights**
83rd to 84th Street between Tenth & Thirteenth Avenues
Ⓜ 79th Street (M/B)

People in Dyker Heights don't waste too many lights on their indoor Christmas trees because from Thanksgiving until Epiphany (January 6), they light up their houses instead.

Drive by at night and see house after house lit up. Homeowners stand outside, sometimes asking for donations to help with the electric bills. Maybe it all started with one neighbor trying to outdo another. But by now, it's a whole neighborhood lighting itself up for the city to see.

FRANK PUGLIESE
Playwright and screenwriter

16.17 **L & B Spumoni Gardens**
2725 86th Street between West 10th & West 11th Streets
☏ 718 449-6921
Open daily for lunch and dinner
Ⓜ 25th Avenue (W); Gravesend-86th Street (N)

🍽 There's one thing New Yorkers will always argue about: pizza. Is it Lombardi's in Little Italy? Joe's on Carmine or Ray's on 11th? Or is it John's in the Village? Some say

Totonno's in Coney Island (pretty great). Others pick
Grimaldi's under the Brooklyn Bridge. (And don't start
with Patsy's.) But I have to say, the best slice is out of
Brooklyn at the Spumoni Gardens. That's right, "the
L & B square."

Pizza and Spumoni: it's a simple combination that has
worked for more than 50 years. There's no real garden at
the Spumoni Gardens, except for the people. There's a
series of outdoor picnic tables and on a summer night
they're filled with screaming families, young girls and their
belly buttons, and boys and men in a collection of baseball
hats. The cars are double-parked curbside and the police
themselves triple-park when the precinct house needs
a few pies. If you've ever been to the Feast of San Gennaro
in Little Italy, then you know what L & B Spumoni
Gardens is like every night, weather permitting.

I'll tell you the secret of their pizza because you couldn't
copy it even if you tried. They put the sauce on top of the
cheese and then put the cheese on top of that.

FRANK PUGLIESE
Playwright and screenwriter

Third Avenue

Years ago, a friend and I decided to walk from one end of
Third Avenue in Brooklyn, following it through Manhattan
into the Bronx and to its end. We would stop, then pick up
the route days, or weeks, later.

The walk reminded me of an old Buddy Hackett joke:
"I just took a trip around the world. If I'd known, I would
have just went to New York."

FRANK PUGLIESE
Playwright and screenwriter

16.18 Joe's of Avenue U

287 Avenue U between MacDonald Avenue & Lake Street
☎ 718 449-9285
Tuesday-Thursday, Saturday 11am-6:45pm; Friday 11am-8pm;
closed Sunday, Monday

Ⓜ Avenue U (F)

🍴 What is a rice ball parmigiana?

The rice ball is made of rice, peas, ground meat, and
cheese, then covered in breadcrumbs and fried. It's then
covered in tomato sauce, ricotta cheese, shaved parmesan,
and baked. It is heavenly. And the best one in New York is
at Joe's of Avenue U, an Italian diner open only for lunch.
I rarely take a flight from Kennedy or head for the beaches
without making the detour and grabbing a few rice balls.

And here's a tip: Joe's is open until the early evening
only on Friday nights, when they have their Sicilian menu,
and a fish special, caught that day.

FRANK PUGLIESE
Playwright and screenwriter

16.19 Enrico Caruso Museum of America

1942 East 19th Street between Avenues S & T
By appointment only, ☎ 718 368-3993

Ⓜ Avenue U (Q)

Five dollars doesn't buy much of anything these days. In
Manhattan, it buys even less: a toasted bagel in a Midtown
deli, a tip for the coat check girl at Balthazar, a taxi ride
from Avenue A to Avenue C. Across the East River in
Brooklyn, however, that same 5 dollars will secure admission to what is arguably the best-kept cultural secret in the
city: the Enrico Caruso Museum of America.

Artistic director Aldo Mancusi has devoted his life (and
most of his home) to documenting the colorful life and
considerable accomplishments of the world's greatest

tenor. Don't smirk. Mancusi isn't just another obsessive-compulsive whose hobby has taken over his abode, like kudzu grown amok. This is a bona fide artistic institution, and Mancusi has the tax-exempt status to prove it, granted by the New York Educational Department in 1989.

The museum's energetic curator/tenant boasts that 2,500 faithful make the pilgrimage to his outer-borough opera mecca every year, but this figure is probably as inflated as Caruso's celebrated ego. Indeed, many opera buffs have never even heard of this place. What they are missing would reduce Pagliacci to tears. After sampling the stentorian Caruso recordings (played on restored gramophones), you'll understand how the big guy managed to perform in front of 50,000 fans in Central Park sans microphone. The museum's music archive is as comprehensive as it gets. In addition to the hundreds of remakes and reissues throughout the years, Mancusi has sourced out and lovingly catalogued 98 percent of Caruso's 265 original presses. In fact, opera scholars frequently seek out Mancusi to study vintage Caruso recordings that digital technology has yet to improve upon.

But this isn't just a bunch of old vinyl. The permanent collection, occupying the entire second floor and spilling over into the bathroom, consists of rare memorabilia that runs the gamut from the mundane (a pair of vintage Rigoletto costumes) to the macabre (a plaster-cast death mask rendered by the famous sculptor Cifariello). Fetishists and groupies will also appreciate the wealth of personal effects Mancusi has accumulated over the years: Sulka neckties, a pack of Turkish cigarettes and a custom tortoiseshell cigarette holder, monogrammed silver flatware from the Knickerbocker Hotel (Caruso lived there before moving to the Vanderbilt Hotel), and a well-preserved pair of black-and-white suede spectator shoes.

Guest speakers are featured regularly, but the highlight of the two-hour tour is an eight-minute home movie of the legend himself, screened in a small theater that seats 20. The herky-jerky silent footage, which shows the operatic icon hobnobbing around Manhattan, is, to use Mancusi's own words, "very dynamic stuff." Those opting for the "Full Monty," however, should call ahead and find out when the next guest singer is booked. These intimate recitals, in which opera singers seem to channel Caruso's harmonic essence from the very artifacts surrounding them, have been known to extend well past museum hours. Antipasti and bottles of Chianti are frequently involved. One recent performer, a Neapolitan baritone with a hearty appetite, was persuaded to join museumgoers at a local trattoria, where he proceeded to reel off Caruso's signature arias between courses.

Since Mancusi's European counterpart, an elderly gentleman in Milan every bit as Caruso-crazed as Mancusi himself, went bust 12 years ago, this two-story Brooklyn dwelling is the last public repository in the world devoted to all things Caruso. But with Aldo now 72, who knows how much longer he'll be around to crank the temperamental gramophones? For the time being, though, Mancusi is open for business and as enthusiastic as ever. "People don't realize how great Caruso was," crows Mancusi. "Not only did he have incredible range—able to sing bass, baritone, and tenor parts—he also had an incredible ability to project his voice vast distances with power." Mancusi merely rolls his eyes when asked how Caruso's voice compares to contemporary tenors. "Pavarotti, Domingo, Carreras . . . please, Enrico would have blown them all off the stage."

RENE CHUN
Journalist

CONEY ISLAND

Mermaid Parade

Parade date and location subject to change

www.coneyislandusa.com

Ⓜ Coney Island-Stillwell Avenue (F/Q/W)

On one invariably sweltering Saturday in late June, a strange and marvelous parade makes its way along a six-block stretch of Coney Island Avenue from the home of the Cyclones (the bright-as-paint stadium for Brooklyn's new minor league baseball team) to the home of the Cyclone (the storied wooden roller coaster at Astroland Park, after which the team is named). Although the Mermaid Parade is less well known than the Greenwich Village Halloween Parade, it's yet another showcase for the local abundance of humor and talent. The inventive costumes—as likely to be worn by spectators as participants—follow an oceanic theme. Neptunes clutching tridents amble alongside flatbeds upon which lobsters and crabs recline. Mostly, though, there are mermaids. Mermaids of every possible description. Following the best equal-opportunity tradition, there are beautiful adolescent mermaids and mermaids no longer in the bloom of youth; female and male mermaids; svelte mermaids and sizable mermaids, including in recent years several very pregnant mermaids. Scaly tails are constructed of everything from bubble wrap to shimmering CDs. Tops are pasties, coconut-shell bras, strategically placed Band-Aids. The music is raucous, from drum bands to the kind with tubas and trombones. The mellow, good-natured and gloriously multicultural mood is especially evident at the hot dog stand on the boardwalk, where the mermaids mingle and take refreshment after the parade is over.

ANN BANKS

Journalist

16.21 **Gargiulo's**
  2911 West 15th Street between Mermaid & Surf Avenues
  ☎ 718 266-4891
  Wednesday-Monday for lunch and dinner; closed Tuesday
  Ⓜ Coney Island-Stillwell Avenue (F/Q/W)

🍴 Food isn't the main attraction here, the atmosphere is—this
  is Al Capone's old haunt. If the huge stuffed octopus that
  decorates the main dining room prompts you to order the
  fried fresh calamari, you won't regret it. After dinner, walk
  across the street to Coney Island; wait a bit before riding
  the Cyclone.
  FISHER STEVENS AND FRANK PUGLIESE
  Actor, director, and co-owner of GreeneStreet Films;
  Playwright and screenwriter

Coney Island Amusements
  Ⓜ Coney Island-Stillwell Avenue (F/Q/W)

16.24 **B & B Carousell**
  1932, W.F. Mangels, builder; George Carmel, carver
  Surf Avenue at West 10th Street

16.25 **Wonder Wheel**
  1920, Charles Herman, inventor
  West 12th Street & the Boardwalk

16.26 **Cyclone**
  1927, Harry C. Baker, inventor; Vernon Keenan, engineer
  834 Surf Avenue near West 10th Street

16.22 **Nathan's Famous**
  1310 Surf Avenue at Stillwell Avenue, ☎ 718 946-2202
  Open daily 8am-2am

  Coney Island is perhaps the least secret place on the
  planet, as it has always advertised itself as strenuously
  as it can. Still, visitors tend not to go there because ►

▶

they feel that Coney has declined sadly since its turn-of-the-century zenith (which is true) and has become a sort of desolate backwater (which is not). Much of the old Coney is gone, but it still offers a trio of wonderful rides that make the visit worthwhile. At the B & B Carousell (*sic*: that's how its maker, William Mangels, himself a Coney native, spelled the word) on Surf Avenue, you can not only listen to an honest-to-God band organ huff out *The Marine Hymn* and *Redwing*, but you can reach out and try to grab a metal ring as your horse glides past the arm that dispenses them. Over on the boardwalk, the Wonder Wheel, which opened in 1920, lifts its steel cages up out of the clamor to where you can see far out into the Atlantic and, on the other side, the towers of Manhattan glinting in the distance. Finally, there's the Cyclone (also see p. 449), built in 1927 and still, in the estimation of many enthusiasts, the single greatest roller coaster. The creature was born here on Coney in 1885, and it is fitting that one of its finest exemplars should still be slam-banging through its high arcs and steel-and-wood thickets. The hot dog also was invented here—or at least has a plausible claim to have been—so after you get off the Cyclone, head down Surf Avenue toward Nathan's Famous, which has been selling the country's best frankfurters since Nathan Handwerker set up his first stand on the site in 1916.

RICHARD SNOW
Editor-in-chief, American Heritage

16.23 Sideshows by the Seashore
Surf Avenue at West 12th Street, ☎ 718 372-5159
Memorial Day to Labor Day
Ⓜ Coney Island-Stillwell Avenue (F/Q/W)

New York City's version of cute seaside amusement park is this gaudy assemblage of rides and carnival booths run by rival companies. The place makes you realize how much Disney airbrushes away.

Careen around the arc of Deno's Wonder Wheel. Up in the sky, above it all and gently rocking (more than you'd care to be), cargo ships out in the Atlantic look like toys and way off in the distance is the Manhattan skyline. This Ferris wheel, built of Bethlehem steel in 1920 and now an official landmark, may outlast us all. Legend has it that a dozen or so co-owners banded together and built it themselves—just so they'd know it had been done right.

Nearby at Surf Avenue and West 12th Street, Sideshows by the Seashore, a little 99-seat nonprofit theater established in 1985, has a cycle of its own to keep up. Shows run continuously on weekends, about 10 short acts in all, strung back to back. The theater charges admission when you go in, and shamelessly tries to shake down the audience for more money later on, before seeing the really good stuff. This is a tongue-in-cheek exercise, a historical throwback, which is how they get away with it. But it is real, too. A lady who proudly grew a full beard got her start here a few years ago. She let everyone stare all they wanted and honed her act before running off to emcee a traveling circus—and to be profiled in *The New York Times*. In a recent performance, a man pushed nails up his nostrils, then pushed a sword down his gullet. A glamorous contortionist lay in a coffin-shaped box. The lid of the box was closed, and sharp blades were pushed through it, from one side to the other. For an extra dollar, you could approach the stage to see how the lady had avoided being cut up—or hadn't. Those who paid looked visibly disappointed; they'd somehow been had. And the show goes on.

BARBARA ENSOR
Writer

Classic Coney Island

Referred to as "Sodom by the Sea" by a rather puritanical *New York Times* in 1894, Coney Island was the summer oasis for working-class city dwellers seeking summer excitement: roller coasters, sideshows, carnival acts, food and more greasy food, the boardwalk, and the beach. Take the F train to the end of the line, ride the Wonder Wheel (the enormous, 150-feet-in-diameter Ferris wheel built in 1920) and the Cyclone (the great wooden roller coaster that has been rumbling, rattling spines, and eliciting screams of fear and delight since 1927), and walk the Boardwalk from Coney to Brighton Beach (see p. 452). Make the pilgrimage to the original Nathan's Famous, which serves more than a million hot dogs a year. Opened in 1916 by Nathan Handwerker, a former employee of Charles Feltman who introduced the frankfurter to New Yorkers in 1887, the wall-to-wall signage survives. They're still grilling the same dogs developed by Nathan and his wife, Ida. The annual Hot Dog Eating Contest takes place on the Fourth of July—the 2001 winner set the record by downing 50 dogs in the allotted 12 minutes. No longer on the boardwalk, but still worth the trip, the Mermaid Parade (see p. 444) attracts all sorts of sea creatures and takes place on the first Saturday after the summer solstice.

The towering 250-foot-high skeleton of the Parachute Jump (relocated to Coney Island from the 1939 New York World's Fair) and the charred frame of the Thunderbolt coaster provide eerie reminders of Coney's heyday.

TRACEY HUMMER AND FREDERIC SCHWARTZ
Writer and Architect

16.26 The Cyclone

1927, Harry C. Baker, inventor; Vernon Keenan, engineer
834 Surf Avenue near West 10th Street
Ⓜ Coney Island-Stillwell Avenue (F/Q/W)

This is the kind of roller coaster they don't make anymore,
and it's such a great ride that even on the ride-all-day park
tickets you can go only five times. Up, up, up you ratchet,
then come hurtling down for a few too-short minutes that
will have you screaming all the way. Go on a weekday and
get in line for the opening ride at noon—the very best car
is the first. Avoid the last car at all costs, unless you like
that whiplash feeling you get after an automobile accident.
Once you're in the seat, the guys who run things will let
you stay on if you pay by the ride, thereby ensuring that
you work your way up to the front car on your second
ride, if not your first. Like everything else in New York,
possession is nine-tenths of the law.
SUSAN WYLAND
Magazine consultant

16.27 New York Aquarium

1955, Harrison & Abramovitz
The boardwalk at the northeast corner of West 8th Street
☎ 718 265-3474
Monday-Friday 10am-4:15pm; Saturday, Sunday 10am-4:45pm;
last ticket sold at 3:45pm daily
Ⓜ West 8th Street-New York Aquarium (F/Q)

In times of tremendous stress, I've gone to the aquarium to
sit at the foot of the large tank there and look at the belly
of a whale.
FRANK PUGLIESE
Playwright and screenwriter

Olde New Yorkese

New York City's blend of immigrants, émigrés, transients, and natives has produced a lexicon that is pleasantly peculiar to New York City. From the beginning of this urban city-state, new and different languages were heard on the street; according to one historian, in 1626, 18 different languages could be heard in the village of Nieuw Amsterdam. However, with the changes wrought by assimilation, technology, economics, immigration patterns, politics, mores, and the city's own ever-changing atmosphere, some words and phrases are either disappearing or becoming as archaic and obscure as Shakespeare's "yclept." Here are some favorites that are fast disappearing from New York's vocabulary:

On Line: When the Internet was just a twinkle in Thomas Watson's eye, New Yorkers wanting to gain admission to Radio City Music Hall or buy tickets for the latest Broadway hit stood on line. The rest of the country stood in line.

Fellow Traveler: Someone whose political beliefs were substantially left-of-center. A "fellow traveler" was not necessarily (frequently not) a member of the Communist Party, but often followed a similar political path.

Red Diaper Baby: Child of parents who were fellow travelers.

Brodie: To do a "Brodie" was to emulate Bowery saloonkeeper and con man Steve Brodie, who won a bet that he would survive a jump off the Brooklyn Bridge. There has been great speculation as to whether he really made the leap, but a Brodie became synonymous with a leap, jump, or fall.

Egg Cream: This ambrosia-like beverage contains neither eggs nor cream. The traditional version of this drink, inhaled in candy stores and luncheonettes throughout the five boroughs, consisted of tooth-rattlingly cold milk, chocolate syrup, and soda water. With the disappearance of soda fountains—the seltzer of soda water spigots was critical to the true egg cream   the beverage and the name are rapidly slipping into memory.

Two Cents Plain: Soda water or seltzer without syrup or flavoring. Usually a six- to eight-ounce cup served at a soda fountain, corner candy store, or luncheonette.

Candy Store: Not to be confused with Godiva, Perugina, or even Fanny Farmer. A true candy store was a neighborhood institution, selling newspapers, cigarettes, and other tobacco products, candy bars, bulk penny candy, and school supplies. A good candy store also had a soda fountain where one could be refreshed with a two cents plain, an egg cream or, in season, a lime rickey, or a Mello Roll.

Halb Viertel: One-eighth of a pound. The late Jerome Weidman, author of *I Can Get It for You Wholesale*, *The Enemy Camp*, and other novels and short stories, noted that the eighth was an unknown measurement in the Bronx, particularly in the heavily Jewish neighborhoods around Pelham Parkway, Mount Eden Avenue, the Grand Concourse, Kingsbridge Road, or Mosholo Parkway. Therefore, if you wanted an eighth of a pound of belly lox, you asked for a halb viertel—Yiddish for half a quarter.

This brief memoriam to our fading New Yorkisms ends with one of my favorites: Does Macy's tell Gimbel's? When the two department stores were fixtures on 34th and 33rd Streets, they were fiercely competitive. Based on that archrivalry, a New Yorker who wanted to assure a friend or relative that they could keep a secret would say, "Does Macy's tell Gimbel's?" With the demise of Gimbel's, that phrase joins the peruke, codpiece, bustle, snood, bobby socks, and rumble seat in the archives of language history.

LEE GELBER
Director of training and tour development,
Gray Line New York Tours

BRIGHTON BEACH

16.28 Brighton Beach
Ⓜ Brighton Beach (Q)

With its Russian character, outdoor shops, and eateries,
Brighton Beach is a good starting point for exploring
Brooklyn's oceanside. Enter the boardwalk at Brighton
Beach Avenue and continue in the direction of Coney
Island, using the parachute jump ride as a landmark.
The walk has a European feeling, especially in the early
evening, with echoes of an Italian *passeggiata*. (You could
also walk on the sand along the surf.) Just before the
aquarium, you'll pass some handball courts, where the
highest measure of this indigenous New York game is still
practiced by greatly skilled talents. End your walk at
Coney Island (see p. 444) with a ride on the Wonder Wheel
or the Cyclone, followed by a world-class frankfurter and
french fries at Nathan's.
SIMON DINNERSTEIN
Artist

Odessa on the Hudson
Ⓜ Brighton Beach (Q)

Brighton Beach ("Odessa on the Hudson" or "Little
Odessa") was and remains a special part of New York's
cultural life, and it's worth spending an evening here—
from 6 p.m., before it gets dark, until 1 a.m. It is preferable
to dispense with dietary considerations for the evening,
and bring a local Brighton acquaintance with you who can
guarantee you a maximum of "bicultural enrichment."
Several items you should know in advance: (a) you have no
chance whatsoever of encountering the so-called Russian
mafia, (b) the culinary predilections of the majority of
Brighton restaurants are not so much Russian as
Ukrainian-Crimean-Moldavian, which doesn't prevent

them from being (occasionally) exceptional; (c) smoked salmon and red caviar should be bought at the Odessa Food Shop (1117 Brighton Beach Avenue, ☎ 718 332-3223) and (d) unfortunately, virtually none of the well-known variety shows, with elements of Russian "restaurant culture," remain in Brighton restaurants—North American show standards only.

YURI MILOSLAVSKY
Writer

SHEEPSHEAD BAY

16.29 Lundy Brothers

1901 Emmons Avenue at Ocean Avenue, ☎ 718 743-0022
Monday-Saturday for lunch and dinner; Sunday for brunch and dinner

Ⓜ Sheepshead Bay (Q)

🍽 Although the hardcore, old-school Lundyites now have a problem with the place, the revamped Lundy's still retains its charm—and the fish is still as fresh as the waitstaff. This is the perfect place for a family-style dinner or a birthday party. Located right on the Sheepshead Bay, the restaurant serves fish that is not caught locally—I promise.

FISHER STEVENS
Actor, director, and co-owner of GreeneStreet Films

Street Games

I grew up on Montgomery Street and Utica Avenue in Brooklyn, where from the age of six, the block was my home. Any city kid would just hang out—which meant doing anything you could create, or nothing at all, with friends. Besides walking and tossing a ball, here are some games passed on from kid to kid.

▶

►

Stick ball: The bat is a broomstick wrapped with tape. The ball is a dead tennis ball. It's played in the schoolyard; draw the strike zone on the wall behind home plate—preferably on a handball court.

Stoop ball: You need a hard, pink Spalding (we called it a "Spaldeen") for this one. Throw it at the stoop and catch it on either a fly or a bounce off the stoop.

Box ball: Players stand at the opposite ends of two sidewalk squares. The rules are like tennis, minus the net. The ball is a Spalding.

Box baseball: Two players stand three sidewalk squares apart. Pitch the ball into the box in front of your opponent, putting English on it to make it harder for him to return with his open hand. Once again, use a Spalding.

Chinese handball: You need a wall or a building in an alleyway. Play like handball, except hit the ball back to the wall on a bounce instead of on a fly. The ball: Spalding.

King, Queen, Jack: Chinese handball but with multiple players, each assigned to his own box. A player is allowed to "baby" the ball, setting up the shot in his own box during play. The King is on the far right, then the Queen and the Jack. Only the King scores points. Other players move up when he misses.

Punchball: Played in the street with a Spalding. Two sewer plates are home base and second base; pick two rear tires on parked cars for first and third base. The "batter" throws the ball up in the air, punches it with his fist and runs. Good players could make it travel one-and-a-half sewers. If cars came down the block during a play, they would wait until it was completed.

Selecting the ball: The right ball for these games is very important. Here's how to pick a good Spalding or its rival, the Pensie Pinkie. Go to the candy store and pick two balls

out of the bucket. Hold them as high as you can and
drop them. Keep whichever one bounces higher until you
have gone through every ball in the basket or worn out
the storeowner's patience.

NORMAN LANES
Cardiologist

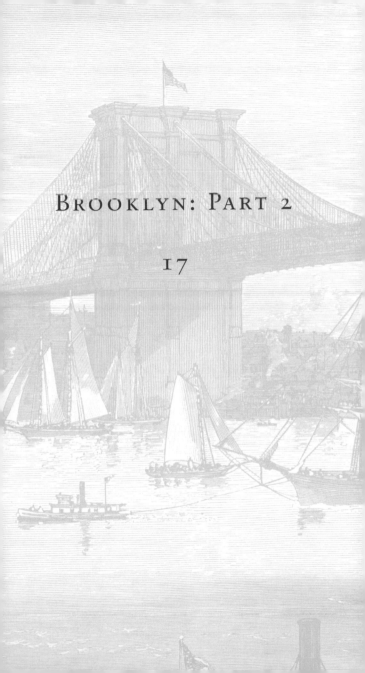

BROOKLYN: PART 2

17

Carroll Gardens, Cobble Hill, Brooklyn Heights, Fulton Ferry, Vinegar Hill, Civic Center, Boerum Hill, Williamsburg & Greenpoint

CARROLL GARDENS

Carroll Gardens Stroll
Ⓜ Carroll Street (F/G)

17.1 **Box Hill**
Smith Street & Second Place

16.4 **Old Stone House**
In James J. Byrne Memorial Playground
3rd Street at Fifth Avenue

17.2 **St. Paul's Episcopal Church of Brooklyn**
1867-84, Richard Upjohn & Son
423 Clinton Street between Carroll & President Streets

17.3 **Former John Rankin House, now the F.G. Guido Funeral Home**
c.1840
440 Clinton Street at Carroll Street

17.4 **Former Rectory, now a residential building**
1893, Woodruff Leeming
255 President Street between Court & Clinton Streets

17.5 **Former Ladies' Parlor and Sunday School, now the South Congregational Church**
1889, Fredrick Carles Merry
358-366 Court Street between President & Union Streets

17.6 Former South Congregational Church, now a residential building
1857
358-366 Court Street at President Street

17.7 Carroll Park
1867
Carroll Street between Smith & Court Streets

17.8 Ferdinando's Focacceria
151 Union Street between Hicks & Columbia Streets
☎ 718 855-1545

17.9 Red Rose Restaurant
315 Smith Street at Union Street, ☎ 718 625-0963
Monday-Friday 4:30pm-11pm; Saturday, Sunday 1pm-11pm

If you are visiting Carroll Gardens from outside the neighborhood, take the F or G train to the Carroll Street stop in Brooklyn. Exit near the front of the train at Smith Street and Second Place. You'll be at the erstwhile summit of Box Hill, site of Fort Box, later renamed Fort Boerum. Here, George Washington watched the Battle of Long Island, the first battle of the American Revolution. It was not a pretty sight. The Americans, trapped on the heights of today's Prospect Point by a British pincer movement, were mauled; survivors retreated across the Gowanus Creek, which lay between the high ground to the east and the shoulder of Carroll Gardens, where you now stand. Many died and 1,300 Americans were captured. Those who survived the swampy rout were aided by a regiment from Maryland who gave covering fire from an old stone farmhouse (see p. 430). The farmhouse dated from the 17th-century Walloon/Dutch settlement here, when a few European souls, having displaced the last Indians, planted orchards and farmed creek oysters to brine and ship to the West Indies. A 1935 re-creation now stands on the far side of the creek, in James J. Byrne Memorial Playground. The ►

►

creek was dredged as a canal in the 19th century.

Story has it that the name Carroll Park (source of the
name Carroll Gardens), was given in honor of Charles
Carroll, Maryland's great Catholic seigneur and signer
of the Declaration of Independence, in respect for the
Marylanders, several hundred of whom died for their
valor. For years, Brooklyn patriots waged a campaign to
dig up the soldiers' bones, which allegedly lie under the
floor of an auto body shop near the Gowanus. While the
bones have gone unexhumed, the name Carroll has gone
from strength to strength. After the mid-1960's landmark-
ing and subsequent gentrification of Cobble Hill, Carroll
Gardens's neighbor to the north, a pioneer real estate agent
began to develop this district under the grand name in an
effort to cleanse it of its old South Brooklyn—or worse,
Red Hook, provenance. So unpopular was the rechristen-
ing among the local working-class population (who saw
the new naming as colonization) that when the agent died,
an unfounded street rumor had it as murder.

If it's daytime and you can tolerate the slightly gritty
walk south on Smith to 3rd Street, turn left and descend
three blocks east to view the industrialized canal at the 3rd
Street bridge. Note as you go the decent brick rowhouses
and ornamented tenements on the block near the high
ground, originally home to small contractors and builders
(mainly Irish), and the change at Hoyt Street to mills,
warehouses, and marble yards as you near the canal. At
the bridge, look north to see Brooklyn's lone skyscraper,
the Williamsburgh Savings Bank Tower, and a glimpse of
the steeple belonging to St. Agnes Church. This church
aimed to reform the brawling Erie Canal boatmen who
wintered on the Gowanus after bringing their grain cargoes
to Red Hook granaries—the neighborhood's 19th-century
economic underpinning. Looking straight ahead, you will
see the heights of Prospect Park above a street that rises in
social and architectural status as it ascends.

Returning to Smith Street by the same route, turn right

and walk to Second Place. Turn left here and walk to
Court Street along the gardens fronting the brownstones
for which the neighborhood is known. You are now in the
high, dry section of a neighborhood which, when built in
the 1860's-1880's, had middle-class aspirations.
Brownstone, the chocolate stone veneer with which genteel
Brooklynites (and Victorian New Yorkers) clad their brick,
was, and is, a badge of arrival. These garden-fronted
streets were virtually unparalleled in the city, a *rus in urbe*,
when they were plotted by surveyor Richard Butts back in
1846 (the year the canal was set to be dredged). Today,
many of the front gardens hold tender Saint Francis images
and the so-called bathtub Madonnas, whose arms stretch
in blessing of passers-by. Some figures have flagstone paths
leading to them, as if one might actually make a pilgrimage
if so inclined. It was the Italian influx from the low-lying
waterfront after the 1930's, when earlier middle-class
English, Irish, German, and Scandinavian residents moved
to farther-away Brooklyn and Long Island, which turned
these miniswards into garden shrines. Southern Italian—
mainly Barinese—culture still pervades the neighborhood
in both language and custom, though this, too, is changing
as older residents die and newcomers from Manhattan are
drawn by civilized housing, comparatively lower rents,
and Old World charm.

Walk north on Court, the neighborhood's main shopping
street, to Carroll Street and turn left on Clinton Street,
the decorous Episcopalian spine that runs from this neighborhood's grand forebear, Brooklyn Heights. The gloomy,
if posh, St. Paul's Episcopal Church on the northeast corner, designed by Richard Upjohn & Son, is one of several
Episcopal sentinels along the leafy thoroughfare.
Catercorner from the church, southwest of Clinton and
Carroll, stands the neighborhood's oldest house and the
finest Greek Revival dwelling in the city. The freestanding
brick mansion at 440 Clinton (c. 1840) was built for a
Manhattan insurance broker. It now houses the F.G. ▶

▶

Guido Funeral Home, whose horse-drawn glass hearse carries Christ's statue through the neighborhood on Good Friday, marking sacred space.

Walk north on Clinton to President Street; turn right, noting several houses on your right whose owners mailed away for a galaxy of architectural add-ons: beetling brows and towering cornices. On your left, at 255 President, the rusticated-stone and curved-brick house, once the rectory of the former South Congregational Church at President and Court, projects a saucy Rapunzel-tower effect while hewing to the standard rectangle plotline. Next door, set back from the street, is the terra-cotta, copper-roofed building that once served as the Ladies' Parlor and Sunday School. The church, whose iron-work lamps, cast to resemble twisted rope, evoke this neighborhood's maritime ties, opened here in 1850, its site supposedly picked by Henry Ward Beecher, preeminent preacher of Brooklyn and perhaps the country. During the Civil War, Mrs. J.T. Stranahan, wife of Brooklyn's great planner/engineer (then apotheosized as the Haussmann of Brooklyn), ran Brooklyn's Sanitary Commission from this complex. So successful was Mrs. J. T.'s commission (which she defended from male takeover), that besides providing prodigious hospital supplies for the Union Army, it put Brooklyn's middle-class womanhood on the map. In general, middle-class women had more influence in Brooklyn, the "city of homes and churches," than in its sister city, New York. Brownstone Brooklyn exalted domesticity, and its newspapers catered to female sensibilities; husbands, largely Manhattan-bound commuters if they lived near Clinton Street, were a less targeted readership. Local papers also pumped up Brooklyn's female persona as a way of differentiating the "good" city of Brooklyn from its hurly-burly rival, New York, and therefore luring more settlement from said wicked city. The characterization was possible due to the hilly topography of Brooklyn, which for nearly a century kept industries (and immigrant workers) out of sight, down by the shore.

The church was co-oped in the early 80's, its desanctifi-
cation unsettling the local Italian youth. But like many city
churches, it had long real estate associations. One impetus
for siting it here was to legitimize a new residential enclave
planned by real estate agents after Brooklyn entrepreneurs
won the right to a local ferry landing. The pretext was
dockage for boats carrying Manhattan funeral parties to
the new Greenwood Cemetery, recently opened on the hills
near Prospect Park. The cemetery founders, ferry entrepreneurs, and agents were, of course, one and the same.
(Under an old colonial law, New York City, then just
Manhattan, owned Brooklyn's East River shoreline, and,
by denying ferry rights, could suppress the outflow
of its upper-middle-class taxpayers. The new ferry not only
increased the possibility of another upscale commuter
enclave, but more importantly, served the booming
shoreside economy of all of South Brooklyn.)

Carroll Park, initially privately owned by surrounding
householders (somewhat like Gramercy Park), was another
effort by real estate agents to confirm the neighborhood's
genteel status. It was secured by an act of legislature the
same year the church arose. Walk east to visit the fenced
enclave, now judiciously divided among arbored sitting
areas, a generously rehabbed children's playground, a ballfield and a bocce court. Old World gender rules prevail at
the last two spaces, which are very much male preserves.

While Barinese culture and custom still infuse the
neighborhood despite demographic reshuffling, innovations
in cargo shipping in the 1960's ended longshore-work, the
main local industry. Nothing substantial arrived to replace
it. At the same time in the mid-60's that the shore industry
collapsed, Robert Moses slashed the BQE through the
community, cleaving it in two at Hicks Street and leveling
its matrix church, Sacred Hearts of Jesus and Mary.
Farther south, the entranceway to the Brooklyn Battery
Tunnel fractured the district's tie to greater Red Hook.   ▶

►

If you would like a glimpse of the waterfront, once so instrumental to this neighborhood, walk north on Court to Union, turning left on Union to cross the appalling ⅊ expressway. At 151 Union is Ferdinando's Focacceria, a Sicilian, not Barinese, restaurant whose embossed-tin interior is the darling of filmmakers seeking Old World essence. The chickpea specialties are good. The cranes visible at the end of the street by the Buttermilk Channel (those are the trees of Governors Island just beyond) represent a last remnant of shipping in the city and stand on the site of the once great Atlantic Basin, built here in the 1840's. The Atlantic Basin was one of the city's few enclosed docking areas at the time, and was built primarily to receive grain boats after the Erie Canal allowed shipments to New York and Brooklyn. Manhattan's financial towers are visible to the north, overlays in the surreal city puzzle. From here you can retrace your steps to Court Street, then walk one block south to President and east, under the London plane trees, along the park to Smith and President. Here is the northern entrance of the same Carroll Street subway stop where the walk began. If you like, before leaving, you might enjoy looping down President Street, between Smith and Hoyt, to see the pristine garden fronts. Note the little houses at the end facing you. They are brick with no brownstone cladding. Despite the respectability of this block—a stately space sheltered by overhanging cornices and graced by lacy ironwork fences— there is something bleak just beyond the frame: the Gowanus and its "unsightly" industries. For good and bad, the veneers in this city are thin. Shapes arise, intersect, dissolve; communities form, disappear, reincarnate. The cozy ⅊ Red Rose restaurant on Smith near the subway, an old Italian veteran, now routinely serves cappuccino, an Italian custom brought to this neighborhood by upscale newcomers from Manhattan. Some of the flotilla of northern Smith Street restaurants, opened in the late 1990's, serve oysters rumored to be from the Gowanus, recently cleansed,

which is, according to some real estate agents, the future
site of yacht marinas and Riviera living.

HOPE COOKE
Writer and urban historian

17.8 **Ferdinando's Focacceria**

151 Union Street between Hicks & Columbia Streets

☎ 718 855-1545

Monday-Thursday 10:30am-6pm; Friday,
Saturday 10:30am-9pm; closed Sunday

Ⓜ Carroll Street (F/G)

🍴 Just across the East River from the Financial District,
Brooklyn Heights was an ur-yuppie neighborhood as long
ago as the late 1940's, the one bit of bourgeois quasi-
Manhattan in the outer boroughs. During the last 30 years
or so, of course, young and youngish writers, editors,
designers and filmmakers, lawyers and bankers—that is,
Manhattanites—have colonized the contiguous neighborhoods for blocks and blocks in every direction. The
mile-long strip of brick and brownstone townhouses
directly south of Brooklyn Heights, neighborhoods
known as Cobble Hill and Carroll Gardens, had been
overwhelmingly Italian. The takeover by "liberals" (as
the local working- and middle-class Italians refer to
yuppies of whatever ideological variety) happened slowly,
until the late 1990's, when a tipping point occurred—
most astonishingly on Smith Street, a main north-south
avenue transformed in about 18 months from a grungy,
tired, uncool commercial strip into a quarter of excellent
and pleasantly stylish restaurants and shops.

In the blocks west of Smith and south of Degraw Street,
artifacts of the old Italian neighborhood remain—the front-
yard statues of the Virgin and Saint Francis, the *Corriere
della Sera* at a couple of newsstands, the storefront social
clubs, a pork store here, a bakery there. But increasingly,
they're starting to seem like vestiges. Which makes a tiny,

unpretentious Sicilian restaurant called Ferdinando's Focacceria, on Union west of Hicks Street (and the Brooklyn-Queens Expressway), all the more precious.

Ferdinando's opened in 1904, and feels closer to that turn of the century than this one. It's dark and a framed pro-Mussolini newspaper front page hangs on the wall. But the place is not unwelcoming and the simple menu is quirkily authentic—in particular the hot, fresh, delicious panelle, a Sicilian chickpea-flour fried bread.

KURT ANDERSEN
Writer

COBBLE HILL

Atlantic Avenue Tunnel
For tour information, contact the Brooklyn Historic Railway Association, ☎ 718 941-3160

Brooklyn's Atlantic Avenue Tunnel was built in seven months in 1844 by 800 Irish workers using the "cut and cover" method, a technique which dates back to ancient Rome. The scale was enormous: it extended 2,750 feet from Columbia to Boerum Streets, was 17 feet high, 21 feet wide, and 30 feet below street level. It was constructed, in part, to solve the technical problem of an incline at the foot of Atlantic Avenue, where the L.I.R.R.'s route started, since the tunnel lessened the effect of the grade at the journey's beginning.

The other motivation behind its creation was the protest of Brooklynites over the noise and soot and smoke created by primitive locomotives. But the tunnel remained open for only 17 years. The last train ran through it in 1859, and it was sealed in 1861, a victim of more local politicking and of the L.I.R.R.'s inability to compete with the new New Haven Railroad and its service to Boston. Abandoned, then forgotten over time, the tunnel became part of urban legend, and now and then there were attempts to find it.

In late 1980, more than a century after the tunnel's closing, and despite the advice of city officials to give up his search for a railroad lost forever, it was rediscovered by Robert Diamond, a Brooklyn native.

President of the Brooklyn Historic Railway Association, Mr. Diamond has obtained permission to develop his find as a museum of sorts. He has called the tunnel a wonder of civil engineering that compares to the Brooklyn Bridge, and he occasionally leads tours through it. Walt Whitman wrote about just this experience below Atlantic Avenue in the 19th century: "The tunnel, dark as the grave, cold, damp, and silent. How beautiful look earth and heaven again, as we emerge from the gloom!" Tourists are encouraged to wear sturdy shoes or sneakers, and to bring a flashlight.

SEAN SWEENEY
Builder

17.11 Sahadi's
187 Atlantic Avenue between Court & Clinton Streets
☎ 718 624-4550
Monday-Saturday 9am-7pm; closed Sunday
Ⓜ Court Street (M/N/R); Borough Hall (1/2/4/5)

🏵 This is the cultural epicenter of Atlantic Avenue's Arabic culture. But a lot of Occidental types shop here, too, for the fresh olives, nuts, and cheeses, and for the boundless geniality of the owners. I felt immediately transformed by its global palate, which reflects the standards of New York City as a whole, and I have been a frequenter here ever since.

RICK MOODY
Writer

17.12 Damascus Bread & Pastry Shop
195 Atlantic Avenue between Court & Clinton Streets
☎ 718 625-7070
Open daily 7am-7pm
Ⓜ Court Street (M/N/R); Borough Hall (1/2/4/5)

🎁 Visiting lower Atlantic Avenue is an immersion in the
culinary delights of Arabic cuisine. The aromas of spices
and olives greet the visitor to Sahadi's. Numerous breads
can be found at Damascus Bakery, and for those in need
of an immediate gastronomic treat, restaurants abound.
MARY ANN HAICK DI NAPOLI
Genealogist

BROOKLYN HEIGHTS

19th-century Brooklyn
Ⓜ Court Street (M/N/R); Borough Hall (1/2/4/5)

17.13 **Former Brooklyn Trust Company, now Chase Bank**
1916, York & Sawyer
177 Montague Street at Clinton Street

17.14 **Brooklyn Historical Society**
1881, George B. Post
128 Pierrepont Street at Clinton Street, 📞 718 222-4111

17.15 **St. Ann's and the Holy Trinity**
1847, Minard Lafever
157 Montague Street at Clinton Street, 📞 718 875-6960

17.16 **Brooklyn Excelsiors Plaque**
133 Clinton Street at Livingston Street

17.10 **Christ Church**
1841, Richard Upjohn; 1917, Louis Comfort Tiffany
320 Clinton Street at Kane Street, 📞 718 624-0083

The neighborhoods of Brooklyn Heights and Cobble
Hill, officially designated as separate districts by both the
real estate industry and the NYC Landmarks Preservation
Commission, are in fact twins of the same era. Three
north-south streets—Hicks, Henry, and Clinton—knit

the two together. These streets contain a time capsule of mid-19th-century, solidly prosperous Brooklyn. A walking tour through these neighborhoods takes less than two hours and covers about a mile and a half, round-trip. Start in late afternoon to see the streets come alive, and stay until dusk, when it becomes easier to sense the present merging into the past.

Begin in Brooklyn Heights at the corner of Clinton and Pierrepont Streets. Here, a 1916 bank with Italian palazzo-like rusticated stone has recently emerged into brightness after a laborious cleaning. Opposite is one of the city's finest Victorian structures, housing the Brooklyn Historical Society. St. Ann's and the Holy Trinity Church, at the northwest corner of Montague and Clinton, is a comforting dark brownstone presence and a cultural focus for the community. Continue to a foursquare 1851 brick house at 133 Clinton, corner of Livingston, with a plaque affixed reading: " . . . former home of the Brooklyn Excelsiors, baseball champions of the United States in 1860. Constructed in 1851, the building was once the Jolly Young Bachelors clubhouse. The Bachelors evolved into the Excelsiors baseball team. One of its pitchers, James Creighton, is said to have tossed the first curve ball. During the Civil War, the Excelsiors introduced the game to soldiers from various states. Because of its popularity, similar teams were established in other cities. Thus baseball as a national sport can be considered as having its origins in Brooklyn."

The block of Clinton Street between Livingston and Schermerhorn is the most consistent exemplar of the good life in Brooklyn in the early 1850's. The street is neither grand nor quaint, yet it conveys a sense of both intimacy and dignity. The three-and-a-half-story rowhouse facades, with stone steps, are set back uniformly, behind a line of low iron fencing. The ground-floor apartments are entered separately by doors at sidewalk level. The sense of privacy created by the fence and the setback diminishes as   ►

▶

darkness falls and lights are turned on. Then both the
street and parlor floors reveal their front rooms and
details: etched glass vestibule doors, spindled grillwork,
steep wood staircases that turn sharply at the second-floor
landing, elaborate interior moldings, and chandeliers hung
from ceiling rosettes.

Clinton Street continues in its 1850's garb across
Atlantic Avenue to Degraw Street, where the Cobble Hill
Historic District ends. Near the southern end of our tour,
architectural grandeur awaits in the brownstone Gothic
Christ Church, constructed in 1841 and designed by
Richard Upjohn, the architect of Grace and Trinity
churches. According to the present church vicar, Ronald T.
Lau, Upjohn's fee for his design was a rent-free pew for
life. The church is constructed of somewhat irregular
brownstone blocks with an inspiringly proportioned,
120-foot-high, four-spire tower. Unusual for its age, the
brownstone has not needed major replacement. This
somewhat shaggy stone has proved to be sound and,
according to its architectural conservators, will be allowed
to continue to weather. The Gothic limestone interior was
completely gutted and renovated in 1917 by Tiffany
Studios, which installed a new altar, reredos, lectern,
and pulpit. In 2000, multiple strokes of lighting shook the
church, causing the tower to shift slightly. Restoration
is planned to maintain the tower's stability.

As dusk descends, retrace your steps north on Clinton,
Henry, or Hicks to see streets come to life with glowing
carriage lamps (some with gas wicks) and lighted houses
revealing unshuttered rooms. The last stop is Montague,
the Heights's main street. In the evening this street has
a relaxed, small-town feel, as well as a wide choice of
restaurants for a drink or dinner, and shops for browsing.
SANFORD MALTER
Architect

17.17 From the Heights to the Hill

Ⓜ Jay Street-Borough Hall (A/C/F)

To see the way New York used to be, you really have to go to Brooklyn. You can hike across the Brooklyn Bridge from Manhattan's City Hall or take the subway to Borough Hall (Brooklyn City Hall before annexation in 1898) and begin in Brooklyn Heights—the first historic district in the city—with its tree-lined streets of manicured 19th-century houses, half predating the Civil War.

Head west on quaint Montague Street to the Promenade, an elevated boardwalk built over the Brooklyn-Queens Expressway, with stunning views of lower Manhattan on one side and of the Heights's finest brownstone backyards on the other side. After resting on a bench or strolling to the Promenade's end, wander south and east along Hicks Street, and then farther south, turning west onto Atlantic Avenue, a gritty commercial strip with Arab bakeries and Mexican restaurants. Traveling south on Clinton Street will bring you to the center of Cobble Hill, where detouring aimlessly brings rewards. When you come upon Court Street, walk south, and at Bergen or Wyckoff cut east until you come to Smith Street, where you'll encounter a new restaurant mecca in the middle of Carroll Gardens. Here there are designer-owned boutiques and artist-run gift shops, sprinkled between bodegas and Italian social clubs. President Street has particularly fine brownstones. Wander about Boerum Hill and Carroll Gardens. No defined route is needed. You'll witness how a generation of New Yorkers raised on *Sesame Street* and *The Cosby Show* is transforming these old-fashioned neighborhoods into small-scale, ethnically diverse settings for real urban life.

JAYNE MERKEL
Journalist

▶

►

RECOMMENDED READING
Clay Lancaster, *Old Brooklyn Heights, New York's First Suburb*, Dover Publications, 1979.
Edwin G. Burrows and Mike Wallace, *Gotham: A History of New York City to* 1898, Oxford University Press, 1998.

A Cinematic Tour of Brooklyn Heights

Ⓜ Clark Street (2); Court Street (M/N/R); Borough Hall (4/5)

Behind the roses and hanging wisteria, New York's first landmarked neighborhood quietly remains much as it did when 19th-century ship captains made their terra firma homes here. The Federalist and Gothic Revival homes date back as early as 1810, but most are from the boom of the 1850's. Sitting high atop the bluff, with the sea air blowing like the horns of eastbound freighters, Brooklyn Heights has become a magnet for filmmakers and writers. Steeped in a rich cinematic history, the Heights has been used by Hollywood as a film set and place of inspiration throughout the years.

We begin at 3 Pierrepont Street (between Columbia Heights and Willow Street), the home of Don Corrado in *Prizzi's Honor*; across the street, at 57 Montague Terrace, Jack Nicholson had his stunning view of the Manhattan skyline. Walk from Pierrepont Street to Willow Street and turn north, and you will pass 151 Willow (between Pierrepont and Clark Streets), the house where Paul Newman in *The Verdict* found out that his star witness had been bought off. Here Brooklyn Heights doubles as Boston. Walking north, you come to the fruit streets: Orange, Pineapple, and Cranberry. Truman Capote penned *Breakfast at Tiffany's* in the bright yellow house on the corner of Orange and Willow. At 9 Cranberry Street (between Columbia Heights and Willow Street), in a garden apartment, Robert Redford held Faye Dunaway hostage in *Three Days of the Condor*. Next door, at Number 11, the three generations of the Castorini family in *Moonstruck* lived in a townhouse, Manhattan's skyline visible in all its glory at the end of the street. On the corner, in front of 81 Columbia Heights (between Orange and Cranberry Streets), Yale of Woody Allen's *Manhattan* purchased a mid-life-crisis Porsche. At Middagh Street (once home to Paul and Jane Bowles before he settled in Morocco and wrote *The Sheltering Sky*), turn left toward Columbia Heights. Nearby, the Brooklyn Heights Promenade has seen its fair share of movie shoots—from *Saturday Night Fever* to *Scent of a Woman*. Like the Brooklyn Bridge, the Promenade is a national treasure, hosting countless screen kisses.

Turn right on Columbia Heights and head down the hill, under the Manhattan Bridge. DUMBO's streets were a set for *Once Upon a Time in America*. For the adventurous, just outside the Heights, at the point where Flatbush Avenue meets the Manhattan Bridge, Robert De Niro was killed in Scorsese's *Mean Streets*.

🍴 After your ramble through the Heights's backlot you will be hungry, so head to Front Street, where you will find Grimaldi's pizzeria. You will have the definitive pizza experience in New York—which means you will be eating the best pizza in the world as you sit among headshots of Frank Sinatra and other Hollywood movers and shakers.

BILLY KENT
Film director and writer

FULTON FERRY & VINEGAR HILL

17.18 **Grimaldi's**

19 Old Fulton Street between Front & Water Streets

📞 718 858-4300

Open daily for lunch and dinner

Ⓜ High Street (A/C)

🍴 Located in the shadow of the Brooklyn Bridge near the Brooklyn Anchorage, this family-owned spot serves the best brick-oven thin-crust pizza in the five boroughs. If you are a newcomer, a few words of caution and advice are in order.

1. Like the sign says: no credit cards, no delivery, and no reservations. And they don't serve single slices, only whole pies.

2. Do not bring the kiddies here after soccer practice. A Grimaldi's pizza, covered with fresh, dare I say robust, toppings, is strictly adult fare.

3. Beware the black olives. They are my favorite topping but they sometimes contain pits. Chew with caution.

4. Not surprisingly, Frank is prominently represented on the walls and in the jukebox. If you just said, "Who's Frank?" stop reading this right now and order in Domino's. You are not ready for a real Brooklyn Italian pizza experience.

5. If you *are* ready for a real Brooklyn Italian pizza experience, order a Manhattan Special soda with your pie. This sweet, coffee-flavored beverage has been a favorite of Italian-American homes, pizzerias, and restaurants for generations. Ordering it is the sign of a true insider, especially since it's not listed by name on the menu. (Why is a Brooklyn-made drink called a Manhattan Special? The factory is located on Manhattan Avenue, that's why.)

6. Be prepared to negotiate with your friends when it's time to dole out the slices. The Grimaldi pizza makers take a devil-may-care approach to sprinkling the toppings and cutting up the pie. If you're not careful, you'll end up with a runt-sized sliver covered with a few bits of topping while the guy across the table gets a slice three times as big as yours.

7. You will be tempted to read the paper placemat that describes the convoluted family feud raging between

Grimaldi's and a rival New York pizzeria, Patsy's. Don't.
Unless you enjoy reading legal briefs, it's too much trouble to
follow and it may distract you from your appetite.

MICHAEL MISCIONE
Writer

Nestled under the Brooklyn Bridge, this family-owned
old-style pizzeria hasn't changed in years, except for the
name (the original was Patsy's). Grimaldi's reputation
rests on the texture of the pizza dough, whose crucial
ingredient is rumored to be Brooklyn water—whatever
that means. Get the one topped with fresh garlic, red
peppers, and onions.

FISHER STEVENS
Actor, director, and co-owner of GreeneStreet Films

17.19 Long Island Safe Deposit Company Building

1869, William A. Mundell
1 Front Street at Old Fulton Street
Ⓜ High Street (A/C)

A little-known and little-noticed two-story iron-front
building stands at 1 Front Street in Brooklyn. Designed
by William A. Mundell and erected in 1869, it occupies
the former site of the old stone farmhouse of the Rapalje
family. Built originally for the Long Island Safe Deposit
Company, it was located at the corner of busy Fulton
Street, close to the ferry to Manhattan.

When the Brooklyn Bridge was completed right over its
head in 1883, the bank and the commuter ferry, along with
the surrounding area, fell into oblivion. For many years,
the little iron bank stood empty. The 1970's saw a revival
in the area, and many empty buildings were put to new
uses. During the past 30 years, the building has served
as a warehouse, a cultural center, a gay bar, and a fine
restaurant, among other enterprises.

Life has not been easy for this little iron-front palazzo,
which has lost its original cornice and rooftop balustrade.

Nonetheless, the building retains its charm through its two iron facades, floor-to-ceiling arched windows, and a chamfered doorway at its corner. Today it stands in the Fulton Ferry Historic District, and serves to remind us of this bustling, mid-19th-century commercial area.
MARGOT GAYLE
Writer and preservationist

17.20 Bargemusic Ltd.

Fulton Ferry Landing, ☎ 718 624-4061
Concert season runs year-round, Thursday-Sunday; schedule information is available at www.bargemusic.org
Ⓜ High Street (A/C)

Conceived and still operated under the individual care of Olga Bloom, Bargemusic offers a unique New York experience. Distinguished musicians play a wide selection of classical chamber music inside a petite concert hall on the barge that remains permanently affixed to the pier beside the Brooklyn Bridge. A full view of Manhattan shimmers across the river through picture windows behind the performers. Intermissions are spent in the fresh air atop the barge, with the activity of ships and ferries steaming up and down the Hudson. Transportation by taxi and subway is easy. On a nice evening, however, approaching Bargemusic across the Brooklyn Bridge (a 15-minute walk) is a sublime experience.
WILLIAM J. WYER
Rare bookseller

17.21 The River Cafe

1 Water Street at Old Fulton Street, ☎ 718 522-5200
Monday-Saturday for lunch and dinner; Sunday for brunch and dinner
Ⓜ High Street (A/C)

¶⟨ Tucked under the Brooklyn Bridge, Buzzy O'Keefe's River
Cafe is New York's most romantic spot for dinner, as well
as one of the finest restaurants in America. Arrive as the
sun sets behind a spectacular view of the downtown
Manhattan skyline and stay late until skyscrapers twinkle
like stars. Bring someone special on a special occasion
and your checkbook, too.
TRACEY HUMMER AND FREDERIC SCHWARTZ
Writer and Architect

17.22 **Brooklyn Bridge Anchorage**
1867-83, John A. Roebling & Washington Roebling
At the intersection of Hicks & Old Fulton Streets, in
the base of the Brooklyn Bridge at Cadman Plaza West
☎ 212 206-6674
Art and music presented in the summer months
Ⓜ High Street (A/C)

Not only does this two-block-long labyrinth hold the
beloved bridge in place, but the man-sized blocks of
granite provided the newly built city with its closest equivalent combination of medieval crypt and ruined castle.
After a summer's stroll across the bridge, the anchorage's
summer exhibitions provide an oasis of cool tranquility.
SEBASTIAN HARDY
Urban planner

17.23 **Fulton Ferry Pier**
Renovated 1976
Foot of Old Fulton Street at the East River
Ⓜ High Street (A/C)

Down on the Fulton Ferry Pier, the site of Brooklyn's East
River ferry landing since the 1640's, you can dream the
harbor through Walt Whitman's eyes. Manhattan Island
is no longer ringed by a forest of masts, but the ferries still
ply the waters to Staten Island and garbage scows scuff

past with their rich ballast. Just ashore from the dock stands the former Franklin House Hotel, where in the 1830's a French dancing master taught neighborhood children quadrilles. An adjoining stable and haybarn provided shelter for the carriages brought over from Manhattan by ferry, as well as the Long Island farmers' wagons en route to city markets. The stable still stands, its roof now forlornly open to the skies. Close by, cabs drop off Manhattanites at the River Cafe (see p. 478)—a barge moored alongside Fulton Dock—and the lights twinkle overhead on the Brooklyn Bridge. Tourists disgorged from New York sightseeing buses are allowed two minutes here to view and photograph Manhattan's nighttime skyline. Some evenings I'll bring a picnic and a guitar and sit by the harbor—in Whitman's words, I am "refresh'd by the gladness of the river and the bright flow."

HOPE COOKE
Writer and urban historian

17.24 Gleason's Boxing Gym

83 Front Street at Main Street, ☎ 718 797-2872
Monday-Friday 6am-10pm; Saturday 8:30am-5:30pm;
closed Sunday
Ⓜ York Street (F), High Street (A/C)

The most famous boxing gym in the world is Gleason's Gym. Mirroring the exodus of artists from the city, Gleason's has moved from Manhattan to the DUMBO section of Brooklyn—and why not? The sweet science has inspired the likes of Hemingway, Bellows, and Scorsese. Virgil's motto hangs inside: "Now whoever has courage and a strong and collected spirit in his breast, let him come forward, lace on his gloves and put up his hands." Taking up the whole second floor of a warehouse, Gleason's Gym is still the home of champions as well as white-collar boxers staying in shape. Four rings, rows of heavy bags, the under-rhythm of fists against speed bags, the smell of sweat. On any given day you can see a sparring session between name fighters. This is not the movies but the real deal. Take the F to York Street, or the A or C train to High Street (all first stops in Brooklyn), collect your spirit, and walk toward the river. If you see men with flat necks, scar-etched eyebrows, and broken noses carrying their gear, you're going in the right direction.

ADAM BERLIN
Writer

Ice Fantasies Inc.

📞 800 NICE-ICE

Say the words "ice queen" and we can all think of plenty of candidates. But an ice man? Meet Joe O'Donoghue, aka Ice Man, who custom-designs over-the-top ice sculptures for clients such as David Letterman and David LaChapelle, Pepsi-Cola, the VH1 Fashion Awards, Annie Liebowitz, Tiffany's, Nobu, and Robert Isabell. My personal favorite was his ultimate no-calorie confection, the ice-cube wedding cake he did for Martha Stewart.

Ice Man got his start at a Hilton Hotel on Long Island. One day when the regular carver didn't show, Joe— a carpenter by trade—whipped out his chainsaw and sculpted a horse's head. Now he's appearing in 9 & Co. commercials, dressed in red leather pants and a wife-beater as he carves a shoe from a block of ice. And you thought your Manolos hurt bad!

DANY LEVY (AND EDITORAL STAFF OF DAILYCANDY.COM)
Founder of DailyCandy.com

CIVIC CENTER

17.25 **Gage & Tollner Restaurant**
372 Fulton Street between Smith & Adams Streets
☎ 718 875-5181
Monday-Friday for lunch and dinner; Saturday for dinner;
closed Sunday

Ⓜ Jay Street-Borough Hall (A/C/F); Court Street (M/N/R);
Borough Hall (1/2/4/5)

🍴 Established in 1879 (when Brooklyn was the third-largest
city in the nation), the restaurant was built to resemble a
late-19th-century Pullman dining car. It has been impecca-
bly restored and maintained. Diamond Jim Brady, Mae
West, W.C. Fields, and Jimmy Durante were some of the
regular patrons. Be sure to be here at dusk when the
gaslight chandeliers, glittering with etched glass, are turned
on. The food is as fine as the atmosphere, with seafood
and steak the specialties.
JAMES J. BRUCIA AND MARGARET BRUCIA
Justice (retired), New York State Supreme Court and Schoolteacher

17.26 **New York Transit Museum**
Located in a decommissioned subway station on the corner
of Schermerhorn Street & Boerum Place, ☎ 718 694-5100
Museum closed for renovations until 2003
www.mta.nyc.ny.us/museum

Ⓜ Court Street (M/N/R); Borough Hall (1/2/4/5)

Best place to go with kids—city kids or out-of-town visitors—when the lines are too long at the American Museum
of Natural History, and when you want more opportunities to "play"—drive a bus, ride a turn-of-the-century
trolley or subway. Fun for kids and their adult companions.
Follow with a snack or meal on Atlantic Avenue (see p. 485)
to experience Middle Eastern cuisine and music.
AMY A. WEINSTEIN
Museum curator

17.28 Junior's Restaurant

386 Flatbush Avenue at DeKalb Avenue, ☎ 718 852-5257
Sunday-Wednesday 6:30am-midnight; Thursday 6:30am-1am;
Friday, Saturday 6:30am-2am

Ⓜ DeKalb Avenue (M/N/Q/R)

🍴 It isn't just "the world's most fabulous cheesecake" that
makes this Googie-style diner in downtown Brooklyn
memorable, it's the way this urban version of an American
classic reflects its locale. As the neighborhood at Flatbush
and DeKalb Avenues changed character, the menu
expanded beyond the pastrami-on-rye and rich desserts
that catered to the original Jewish clientele to please a
broader audience. At Sunday-morning brunch, "alternative" 20-somethings in jeans and slogan T-shirts mix with
girls in fluffy dresses and their formally dressed families
arriving directly from church. Rarely do food and ethnicity
blend as interestingly and authentically as they do here.
JAYNE MERKEL
Journalist

BOERUM HILL

Brooklyn Academy of Music

17.29 BAM Opera House

30 Lafayette Avenue between Ashland Place & St. Felix Street
☎ 718 636-4100

Ⓜ Atlantic Avenue (Q/1/2/4/5)

17.30 Harvey Lichtenstein Theater

651 Fulton Street between Ashland & Rockwell Places
☎ 718 636-4100

Ⓜ Nevins Street (1/2/4/5)

The Brooklyn Academy of Music, better known by its hip
acronym, BAM, is New York's liveliest performing arts ▶

►

center. This old opera house and its various ancillary
spaces, built when Brooklyn's original academy burned
down in 1903, has long been the city's top presenting site
for contemporary dance, theater, and music—much of it
from abroad. One also sees the occasional classic drama
and visiting opera company here, but BAM's core identity
is with the cool and the curious. Heavily dependent
upon city funding, BAM's artistic scope has changed
considerably over the years. The complex once had five
theaters, but three of BAM's performance venues were
recently converted to other uses, including a movie
multiplex and a restaurant. Only two stages remain today,
but they are glorious: the BAM Opera House (once
a subway-circuit touring site for the Met Opera and other
high-end companies, but now home to the avant-garde
Next Wave Festival) and the nearby Harvey Theater
(originally the Majestic, but renamed for BAM's longtime
director Harvey Lichtenstein). The BAM Opera House
is a prime example of restored 19th-century theater
glamour, made all the more handsome by contrasting
with the modern work seen on its stage, while the Harvey
is a deconstruction casebook. Most of this theater's
beautiful decayed plaster was, in fact, designed by architect
Hugh Hardy, who modeled his renovation on Peter Brook's
Bouffes du Nord Theatre in Paris. The work presented here
changes from year to year and month to month. Look for
the latest performance schedule and be prepared for a long
subway or taxi ride. The quality may be variable, but the
level of invention is high.

ROBERT MARX
Essayist, producer, foundation executive

17.32 Bergen Beat Cafe

440 Bergen Street at Fifth Avenue, ☎ 718 241-1891
Monday Friday 7am-10pm, Saturday, Sunday 9am-10pm

Ⓜ Seventh Avenue (Q); Bergen Street (1/2)

🍴 Nestled between Fifth and Sixth Avenues on Bergen Street, two blocks south of Flatbush Avenue, Bergen Beat awaits. In the comfort of the vintage and retro chairs in this chill lounge, you can recover from your hangover listening to the beats you grooved to just the evening before. If the inside is too hip for you, enjoy the front patio and the view of owner, Jai's (aka DJ Skobadelic) beat-up and deliciously unpretentious Vespa. The friendly waitstaff serves everything from regular coffee to chai Kashmiri (tea, for those of you not in the know), with your choice of anything from Nutella and banana on panini to a scrumptious plate of Schinken (a German smoked ham) and various cheeses. They love their grooves as much as their food at this cozy little Brooklyn spot.

NAOMI BOMBARDI-WILSON
Filmmaker and producer

Atlantic Avenue Shopping

Ⓜ Atlantic Avenue (Q/1/2/4/5)

🏬 Brooklyn's Atlantic Avenue harbors one of the well-kept secrets of our city—perhaps because you have to leave Manhattan to get to it. Take the subway to Atlantic Avenue and you'll be at the junction of Fourth, Atlantic, and Flatbush Avenues. Get on Atlantic and walk west in the direction of the stores.

Ask in almost any of the stores for the free walking-and-shopping guide to the 11 blocks from Fourth Avenue to the East River. With the guide in hand, you can juxtapose photographs of what once was with what you now see.

You'll find a blossoming renaissance at the turn of this century, just as there was one at the turn of the last.   ►

▶

Serendipitously, some of the best of the last century's furnishings—now antiques—can be found a few blocks up, some even housed in period storefronts. Trendy and long-established restaurants line the avenue and neighboring blocks. In the 1930's, Middle Eastern specialty foods arrived; today, still family-run, many of these establishments located around Court Street carry food from all over the world. Wander in and enjoy the delicious sights and smells. And as you stroll down the avenue, check out the many boutiques for modern fashion and home furnishings.
BETSY KISSAM
Writer

WILLIAMSBURG

17.33 **Peter Luger**
178 Broadway between Bedford & Driggs Avenues
☎ 718 387-7400
Open daily for lunch and dinner
Ⓜ Marcy Avenue (J/M)

🍽 The best steak in the world. Hardwood floors, tin ceilings, paneled walls, bare wood tables, cigars, and lifetime waiters take you back to a turn-of-the century beer hall. Opened in 1887, it was originally Charles Luger's Cafe, Billiards and Bowling Alley. Start with a Dewar's on the rocks and the jumbo shrimp cocktail, followed by shared sides of thick-sliced tomato and onions, German fried potatoes, and creamed spinach, followed by platters of massive, marbleized dry aged porterhouse, cooked to perfection. Have your bachelor party here or go with a bunch of guys after a Knicks game.
FREDERIC SCHWARTZ
Architect

17.34 Pete's Candy Store

709 Lorimer Street between Frost & Richardson Streets
℡ 718 302-3770
Sunday-Tuesday 5pm-2am; Wednesday-Saturday 5pm-4am
Ⓜ Lorimer Street (L)

🍴 In the infamous words of Ogden Nash, "Candy is dandy, but liquor is quicker." But seriously: why choose? Pete's Candy Store is an out-of-the-way bar that serves candy-flavored cocktails to tickle even the most rational adult's inner child. Selections change every four to six months, but on the regular menu: a sweet vanilla shanti, a blood-orange martini that tastes like an orange sourball, the "egg scream" spiked with Kahlua, and a mojito chock-full of crushed fresh mint (this one tastes like an old-fashioned peppermint stick). Regrettably, Lynchburg lemonade is off the menu, but who knows? Maybe the spiky-haired bartender will make one for you on the spot.

Traditional quaffs include Manhattans, Stoli martinis, and Brooklyn Lager, as well as traditional, pub-style toasted sandwiches to soak it all up. Best of all, the prices will remind you of the old penny candy store.
DANY LEVY (AND EDITORAL STAFF OF DAILYCANDY.COM)
Founder of DailyCandy.com

17.35 Feast of Our Lady of Mt. Carmel and Saint Paulinus

Havemeyer Street between North 8th & North 11th Streets
Feast held in July, ℡ 718 384-9848
Ⓜ Bedford Avenue (L)

The best-known Italian-American street festival in New York (and perhaps the country) is the Festa di San Gennaro, held each September on Mulberry Street. I advise you to avoid it and, instead, wait for the smaller, lesser-known, and more authentic feasts in outlying areas. My personal favorite is the Feast of Our Lady of Mt. Carmel and Saint Paulinus in Williamsburg.

This festival commemorates the fifth-century rescue of the town of Nola in southern Italy. It's an event not unlikely for the region, but one that most researchers consider apocryphal. Pirates (the event depicts them as "Turks," but no one really knows for sure) had abducted for slavery a number of townspeople, including the only child of a local family. The Bishop of Nola (aka Saint Paulinus) offered himself as a substitute for the boy. The legend tells us the bishop so impressed the pirates with his courage and nobility that they released him and all of the other townspeople. They hit the high seas, never again to return!

You will, of course, see the standard accoutrements of all *feste*: gambling booths, sausage-and-pepper merchants, and even one marvelous painted sideshow wagon ("See the Island Princess: World's Smallest Woman!"), but all of it is merely an opening act, the prelude to what everyone has come here for: the dancing of the *giglio*. As far as I'm concerned, it's the closest thing we have to the Hindu festival of Jagannath.

The *giglio* (Italian for lily) is an 85-foot-high wood, aluminum, and painted papier-mâché tower surmounted by a figure of Saint Paulinus. Images of the Virgin, saints, and cherubs (or *putti*) adorn its sides. Including its platform, which also carries a male singer and a brass band, its estimated weight is 8,000 pounds (the lead trumpeter alone contributes a goodly portion). A *paranza* of 125 men carries it, all of them in red berets and white T-shirts bearing the words, *O' giglio, e paradiso*. There's also an immense wooden boat, with its own band and a statue of the bishop himself, carried by another 125-man *paranza* approaching from the opposite direction.

The bands play music composed specifically for the carrying of the *giglio*: traditional Neapolitan songs and crowd-pleasers such as "My Way" and "Rocky."

The *giglio* is, by far, the tallest thing in the immediate area—a typical urban neighborhood of modest four- and five-story dwellings. When the procession lumbers through, the crowds, fueled by Budweiser and *vino da tavola*, part to let them through.

Inches away from the tower, its companion ship, and their brave armies of musicians and bearers, you join the crowd's wild cheering.

KATHRYN NOCERINO
Poet and fiction writer

17.36 **Plan-Eat Thailand**
141 North 7th Street between Bedford & Berry Streets
☎ 718 599-5758
Open daily 11:30am-1am
Ⓜ Bedford Avenue (L)

🍴 The new bohemian scene, Williamsburg, is a spillover of sorts from the East Village. But the real art crowd came here 20 years ago. They were pioneers who suffered a long time without services, especially dining, Manhattan-style. Planet Thai changed that, becoming one of the first restaurants in the area to cater to the new generation in Williamsburg, and to serve innovative ethnic food in a neighborhood dominated by Old World cuisines.

The original restaurant opened on an obscure corner and was immediately patronized by the art locals, newcomers to Williamsburg, and, increasingly, Manhattanites who had their ears to the ground. Now, of course, Williamsburg is a desirable destination and, accordingly, Planet Thai has moved down the street to its current larger location, which accommodates the growing neighborhood. The new restaurant is big, noisy, and crowded, with an expanded menu that includes other Asian cuisines. But Planet Thai is still a phenomenon. The food is good and reasonably priced, and about as authentic as you'll get, short of a trip to Bangkok.

DAVID WINTER
Art dealer

`17.37` Galapagos
70 North 6th Street between Wythe & Kent Streets
℡ 718 782-5188
Monday-Thursday 6pm-2am; Friday, Saturday 6pm-4am;
Sunday 6pm-2am
Ⓜ Bedford Avenue (L)

Located in an old mayonnaise factory on a desolate street,
this bohemian mixed-use multiplex offers its neighbors
a ground-floor indoor reflecting pond, lit at night with
floating candles. Inside, the space offers dance, music,
and revival films, interspersed with the products of local
filmmakers. During the summer, the films move up and
out to the roof, where breezes and the Manhattan skyline
provide distractions.
SEBASTIAN HARDY
Urban planner

GREENPOINT

Old World Flavors
Ⓜ Greenpoint Avenue (G)

🎁 The Polish neighborhood around Greenpoint and
Manhattan Avenues in Greenpoint gives the impression
of being in a small city transplanted from Europe: blocks
of eclectic and undatable three- and four-story buildings
housing an array of interesting small businesses, in almost
all of which Polish is the language of choice. Two food
stores of note are Starapolski Meat Market (912 Manhattan
Avenue), worth a trip for its range of pierogi; and
Piekarnia Staropolska (926 Manhattan Avenue), a bakery
known for its extravagant fruit babkas. There are many
bookstores, such as Ksiegarnia Literacka (161 Java Street)

and Polska Ksiegarnia (946 Manhattan Avenue), the latter
of which has Harry Potter in Polish. Restaurants such as
Polska Restauracja (136 Greenpoint Avenue), with good
food and indifferent ambience, abound. Around the shopping center is a periphery of cheerful, tidy residential blocks.

THOMAS HEFFERNAN
Writer

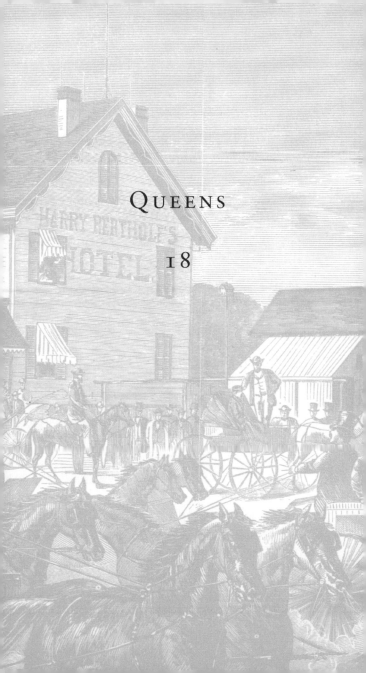

QUEENS

18

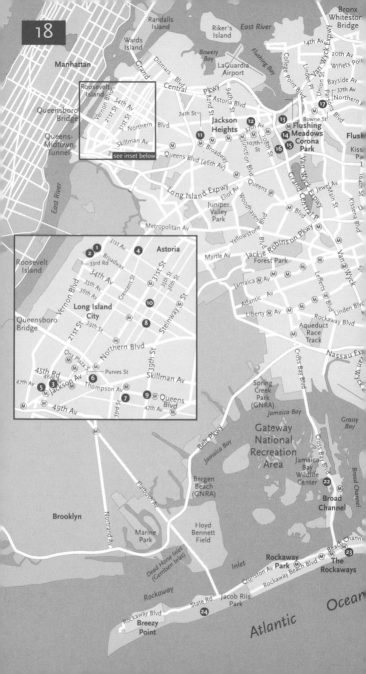

Long Island City, Astoria, Jackson Heights, Flushing Meadows-Corona Park, Flushing, Floral Park, Douglaston, Jamaica Bay & The Rockaways

LONG ISLAND CITY & ASTORIA

18.1 **Socrates Sculpture Park**
1986, Mark Di Suvero
On the corner of Broadway & Vernon Boulevard
☎ 718 956-1819
Open daily 10am to sunset
Ⓜ Broadway (N/W)

Here's a wonderful, free, and major outdoor sculpture museum, local family park, and studio facility in Long Island City. It's set on the edge of the East River, with the towers of Manhattan as a backdrop. The best way to appreciate its setting is to take the N subway train from Manhattan to the fourth stop in Queens and get off at Broadway in Astoria. Descend the elevated platform and walk west along Broadway through a neighborhood that has become a primary destination for incoming immigrants to this country. After eight or 10 blocks you'll march straight into the park, once an abandoned dump, now a fantasy world of artistic imagination, with monumental sculptures casually jutting up from and sprawling across the landscape. On a recent spring weekend, I stood in front of the top four feet of a full-size Brooklyn townhouse of the sort the artist grew up in, the rest of the building seemingly sunk into the earth. Beyond, in the water just offshore, was a gathering of oversize teacups, each on top of a long slim rod. Families strolled, a boy climbed to the top of an iron sculpture, somehow adding to its message.

Behind a chain-link fence other works in progress rose against the sky. A bulletin board announced an outdoor summer movie program. For the visitor, the visual stimulation is almost overwhelming in this blending of life and art, New York style.

STAN MACK
Cartoonist and reporter

Number 7 Train Through Queens

18.2 Isamu Noguchi Garden Museum
(see p. 499)

18.3 P.S. 1 Contemporary Arts Center
1997, expanded as arts center by Frederick Fisher
22-25 Jackson Avenue at 46th Avenue, ☎ 718 784-2084
Wednesday-Sunday noon-6pm; closed Monday, Tuesday
Ⓜ 23rd Street-Ely (E/V); 45th Road-Court House Square (7); 21st Street (G)

18.12 Former Home of Louis Armstrong
1910, Robert W. Johnson
34-56 107th Street between 34th & 37th Avenues
Currently being converted into the Louis Armstrong House Museum
Ⓜ 103rd Street-Corona Plaza (7)

18.13 Shea Stadium
126th Street & Roosevelt Avenue
For ticket information, ☎ 718 507-8499
Ⓜ Willets Point-Shea Stadium (7)

18.14 Arthur Ashe Stadium
National Tennis Center, inside Flushing Meadows-Corona Park, ☎ 718 760-6200
Ⓜ Willets Point-Shea Stadium (7)   ▶

►

Get on the Number 7 train, which is a world unto itself.
Ride in either the front or back car and look out the win-
dow as you cross the train yards and leave the city,
heading through Queens, where I grew up. Get off at
Vernon Boulevard and walk over to the Noguchi Garden
Museum, which is as far as you can get from the pace of
Manhattan. Half of Noguchi's ashes are buried here; the
other half, in Japan. Wise man. His sculpture resonates to
perfection in these gardens he designed. Also see P.S. 1's
Contemporary Arts Center before you leave Long Island
City. Get off at 74th Street and you're in Bombay. Buy
material for a sari, get a great meal, listen to the ragas
crooning out of the shops. Get off at 82nd Street, which
was my stop as a kid, and you're in South America.
The combination of the faux Tudor architecture and
the Spanish signage tells you all you need to know about
America, or at least about New York's constant reinvention; it is vibrancy itself. Get off at Junction Boulevard
and find the home of Louis Armstrong. At Willets Point,
see the remnants of the 1963 World's Fair and go either
to Shea Stadium or Ashe Stadium, depending on the
season, for the Mets or the tennis. Get off at the end of the
line in Flushing and just walk around. You'll find yourself
in Asia. There are a few other ethnic groups I'm sure I've
missed, traveling on the city's own equivalent to the
Trans-Siberian Railroad.

JOHN GUARE
Playwright

18.2 Isamu Noguchi Garden Museum

1985, Shogi Sazao

Due to renovations, the museum is temporarily located at
36-01 43rd Avenue at 36th Street, ☎ 718 721-1932
Wednesday-Friday 10am-5pm, Saturday-Sunday 11am-6pm;
closed Monday, Tuesday

Ⓜ 33rd Street (7)

The museum will move back into its usual premises in 2003.
32-37 Vernon Boulevard at 33rd Road, ☎ 718 721-1932

Ⓜ Broadway (N/W)

A short subway ride from Manhattan, then a short walk
through a safe but unprepossessing neighborhood, and
you're in one of those sublime enclaves that make New York
seem like the most serene spot on the globe. The so-called
indoor/outdoor gallery on the ground floor and the garden it
leads into are showcases for Noguchi's large works in stone,
a substance he is said to have found a source of consolation.
Whatever Noguchi himself may have meant, the consoling
effect is palpable. So is the exhilaration.

This site was Noguchi's office, studio, and storage facil-
ity from 1975 on. It was dedicated as a museum in 1985.
ROSLYN SCHLOSS
Editor

Located in a quiet corner of Long Island City, Queens,
is the museum that Isamu Noguchi (1904-1988) built to
house his personal collection. This spare and unique
museum presents the rare opportunity to see a huge body
of Noguchi's work gathered in the setting he designed for
it. Though the journey to the museum can seem daunting,
upon arrival, one finds a sanctuary of calm, filled with
unique examples of the artist's work. Primarily large
sculptures of hand-worked stone, the pieces reveal the
magic of Noguchi's originality and freshness in both
conception and execution. I am particularly fond of the
piece titled *The Well*, in which a simple stone and the
essence of a fountain are fused to become an archetypal

image made manifest. This quiet piece sits still in the garden and only upon close inspection reveals its secret.

In addition to his large stone pieces, the museum houses examples of Noguchi's landworks, gardens, and theater designs. But perhaps the most unexpected treat is the minimal cafe, populated with a rich sample of the myriad designs of Noguchi's *akari*, or light sculptures. The entire catalog of these magical lamps, which glow like a night moon, is available for sale at the museum, making it possible to take home with you a piece of lit sculpture—one of the artist's most lasting gifts.

CAROLYN CARTWRIGHT
Feature-film set decorator and interior designer

A rare opportunity to experience the power of sculpture and its dialogue with nature. It is a wholly unexpected encounter in New York City—subterranean, poetic, and visually breathtaking. Noguchi's sculpture garden provides for an understanding of abstraction in nature and in our urban experience.

CLARE BELL
Director of exhibitions, PaceWildenstein

Two Worlds

18.2   **Isamu Noguchi Garden Museum**
(see p. 499)

18.4   **Rizzo's Italian Village**
31-01 21st Street at 31st Avenue, ☎ 718 728-9573
Wednesday-Sunday for lunch and dinner; closed Monday, Tuesday
Ⓜ Broadway (N/W)

The gardens are dramatically different from one season to the next, so the time of year you visit will determine the gardens you will see. Designed as a journey through his career, this museum treats the visitor to the extraordinary range of work by Noguchi. To me, it is a completely inspiring New York experience, at once of the city and also removed from it.

My personal twist is to couple a visit to Noguchi with a meal at a restaurant called Rizzo's. I first ate at Rizzo's with Uko and Hideko Morita. (Uko was one of Noguchi's many assistants almost a quarter-century ago when he worked out of a nearby factory space. Almost every day Noguchi and his assistants would come here for lunch.) To contrast this Old World, garish Italian restaurant with the perfectly minimal designs Noguchi favored is simply beyond words. And really, the food's not bad....

LAURIE MCLENDON
Retailer

18.3 P.S. 1 Contemporary Arts Center

1997, expanded as arts center by Frederick Fisher
22-25 Jackson Avenue at 46th Avenue, ☎ 718 784-2084
Wednesday-Sunday noon-6pm; closed Monday, Tuesday
Ⓜ 23rd Street-Ely (E/V); 45th Road-Court House Square (7);
21st Street (G)

A perfect postscript to formal education, this century-old public school now houses artists and galleries, temporary and permanent, inside and out, in a continually evolving reuse of the fabric of the structure. Walk the three-dimensional labyrinth of halls and stairs, compare the juxtaposed life and lifelessness of the old and new, and above all, feel the brilliantly sharp edge of the art. See the James Turrell at dusk and ascend the stair to the roof. P.S. 1 continues as fresh as the seeing and making of art—a place of beginnings.

JAMES L. BODNAR
Architect

18.5 Manducatis

13-27 Jackson Avenue at 47th Avenue, ☎ 718 729-4602
Monday-Friday for lunch and dinner;
Saturday, Sunday for dinner only
Ⓜ Hunters Point Avenue (7); 21st Street (G)

🍴 Go with a gang. Do not order from the menu, but ask Vincenzo and his wife, Ida, to bring you what's good. Roasted peppers with amazing mozzarella, then probably stewed eggplant bruschetta, fettucine with fresh tomatoes and shitake mushrooms, some veal in lemon sauce, salad, sensational bread. If she has the time, Ida might talk to you about being bombed out of Monte Cassino as a child, and of the relatives Vincenzo lost in the destruction of Naples. (He went out for a loaf of bread one morning and came home to a pile of smoking rubble.) Two Italians fleeing American bombs half a century ago, they met in Italy and fell in love in New York. She still cooks the very best cucina casalinga I've tasted outside of Calabria. Very, very good value if you manage to avoid the temptations of a stunning wine list.

ROGER MICHELL
Director

18.6 The Sculpture Center

44-19 Purves Street at Jackson Avenue, ☎ 718 361-1750
Closed for renovations until Fall 2002
Ⓜ 23rd Street-Ely Avenue (E/V)

The center's new facility contains within its singular space perhaps the most powerful volume for the exhibition of art in New York City. This industrial hall, with its soaring overhead gantry, trusses, and monitor running the length of the building, suggests the heavy lifting of railroad cars of its past, and a future with the likes of Serra and Di Suvero. The collaboration of Maya Lin and David Hotson on a small addition and interiors will contribute a simple elegance to this structure's totally tough texture, for the exhibition of serious emerging artists.

JAMES L. BODNAR
Architect

18.7 MoMA QNS

2002, Michael Maltzan and Cooper, Robertson & Partners
45-20 33rd Street between 47th Avenue and Queens Boulevard, in the former Swingline building, ☎ 718 389-4729
Ⓜ 23rd Street-Ely Avenue (E/V);
45th Road-Court House Square (7)

Note: In 2002, MoMA will temporarily relocate to its Queens location while the 53rd Street building undergoes renovation. The renovation is scheduled for completion in 2005.

"The City Rises"
1910, Umberto Boccioni

The painting by Umberto Boccioni known as *The City Rises* is a big, frenzied canvas of men and horses erecting a building, but so fraught with life that when I first saw it I thought the title meant a city rising up in revolt. Most people are rushing past to see Van Goghs and Picassos, but in Boccioni's work I see all the fantasy and optimism of New York City.

SALLIE TISDALE
Writer

Ludwig Mies van der Rohe Archive
By appointment only

The Mies van der Rohe Archive at the Museum of Modern Art, open to the public by appointment, isn't so important for its own architectural qualities as for the architectural treasures within it. Ensconced in a 10-foot-by-20-foot room, the architect's letters, papers, photographs, and drawings—20,000 of them—reach to the 12-foot ceiling. Standing here, you are literally surrounded by his lifework. For an

architect, opening the door to the archive gives the same
thrill as Howard Carter might have received peering into
Tutankhamen's tomb. "What do you see?" they asked him.
"Wonderful things."

To your right are four cabinets of flat files, six feet
tall and about four feet wide, with dozens of drawers
containing the unframed drawings in Mylar sleeves. Above
that are the tills with the most exhibited drawings, kept in
their frames for protection. Ahead of you are the lateral
files containing Mies's photography collection, documenting his own work. Above them are shelves with archival
boxes with the architect's correspondence, notebooks,
various legal papers, magazines he collected, and other
flat material.

To the left, a custom-made cabinet with eight-foot-wide
drawers holds Mies's oversize drawings, principally the
full-scale drawings he made of his furniture designs. Above
that are hundreds of rolls of working construction drawings that still need to be treated by conservators.

When Mies left Berlin in 1938 to teach at the Illinois
Institute of Technology in Chicago, he left his archive in
the care of his professional collaborator and companion,
the designer Lilly Reich. After the Allies began bombarding
Berlin, Reich and one of Mies's former students transferred
all the material to a barn in what became East Germany
for safekeeping. It remained there until Mies was able to
secure permission from the government to bring it to the
United States. In 1968 Mies bequeathed the drawings to
the Museum of Modern Art.

The Mies archive will be on the move again shortly.
It will be transferred to MoMA QNS in Long Island City,
the provisional home of the museum while its 53rd Street
home is renovated and expanded to the designs of Yoshio
Taniguchi. In the study center at MoMa QNS, designed
by Michael Maltzan and Cooper, Robertson & Partners,
the architectural features of the archive will be a bit more

spacious, but not enough to dilute the unique experience of having a lifetime's work within reach.

TERENCE RILEY
*Chief Curator of Architecture and Design,
The Museum of Modern Art*

"Red and Blue Chair"

1918, Gerrit Thomas Rietveld

Almost immediately from its appearance in 1918, Gerrit Rietveld's *Red and Blue Chair* became a formidable icon of the radical inception of the modernist development. For me, this chair and the aesthetic it conveys establish a point of reference and departure for my own work, which also derives from an attempt to start from scratch. It allows me to imagine what must have been, even for the principal founders of modernism—indeed, particularly for them—quite a disruptive shift in orientation; a work that elicits something of the original strangeness, the putting-into-question, that characterizes the beginnings of modern furniture design, but without eluding or repudiating that inheritance, whose deepest charms remain.

ED WEINBERGER
Furniture designer

"The Red Studio"

1911, Henri Matisse

The Museum of Modern Art is one of New York City's most precious treasures; it is not a secret. But, even in that unsurpassed collection of more than 6,000 drawings, 40,000 prints and illustrated books, 25,000 photographs, 3,200 paintings and sculptures, 24,000 works of architecture and design, and 15,000 films and videos, grateful frequent visitors necessarily have special favorites.

My favorites are a shifting group and the competition among them for first place is often intense; when I am asked to name the work to which my attachment

is the most intimate and intense, I fall into a state of high
anxiety. That is because other works that mean to me as
much—or almost as much—will have been slighted. Thus
it is with a trembling hand that I write out the name of
The Red Studio (1911) by Henri Matisse.

The Red Studio is a horizontal rectangle painted red
(almost that of a ripe tomato). The paintings Matisse hung
in this space are his own; some of them we recognize or
think we recognize. Closer to the viewer are a table bearing
a Matisse ceramic plate, a glass, a vase, and a couple of
other objects, and a high-backed chair. Under the paintings
that hang on the wall we find a chest of drawers, sculptures
on high stands, an empty gilt frame, more paintings—some
leaning against the wall, some against the frame—and an
armoire. Also against the wall is placed a grandfather
clock, outlined in yellow, with a blue-and-white face that
has no hands. It bisects the painting. A sliver of a window
lets in a pale blue-and-white day. This is one of Matisse's
flat paintings—like MoMA's *Piano Lesson* (1916), also by
Matisse—that would have us think, until we look carefully,
that the master had abandoned the use of perspective.
After a while, we discover how subtly in fact he has used
it, creating the illusion of depth with details we may not
have grasped: the angles at which the frame and certain of
the standing paintings are inclined, the way we seem to
look at the studio through the armature of the high chair.

The studio is empty. I have always loved Matisse's interiors, and still think that some day, if I am lucky, I will live
in a space that looks as though he had painted it. I would
happily move into the idealized and intensely personal
space of *The Red Studio*.

LOUIS BEGLEY
Attorney and writer

Art in Astoria

18.7 **MoMA QNS** (see p. 503)

18.8 **American Museum of the Moving Image**
35th Avenue at 36th Street, ☎ 718 784-0077
Tuesday-Friday noon-5pm; Saturday, Sunday 11am-6pm;
closed Monday
Ⓜ Steinway Street (R/V/G); Broadway (N)

18.3 **P.S. 1 Contemporary Arts Center** (see p. 501)

Long Island City has been developing a chic enclave of
modern artists and actors. With everything from Kauffman
Astoria Studios and Silvercup Studios to the American
Museum of the Moving Image, P.S. 1 (affiliated with
MoMA; and the soon to be temporarily relocated headquarters of MoMA itself, Astoria/Long Island City has
become a cultural and culinary haven for the authentic. It
is also, at present, still much more affable and affordable,
all around, than its more gentrified cousin, Manhattan.
NINA FIORE
Internet producer

18.9 **Hemsin**
39-17 Queens Boulevard at 39th Street, ☎ 718 937-1715
Open daily for breakfast, lunch, and dinner
Ⓜ 40th Street (7)

🍴 Hemsin, a remote region in northeastern Turkey, borders
the shores of the Black Sea. Set in the valleys of the Kackar
Mountains above the forests of the Rize country of
Arderen and Pazar, Hemsin is the eponymous home to a
kind of small, highly prized fish, a rare breed of sheep, and
bees that hive only in birch trees.

It's also one of the most interesting and authentic
Turkish bakeries and restaurants in New York City.
Located about two miles from the Queensboro Bridge,

Hemsin is in the center of what is rapidly developing into one of the city's newest arts districts. P.S. 1, an affiliate of the Museum of Modern Art and New York's premier contemporary art center; the Noguchi Studio (see p. 499); Socrates Park (see p. 496); MoMA QNS; the Museum of Modern Art's Long Island City branch; and the Sculpture Center (see p. 502), among other venues, are all within walking distance of the restaurant. From the superb lah-macum, a kind of Turkish pizza, to outstanding mezze— Turkish appetizers that range from various eggplant dishes to stuffed grape leaves—and burek (cheese- or meat-filled pastries) as well as perfectly grilled chicken and lamb kebabs, Hemsin has the look and feel of the most memorable Turkish restaurants along the European and Asian coasts of the Bosphorus, from Istanbul to the mouth of the Black Sea. It is simple but superb.

GLENN LOWRY
Director, The Museum of Modern Art

18.10   **S'Agapó Taverna**

34-21 34th Avenue at 35th Street, ☎ 718 626-0303
Open daily noon-2am

Ⓜ Broadway (N/W), Steinway (R)

🍴 While New York has been overtaken with an explosion of Greek restaurants, S'Agapó ("I love you" in Greek) offers something extra. The superb and very authentic appetizers that owner Costantin Lambrakis creates are made with his own extra-virgin olive oil—especially imported from Crete. Ask for maidanouri, a parsley dip; piperossi, a hot pepper dip; haloumi, fried Greek cheese; and vlahopita, a quiche-like pie made with herbs.

RINA ANOUSSI
Travel agent

JACKSON HEIGHTS

18.11 Jackson Heights Tour

Ⓜ Jackson Heights-Roosevelt Avenue (E/F/R/V/G);
74th Street-Broadway (7)

New York's vaunted sense of energy is felt in many neighborhoods—the streams of pedestrians in Midtown, the lunch-hour rush on Wall Street, the fans on the ramps at Madison Square Garden surging into a Knicks game. High energy gets an immigrant flavor in Jackson Heights, Queens, especially at the intersection of Roosevelt Avenue and Broadway, easily reachable by subway. Indians, Pakistanis, Argentineans, Uruguayans, Peruvians, Chinese, Thais, and several other ethnic groups live and shop together in this tightly packed neighborhood. The elevated Number 7 train track that runs over Roosevelt Avenue recalls an earlier New York, but the pushcarts here sell mangoes, tacos, and freshly squeezed sugarcane juice.

Shops display sari silks and elaborate gold jewelry on 74th Street; supermarkets sell tiffin sets and bamboo steamers; appliance stores advertise roti and tortilla makers. Good eats abound—rotisserie chickens coated with South American spices are served with baked potatoes or yucca, while an empanada from one of the bakeries along 37th Road is good walking-around food. The Jackson Diner (37-47 74th Street between 37th and Roosevelt Avenues, ☎ 718 672-1232), named for a former American-style diner on the same block, is now an Indian restaurant with some of the best Indian food in all of the city. Their recently renovated space can be thought of as an emblem of this neighborhood—the heart of tradition in the body of the new.

CHARLES SUISMAN AND CAROL MOLESWORTH
Authors

FLUSHING MEADOWS-CORONA PARK

18.15 ### Queens Museum of Art

New York City Building in Flushing Meadows Park

☎ 718 592-5555

Tuesday-Friday 10am-5pm; Saturday, Sunday noon-5pm;
closed Monday

Ⓜ Willets Point-Shea Stadium (7)

Panorama of the City of New York
Panorama Gallery

I am the proud landlord of a red-brick apartment building.
It's three inches tall and sits on my mantelpiece.

My little piece of Gotham real estate was once part
of the Panorama of the City of New York, a scale model
of the five boroughs that's one of the few holdovers from
the 1964 World's Fair. As a jaded native, I'm not easily
impressed by New York attractions, but the Panorama
leaves me speechless every time I see it. Containing some
835,000 teensy-weensy buildings, it fills a floor space the
size of two N.B.A. basketball courts. Every dwelling and
large structure in the city is represented. The Statue of
Liberty could fit in a coffee mug. The deck of the Brooklyn
Bridge looks like a yardstick. Every few minutes the room
dims to mimic nightfall and the tiny windows glow just
like the real thing.

For years the Panorama was allowed to get dusty and
out-of-date, but in the mid-1990's it underwent a sort of
urban renewal. The whole thing was given a thorough
vacuuming. Then, long-gone structures were unceremoni-
ously plucked out with pliers and newly built ones were
glued in their place. During a visit to the makeover site I
was given permission to keep a few of the little buildings
I found in a bucket filled with the castoffs from the miniature metropolis. Alas, like so many New York historic
preservation efforts, I was only able to rescue a tiny

percentage of the many structures that ultimately wound up in a trash heap.

MICHAEL MISCIONE
Writer

Tennis Tickets

New York Junior Tennis League
24-16 Queens Plaza South at Crescent Street
☎ 718 786-7110
Ⓜ Queensboro Plaza (N/W/7)

The U.S. Open is one of New York's premier sporting, as well as social, events. And it is one of the four most important tennis events in the world. Despite, however, the recent 300-million-dollar renovation of its stadium and increased spectator occupancy, due to its international and national popularity, even the most well-connected New Yorker finds getting tickets to be a task. One of New York's best-kept secrets is being able to purchase U.S. Open tickets through the New York Junior Tennis League. Although tickets are sold at a markup, proceeds go to a charity founded by Arthur Ashe and are, therefore, tax-deductible. And you can generally get tickets up to the day before the event.

CHRISTINE KRAFT SCHUFF
Special events, Tennis Week *magazine*

18.16   Queens Zoo
53-51 111th Street at 53rd Avenue, in Flushing Meadows Park
☎ 718 271-7761
Open daily 10am-4:30pm
Ⓜ 111th Street (7)

Aviary
1964, Buckminster Fuller
North side of zoo

If the time comes when you get tired of sitting around the house reading Buckminster Fuller's *Untitled Epic Poem on the History of Industrialization*, you might want to head out to the aviary at the Queens Zoo, which is the only substantial geodesic dome in the five boroughs. It was designed by Fuller for the 1964 World's Fair, where it served as the Winston Churchill Pavilion. Today it houses a small community of wild turkeys, cattle egrets, magpies, robins, and buffleheads (a sort of compact black-and-white subaqueous duck).

This place has very good chi. The dome is 60 feet high and open to the elements. Trees grow in it: oaks and birches. Its triangular panels, which make up its miraculous weight-bearing canopy of hexagons and pentagons, are covered with a stiff wire mesh that keeps the birds in and lets the sun and rain through. When it snows heavily, the snow fills in the panels and makes the whole place into a kind of translucent igloo. There is a winding anamorphic pathway that grades gently upwards until you are high among the branches, then you wind back down. Do a few circuits. Go on a weekday, when the wage-slaves are shackled to their desks, and you will have the place to yourself.

CHRISTOPHER CAHILL
Poet and novelist

FLUSHING

18.17 **Bowne House**
1661, John Bowne
37-01 Bowne Street between 37th Avenue & Northern Boulevard, ☎ 718 359-0528
Regular hours suspended due to renovation; call for an appointment
Ⓜ Flushing-Main Street (7)

Out in Flushing is a small, wooden house, that was lived in
by an English Quaker named John Bowne about 350 years
ago. Its story, as I heard it, goes like this. At that time,
Flushing was controlled by Peter Stuyvesant, the Dutch
governor of New Amsterdam, a little town of about 3,000
people at the south end of Manhattan Island. Stuyvesant
let it be known that nobody should practice any religion
except the Dutch Reform Church. He arrested Bowne, put
him in a dungeon. And then in court, Bowne refused to
take off his hat, saying, "I only take off my hat in the presence of God." Back to the dungeon.

Now the other colonies along the coast were asking if all
this was necessary. And Stuyvesant told the jailer, "Leave
the door open, let the fool escape." But Bowne refused
to escape. He said, "I demand a fair trial." And Stuyvesant,
to get rid of him, said, "Well, you can go to Amsterdam,
Holland, and argue your case with the Dutch West India
Company." Stuyvesant then told the captain to drop off
Bowne in Dublin and sail away without him. But Bowne
found some Quakers in Dublin, passed the hat, and got
enough money to go on to Amsterdam in another boat.
After two years, and probably a good deal of work and
money to Dutch lawyers, he got a slip of paper saying
he had a right to be a Quaker in New Amsterdam. He
sailed back, and grudgingly Stuyvesant said, "OK, OK."

Who is the real hero? Bowne's wife, who kept the farm
up and took care of the children for two long years while
he was away. I guess some of his Quaker neighbors helped
out. They weren't allowed to formally practice their
religion, but I guess they were in touch with each other.

At any rate, it's a landmark in American freedom of
religion, a story that should be remembered. The Bowne
house still stands in Flushing—a Korean neighborhood now!
PETE SEEGER
Musician

FLORAL PARK

18.18 Queens County Farm Museum

Farmhouse built c. 1772

73-50 Little Neck Parkway, Floral Park, ☎ 718 347-3276
Monday-Friday 9am-5pm; Saturday, Sunday 10am-5pm
Ⓜ Kew Gardens-Union Turnpike (E/F), then take the Q46 X
bus east on Union Turnpike to Little Neck Parkway, walk
north three blocks

Its flat, well-drained, and extremely fertile soil makes Queens
an ideal spot for farming. As far back as the 18th century, this
borough was literally the market garden for Brooklyn and
Manhattan, its orchards, farms, greenhouses, and nurseries
supplying copious amounts of fruit, vegetables, and flowers to
its urban neighbors on a daily basis. Sadly, the pressures of
housing an expanding population forced most farms out; by
1920, they were almost all gone. The Queens County Farm
Museum is a last vestige of this rich agricultural past.

The museum, on 47 acres in Floral Park, is a remnant
of a much larger farm established in 1772 by Jacob
and Catherine Adriance. They built the Flemish-style
farmhouse that still stands, although subsequent owners
have added to it. By 1900, the farm was the second largest
in Queens, and was valued at 32,000 dollars. In 1926, the
owner sold the property to the State of New York, which
made it part of the nearby Creedmoor Psychiatric Center.
The farm provided fresh produce for the institution, where
working the fields and caring for livestock were considered
therapy for the patients. Creedmoor stopped farming in
1960, and in 1973, when the state put the property up for
sale, area residents banded together to save the farm and
open land. The farmhouse, its outbuildings and the seven
acres around it now comprise the farm museum, which has
been designated both a national and city landmark.

The Farm Museum gives visitors the opportunity to
experience a farm firsthand, a unique thrill for many of us,

but especially for city schoolchildren, who come here in busloads (half a million visitors a year). This is not the neat and tidy farm of nostalgic dreams, but instead a very real, rough and tumble place, which feels, sounds, and smells like a working farm. The museum's particular mission is to teach visitors about Queens's agricultural history. To that end, there is an orchard (three acres of apple, pear, peach, and plum trees) and plenty of livestock, including several Suffolk sheep, pigs, an Ayreshire cow, and a hundred or so laying hens. More than an acre of planting fields are filled with crops—pumpkins, beans, squash, corn, eggplants, and tomatoes—much as they would be on a typical truck farm. The staff and volunteers hand-weed the fields, employ natural pest-control techniques and spread compost from their own barnyards. Beehives produce honey, and the pond is home to a number of ducks and geese. There is also a small greenhouse dating to the Creedmoor period; it has been recently rebuilt to recall Queens's status as the birthplace of the American horticultural industry.

Behind the farmhouse is a small herb garden, surrounded by a traditional picket fence and filled with plants used in the 18th and 19th centuries for treating the sick, dyeing yarns, brewing teas, and seasoning food. Although there is no record of an herb garden in precisely this spot, farms typically had this kind of garden near the house, so that the herbs used in everyday household activities were within reach. Besides the herbs, the beds are filled with strawberries, rhubarb, asparagus, lavender, asters, and hollyhocks.
NANCY BERNER AND SUSAN LOWRY
Landscape consultants and garden writers

A case of *rus in urbe* if ever there was one. Or at least *rus in suburbe*. This 47-acre working farm and open-air museum is a good place to experience the sights, sounds, and smells of farm life. Episodes of *Sex and the City* and *Law and Order* were filmed here.
KATHARINE RISTICH
Editor

DOUGLASTON

Where the Wild Things Are

New York City's many huge, naturalistic parks are among its best-kept secrets, and the variety and quantity of renewable wild edible and medicinal plants and mushrooms elude the knowledge of most New Yorkers.

Everyone knows about Central Park, but few visitors to the city explore Forest Park, Cunningham Park, or Alley Pond Park (all in Queens), Inwood Hill Park in Manhattan, or Prospect or Marine parks in Brooklyn. I've explored these and other overlooked natural habitats, and have collected and used an array of tasty, healthful wild plants most people destroy as "weeds." You may fall in love with the lemony flavor of wood sorrel or the spinach-like taste of lamb's quarters. After trying wineberries, you'll never want to buy the related commercial raspberries again. And the chicken mushroom, much better than any commercial mushroom, really does taste like chicken. Sometimes more than 30 pounds emerge from dead trees or logs in the woods.

"WILDMAN" STEVE BRILL
Naturalist

RECOMMENDED READING
Steve Brill, *Identifying and Harvesting Edible and Medicinal Plants in Wild (and Not So Wild) Places*, William Morrow, 1994.

18.19 **Douglaston**
Northeastern Queens
Long Island Railroad (Port Washington line) to
Douglaston Station, or
Ⓜ Main Street-Flushing (7), then Q12 bus to
Douglaston Parkway

In the farthest northeast corner of Queens sits the neighborhood of Douglaston. Recently made a historic

district, Douglaston was a planned railroad suburb, with
its most significant houses built at the turn of the last century and into the 1920's. Take the Long Island Railroad
Port Washington Line to the Douglaston Station and walk
north past the collection of shops, the public school, and
the neighborhood church to the well-groomed and densely
sited blocks of elegant houses. Streets are defined by big
old trees, and you can walk the whole place in an hour.
Take a lunch and sit by Little Neck Bay; Manhattan feels
a world away.

DEBORAH BERKE
Architect

JAMAICA BAY & THE ROCKAWAYS

John F. Kennedy International Airport
Bus service information, ☎ 718 875-8200

18.20   **Former Pan American Airways Terminal, now Terminal 3**
1961, Tippetts-Abbett-McCarthy-Stratton; Ives, Turano &
Gardener, associate architects
Entrance off the Van Wyck Expressway

18.21   **Former Trans World Airways Terminal, now Terminal 5**
1962, Eero Saarinen, Kevin Roche co-designer
Entrance off the Van Wyck Expressway

I was born in Queens, right off the Van Wyck Expressway,
a few minutes from JFK (then known as Idlewild Airport).
As a child, my first memories of architecture were the
now-neglected Pan Am Terminal (1961) and the Jet Age
icon, the TWA Flight Center (1962). Once the home
of the world's most successful airline, Pan Am's four-acre
elliptical, cantilevered roof is a giant hovering umbrella for
boarding jumbo jets. A marvel of engineering designed by
Tippetts-Abbett-McCarthy-Stratton, the concrete, cable-
supported roof is now barely visible, but its gravity-   ►

►

defying memory still remains. Eero Saarinen and Associates's
TWA Terminal is soaring and surreal, an expressionistic,
total "whammo" of a masterpiece. TWA is the ultimate big
bird, ready to soar, a testament to the freedom of flight
and an architect's dream.
FREDERIC SCHWARTZ
Architect

18.22 **Jamaica Bay Wildlife Refuge**
Visitors' Center is located at Cross Bay Boulevard,
Broad Channel, ☎ 718 318-4340
Open daily 8:30am–5pm
Ⓜ Broad Channel (A/S); walk west to Cross Bay Boulevard,
then 1/2 mile north
Bus information: Triboro Q53 from Roosevelt Avenue-
Jackson Heights to Jamaica Bay Wildlife Refuge

Broad Channel Bird Preserve, part of the Gateway
National Recreation area, is about half a mile north of the
Broad Channel subway stop in Queens on the A train, and
a world away from the clamor of the city. It was built on
land created when Big Egg Marsh, the Raunt, Goose
Creek, Black Bank Marsh, and Ruler's Bar Hassock were
combined with Broad Channel into one island. The park
is divided in half. The East Pond was created more for
birds than for people. The large artificial lake, a favorite
stopping place for migrating birds, can be seen from a few
viewpoints, but is mostly hidden. The best view is actually
from the subway, which runs right along one edge. The
trails here are somewhat marshy, passing through tall
reeds. There is a bird blind, and a tiny frog and turtle pond
known as Big John's Pond after the bulldozer operator
who made it. The more accessible West Pond Trail is a flat,
beautifully maintained one-and-three-quarter-mile loop
around a smaller lake also popular with birds. The trail
passes through woodlands, marsh, dunes, and beach, past
shipwrecks and cormorant platforms. Even if you don't

know much about birds, you will probably be able to spot snowy egrets, herons, ibis, swans, or plover among the more familiar ducks and geese. If you see anything more exotic, a friendly birdwatcher is usually around to tell you what you've found. Because the preserve is on the Atlantic flyway, a major migratory corridor, about 325 species of birds have been spotted passing through. Native cactus plants at the beginning of the trail are a reminder that New York's climate is semitropical. Other areas have been designed to attract butterflies, bats, owls, and even snakes. A sandy side trail is closed to the public during the diamondback terrapin nesting season (June and July). The rest of the year, a bench perched on the crumbling sandy bank of the turtle beach is an ideal spot to watch the sun set into Jamaica Bay with the Manhattan skyline in the background. The view that perhaps best epitomizes this piece of wildland within the city can be seen facing west over the pond. The spire of the Empire State Building appears to rise from the middle of a green, grassy hill, and if your timing is right, you can watch the airplanes leaving Kennedy Airport, seemingly rising to join a flock of wild geese as they take off from the lake.

JANET B. PASCAL
Writer and editor

A visit to the Jamaica Bay Wildlife Refuge makes you feel as if you have spent a day in the country. The sense of being transported to a distant world begins on the A train as it crosses over Jamaica Bay and leaves you on the island of Broad Channel. The town is like a small New England fishing village, with its lovely wooden church and houses built on stilts over the water, each with its own motorboat. The entrance to the refuge is through the ranger station, where one can find out about the latest bird sightings and buy postcards and nature guides. No food is allowed inside the refuge, but the rangers have thoughtfully provided picnic tables for those who bring their own lunch.

The stars of this sanctuary are the birds. For the serious birdwatcher, there is the thrill of anticipation as one sets out hoping to see a rare bird to add to one's life list. One usually begins the bird walk by going around the freshwater pond, where snowy egrets stalk fish, ruddy ducks dive for vegetation, cormorants dry their wings in the breeze, and glossy ibises sail majestically overhead.

After completing the pond trail, one enters the garden area, specially planted with trees and bushes that attract tree birds. Here a sharp eye and a lot of patience are needed to spot the birds as they flit rapidly from tree to tree. One can be rewarded with glimpses of brilliantly colored warblers, mewing catbirds, rufous-sided towhees, and a host of other species whose calls create a symphonic accompaniment as one walks along the trail.

To fully enjoy the birding experience, binoculars and a bird book are a must, although many of the other visitors to the refuge are bird and nature enthusiasts happy to share their knowledge with the novice. Walking is the only mode of transportation allowed. For the visitor who wants a quiet communion with nature, Jamaica Bay is truly a sanctuary from the turbulence of city life.

SUSAN L. BRAUNSTEIN
Curator of archaeology and Judaica, The Jewish Museum

18.23 Urban surfing: Beach 90

Calling the Rockaway Beach Surf Report (☎ 718 474-9374) is a good way to start, due to the inconsistent nature of East Coast waves. But if the conditions come together, the surf at Rockaway Beach provides urban surfers with good reason to grab a board and head for the A train. Ride to Broad Channel, then switch to the shuttle (S) train. It will drop you off at Beach 90, where on a good day you can find some of the sweetest barrels on the East Coast. The gritty urban landscape viewed from the ocean creates an amazing contrast. One thought dominates the subway ride

back to town after surfing a hefty hurricane swell: they
have no idea. Recommended for spectators as well as
the hardcore.
BILL KOMOSKI
Artist

18.24 A Day at the Beach: Fort Tilden

Western edge of Rockaway Peninsula, west of Jacob Riis Park
☎ /18 318-4300

Ⓜ Flatbush Avenue-Brooklyn College (2/5), then Q bus; or
Rockaway Park (A/S), then Q35 bus or Q22 bus

Much of Jacob Riis Park on the western end of the
Rockaway Peninsula is a typical New York City beach—
a boardwalk, lifeguards, crowds, and a Robert Moses
bathhouse. If you take the Q35 bus, however, past the
huge parking lot all the way to Fort Tilden, now part of
Gateway National Recreation Area, you come to the last
remaining natural dunes within the city limits. The beach
here is nearly as lovely as the more famous beaches of
Fire Island and the Hamptons, and rarely are there many
people around. It is a nesting area for snowy plovers, and
in the fall, migrating monarch butterflies often pass
through. Fort Tilden, founded in 1917, was rebuilt during
World War II to guard against German U-boats, some of
which actually did get as far as the Rockaways and even
into New York Harbor. Now the fort buildings are mostly
abandoned, crumbling ruins, completely overgrown and
almost invisible under the drifting sand. Several trails lead
to the top of the old batteries. They are steep and narrow,
but if you climb them you are rewarded with magnificent
views out to sea and back to Manhattan. (Be sure you
know what poison ivy looks like—it thrives in the dunes.)
If you're feeling ambitious and you're willing to climb over
a few seawalls, you can walk about three miles along

the beach, all the way to the tip of Breezy Point. A beach club blocks the beach at one spot, but because the tip of the point is National Park land, you will be allowed to pass through. This is a favorite nesting territory for black skimmers, and if you startle them, huge calling flocks will dive at you, filling the air. There is no public transportation beyond Fort Tilden, so be sure to leave enough time and energy to walk all the way back the way you came.

JANET B. PASCAL
Writer and editor

STATEN ISLAND

19

Newark
Bay

Bayonne
Bridge

Richmond Terrace

Staten Island Expwy

Arthur Kill

Goethals
Bridge

Forest Avenue

Port Richmond Av

Jewett Avenue

Willowbrook Pky

South Avenue

Prall's
Island

Staten Is

New
Jersey

Victory Blvd

Willow
Brook
Park

Rockland Avenue

Forest Hill Rd

Fresh
Kills
Park

Richmond Hill Rd

La Tourette
Park

Hig
Roc
Par

Fresh Kills
Landfill

Richmond Avenue

Island
of
Meadow

Fresh
Kills
Park

Richmond Rd

New
Jersey

Arthur Kill

Arthur Kill Rd

West Shore Expwy

Huguenot Avenue

Woodrow Rd

Arthur Kill Rd

Giffords Ln

Evergreen
Park

Nelson Avenue

Amboy Rd

Great Kills
Harbor

Clay Pit
Ponds
State Park
Reserve

Arthur Kill Rd

Bloomingdale Rd

Foster Rd

Korean War Veterans Pkwy (Richmond Pkwy)

Richmond Avenue

Arden Avenue

Blue Heron
Pond Park

New
Jersey

Arthur Kill

Outerbridge
Crossing

Seaside Avenue

Wolfes
Pond
Park

Amboy Rd

Page Avenue

Tottenville

Hylan

Blvd

9 Conference
House Park

Raritan
Bay

Atlantic

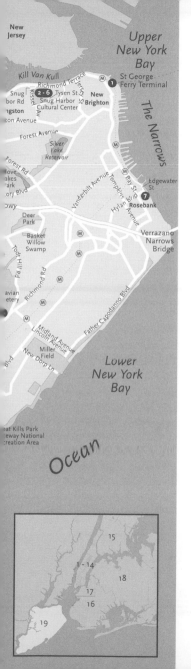

New Brighton, Livingston, Rosebank, Todt Hill & Tottenville

NEW BRIGHTON & LIVINGSTON

Snug Harbor Cultural Center
1000 Richmond Terrace between Tysen Street &
Snug Harbor Road, ☎ 718 448-2500
Open daily 8am-midnight
Ⓜ Whitehall Street (N/R) or Bowling Green (4/5) to the
Staten Island ferry, then the S40 bus or the S1 to Snug
Harbor gate

19.1 **Staten Island Ferry**
☎ 718 815-BOAT
Ferries run 24 hours

19.2 **Chinese Scholar's Garden**
Staten Island Botanical Garden
Winter: Wednesday-Sunday 10am-4pm; closed Monday,
Tuesday; Spring, Summer, Fall: Tuesday, Wednesday,
Thursday, Saturday, Sunday 10am-5pm; Friday 10am-9pm;
closed Monday

19.3 **Staten Island Botanical Garden**
Snug Harbor Cultural Center
☎ 718 273-8200
Open 8am to dusk

19.4 **Staten Island Children's Museum**
Snug Harbor Cultural Center, located behind the chapel
☎ 718 273-2060
October-June: Tuesday-Sunday noon-5pm; closed Monday
July-September: Tuesday-Sunday 11am-5pm; closed Monday

19.5 Children's Maze
Staten Island Botanical Garden
Tuesday-Sunday 10am-5pm; closed Monday

19.6 Antique Rose Garden
Staten Island Botanical Garden
Tuesday-Sunday 10am-5pm; closed Monday

When you take the ferry to Staten Island (and this is a trip
that should be high on your list), you'll be using a staple
transport of the earliest colonial times. True, it was
powered with muscle and oar in the days of Peter
Stuyvesant, and subject to the dreadful whims of Neptune,
but, though fuel-powered today, the ferry is still the only
municipal link with the sister island of Manhattan and
offers a stunning view of the Statue of Liberty. A delight
awaits you in this southernmost borough in the form of an
exquisite Chinese Scholar's Garden, which came into being
in 1999, a reflection of the increasing Asian population.
It is to be found to the north, on the broad band of
Richmond Terrace in an area designated as the Snug
Harbor Cultural Center, reachable by walking from the
ferry or a bus. The very idea of such a poetic oasis would
have thrilled the mid-19th-century visitor Henry David
Thoreau, who was ever looking to extricate himself from
urban confinements. This famed New England naturalist
was engaged as a tutor here and wrote to his sister in
a letter of 1843, "the whole island is like a garden and
affords very fine scenery." What Thoreau enjoyed most
were the unending Staten Island views of the ocean, which
held him in thrall. "My life is like a stroll upon the beach /
as near the ocean's edge as I can go," are the beginning
lines of a poem he conceived while strolling the Atlantic.

Staten Island was once famed for the complex known as
Sailors' Snug Harbor, the grounds on which you now

▶

▶

find yourself. This was a haven endowed by a 19th-century
philanthropist "for the purpose of maintaining and supporting aged, decrepit and worn-out sailors." There was
assuredly a need for such an asylum in the vast port region
of New York, where for two and a half centuries a robust
percentage of the population was maritime. This refuge for
sailors opened in 1833 in an imposing, Greek Revival-style
edifice with 23 occupants; it eventually expanded to 60
buildings. Thoreau tramped the grounds with great interest
as, meanwhile, the grandeur and munificence of Sailors'
Snug Harbor were becoming legendary. When Theodore
Dreiser visited in 1904, he wrote of "the orderly and palatial buildings, the beautiful lawns and flowers, and then
the thousand and one characters who . . . found their
way" to the harbor. In a spoof on the splendor of the
place, the local weekly *Independent* remarked in a 1908
issue that the sailors enjoyed "breakfast on plovers' eggs
and terrapin, lunch on paté de foie gras, and [they] dine
on canvas-back duck, with dry Champagne."

Today on the grounds of the former Sailors' Snug
Harbor, you can visit the Staten Island Botanical Garden,
the Children's Museum, and the Children's Maze, as well
as a model farm with a vineyard. You will find when you
visit the Antique Rose Garden on these grounds that,
among the numerous breeds of roses blooming there, some
strains date from the year 1400. Staten Island's history
assuredly does not go back as far as the Renaissance, but
there is a scene of old that you can bear in mind as you
visit this borough. On July 12, 1776, four days after the
American colonists made their bold Declaration of
Independence, a British fleet dropped anchor off Staten
Island. It was comprised of 52 warships and 427
transports commanded by General Sir William Howe.
Together with the 32,000 troops already encamped on the
island, this vast fleet comprised the largest expeditionary
force ever assembled in the 18th century. The military
coats of the alighting soldiers created a sea of red on the

island that presented a sight as magnificent as it was menacing. A bloom of Renaissance roses offers a more tranquil scene.

GLORIA DEAK
Writer

ROSEBANK

19.7 Alice Austen House Museum

2 Hylan Boulevard between Bay & Edgewater Streets
☎ 718 816-4506
Thursday-Sunday noon-5pm; closed Monday-Wednesday;
closed January and February

Ⓜ Staten Island ferry, then the S51 bus from the terminal
to Bay Street/Hylan Boulevard

Perched on a hill overlooking the Narrows, with a panoramic view extending from the Verrazano Bridge to the Statue of Liberty, stands the perfect Victorian vine-covered cottage, the Alice Austen House Museum. Gingerbread touches decorate the roof, porch, and gabled windows of the white clapboard house. The rough-cut grass sloping down to the water is dotted here and there with old-fashioned shrubs, and large shade trees line the pebbled path and guard the house. Close your eyes and you can almost see pioneer photographer Alice Austen running out of the front door with her camera in one hand and tennis racket in the other. Austen, who lived in this cottage—then called Clear Comfort—for almost 80 years, was a passionate photographer and left a fascinating and extensive record (almost 3,000 negatives) of daily life at the turn of the century. Her subjects were her peers in the moneyed, genteel enclave of summer homes on Staten Island, as well as shoeshine boys, washerwomen, and immigrants on the streets of Manhattan. She recorded her friends and neighbors playing tennis, learning to cycle, and driving the earliest motorcars. Although she never married, she and her companion of 55 years, Gertrude Tate, seem to have enjoyed an extensive social life. When Austen lost all her inheritance in the stock market crash of 1929, she and Tate tried to support themselves by turning Clear Comfort into a restaurant. Sadly, Austen eventually had to leave her home, moving to the city poorhouse. Only just before her death in 1952 was her work recognized and published.

Clear Comfort was opened as the Alice Austen House Museum in 1985. Inside, the small, slightly shabby rooms, busy wallpaper, and dark furniture feel right for the period, and changing exhibitions of Austen's photographs and a short biographical film narrated by one of her acquaintances (the voice reminiscent of films of the 30's and 40's) shows vintage footage of life on Staten Island during her time.

NANCY BERNER AND SUSAN LOWRY
Landscape consultants and garden writers

TODT HILL

19.8 Moravian Cemetery

2205 Richmond Road, entrance on Todt Hill Road or Richmond Road, ☎ 718 351-0136
Open daily 8am-6:30pm

Ⓜ SIRT to Grant City; walk west on Lincoln Avenue, then turn left on Richmond Road

Ride the Staten Island ferry and visit the Moravian cemetery. Members of New York's most famous families are buried in this beautifully landscaped spot, though the Vanderbilt Mausoleum is not, regrettably, open to the public.

VICTORIA NEWHOUSE
Writer

TOTTENVILLE

19.9 **The Conference House**

1680

7455 Hylan Boulevard, in Conference House Park

☎ 718 984-2086

April 15th to mid-December: Friday-Sunday 1pm-4pm

Ⓜ Staten Island ferry, then the S78 bus to the end
of Hylan Boulevard

Oh, those Manhattan songwriters. The Bronx may be up,
but the Battery certainly isn't down. Tottenville is.

Tottenville, Staten Island, is the southernmost tippy-tip
of New York City (and New York State, for that matter).
In the 19th century, the area was famous for the delicious
oysters that were harvested in the nearby waters. But
while the oyster beds died long ago, another historical
vestige remains: a 17th-century stone manor house
overlooking the shore known as the Conference House
of the Billopp House.

The house was the site of a brief, little-known episode
of Revolutionary War history. On September 11, 1776, a
small delegation of Americans that included Benjamin
Franklin and John Adams met here with British Admiral
Lord Richard Howe in a failed attempt to settle the
escalating hostilities. The Americans rejected the British
peace proposal because it did not recognize the independence of the colonies.

The original stone structure was built around 1680 by
British sea captain Christopher Billopp. Over the centuries
the house endured various additions and incarnations.
Once, for example, it served as a rat-poison factory. In
1926 the property was deeded to the City of New York.
The house was restored and opened as a museum in 1937.

One rainy afternoon a couple of years ago I attended
the annual re-enactment that the Conference House stages
to mark the famous 1776 treaty summit. Part history

festival, part block party, the daylong event featured a friendly hodgepodge of house tours, craft exhibits, vendors, musicians, balloon twisters, puppet shows, and nature walks. At the appointed hour, a rowboatful of Revolutionary War buffs in period costumes, representing the American delegation, trooped up the shore to the house, where they were met by Lord Howe. My heart went out to the hapless guy portraying His Lordship. He probably came late to the re-enactor's meeting. All the good parts were taken and he got stuck playing the villain.

MICHAEL MISCIONE
Writer

BIOGRAPHIES

ROBERT KAHN, series editor and creator of the City Secrets series, is an architect in private practice. His work has been widely published. He has taught design, most recently at Yale University. He is the recipient of the Prix de Rome in Architecture from the American Academy in Rome. He lives with his wife Fiona in New York City and Shelter Island.

THE MUNICIPAL ART SOCIETY is a private non-profit membership organization whose mission is to promote a more livable city. Since 1893, the society has worked to enrich the culture, neighborhoods, and physical design of New York City. The MAS advocates for excellence in urban planning, contemporary architecture, historic preservation, and public art.

THE NEW YORK TIMES NEEDIEST CASES FUND. On Christmas day, 1911, Adolph S. Ochs, publisher of the New York Times, went out for a walk after a big turkey dinner, and encountered a shabbily dressed man on the street. The man said he had just been given Christmas dinner at a Y.M.C.A. but had nowhere to sleep. The publisher looked him over, decided he looked respectable and gave him a few dollars and his card. "If you're looking for a job," he said, "come see me tomorrow."

The encounter left the publisher thinking about charity. The next year, he sent a reporter to several of the city's private welfare agencies to collect stories about the poor. He had a plan: to publish stories about the Hundred Neediest Cases in New York. The appeal would be made not with a direct request for money but with the facts of their lives. These small chronicles, it turned out, sounded a powerful call.

The campaign began December 15, 1912. All told the Fund has raised $118 million in its 90 years. The campaign, no longer limited to a hundred specific cases, distributes its funds to seven participating social welfare agencies. They serve people of all ages and background and in every borough. For more information, log on to www.nytco.com/foundation.

Adapted from an article in *The New York Times*.

INDEX OF RECOMMENDED READING

Oliver E. Allen, *Tales of Old TriBeCa: An Illustrated History of New York's Triangle Below Canal*, The TriBeCa Tribune, Inc., 1999.

Mardges Bacon, *Ernest Flagg: Beaux-Arts Architect and Urban Reformer*, MIT Press, 1986.

Geoffrey R. Bartholomew, *The McSorley Poems: Voices from New York City's Oldest Pub*, Charlton Street Press, 2001.

Adam Bartos and Christopher Hitchens, *International Territory: The United Nations 1945-95*, Verso, 1994.

Barry Bergdoll, Janet Parks and Hollee Haswell, *Mastering McKim's Plan: Columbia's First Century on Morningside Heights*, Columbia University Press, 1997.

Elizabeth Blackmar and Roy Rosenzweig, *The Park and the People: A History of Central Park*, Cornell University Press, 1998.

Eric Blau, *The Hero of the Slocum Disaster*, Mosaic Press, 1997.

Steve Brill, *Identifying and Harvesting Edible and Medicinal Plants in Wild (and Not So Wild) Places*, William Morrow, 1994.

Edwin G. Burrows and Mike Wallace, *Gotham: A History of New York City to 1898*, Oxford University Press, 1998.

Caleb Carr, *The Alienist*, Bantam Doubleday Dell, 1995.

Andrew Carnegie, *The Gospel of Wealth*, Applewood Books, 1998.

Ron Chernow, *The House of Morgan: An American Banking Dynasty and the Rise of Modern Finance,* Simon & Schuster, 1991.

Judi Culbertson & Tom Randall, *Permanent New Yorkers: A Biographical Guide to the Cemeteries of New York*, Chelsea Green Publishing, 1987.

Howard Dodson, Christopher Moore & Roberta Yancy, *The Black New Yorkers: The Schomburg Illustrated Chronology*, John Wiley & Sons, 2001.

Andrew Scott Dolkart, *Gramercy, Its Architectural Surroundings: Preserving the Neighborhood's Important Contributing Buildings*, Gramercy Neighborhood Associates, 1996.

Andrew Scott Dolkart, *Morningside Heights: A History of Its Architecture and Development*, Columbia University Press, 2001.

Helen Epstein, *Joe Papp: An American Life*, Da Capo Press, 1996.

Louisa Ermelino, *The Black Madonna*, Simon & Schuster, 2001.

Stephen Garmey, *Gramercy Park, An Illustrated History of a New York Neighborhood*, Balsam Press, 1984.

Michael Gold, *Jews Without Money*, Carroll & Graf Publishers, Inc., 1996.

Judith Mara Gutman, *Raging Bull of American Culture, A Life of Alfred Stieglitz* (forthcoming).

Ricky Jay, *Jay's Journal of Anomalies*, Farrar, Straus & Giroux, 2001.

Ricky Jay, *Learned Pigs and Fireproof Women*, Farrar, Straus & Giroux, 1998.

Alfred Kazin, *A Walker in the City*, Fine Communications, 1997.

Clay Lancaster, *Old Brooklyn Heights, New York's First Suburb*, Dover Publications, 1979.

Le Corbusier, *Towards a New Architecture*, Dover Publications, 1986.

Le Corbusier, *When the Cathedrals Were White*, 1947, o.p.

P.W. Lehmann, *Roman Wall Paintings from Boscoreale in the Metropolitan Museum of Art*, Archaeological Institute of America, 1953, o.p.

David Levering Lewis, *When Harlem Was in Vogue*, Penguin, 1997.

John Marin: New York Sketches, exhibition catalogue published by Kennedy Galleries, 1990.

Joan Maynard and Gwen Cottman, *Weeksville Then and Now*, Society for the Preservation of Weeksville and Bedford-Stuyvesant History, 1983.

Joyce Mendelsohn, *Touring the Flatiron: Walks in Four Historic Neighborhoods*, New York Landmarks Conservancy, 1998.

Joseph Mitchell, *McSorley's Wonderful Saloon*, Pantheon Books, 2001.

Joseph Mitchell, *Up in the Old Hotel and Other Stories*, Random House, 1993.

Money Matters: A Critical Look at Bank Architecture, McGraw Hill with the Museum of Fine Arts and the Parnassus Foundation, 1990.

W. G Rogers, *Wise Men Fish Here: The Story of Frances Steloff and the Gotham Book Mart*, Booksellers Publishing Inc., 1994.

Henry Roth, *Call It Sleep*, Farrar, Straus & Giroux, 1991.

Edna St. Vincent Millay, "First Fig," *A Few Figs From Thistles*, 1922.

J.D. Salinger, *The Catcher in the Rye*, Little, Brown & Co., 1991.

Beth L. Savage, ed., *African American Historic Places*, John Wiley & Sons, 1994.

Charles Schumann, *American Bar: The Artistry of Mixing Drinks*, Abbeville Press Inc., 1995.

Kenneth Silverman, *Houdini!!!: The Career of Ehrich Weiss*, HarperCollins, 1997.

Ellen M. Snyder-Grenier, *Brooklyn! An Illustrated History*, Brooklyn Historical Society, Temple University Press, 1996.

Robert A.M. Stern, Thomas Mellins and David Fishman, *New York 1960: Architecture and Urbanism Between the Second World War and the Bicentennial*, Monacelli Press, 1995.

Hildegarde Hoyt Swift and Lynd Ward, *The Little Red Lighthouse and the Great Gray Bridge*, Harcourt, 1983.

Joseph Frazier Wall, *Andrew Carnegie*, University of Pittsburgh Press, 1989.

Norval White & Elliot Willensky, *AIA Guide to New York City, Fourth Edition*, Three Rivers Press, 2000.

Walt Whitman, "City of Ships," from *Leaves of Grass*.

Marie Winn, *The Red-Tails in Love: A Wildlife Drama in Central Park*, Pantheon Books, 1999.

Yasuo Yoshida, et al., *Japanese for Beginners*, Barron's Educational Series, 1992.

Bonnie Young, Malcolm Varon and the Metropolitan Museum of Art, *A Walk Through the Cloisters*, Harry N. Abrams Inc., 1990.

INDEX OF CONTRIBUTORS

Philip E. Aarons is a principal and founding partner of Millenium Partners, a national developer of large-scale mixed-use urban projects. He is also on the board of directors for Creative Time, Printed Matter, Ballet Tech and the Skyscraper Museum. p. 60

Margot Adler is the New York correspondent for National Public Radio and the author of *Drawing Down the Moon*. pp. 149, 330, 332, 334, 340

Nadia Aguiar is pursuing an M.F.A. in creative writing at Columbia University. p. 358

Dan Algrant is a New York filmmaker. His credits include *Anthing for Jazz*, a portrait of Jaki Byard, episodes of the television series *Sex and the City*, feature films *Naked in New York*, and most recently, *People I Know*. p. 274

Myra Alperson is a writer and tour leader who for eight years led "Hungry Pedalers Gourmet Bicycle Tours" through New York City's five boroughs. Now the editor of *NoshNews*, a newsletter exploring the city's best ethnic markets and eateries, she also leads NoshWalks through many of the city's neighborhoods. pp. 414, 438

William Ambler received his B.A. from Princeton University in 1988 and his M.A. from the Courtauld Institute in 1992. He is currently a doctoral candidate at the Institute of the Arts at New York University and a curator at the Hispanic Society of America. p. 390

Kurt Andersen is a novelist (*Turn of the Century*), essayist (*The New Yorker, The New York Times Magazine*), public radio host (Studio 360), and former editor (*Spy, New York*). p. 467

Rina Anoussi is president of The Travel Business. p. 508

Nicholas Arcomano is former senior attorney at BMI, vice president and counsel, SESAC Inc., specializing in copyright law. He is a member of ALAI, International Organization for Protection of Literary Artistic Property. p. 83

Dr. María Arrillaga was a 1996 fiction finalist at the Institute of Latin American Writers. In Puerto Rico, she has won literary awards for poetry, essays and fiction. She is a professor at the University of Puerto Rico. pp. 338, 435

Dennis Ashbaugh is an artist living in New York City, a Guggenheim Fellow whose work is in the collections of most major art museums, and a surfer. p. 260

Jane Avrich is a fiction writer who lives in New York City. She teaches English at St. Ann's School in Brooklyn. p. 351

Ann Banks is a journalist who has written for *The New York Times Magazine, Condé Nast Traveler* and many other publications. She is the author of seven children's books and editor of *First Person America*. pp. 272, 444

Dennis Barone is the author of *The Returns, Temple of the Rat, Separate Objects: Selected Poems* and *Echoes*. He received the America Award in fiction in 1997. In 1992, he held the Thomas Jefferson Chair, a distinguished Fulbright Award in the Netherlands. p. 156

Jack Barth is an artist who lives in New York City. p. 299

Pamela Bayless has been an editor at *Newsweek International, SELF* magazine and *Crain's New York Business*; worked in communications for CUNY and the Y.M.C.A. of Greater New York; and is now a writer and communications consultant. She holds a B.A. from the University of Kansas and a M.A. in journalism from Columbia University. pp. 340, 382

Louis Begley is a lawyer and novelist living in New York City. His most recent novel is *Schmidt Delivered*. p. 505

Clare Bell is director of exhibitions at PaceWildenstein and the former chief curator at the Museum of the City of New York. A former curator at the Solomon R. Guggenheim Museum, she is the author of *Jim Dine: Walking Memory*. pp. 338, 500

Barry Bergdoll was trained at Columbia and Cambridge universities in architectural history, and as an intern at the New York City Landmarks commission. On the faculty of the art history department at Columbia, he specializes in the architectural history of 19th- and early 20th-century France and Germany, but he never stops looking on his own and with students, at the urban fabric of New York. pp. 91, 214, 337, 375

Deborah Berke is a professor of architecture at Yale University and maintains an architectural practice in New York City. She is the co-editor of *The Architecture of the Everyday*. p. 315, 409, 516

Adam Berlin received his M.F.A. from Brooklyn College. His first novel, *Headlock*, was published in 2000. pp. 38, 480

Nancy Berner is an associate editor of the Children's Book Committee at Bank Street College. She also regularly volunteers at the Conservatory Garden in Central Park, and, with Susan Lowry, is co-author of *Garden Guide: New York City*. pp. 514, 529

Frederick Biehle is a professor of architecture at Pratt Institute in Brooklyn and a partner in Via Architecture Studio. He is a 1987 architecture fellow of the American Academy in Rome. p. 24

Lucienne S. Bloch has received fellowships from the New York Foundation for the Arts and Yaddo, among others. She is the author of *On the Great-Circle Route* and *Finders, Keepers*. p. 281

Sandra Bloodworth is the director of Metropolitan Transportation Authority Arts for Transit. An artist with a background in design, art and the public process, she teaches urban development and visual arts at New York University. p. 267

James Bodnar is an architect in private practice in New York City. pp. 86, 501, 502

Naomi Bombardi-Wilson co-founded Ms. Chief Productions, the first film production company whose main focus is to enhance and promote women and their talents in and through film, and the film community. She is the director of two shorts and is developing a feature slated for production in winter 2002. p. 485

James Boorstein is writing a book about walking around the outer edge of Manhattan Island. He has restored museum period rooms in New York and Los Angeles, and has shown his conceptual site-specific sculpture in the U.S. and Europe. p. 397, 399

Lana Bortolot is a writer and editor based in New York City. She writes on cultural travel, and has been a copywriter for such magazines as *Guns and Ammo*, *Sassy* and *The New Yorker*. pp. 53, 164, 171, 213, 228

A New York native, Alexander R. Brash is chief of the Urban Park Rangers, City of New York Parks

& Recreation, which oversees the city's 1,580 parks. pp. 17, 328

Susan L. Braunstein is curator of archaeology and Judaica at the Jewish Museum. She holds a Ph.D. in ancient Near Eastern archaeology from Columbia University and is on the faculty of the Jewish Theological Seminary of America. pp. 309, 519

"Wildman" Steve Brill, a naturalist, leads wild food and ecology tours through greater New York City and is the author of *Identifying and Harvesting Edible and Medicinal Plants in Wild (and Not-so-Wild) Places*, and *The Wild Vegetarian Cookbook*, but is best known for having been arrested and handcuffed by undercover park rangers for eating a dandelion in Central Park. p. 516

Katey Brown is an art historian with the University of Georgia studies abroad program. pp. 279, 295

The Honorable James J. Brucia is a Justice (retired) of the New York State Supreme Court. pp. 47, 199, 482

Margaret Brucia is a retired schoolteacher. pp. 199, 482

Margaret A. Brucia is a Latin teacher. In 1992, she was a fellow at the American Academy in Rome in post-classical/humanities studies. pp. 149, 262

John Bryant is the author of *Melville and Repose* and *The Fluid*

Text. He is the editor of *Leviathan: A Journal of Melville Studies* and of *Melville's Tales, Poems, and Other Writings*. p. 15

Mario Buatta, the "Prince of Chintz," was born in New York and has worked there in the interior design profession for more than 40 years. p. 347

Melvin Jules Bukiet is the author of six books of fiction, most recently *Strange Fire* and *Signs and Wonders*, and is the editor of *Neurotica*. A collection and an anthology are forthcoming. p. 370

Peter Burchard is the author of 25 books, both fiction and nonfiction. He has focused on black studies and New York City history. He was a Guggenheim fellow in 1966, and since then, has received several national awards. His book *One Gallant Rush: Robert Gould Shaw and His Brave Black Regiment* was a major historical source for the motion picture *Glory*, which won three Academy Awards. His latest book, *Lincoln and Slavery*, was published in 1999. pp. 124, 127

Christopher Cahill, a poet and novelist, is editor of *The Recorder*. He is director of Institute for Irish American Studies at the City University of New York. pp. 170, 512

Don Camp, an experimental photographer, has received grants and fellowships from the Guggenheim Foundation, the National Endowment for the Arts, the Pew Charitable Trust and the Pennsylvania Council on the Arts. He has been a visiting artist at the American Academy in Rome. His work is in the collections of the Solomon R. Guggenheim Museum and the Philadelphia Museum of Art, among others. p. 119

George Campbell Jr. is president of the Cooper Union for the Advancement of Science and Art. He earned a Ph.D. in theoretical physics from Syracuse University and is a graduate of the Executive Management Program at Yale University. A recipient of the 1993 George Arents Pioneer Medal in Physics, he is a fellow of the American Association for the Advancement of Science and the New York Academy of Sciences. He has published numerous papers and is co-editor of *Access Denied: Race, Ethnicity and the Scientific Enterprise*. p. 124

Sarah Caplan studied art at Oberlin College and the Parsons School of Design. For the turn of the millennium she brought back the notorious Pop Art paper dress under her label MPH. The dresses were sold around the world and were accepted into the permanent collection at the Museum at the Fashion Institute of Technology, New York. She also works as a freelance graphic designer and is co-author of the upcoming guide to shopping in SoHo and NoLIta, *The Index*. pp. 79, 274

Carolyn Cartwright has decorated 10 feature films and has worked with Sidney Lumet, John Sayles,

Robert DeNiro, Spike Lee, Luc Besson and Ed Harris. She lives and works in New York City. pp. 40, 123, 499

Giorgio Cavaglieri, an architect, has won the Gold Medal of the Architectural League of New York; the Medal of Honor of the New York Chapter of the American Institute of Architects; the Presidential Citation of the National American Institute of Architects; fellowships from the American Institute of Architects and the NIAE; and 35 other professional awards from various professional and civic groups. p. 336

Robin Cembalest is the executive editor of *ARTnews*. She has contributed to *The New York Times*, *The Wall Street Journal*, and many other publications in the United States and Spain. In 1994 she won a Society of the Silurians Award for Arts/Cultural Reporting and a National Headliner Award for her coverage of the Hispanic Society of America in *ARTnews*. p. 390

Walter Chatham is an architect practicing in New York and Miami. He is a fellow of the American Academy in Rome and a past president of the Architectural League of New York. p. 33, 332

David Childs is a consulting design partner to Skidmore, Owings & Merrill New York. His current projects include the new New York Stock Exchange and the new Pennsylvania Station at the historic

Farley Post Office building. He serves on the board of the American Academy in Rome, the Museum of Modern Art, the Municpal Art Society, the New York City Partnership, and the National Building Museum. pp. 20, 25

Rene Chun, a freelance journalist, has been a New Yorker for 17 years. p. 441

Mary Clarke has been an editor at magazines such as *Seventeen*, *Redbook*, and *Sassy*. She is currently beauty director at *Modern Bride* and contributing editor at *Index* magazine. She was born and raised in New York City, where she still lives. pp. 170, 228

Robin Clements teaches Latin, history, and carpentry at St. Bernard's School in New York City. p. 39

Stacy Cochran has written and directed three feature films: *Drop Back Ten*, *Boys* and *My New Gun*. She produced and directed *Richard Lester!* a documentary about the director and several short films. She graduated from Williams College and received an M.F.A. in film from Columbia University. p. 119

Jim Coddington is chief conservator at the Museum of Modern Art. p. 263

Phyllis Samitz Cohen is the director of the Adopt-A-Monument and Mural program for the Municipal Art Society of New York. In 1993, she received the Special Recognition Award from the Art Commission of the City of New York. p. 410

Pier Consagra is an artist who lives and works in New York City. He is an adjunct professor at Columbia University, and has also taught at Bard College and Cooper Union. pp. 191, 288

Robert Cook is a partner in the law firm of DeForest & Duer, where he specializes in land-use matters in the City of New York. He is the author of a book, *Zoning for Downtown Urban Design*, chairman of the Zoning Committee of Citizens Housing and Planning Council and former chairman of the Committee on Land Use Planning and Zoning of the Association of the Bar of the City of New York. p. 31

Hope Cooke, a writer and urban historian, is the former Queen of Sikkim and author of *Time Change: Teaching the Magic of Dance* (with Jacques D'Amboise) and *Seeing New York*. pp. 460, 479

Alexander Cooper is an architect and partner in Cooper, Robertson & Partners, designers of the Hudson River esplanade and Stuyvesant High School in Battery Park City. He developed the expansion program for the Museum of Modern Art and serves as consulting architect for the new MoMA building. He also has served as director of design for New York's Housing and Development Administration, director of Columbia University's urban design program and as New York City planning commissioner. p. 408

Avery Corman is the author of *Kramer vs. Kramer, Oh, God!* and

The Old Neighborhood. A frequent contributor to *The New York Times*, he is working on a new theater piece for Broadway. p. 413

Alfred Corn is the author of 12 books and is a professor in the M.F.A. program of the School of the Arts at Columbia University. p. 400

Theresa Craig is the author of *Edith Wharton: A House Full of Rooms—Architecture, Interiors and Gardens*. She teaches literature at City University of New York and humanities at the New School University. pp. 30, 222

Michael Cunningham's novel, *The Hours*, won the 1999 Pulitzer Prize in Literature and the PEN Faulkner Award. His other novels include *A Home at the End of the World* and *Flesh and Blood*. p. 107

Phillip Danzig is an architect active in the community murals movement. He works primarily in tile. p. 378

Gloria Deák is the author of many books concerned with American cultural history, including *Picturing America* and *Picturing New York*. pp. 103, 526

Kathleen DeMarco is a writer and film producer who has lived in the West Village of New York City since 1993. pp. 16, 43, 44, 62, 67, 87, 364

Lisa Dennison is the deputy director and chief curator at the

Solomon R. Guggenheim Museum. She is responsible for collections and exhibition programming at the Guggenheim Museums in New York, Venice, Berlin and Bilbao. She received a B.A. from Wellesley College and an M.A. from Brown University. p. 307

Lorraine B. Diehl is the author of *The Late, Great Pennsylvania Station*. She conducts tours of the remnants of the old Penn Station and writes a weekly feature for the New York *Daily News* describing overlooked Manhattan history. She is currently working on *Horn & Hardart: The Automat in America*. p. 337

Mary Ann Haick Di Napoli is a genealogist, educator and chronicler of the early history of the Arab-American community around Atlantic Avenue. She is a licensed New York City tour guide. p. 469

Simon Dinnerstein is an artist and professor of fine arts at the New School and Parson's School of Design. He has had 17 one-man exhibits, and been the recipient of the Rome Prize and a Fullbright Grant. pp. 279, 452

Kim Dramer is a Ph.D. candidate in art history and archaeology at Columbia University. She moved from Harlem Heights to Hudson Heights three years ago and was thrilled with the rocky cliffs and the rocking bunch of women who have lived there over the centuries. She highly recommends the pickled herring at Smart Choice. pp. 392, 401

Laurie Duchovny is a writer who lives in Greenwich Village. She taught at St. Ann's School for 10 years. She is a member of the Writer's Room and is the author of the forthcoming *The Index*, a shopping guide to SoHo and NoLIta. p. 150

Bruce Ducker is the author of six novels, including *Bloodlines* and the prizewinning *Lead Us Not Into Penn Station*. pp. 137, 140

Alexander Duff started his entertainment career as a restaurant and nightclub owner. He is co-owner of Groovejet Records LLC, produces nightclub events in non-nightclub spaces, and specializes in corporate-sponsored electronic concerts. He recently released a compilation of electronic music called *Groovejet*. pp. 61, 157, 245

Barbara Ensor is a writer who lives with her husband and two children in Brooklyn, New York. p. 446

Louisa Ermelino was born and reared in Greenwich Village, where she still lives. She is the author of the novels *Joey Dee Gets Wise*, *The Black Madonna* and *The Sisters Malone*. Chief of reporters at *InStyle* magazine, she has worked at *People, Time* and for the television show, *Top Cops*. p. 80

Fernando Ferrer is the former Bronx borough president and a former New York City council member. An award-winning engineer of the nation's largest housing revival, he is a recipient of the RPA STAR and LaFarge Memorial awards, among others. pp. 411, 421

Matthew Field has edited more than 50 books on magic and is the video reviewer for *Genii*, the international conjurers's magazine. p. 118

Nina Fiore was born and reared in Astoria, Queens, to immigrant parents who hailed from the same small town in Southern Italy. She graduated from Harvard in 1994 with a degree in fine arts, and has worked in Internet production at Merrill Lynch and Viacom. p. 507

Jane Fisher is an independent consultant in publishing and direct marketing, whose career has included stints at such companies as Oxford University Press, Macmillan, Condé Nast, and Scholastic. pp. 43, 50, 90, 229

David Fishman is co-author of *New York 1960: Architecture and Urbanism between the Second World War and the Bicentennial* and *New York 1880: Architecture and Urbanism in the Gilded Age.* pp. 260, 263

Christopher Forbes shares responsibility for the advertising sales activities of Forbes Magazine. An art history major, he also served as the first curator of the magazine's extensive art collection. pp. 100, 434

Bruce S. Fowle is the principal in charge of design at Fox & Fowle Architects. His work has been widely published and includes numerous award-winning projects. He is a member of the American Institute of Architects' College of Fellows, Academician of the National Academy of Design and a founder of the New York chapter of Architects, Designers and Planners for Social Responsibility. p. 232

Alex M. French is pursuing his M.F.A. in nonfiction writing at Columbia University. p. 63

M. Paul Friedberg, professor emeritus at City College New York, is an award-winning landscape architect and designer whose published work has appeared in *Play and Interplay* and *Handcrafted Playgrounds*. p. 378

Margot Gayle was born 93 years ago in Kansas City, Missouri. Before finding her calling as a preservationist, she worked as a journalist and radio scriptwriter. In 1966, she was a co-founder of the Victorian Society in America. Her work helped arouse public interest, leading to the designation of SoHo as the cast-iron historic district in 1973. Among her books are *Cast Iron Architecture in America: The Significance of James Bogardus* and *Cast Iron Architecture in New York.* pp. 311, 477

Joan H. Geismar has been an urban archaeologist in the New York metropolitan area for 20 years. She was designated a New York Centennial Historian of the City of New York in 1999. p. 15

Lee Gelber is director of training and tour development for Gray Line New York Tours. pp. 249, 450

Estelle Gilson, born and educated in New York City, has received numerous awards for journalism and translation. She is the translator (from Italian) of works by Umberto Saba, Massimo Bontempelli, and Giacomo Debenedetti, and (from Hebrew) of poet Gabriel Preil. "New York," her version of Juvenal's "Third Satire" appears in Penguin's *Juvenal in English*. p. 398

Kenneth Seeman Giniger is a book publisher, editor and anthologist in New York City. p. 220

Scott Glass is an architect at Rogers Marvel Architects in New York. He is a founder of BDDW Inc., a design and manufacturing firm concerned with the complicated relationship between the idea and the act of building. p. 283

Adam Glick is president of Jack Parker Corporation. p. 189

Maryellen Gordon is a New York-based journalist. A deputy editor at *Glamour* magazine, her previous work appeared in publications such as *Elle*, *Harper's Bazaar*, *The New York Times* and *Women's Wear Daily*. Her major honor is to have made a good living as a freelance writer. pp. 24, 145

Alexander Gorlin is an architect based in New York and author of *The New American Townhouse* and subject of a monograph, *Alexander Gorlin: Buildings and Projects*. p. 206

John Guare is a playwright based in New York City whose work includes *The House of Blue Leaves* and *Six Degrees of Separation*, which received the New York Drama Critics Circle Award and was made into a feature film. pp. 110, 240, 275, 325, 497

Agnes Gund has been a trustee of the Museum of Modern Art since 1976 and has served as its president since 1991. In the mid-1970's, as an advocate of arts education, she founded Studio in a School to place professional artists as teachers in public schools. She is affiliated with a number of nonprofit arts institutions including the Wexner Center for the Arts, the American Academy in Rome, the Romare Bearden Foundation and the J. Paul Getty Trust. pp. 278, 418

Judith Mara Gutman is a writer, lecturer and part-time academic. The author of seven books and nearly 100 articles, she has completed a biography, *Alfred Steiglitz, Raging Bull of American Culture*, written with exclusive access to the largest and still-closed Stieglitz archive. She is a member of PEN and its Freedom-to-Write committee, the Authors' Guild and AICA. pp. 26, 145

Born in New York City and raised by two architects, Sebastian Hardy has been exploring New York City without supervision since he was old enough to unlock the front door. pp. 141, 167, 377, 479, 490

During the week, Kate Hartnick runs a marketing consulting firm that works chiefly with media companies, educational and cultural organizations and B2Bs. On the weekend, she is an avid urban explorer. pp. 146, 361

Elizabeth Hawes is a writer whose work has appeared in *The New Yorker* and *The New York Times Magazine*, among other publications. She is the author of *New York, New York: How the Apartment House Transformed the Life of the City 1869-1930*. She is currently at work on a book about Albert Camus. p. 428

Angela Hederman is editor and publisher at The Little Bookroom. pp. 73, 234

Thomas Heffernan is the author of *Stove by a Whale* and *Wood Quay: The Clash Over Dublin's Viking Past*. He is a former president of the Melville Society. pp. 437, 490

Steven Heller is an art director, author and co-chair of MFA/Design at the School of Visual Arts. His recent books are *Graphic Design Reader* and *Counterculture: The Allure of Mini-Mannequins*. pp. 111, 121, 190

David Hellerstein, M.D. has won the Pushcart Prize best essay award and several MacDowell Colony fellowships. He has published four books and has written for many magazines. He is the author of *Battles of Life and Death, A Family of Doctors* and *Stone Babies*. He is chief clinical director of the New York State Presbyterian Institute. p. 243

Skot Hess won the 1999 Jury Award for outstanding solo performance at Fringe Festival, New York City, for a 21-character solo show, *B.J.: The Trail of a Transgender Country Singing Star.* p. 110

Chester Higgins Jr. is a traveler, author, and staff photographer for *The New York Times*. p. 365

Philip Hoare's books include *Serious Pleasures: The Life of Stephen Tennant, Noel Coward: A Biography, Oscar Wilde's Last Stand* and *Spike Island*. p. 182

Sam Hoffman's first film, *The Ride Home*, played at festivals in the United States and around the world. He has been an assistant director on more than 20 films for directors including Woody Allen, Wes Anderson, and Nicholas Hytner. p. 185

Peter J. Holliday is a historian of classical art and archaeology at California State University at Long Beach. pp. 287, 343, 373

Rachael Horovitz is a film producer and executive based in New York City. p. 116

Marie Howe is a poet and the author of *The Good Thief* and *What the Living Do*. She is on the writing faculties at Sarah Lawrence College and Columbia University, and has received grants and fellowships from the National

Endowment for the Arts, the Guggenheim Foundation, Radcliffe College and others. pp. 69, 83

Tina Howe is a playwright, whose work includes *Painting Churches*, *Coastal Disturbances*, and *Prides Crossing*. She is the winner of many prizes. p. 326

Tracey Hummer is a New York-based writer and editor covering art, architecture, and design. She is an editor with *Art in America*, and a former managing editor of *Artforum*. pp. 26, 49, 86, 123, 162, 170, 227, 245, 246, 274, 318, 380, 448, 478

Johanna Hurwitz is the award-winning author of more than 50 popular children's books. She lectures to students, teachers, parents and librarians from Mississippi to Mozambique. p. 230

Richard Hyland is a distinguished professor at the Rutgers University School of Law in Camden, NJ. p. 241

Colta Ives is a long time curator of drawings and prints at the Metropolitan Museum of Art. She has been organizer and catalogue author for exhibitions on Bonnard, Daumier, Degas, Goya and Toulouse-Lautrec and wrote commentary for Robert Rauschenberg's book of New York photographs, *Photos In + Out City Limits: New York C.* p. 242

Thomas Jayne is head of Thomas Jayne Studio Inc. He holds an M.A. in American architecture and decorative arts from the Winterthur

Program. *House Beautiful* has named him one of the 14 "future hall-of-famers" in the decorating world. p. 223

John Jiler is the author of *Avenue X*, a musical, which won the Richard Rodgers Award and the Kleban Award. His novel, *Sleeping with the Mayor*, was chosen as a *New York Times* "most notable" book in 1997. p. 244

Fenton Johnson is a novelist, memoirist and a regular contributor to *Harper's Magazine*. He is a literature fellow of the National Endowment for the Arts. p. 304

Philip Johnson came to prominence in the 1930's as the first director of the Department of Architecture at the Museum of Modern Art. His work as an architect, curator and critic has continued ever since. The Seagram Building is home to his firm, Philip Johnson/Alan Ritchie Architects. p. 260

Celedonia Jones is the Manhattan Borough Historian. In 1998, he was designated one of New York City's Centennial Historians. p. 392

Lawrence Kahn is a professor emeritus of pediatrics at Washington University in St. Louis. Currently, one of his major activities is leading a group from the Lifelong Learning Institute in reading and interpreting all of Shakespeare's plays. Beyond that, he takes great pleasure in the practical application of his son's *City Secrets*. p. 306

Robert Kahn, the series editor and creator of *City Secrets*, is an architect in private practice, whose work has been widely published. He has taught design, most recently at Yale University. He is a Rome Prize winner in architecture from the American Academy in Rome. He lives and works in New York City. pp. 88, 93, 193, 256, 275, 284

Maira Kalman is the author/illustrator of 10 books including *Max Makes a Million, Next Stop, Grand Central* and *What Pete Ate*. Her work appears in *The New Yorker*, *The New York Times* and *New York Magazine*. p. 152

Paul Kane is a professor at Vassar College. He was a Guggenheim fellow in 1998-99. p. 176

David Bar Katz is a writer and director in every medium other than comic books, though he hopes to break into them soon. p. 133

Robert Kaufelt is the proprietor of Murray's Cheese Shop, one of Greenwich Village's oldest continuously running businesses. He writes and teaches about food and lives in Greenwich Village with his wife, Patricia, an artist; and their two dogs, Fannie and Louie. p. 64

Edmund Keeley is a novelist, translator, critic and the author of 32 books. A former president of the PEN American Center, he received the Rome Prize from the American Academy in Rome, and the Academy Award in literature from the American Academy of Arts and Letters, as well as the Ralph Manheim Medal for Translation. He is the Charles Barnwell Straut English professor emeritus at Princeton University. p. 70

Betty Keim, an editor, writer and musicologist, has written articles on Native American and Spanish music, and scripts for documentary films on American architecture. She is the owner of a production company that develops books, catalogues and art-related products for publishers and art organizations. p. 265

Billy Kent graduated from Vassar College and the American Film Institute, then began his film career at MTV. He has directed hundreds of television commercials and his short films (*Egg Salad, Five Shorts*) have been honored at the Sundance Film Festival, the Metropolitan Museum of Art, and the Monte Carlo Film Festival. His first feature film, *The Oh in Ohio*, is in production. p. 474

Dave King is a writer and editor. He is on the faculty of the English department of Baruch College, New York. p. 66

Binnie Kirshenbaum is the author of *Hester Among the Ruins, Pure Poetry, A Disturbance in One Place, History on a Personal Note* and *On Mermaid Avenue*. p. 191

Betsy Kissam, the author of the *Atlantic Avenue Walking Guide*, is a freelance writer. p. 485

Howard Kissel is the theater critic for *The Daily News*, New York. He also writes about the arts. p. 360

Susan Kleinberg has exhibited at the Venice Biennale, the American Center in Paris and the Castelli Gallery. She has been a visiting artist at the American Academy in Rome. p. 221

Edward I. Koch was the mayor of New York City from 1978-1989. p. 287

Bill Komoski was born and raised in New York City. He is a painter and a teacher at New York University and the School of Visual Arts. He has been surfing since age 11. pp. 172, 242, 520

Joyce Kozloff is an artist who lives in New York. An activist in the feminist art movement for more than 30 years, she was an early Pattern & Decoration painter in the 1970's and has subsequently worked in the field of public art. Her art of the last decade has been cartographic. *Targets*, a 108-inch diameter wooden globe which can be entered, is painted on the inside with aerial maps of all the countries the U.S. has bombed since World War II; it is currently traveling nationally. pp. 187, 342, 402, 435, 436

Max Kozloff, a former editor of *Artforum*, is a freelance art and photography critic based in New York City. p. 434

Gail Kriegel is a playwright, librettist and Rockefeller Foundation fellow. Her work was chosen as First Official Selection at the Cork International Film Festival. pp. 29, 31, 49

Evelyn and Peter Kraus are the owners of Ursus Books and Prints, specializing in art books, rare books of all kinds, and decorative master prints. p. 139

Alisa LaGamma is an art historian and curator at the Metropolitan Museum of Art, where she curated the exhibition, "Art and Oracle: Spirit Voices of Africa." p. 293

Anne Landsman's first novel, *The Devil's Chimney* was nominated for the PEN/Hemingway Award, the Janet Heidinger Kafka Prize, QPB's New Voices Award and the M-Net Book Prize. She has been awarded fellowships from the Sundance Institute, the MacDowell Colony and Yaddo. p. 313

Dr. Norman Lanes is a cardiologist in private practice in New York City and a police surgeon for the New York Police Department. He grew up in Crown Heights, Brooklyn. p. 453

Shirley Lauro, a playwright and novelist, is a Guggenheim fellow and the author of the Tony-nominated drama, *Open Admissions*, as well as *A Piece of My Heart* and *The Contest*. p. 303

Richard Lavenstein is a principal at Bond Street Architecture & Design. pp. 100, 264

Jane Daniels Lear is a senior editor at *Gourmet* magazine. pp. 154, 312

Dany Levy, a journalist known for her content-mining abilities and creative voice, began her career in 1994 at *New York* magazine. There she revamped and edited the "Sales and Bargains" section in 1996 and subsequently created the "GothamStyle" section for the same publication in 1998. She has also written for *The New York Times*, *Martha Stewart Living*, and *Time Out New York*. pp. 87, 138, 141, 152, 481, 487

Hilary Lewis is an urban planner and architectural historian who writes frequently on the built environment. She is the co-author of *Philip Johnson: The Architect in His Own Words* and author of the upcoming *Philip Johnson: Fast Forward*. p. 263

On her thirtieth birthday, Renee Lewis moved to New York from Ohio with the goal of living the artist's life. She is a designer of jewelry and vintage couture. p. 194

Laura Linney is an actress who was born in Manhattan and has lived there her entire life. Working in film, television, and on stage, she was nominated for an Academy Award for *You Can Count On Me*. She portrays Maryann Singleton in Armisted Maupin's *Tales of the City* series, and can frequently be found on stage in New York City theaters large and small. p. 318

Laurie Lisle is the author of biogra-phies of Georgia O'Keeffe and Louise Nevelson, as well as a book about childlessness. p. 177

Robert Livesey is director of the Knowlton School of Architecture at the Ohio State University. pp. 13, 261

Iain Low holds B.Arch and M.Arch degrees. He was a visiting fellow at the American Academy in Rome in 1994-95. p. 95

Born in New York City, Glenn Lowry is the director of the Museum of Modern Art. He was curator of Islamic Art at the Freer and Sackler Galleries at the Smithsonian Institution, Washington, D.C. pp. 298, 507

Susan Lowry worked for 10 years as a television journalist in Canada and the United States before switch-ing fields and earning a degree in landscape architecture. She lives in New York City, where she also vol-unteers at the Conservatory Garden in Central Park. She is co-author, with Nancy Berner, of *Garden Guide: New York City*. pp. 514, 529

Frank Lupo is design director of Perkins & Will New York, and the current president of the Architectural League of New York. p. 431

Stan Mack is the creator of the cartoon strip, "Real Life Funnies," which ran in *The Village Voice*, and is a former art director of *The New York Times Magazine*. His books include *The Story of the Jews, a 4,000 Year Adventure*. p. 496

Jon Madof is a musician and publicist based in Brooklyn. He leads Rashanim, an ensemble that explores Jewish and Middle Eastern music with a New York flavor. He has been profiled in *The Philadelphia Inquirer* and on WNYC-TV, and performs regularly at The Knitting Factory. pp. 140, 429

Sanford Malter received his degree in architecture from Cornell University, and is founder of the architectural preservation firm of Malter & O'Donnell. He has been a consultant for historic preservation projects throughout New York City and is a contributor to *Picturing New York* by Gloria Deák. p. 470

Charlotte Mandel, a poet, is the author of *Sight Lines, The Marriages of Jacob*, and *The Life of Mary*. p. 257

William Muir Manger Jr. is the chairman of the director's council of the Museum of the City of New York. p. 419

Maria Manhattan is an artist who was born and reared in New York City. As a child, she, her brother and parents spent their summer vacation days visiting historical landmarks in and around New York. p. 101

Brice Marden is a painter who lives in New York City. p. 280

Helen Marden is a painter who lives in New York City. pp. 203

Charles Marsden-Smedley is a museum and exhibition designer based in London. p. 12

A native of Birmingham, Alabama, Hugh Martin started his career in New York as a vocal arranger. With Ralph Blanc, he wrote *Meet Me in St. Louis* for Judy Garland. Two songs from the score, "The Trolley Song" and "Have Yourself a Merry Little Christmas," have become classics. pp. 224, 279, 401

Robert Marx has been the director of the theater program at the National Endowment for the Arts and the New York State Council on the Arts, and was executive director of Lincoln Center's New York Public Library for the Performing Arts. He is an essayist on theater and opera, has produced off-Broadway plays, and is the voice frequently heard on the intermission features of the Metropolitan Opera's radio broadcasts. pp. 418, 483

Joseph Masheck, Ph.D., former editor of *Artforum* (1977-80), studied art history at Columbia under Rudolf Wittkower and Dorothea Nyberg, and has taught at Columbia, Harvard and Hofstra universities. He also studied aesthetics at Trinity College Dublin, and is a fellow of the Royal Society of Arts. pp. 25, 195, 259, 266

Michael Massing is a magazine writer and the author of *The Fix*, a critical study of the U.S. war on drugs. pp. 356, 357

Terry Mayer, a bellologist, designs miniature bells as jewelry and is a collector of international bells. She lectures on bells, has been president of the Metropolitan New York

Chapter of the American Bell Association for 12 years, and is a native New Yorker. p. 249

Joan Bacchus Maynard is a preservation activist and executive director emeritus of the Society for the Preservation of Weeksville. She was a founder of Weeksville Society, was the organization's director for 25 years, and is a Crown-in-Shield Awardee of the National Trust for Historic Preservation. p. 437

Laurie McLendon is the owner of Papivore, a stationery store in New York City. pp. 194, 277, 500

Richard Meier received his architectural training at Cornell University and established his own office in New York City in 1963. His international practice has encompassed major civic commissions in the United States and Europe, and he has received the highest honors in the field including the Pritzker Prize for Architecture. Among his most well-known projects are the acclaimed Getty Center in Los Angeles, the Barcelona Museum of Contemporary Art, and the City Hall and Central Library in The Hague. p. 258

Jayne Merkel is an architectural historian and critic who contributes regularly to *Architectural Design* in London. A former editor of *Oculus*, the monthly magazine of the AIA New York Chapter, she has also written for *Architectural Record, Art in America, Artforum, Connoisseur, Design Book Review*, and served for 11 years as architecture critic of *The Cincinnati*

Enquirer. She has taught at various colleges and curated numerous museum exhibitions. pp. 183, 473, 483

Joseph G. Merz is an architect in Brooklyn Heights, New York. He and his wife, Mary C. Merz, were formerly curators of Prospect Park. p. 432

Danny Meyer opened New York's Union Square Cafe in 1985 and Gramercy Tavern in 1994. Both have received numerous accolades, including recognition in the 2000 Zagat Restaurant Survey as the city's Number 1 and Number 2 favorites respectively. He co-authored the *Union Square Cafe Cookbook*, and *Second Helpings from Union Square Cafe*. Among his many honors are the 1996 James Beard Humanitarian of the Year Award and the IACP Restaurateur Award for Excellence. He is the proprietor of Eleven Madison Park and Tabla. p. 189

Alec Michod earned an M.F.A. at Columbia University. He works at VHI, writes for the *A&F Quarterly* and has just completed a novel. p. 201

Roger Michell is a film and theater director of, among others, *Persuasion, Notting Hill*, and *Changing Lanes*. p. 502

Dana Micucci is a New York-based journalist specializing in the arts. She has written for *The International Herald Tribune, The Chicago Tribune, Architectural*

Digest, Harper's Bazaar, Art & Antiques. She is the author of *Artists in Residence* and *Best Bids: The Insider's Guide to Buying at Auction.* p. 165

Yuri Miloslavsky is a fiction writer, literary scholar, and journalist who received his Ph.D. in Russian literature from the University of Michigan. Born in Russia, he is a Russian Writers Union member, PEN member, and an honorary fellow of writing at the University of Iowa. He has published five books of fiction, as well as many cultural and political essays. pp. 312, 452

Michael Miscione is a native New Yorker who writes about New York City history when people pay him. And even when they don't. pp. 152, 339, 357, 412, 422, 430, 475, 510, 531

Carol Molesworth and Charles Suisman are the authors of the *Manhattan User's Guide* newsletter and book, the *New York Holiday Guide* and the *New Yorker Guide to Hotels in New York City.* pp. 177, 207, 509

Rick Moody is the author of several novels including *The Ice Storm* and *Purple America*, and a collection of short stories titled *Demonology.* p. 469

Christine Moog is a graphic designer. pp. 82, 166, 402

Richard Mooney is retired from the Editorial Board of *The New York Times*, where he wrote on city affairs—economic, cultural and

political. He is writing a biography of Nathan Hale. pp. 276, 302

Christopher Paul Moore is the author of *Santa and Pete: A Novel of Christmas Present and Past* and co-author of *The Black New Yorkers: 400 Years of African American History.* He has been a member of the New York City Landmarks Preservation Commission since 1995 and is a 12th-generation descendant of Manhattan's first African, Dutch and Native American community. pp. 20, 48, 383, 384, 385

Rob Morrow's credits as an actor include *Northern Exposure*, *Quiz Show*, and the new Showtime original series *Street Time.* His most recent project is *Maze*, an independent feature, in which he wrote, directed, produced, and starred. p. 286

Gregory Mosher is a director and producer. He was director of Lincoln Center Theater from 1985 to 1992. pp. 78, 222, 341

Muntadas is a visual artist who lives where he works and works where he lives. p. 212

Geraldine Nager is a senior vice president in the Private Client Services Group of Sotheby's New York. p. 317

Victoria Newhouse is the author of *Toward a New Museum.* pp. 391, 530

Kathryn Nocerino, a native New Yorker, is a writer and reviewer of poetry and short fiction. Her fiction appears in *Growing up Ethnic in America* and *Identity Lessons*. Her poetry books are: *Death of the Plankton Bar and Grill, Candles in the Daytime*; and *Wax Lips*. Two of her poems were set to music by the American composer Charles Bestor. pp. 349, 487

Starr Ockenga is a garden photographer, writer, and lecturer. Her most recent book is *Eden on Their Minds: American Gardeners with Bold Visions*. p. 197

Georgia O'Neal is a native New Yorker born and bred on the Upper West Side. pp. 122, 363

Sally Ordway is a playwright and librettist and writer-in-residence at Encompass Music Theater in New York. She has received National Endowment for the Arts and CaPs grants, as well as fellowships from the MacDowell Colony, Yaddo, and the Edward Albee Foundation. Her plays have been produced by Mark Taper Forum (Los Angeles) and Playwrights Horizons (New York City), among other venues. p. 195

Al Orensanz, the director of the Angel Orensanz Foundation, was born in Spain in 1949. He has a Ph.D. in sociology from the New School University. He is the author of five books on sociology and the semiology of urban communities and received the Award of British Council from Beijing University. p. 132

Nadine Orenstein is an associate curator in charge of the German and Netherlandish Old Master prints at the Metropolitan Museum of Art. pp. 277, 356

Janet B. Pascal, a production editor at Viking Children's Books, has been exploring the nooks and crannies of New York for the past 12 years. The author of *Arthur Conan Doyle: Beyond Baker Street*, she is currently working on a biography of New York urban reformer Jacob Riis. pp. 51, 112, 125, 167, 169, 294, 518, 521

Raymond R. Patterson (1929-2001) is remembered as a poet, English professor emeritus at the City College of New York, and founder of the college's annual Langston Hughes Festival. p. 380

Andrew S. Paul has been general counsel of a large hedge fund for almost 13 years. Accordingly, he says, he rarely sits with his back to the door and never near an open window. pp. 67, 108

John Penotti founded GreeneStreet Films, a premiere film production and finance company located in New York City. As a film producer, he has made, to date, nine theatrical features, including the award-winning film adaption of Herb Gardner's *I'm Not Rappoport* and John Turturro's *Illuminata*, and the studio releases, *In the Bedroom* and *Pinero*. pp. 139, 433

Peter Pennoyer, principal of Peter Pennoyer Architects, P.C., has designed houses from New York to

California. The firm's commissions have included the Mark Hotel and renovations to the Colony Club. He serves as a trustee of the New York Architectural Foundation, the Municipal Art Society and the Institute of Classical Architecture. p. 21

Matteo Pericoli was born in Milan in 1968 and has worked as an architect and illustrator in New York since 1995, including three years with Richard Meier & Partners. *Manhattan Unfurled*, two 37-foot-long drawings of the east and west sides of Manhattan, was nominated for the Brendan Gill Award by the Municipal Art Society of New York. p. 173

Caitlin Petre is a highschool senior in New York City. She plans to attend college in 2002 and study to become either an actress or a writer. p. 198

Jean Parker Phifer is president of the Art Commission of the City of New York. She received her B.A. from Yale University in 1974 and her M.Arch. from Columbia University in 1977. pp. 304, 324, 330

Robert Phillips is the author and editor of more than 30 books. He received an award in literature from the American Academy of Arts & Letters and is currently the Moores's professor of English at the University of Houston. p. 240

Melissa Holbrook Pierson is the author of *The Perfect Vehicle* and *Dark Horses and Black Beauties*. p. 433

Lisa B. Podos is the director of public programs at the Bard Graduate

Center for Studies in the Decorative Arts, Design and Culture. p. 308

Sam Posey is a racecar driver, an artist, and a designer. He has competed in the Indianapolis 500, the United States Grand Prix, and the 24 Hours of Le Mans, where he set the lap record with a Ferrari that had a top speed of 248 mph. p. 327

Gerald Posner is the author of seven books on subjects ranging from major political assassinations to Nazi war criminals to Triads and the heroin trade. He is an occasional contributor to leading national magazines on political and investigative issues. p. 102

Frank Pugliese is a playwright, screenwriter, director, and teacher. pp. 201, 415, 439, 440, 441, 445, 449

Anna Quindlen is the author of three bestselling novels and won the Pulitzer Prize for her opinion columns. p. 21

Michael Ratcliffe is a former literary editor and chief book critic of *The Times* in London, and a former theater critic and literary editor of *The Observer*. Now working freelance, he has written on opera in Britain, on European travel for *The New York Times*, and has led specialist cultural tours to Prague, Vienna, Provence, and Berlin. pp. 231, 301

Jean Rather is a painter and a member of the Art Commission of the City of New York. p. 278

Peter Reed joined the Museum of Modern Art in 1992 and has organized a number of exhibitions, including "The United Nations in Perspective" (1995) and "Alvar Aalto: Between Humanism and Materialism" (1998). He received his M.A. and Ph.D. in art history from the University of Pennsylvania. In 1998 he was knighted by the president of Finland with the Order of the White Rose. p. 247

David L. Reese is curator of Gracie Mansion and has served on the advisory board of the Mount Vernon Hotel Museum, the Morris Jumel Mansion and the American Friends of Attingham Summer School. He has lectured on 19th-century architecture and decorative arts and contributed the chapter, "American Beaux Arts, 1870–1926," in *The Elements of Style: A Practical Encyclopedia of Interior Architectural Detail.* pp. 316, 403

Janelle Reiring owns Metro Pictures gallery. p. 163

Ronnette Riley is an architect in private practice in New York City. p. 206

Terence Riley is chief curator of architecture and design at the Museum of Modern Art. pp. 169, 503

Katharine Ristich is an editor at theheart.org. A graduate of Mount Holyoke College, she has written music reviews for *Spin* magazine. pp. 280, 401, 420, 515

Kevin Joseph Roach is the resident set designer for the Swedish Cottage Marionette Theatre in Central Park. He has designed sets for *The Blue Man Group*, the "Fire Zone" at Rockefeller Center, and for 12 years was official set designer for the 52nd Street Project, a non-profit organization that brings together children from the Hell's Kitchen neighborhood and professional theater artists. p. 333

Donald Robertson has worked in magazine publishing for more than ten years, and has redesigned and/or launched magazines such as *American Marie Claire*, *Cosmopolitan* and *YM*. Currently the creative director at *Glamour* magazine, he lives in Pelham, New York with his wife and two children. pp. 197, 408

Roxana Robinson is the author of three *New York Times's* Notable Books, including *Georgia O'Keeffe: A Life* and *This Is My Daughter*. She is a New York Public Library Literary Lion and a Guggenheim fellow. p. 330

Gina Rogak is a native New Yorker and director of special events at the Solomon R. Guggenheim Museum. p. 324

Ralph M. Rourke is the director of the Hall of Fame for Great Americans. p. 412

Glen Roven, an Emmy award winner, lives in London and New York City. His first Broadway musical, *The 5,000 Fingers of Dr. T,* opened in fall of 2002. p. 345

For 60 years, Pete Seeger has been singing and song-leading at schools, camps, colleges, unions and peace rallies. pp. 32, 144, 403, 512

Renée Shafransky is a writer whose work has appeared in *The Village Voice* and *Condé Nast Traveler*. She has written screenplays for Columbia, Universal, and Disney studios, and TV scripts for PBS and HBO. She has a private psychotherapy practice in New York City, was ordained a minister in June 2001 and is working on her first novel. p. 372

Samuel Shem is a Harvard medical doctor, a Rhodes scholar, and the author of the novels *House of God* and *Mount Misery*, as well as the play, *Bill W. and Dr. Bob*. p. 196

Alix Kates Shulman has written four novels, including *Memoirs of an Ex-Prom Queen*, two memoirs, including the award-winning *Drinking the Rain*, and two books on anarchist-feminist Emma Goldman. pp. 69, 70

Joan Silber is the author of the novels, *Household Words* (winner of a PEN-Hemingway award), *In the City*, and *Lucky Us*, and the story collection, *In My Other Life*. Her fiction has appeared in *The New Yorker*, *Ploughshares* and *The Voice Literary Supplement*. She has received grants from the National Endowment for the Arts, the New York Foundation for the Arts and the Guggenheim Foundation. pp. 94, 122

Amy Sillman is a painter who lives in New York. She has received fellowships from the Guggenheim Foundation, the Tiffany Foundation, and the National Endowment for the Arts. She teaches part time at Bard College. p. 296

Nathan Silver is an architect, critic, educator and author of books on architecture and design. His book, *Lost New York*, was nominated for the National Book Award. Now based in London, he has been architecture critic of the *New Statesman* and head of a school of architecture. He studied and worked in New York for many years and still considers it home. p. 174

Stefanie Silverman is an architect, graphic designer and Jill-of-all-trades living in New York City. p. 143

Deborah Skelley has held executive positions at Paramount and Sony Studios and is a former motion picture agent in the New York office of the William Morris Agency. p. 272

Rebecca Smith is an artist who has exhibited nationally and internationally since 1979. p. 379

Richard Snow is the editor-in-chief of *American Heritage* magazine and the author of several books, including two historical novels and a volume of poetry. pp. 221, 244, 445

Andy Spade co-founded American accessories brand "kate spade" with his wife, Kate Spade, and serves there as CEO and creative director.

He recently launched JACK SPADE, a line of accessories for men, which was nominated for the Perry Ellis award for New Accessories Talent by the CFDA. p. 82

American accessories designer Kate Spade has been honored by the CFDA, winning the Perry Ellis award for New Accessories Talent in 1996, and Accessory Designer of the Year in 1998. She also was included in the 1999 National Design Triennial. p. 286

Elissa Stein is a graphic designer, illustrator, and writer of off-beat and often quirky books. pp. 106, 417

Robert S. Steinbaum is publisher of *The New Jersey Law Journal*, a publication of American Lawyer Media. p. 196

Fisher Stevens was whisked away to Greenwich Village from Chicago when he was 12- years-old. He has acted in numerous films, television, and Broadway shows including *Flamingo Kid, Short Circuit, Brighton Beach Memoirs, A Perfect Ganesh* and recently directed *Just a Kiss*. pp. 415, 445, 453, 477

Eric Stoltz is an actor and director who has appeared in films, television, and on Broadway. pp. 14, 61, 63, 91, 149, 166, 206, 272, 355

A West Villager since 1961, George C. Stoney is a filmmaker and a professor of film at New York University's Tisch School of the Arts. Washington Square was a featured location in *Metropolis: Creator or Destroyer?*, his PBS documentary series inspired by the urbanist Jane Jacobs. p. 199

Sarah Stonich is the author of the novel, *These Granite Islands*. She also writes essays and short fiction. She lives in St. Paul, where she is working on a new novel. p. 285

Mark Strand is a poet. He teaches at the University of Chicago. His most recent book of poems, *Blizzard of One*, won a Pulitzer Prize in 1999. pp. 92, 226

Alexandra Styron attended Columbia University, and has been a New York City resident for 17 years. *All the Finest Girls*, a novel, was published in spring 2001. p. 184

Charles Suisman and Carol Molesworth are the authors of the *Manhattan User's Guide* newsletter and book, the *New York Holiday Guide* and the *New Yorker Guide to Hotels in New York City*. pp. 177, 207, 509

Sean Sweeney is a builder, New York resident, and fourth generation Greenwich Villager. p. 468

Lionel Tiger is Darwin Professor of Anthropology at Rutgers University. Among his books are *Men in Groups, The Pursuit of Pleasure* and *The Decline of Males*. p. 173

Sallie Tisdale is the author of six books, most recently *The Best Thing I Ever Tasted*. p. 503

Karen Moody Tompkins is an artist whose work has been included in numerous exhibitions as well as in museum and corporate collections. pp. 335, 364

Gwendolyn Toth is director of ARTEK and music director of St. Francis of Assisi. She specializes in historical performance on a multitude of keyboard instruments, including harpsichord, organ, fortepiano, virginal, clavichord, and lautenwerk. p. 200

Thorin Tritter earned his Ph.D. in American History at Columbia University. He has led historical and architectural tours of New York City for seven years and has worked with a number of historical organizations including the New York Historical Society, the Lower East Side Tenement Museum, the Museum of Chinese in the Americas and Big Onion Walking Tours. He currently is teaching at Princeton University. pp. 38, 348, 371

Susan Tunick is an artist working in ceramic and is president of the Friends of Terra Cotta, a national preservation organization. She has written extensively about architectural ceramics, including *Terra Cotta Skyline*. pp. 90, 205

Jane Tucker Vasiliou, Ph.D., is an independent scholar living in New York City. p. 347

Anita Velez-Mitchell has received four Ibero-American Writers Awards for her short stories, poetry and essays, which have appeared in

Helicon 9, News Letters, The Institute of Puerto Rico Journal and other publications. p. 314

Thomas Von Essen was appointed a New York City firefighter in 1970, president of the firefighters's union in 1993, and commissioner in 1996. He has four wonderful kids, and a wife—also wonderful. p. 363

Gerald Weales is emeritus professor of English at the University of Pennsylvania. He is a former drama critic for *The Reporter* and *Commonweal* and the author of many books on theater and film, as well as a novel and several children's books. p. 378

Ed Weinberger, who has lived in New York City all his life, designs furniture. p. 505

Holding a master's degree in the history of decorative arts from the Cooper-Hewitt, National Design Museum, Amy Weinstein is a 20th-century material-culture associate at the New-York Historical Society. Previously, she was assistant curator at the Museum of the City of New York where she was responsible for the museum's renowned toy collection. p. 482

George Weissman is the retired chairman of Philip Morris Companies Inc. and the chairman emeritus of Lincoln Center for the Performing Arts. p. 341

Marjorie Welish is the author of *Signifying Art: Essays on Art after 1960* and *The Annotated "Here" and Selected Poems.* She has received grants from the Howard Foundation, the New York Foundation for the Arts, the Fund for Mutual Understanding, and the Pollock/Krasner Foundation for the Arts. p. 94

Fred Wessel is an artist and professor at the Hartford Art School, University of Hartford. He is the director of Workshops in Italy (www.workshopsinitaly.com), a series of workshops in painting and the art of the Italian Renaissance for artists and art-lovers. p. 300

Rachel Wetzsteon is the author of two books of poems, *The Other Stars* and *Home and Away.* p. 377

Gordon Whiting is an executive director at W. P. Carey & Co. LLC, a real estate investment banking firm based in New York City and is a member of Holland Lodge No. 8, F.&A.M. p. 192

Kassy Wilson is manager of published media at the Museum of The City of New York. She has lived in New York City for more than 20 years. p. 331

David Winter is a dealer of anonymous art and photography. p. 489

Elizabeth Winthrop is the author of more than 50 books for children and adults, including *Island Justice* and "The Golden Darters," a selection of the 1992 *Best American Short Stories.* p. 305

William J. Wyer is a partner in Ursus Rare Books Ltd. pp. 211, 478

Susan Wyland, a magazine consultant, is the former editor of *Martha Stewart Living* magazine, the former vice president and editorial director of Disney's Family.com and the founding editor of *Real Simple* magazine. pp. 192, 449

Cynthia Zarin is the author of three books of poetry and several books for children. She has taught at Yale and Princeton Universities and is artist-in-residence at the Cathedral of St. John the Divine. p. 372

James Zug is a writer who lived for four years off Sixth Avenue in the Village. He now lives with his wife along the Hudson River. p. 102

GENERAL INDEX